GEORGE SYLVESTER MORRIS

GEORGE
SYLVESTER
MORRIS

HIS PHILOSOPHICAL CAREER
AND THEISTIC IDEALISM

MARC EDMUND JONES

GREENWOOD PRESS, PUBLISHERS
NEW YORK   1968

CONTENTS

To Priscilla
Lovely companion in
the great adventure

FOREWORD

THIS study is inescapably as much an outline of the author's own thinking as an analysis of George Sylvester Morris and the dynamic idealism developed at the University of Michigan. The assumption underlying every point brought forward in the following pages is that no man can be separated from the general milieu in which he matures and shapes himself, least of all the thinker whose principal stock in trade is the abstractions or generalizations that must remain far more rooted in collective than individual experience. The fact that Morris is presented here in the form of a wholly sympathetic exposition of his philosophy, instead of a critical rejection of his point of view or a dispassionate and historical evaluation of the ideas he has worked out or made his own, is the result of converging personal compatibilities in the social matrix of American thought. However, the principle would hold no less were Morris under attack by someone who had little intellectual traffic with the idealistic concepts. True, there is a school of thought which presupposes ideas to have an existence of their own in a special realm of mind, and which in consequence does not hesitate to discuss philosophy and philosophers in a social vacuum of sorts—proceeding to trace out lines of influence from one metaphysical entity or relationship to another—but such rational extremism is of a piece with the mechanical type of speculation against which Morris' whole career was most characteristically a protest.

The purpose of a foreword in any volume, except as it offers a repository for afterthoughts in the paradoxical fashion encouraged by the conventions of modern book-making, is presumably to provide the student—or the reader astute or concerned enough to recognize the need— with some broad overview of the context in which the chapters have been written. Any subject matter short of pure mathematical science is filtered through an intricate screen of prejudices, even in the case of the most skilled and wholly objective writers, and it is altogether too bad that an author usually seems to be displaying his egotism when he attempts to sketch in the various orientations of his creative struggle. His predilections are a part of him, and so a prime ingredient in his book, and who is as well equipped as himself to acquaint the reader with their consequences.

The basic problem in the present study, as in practically every possible aspect of human development, is the extraordinary complexity of the subject matter. When it seemed, after several years of work, that an analysis of the life and writings of George Sylvester Morris was the best immediate form for the author's total project of intellectual reconstitution (his effort to evolve, refine and validate a sort of functional indeterminacy), and when all the Morris source materials were located and examined rather thoroughly, a real obstacle developed in the fact that no ordering principle had appeared to serve as a unifying element running through the whole. The interpretation of an Aristotelian mean as a reconciliation of all dualisms was evident as a central and perhaps most important factor from the beginning, but the dilemma of the author was the same one which Morris himself apparently had faced, namely, a realization that any lean upon a purely logical device meant the acceptance and use of the very sort of rational schematism to which both the author and the subject of his study were unalterably opposed. The epistemological duality forever turning up in nature was not a metaphysical actuality, but an endowment of mind, and the impasse in the philosophical speculation was a simple failure to get on beyond this first critical insight, or to press on in terms of what John Dewey in 1886 identified as the psychological standpoint. In the end the ordering principle for an understanding of the ideas and achievements of Morris, such as would stand up under criticism, was the functional concept revealed in the unswerving determination by Morris to find a formulation for his evangelistic convictions within the framework of scientific and historical criteria. His personal integrity of mind in the light of his intellectual milieu was the clue to the meaning of his statements and the import of his conclusions.

Two blind spots contributed to the disorganization of the materials in the author's early analysis through the first two years of work on Morris in the Graduate School of Columbia University, and both of them were responsible for much agony of thought as exhibited by Morris himself through two decades of groping from his first speculations at Dartmouth College and Union Seminary on through his professorship of modern languages at the University of Michigan. The first of these intellectual blocks appears particularly incomprehensible in afterview, and yet it was an honest heritage of these recent centuries when the presuppositions of naïve rationalism are so strongly entrenched, and when secular thinking acquires a halo of intelligence somehow denied to any frank or honest theological realization. Theism can be a very great asset to the thinker outside as well as inside the churches of today, rather than the reverse, but this fact apparently goes unsuspected by everyone, even in the areas of pure religious dogmatism, since few see that theism is far more than an expression of faith.

The second of the blind spots lies in the field of technical philosophy, and it is the result of a failure to achieve an insight so absurdly simple that it long eluded Morris—who was expecting a greater profundity to match the discouraging complexity and depth characterizing the problems of Christianity as he viewed them—and at first the presence of this particular block to his thinking was not even recognized in Morris by the author. It is Morris who has, perhaps quite uniquely, discovered that a naïve organicism can be taken from Hegel quite independently of the mechanical and artificial system-building which proved so fascinating to the German mind, and that this basically Heraclitean universality and integrity of flux can then be used for the recovery of what well may be the real Plato and Aristotle, thereupon constituting what Herbert Schneider has identified as dynamic idealism. The theistic reconciliation of man and his world was what fundamentally gave order and understandable direction to the life of Morris, and it was the Hegelian organicism which provided the capstone for his career and now makes it possible to view his work as a contribution of genuine if potential significance to an atomic age.

The actual genesis of this study, together with the several collateral lines of development with which it is integrated (but which have little direct connection with Morris), was in the accident of some five or six of the author's boyhood years, spent in Chicago on Fifty-third Street near Kimbark Avenue during the establishment of John Dewey's original experimental school more or less around the corner. Had he attended that institution, so important in the history of American education, results in his own life might have been different. Instead, the new ideas were discussed in his hearing, always more or less critically, and an inchoate but definite fascination probably laid the ground for the later and much greater impact of Dewey's ideas. It was at the experimental high school of the University of Chicago, immediately after Dewey himself had left for Columbia, that the processes of speculative thought in the author's formative mind were given an important and very early stimulus. Two of the instructors in particular made a contribution for which no adequate appreciation can ever be expressed, especially after so great a lapse of time. Of these Frank Barnes Cherington in English awakened a discriminative approach to literature which has had its fruits in whatever may be claimed for a life given over very largely to work as a writer and editor. Indeed, few individuals have been as fortunate in the quality of their literary mentors when, to Cherington's stimulation, is added that of Benjamin F. Stelter at Occidental College.

Much more important, however, as far as the development of the author's philosophical thought is concerned, was the impact of Frederick Newton Williams, the art teacher at University High School. It is unfortunate that his career was clouded by subsequent scandal, but at least one young student was spared the species of shock reserved for others of the teenage boys, and was introduced instead to fascinating areas of investigation relative to Egyptian art, phallic symbolism and the whole field of the occult in rather broad or preliminary terms. It was an experience where seeds were sown in very fertile ground thanks to earlier encounters with Christian Science and Theosophy, and to a curious emphasis upon the first of these interests during the boyish adventure of many summer evenings spent climbing all over the structure as the First Church of Christ, Scientist, was erected in Chicago not many blocks from a prior residence. As if these heterodox impacts were not enough to encourage an originality of thinking, for better or worse, the encounter with astrology at David Wark Griffith's studio in Los Angeles, just six years after leaving high school, provided a climax of *outré* outreachings of the mind in a mode of psychological analysis which has proved to be of very great service in screening out certain fallacies of philosophical assumption such as might otherwise have gone completely unsuspected, but which also has been of exceptional disservice as far as a normal intellectual career is concerned. Only the individual who has been through the experience can know what a pariah the occultist will find himself to be in almost every conventional group of modern people.

The nostalgic eye often looks back upon the nineties as a time of great social and intellectual unities, but actually the sensitive mind of the era was continually exposed to the stresses and strains of a society that had no clear or effective idea of itself and of an age that had little sure religious or philosophical anchorage. The constant bickering between the Protestant and Catholic branches of the author's own family early prejudiced his mind against any theistic influence or guidance, had there been anyone capable of giving this. He had to wait for the very sage intellectual mentorship of David James Burrell, of Princeton Seminary, before he found himself equipped with the intellectual tools and correctives which have enabled him to approach Christian theism at all intelligently.

Like Morris, however, he had in his background, unshakable
and without ever even the slightest moment of emotional or
rational doubt or distrust, the quality of religious experience
which had dominated the Vermont milieu of Morris through
pietistic infiltrations. In the author's case this was mainly the
impact of one of America's emotionally best balanced holiness
movements, the Christian Endeavor Society, founded by Francis E. Clark, and now headed by Daniel A. Poling, both warm
personal friends to whom a very great debt of gratitude can
here be acknowledged. Christian Endeavor proved to be something inspirationally vigorous enough in orthodox lineaments
to serve as a very needed rectification for the extremisms which
the young thinker subsequently encountered in various fields
of the occult.

The problems of a religious conviction acquired just before
the high school years—again paralleling the case of Morris
rather closely—were not in matters of faith, or in the reality
and validity of a Christian experience, but were a proposition
of the intellectualization which might provide a seeking mind
with a halfway adequate account of man and his world. It
was in line with the author's need here, as it became more and
more obvious each year, that the course of wisdom seemed
to dictate a formalization of what in days of early dramatic
writing had been a widely ramified but not at all unified self-
education. In 1929, therefore, began the centralized line of
endeavor which now has culmination in the present volume.
The many acknowledgments to be made can never match, in
graciousness, the co-operation given the enterprise on every
hand. Occidental College, in Los Angeles, extended an extraordinarily warm welcome to its new student, especially in the
persons of President Remsen Du Bois Bird, Arthur Gardiner
Coons who was then dean of men and is now president
in turn, Professor Stelter who already has been mentioned,
Thomas Gregory Burt in philosophy, Frank Jason Smiley and
Hazel Elizabeth Field in science, Florence Norma Brady the
registrar, and innumerable others. The closest personal friendship developed with J. Hudson Ballard in the Department

of Religion, and it was through the wise counsel of this best of friends, when depression conditions compelled the abandonment of all plans for the Ph.D. degree, that the author proceeded into the ministry, and with his lady came to know a richness of living and service to which he has not yet been able to pay full tribute.

The five years' pastorate in the Sacramento Valley provided high opportunity for carrying the presentation of a modern theism very directly into the everyday life of a community self-contained enough to be seen as a single milieu by the participants in its total drama. Here was the full demonstration, at least to the author's satisfaction, that Christian theism can stand on its own feet without resort either to a dogmatic refusal to face modern secular thinking on the one hand or, on the other, to a compromise with essentially secular or mechanico-rational concepts by surrendering or denying the transforming power of a dynamic spirituality. From the actual ministration to a church congregation, with a complete sharing in all community activities, came the real buttressing for all later analysis of the theological insights coming forward in the present study of Morris.

As necessary preparation for the pastorate, the three years in the San Francisco Theological Seminary at San Anselmo, California, contributed primarily to the same testing and refining of theistic realizations which had first been strengthened through Christian Endeavor activities and field work. They also made it possible to begin a pressing back into Hebrew sources and materials, a phase of the author's total intellectual project into which this Morris volume fits as perhaps a convenient keystone for the whole. The death of Mahatma Gandhi (within a relatively few days of the final examinations for the doctorate on the basis of the Morris contribution) gave him a most unexpected opportunity for an exposition of theistic ideas in their East India setting, and the book *Gandhi Lives* in consequence has come off the presses some seven or eight months before this text first reaches the reader. What may well be the next step in the reorientation of theistic concepts in the history of religion and theology is in connection with the Hebrew insights, if it becomes possible to complete a considerable degree of work on Solomon ben Judah ibn-Gabirol as the relatively recent figure most important in this connection. The Seminary experience was wonderfully rewarding, blessed with the friendship of President William Henry Oxtoby in very great particular, together with his son Gordon Corning Oxtoby in Hebrew, Edward Arthur Wicher in Greek, and all the other true souls to whom the reminiscent heart would reach.

The completion of the doctorate in philosophy has been slow, the considerable loss of time complicated by increasingly upset conditions in the economic life of the country through the whole period centering around World War II. The opening of opportunities for free lance editorial work in New York made Columbia University possible as a field of operation, but the lack of any clear choice of subject matter provided a great initial difficulty. The author was quite unwilling to defend ideas which as yet were tentative and without adequate orientation in the history of philosophy. Since his interest was on the epistemological or logical side, and since he was thoroughly a product of the Dewey impact—however much he leaned personally to the theistic and religious rather than the secular and starkly philosophical side of the coin—the first move was made in the field of education, and the idea of a dissertation on the problem of the communication of ideas was accepted tentatively under the sponsorship of William Heard Kilpatrick, of Teachers College. The project took tangible form rather gradually as a survey of the educational literature in the years when Dewey was building his experimental work at the University of Chicago, and when the author himself was facing the problem however unknowingly as a young groping mind in the same intellectual climate.

The enterprise was fruitless, largely because it proved impossible to screen out an integrating conception from the mass of periodical literature. With the retirement of Kilpatrick,

John L. Childs came into the picture, and suggested that
the best procedure in getting at the epistemological problem
would be to make an analysis of the early ideas of John Dewey,
dealing with Dewey's transition from a naïve acceptance of
British Hegelianism to his development of his own psychological and behavioristic point of view of a more secular sort.
This suggestion had its ultimate fruits in the realization that
communication of ideas is dynamic or psychological, willy-
nilly, and it was this investigation that led back ultimately
to Morris as the original mentor of Dewey. More and more
the intellectual struggles of Morris rather than Dewey seemed
to be leading to the heart of the problem, at least as the author
saw this and found it paralleled in his own experience. The
wider point of view took the matter out of the field of education, but the years of warm fellowship with the faculty and
students at Teachers College have made a very real contribution to the whole effort. It will never be possible to say
enough by way of appreciation, not only for the generous
assistance given by the two professors named, but also by
Dean William Fletcher Russell, Bruce Raup and Gertrude
Belser among many others.

It was Herbert Wallace Schneider who saw the full possibilities of a study based directly on the life and writings of Morris,
and who has given unsparingly of himself in helping the
author get to the bottom of the many difficulties arising in the
course of the research. Herbert Schneider's knowledge of American philosophy and philosophical history made it possible
to complete the work many years earlier than would have
been the case had it been necessary to run down every avenue
of side investigation in more or less blind fashion. He is
gifted with one of the finest editorial minds the author has
ever encountered. The other members of the Department of
Philosophy in the Columbia graduate faculty have been whole-
heartedly co-operative at all times, including John Herman
Randal, Jr., Irwin Edman, Ernest Nagel and Horace Leland
Friess in particular. Quite individual thanks are due Joseph
L. Blau and Shirley Carson O'Connell. Dorothy King of the

University of Michigan historical collections, now at Smith College, was particularly helpful in making needed Morris and Wenley materials available.

The author's secretary, Elsie Boyle, has typed and retyped versions beyond remembrance in the course of the writing, and has taken full responsibility all through for the technical integrity of the manuscripts as far as spelling, punctuation and style are concerned. She has checked the manuscript, and in some cases the proofs, against the source materials, and has helped at all points in the proofreading and other details of book publication. Robert Hartley has given generously of his time in reading the final manuscript and all proofs. Emily Lindahl has helped with the indexing. Through the kindness of Alma Lissberger the final stages of the study have been very greatly expedited.

New York City, August 6, 1948

ROBERT MARK WENLEY'S INTERPRETATION

A VERY thoroughgoing account of Morris' early life and background is provided by Robert Mark Wenley's *The Life and Work of George Sylvester Morris, a Chapter in the History of American Thought in the Nineteenth Century*.[1] The volume was sponsored by the executive board of the Graduate School of the University of Michigan. Professor Wenley (a Scotsman, born at Edinburgh in 1861, died at Ann Arbor in 1929), succeeded to Morris' chair at Michigan in 1894—following John Dewey, who was the immediate successor of Morris—five years after Morris' death. Wenley began his researches for the book in the summer of 1910, and he explains that the more than twenty years intervening since the death of his subject had permitted the lapse of "facts indispensable to an adequate biography." He found he had to remain uninformed in connection with various important points because "those who could have set the situation in proper perspective from personal knowledge had passed away." [2] He had the assistance of Mrs. Morris and Miss Ethel Morris (the daughter, of the two Morris children), and particularly valuable help from Morris' favorite niece, Mrs. Kate Morris Cone (who had written a detailed account of the life and character of Morris' father), and of President

---

[1] New York, Macmillan, 1917. [2] *Op. cit.*, page vi.

1

James B. Angell of Michigan University, under whom Morris taught for eighteen years.

Wenley spent more than five years on his manuscript, and it is exceedingly unlikely, three decades later, that anything further of real moment can be added to the historical biography. No primary materials have been discovered other than those mentioned in Wenley's book, and in consequence there is no additional evidence to rectify his account on the factual side. His treatment of Morris' life and career is an evident labor of love. The portrait is sympathetic. It possesses an unusual degree of warmth, and at times even a poetic charm. Lacking satisfactory sources, in the form of direct and detailed contemporary record, Wenley has principal recourse to the reminiscent accounts and observations of various individuals who knew Morris personally, including many who had studied under him or had professional contacts with him of one sort or another. It is this circumstance which gives the account its particular richness. The materials on the whole, however, are somewhat loosely organized. The general plan is a twofold division, first presenting a historical sketch of the life and then following this with "an estimate of Morris as a thinker" which runs to about equal length. Background information is preserved in generous detail throughout the pages, and the volume is indispensable for any examination of Morris as a personality.

The present analysis is concerned primarily with the philosophical contribution of Morris to the history and course of American philosophy, and it leans heavily upon Wenley's researches for its general overview of the more intimate events in Morris' life. Apparently all source materials utilized by Wenley are available, most of them in the historical collection at the University of Michigan. While many of these were consulted, in the course of this later study, all references through the following pages in connection with Morris' personal life are to Wenley's book, since it is more generally accessible. For other than the details of home life and background—that is, schooling and travel, the adventuresome incidents in professional adjustment, the recollections of those who knew Morris in or out of the classroom, and the like—Wenley's account is of debatable value. He is very prone to bring in other writers to speak for Morris, such as Lotze and Edward Caird, without a by-your-leave from either Morris or the people quoted, and at times he seems to draw heavily on a commonplace book of his own fabrication.[3] Many of his pages are far more an exposition of presumably inevitable effects of a New England Puritanism upon Morris as a convenient *tabula rasa* than any descriptive analysis of Morris' own individual—indeed, actually unique—intellectual development.

Wenley's interpretation of Morris is based on two primary theses which determine the nature of his exposition and the direction of his various conclusions. The first of these is the assumption that Morris started out with an unquestioning pietistic faith which crumbled under the onset of the mounting scientific criticism during the latter part of the nineteenth century, only to recover it through a newly rationalized Christian spiritualism in the latter years of the Michigan professorship. The other thesis,

---

[3] For example, such curious side allusions as to Colenso, a British defeat during the Boer War in 1899.

somewhat related to the first, is that Morris' thinking went through a series of clearly demarked intellectual cycles, beginning with (1) a naïve superficiality of undergraduate days, passing into (2) a wholly uncritical acceptance of British empirical thought and then moving through (3) a Neo-Kantian phase into (4) a relatively orthodox or onto-logical Hegelianism. The first of Wenley's two theses, which posits a middle period of spiritual doubt in Morris' life, is rejected by the present study as not borne out by the evidence. Instead, a simpler and alternative hypothesis is adopted to account for the known facts in connection with Morris' faith, namely, that it remained unshaken and that his problem rather was to achieve an adequate in-tellectualization for those convictions which seemed thor-oughly grounded in his own inner experience. Morris does not show signs of any battle within himself on the psycho-logical side of his interest, but does appear to have been caught up and challenged to a great agony of creative thinking by the purely rational difficulties he encountered on the philosophical side.

As for Wenley's other hypothesis, it is modified rather than rejected in the course of this re-examination of the basic materials. There is no mistaking the marked chapters in Morris' intellectual progress, but there are no signs of a logical discreteness in these periods, that is, each new one largely excluding the preceding one as an antithesis, and so calling for a synthesis and a fundamentally different species of ideation in an overformal Hegelian dialectic. John Dewey, who probably knew Morris' technical back-ground in philosophy as intimately as any individual, has pointed out in a letter written to Wenley, in December,

1915, that Morris thoroughly fused his earlier Aristotelianism and later German idealism.[4] Dewey defined Morris' Hegelianism, the "organic relationship of subject and object, intelligence and the world . . ." as "the supreme instance of the union of opposites," and said that "epistemologically he was a realist—close to a common-sense realist," adding that "it has always seemed to me that he showed a truer historical instinct in his opposition of Hegel and Kant than has that line of commentators who have treated Hegel as a Kant freed from inconsistency." In other words, according to Dewey, Morris saw Kant as "a phenomenalist, an agnostic," and it is precisely such a Morris that emerges in the present study.[5]

Wenley has misunderstood Morris most seriously when he fails to recognize this epistemological experientialism to which Dewey later called attention. Wenley's own Hegelianism was not a literal discipleship, but it was completely ontological—i.e., a gospel revealing the nature of man and his world—and as such neither representative of Morris nor capable of interpreting him correctly. Dewey, writing to Wenley in 1915, did not feel himself in a position to "expound the idealism which won the ardent loyalty of Morris" three decades before, but he did venture to "comment upon it from the standpoint of the impressions left upon a student. It was, all the way through, an objective and ethical idealism. He effected in himself what many book-scholars would doubtless regard as impossible—a union of Aristotle, Fichte and Hegel. The world, the world truly

---

[4] A process which will be brought out in some detail, and in confirmation of this first-hand judgment. Cf. pages 154, 156, 160.

[5] Cf. Wenley—as all references to The Life and Work of George Sylvester Morris are identified from this point forward—pages 316-8.

seen, was itself ideal; and it was upon the ideal character of the world, as supporting and realizing itself in the energy of intelligence as the dominant element in creation, that he insisted." [6] This almost naïve organicism, in which physical things were teleologically complementary to an ideal or spiritual reality that existed because it made itself manifest continually and in totally unconditioned fashion, was the philosophical formulation of the basic theism—first expressed out of Aristotle in terms of final cause, and then more satisfactorily out of Hegel in the form of a completely personalized universe—which Wenley, with the perspective of a more rational mechanism, was never able to recognize.

The indifference of Wenley to any true organic view is shown in an address prepared for delivery as the seventh annual Howison Lecture at Berkeley, California, in 1929, which he did not live to present in person, but in which he gives the framework of his own thinking at the end of his career. "The vapid prejudice, attractive because so simple, that Howison and his group reproduced German Idealism, is too naïve for serious consideration. What happened was this: the first generation of British Idealists had found a gospel, a way of deliverance from what seemed to them the hidebound futilities of national thought. Thomas Hill Green may have preached Hegel in the latest fifties; he preached 'with the accent of a Puritan' who held 'that it is only in word, or to the intellectually dead, that the creed of the present is the same as the creed of the past.' This understood, we must take Edward Caird's declaration to heart seriously: 'the days of discipleship are past.' British

---

[6] *Ibid.*, page 316.

conditions in Palmerston's old age forbade compliant discipleship, keen sense of obligation despite. American conditions, in their turn, differed widely from British; in especial, there were few, if any, teachers whose persuasiveness lent them formative power. No men appeared in the mould of Edward Caird, T. H. Green, and William Wallace; no preacher of John Caird's tremendous appeal broadcast the doctrine to the people; no theologian of weight, like A. M. Fairbairn, trained young ministers. Had Idealism been served thus on this side, 'it would have swept the country,' as Stanley Hall once said to me."

Then he adds, in a footnote, "I like to surmise that G. S. Morris might have achieved something of the kind at Michigan. But his career was truncated at both ends. His ten years, after 1870, in the Chair of Modern Languages, and his early death at forty-eight (March, 1889), were real mischances." [7] It is with this remarkably casual reference to Morris, twelve years after writing the book on the life and work of his predecessor, that Wenley gives an intimation of his peculiar interpretation of the aims and achievement of Morris. The latter's formulation of a distinctive idealism, quite different from the British, simply escaped Wenley's notice.

Wenley starts his outline of Morris' intellectual development with a clear statement of the problems he had faced as a biographer. "When we come to attempt an estimate of Morris as a thinker, several difficulties must be acknowledged, and borne in mind throughout. First, materials for an intimate review of his entire mental history are lacking. Till the year 1874, when the Ueberweg translation and

---

[7] *'Tis Sixty Years Since*, University of California Press, 1929.

the articles on Trendelenburg were published, we find ourselves compelled to fall back upon such general considerations as we may derive from the tendencies of New England culture taken as a special phenomenon. No doubt these are definite enough. But, second, documentary evidence fails us to mark the steps whereby he passed from childhood faith to a more or less sceptical mood. Personal recollections, too, are scanty. For, sensitive and shy, he never wore his heart on his sleeve." At a later point in his exposition Wenley then reveals the characteristically narrow perspective which provides the psychology of his approach. "It is by no means easy to disentangle the essential presuppositions pertinent to such views, especially when the material before us happens to be the random, pietistic phrases of an immature undergraduate. Nevertheless, the attempt cannot be avoided, because it is evident that Morris, the thinker, was influenced throughout life by this, his starting-point, far more profoundly than by any other single consideration. To liberate himself from it or, at all events, to rethink it, remained his prime object as it was his paramount need. He began and ended a 'Christian spiritualist.' " All evidence, contrariwise, shows the rethinking of the problems of Christianity to have been the primary interest of Morris. There is no actual support for Wenley's picture of him as the victim of a deleterious early New England conditioning.[8]

Morris gained an enduring religious faith from his Puritan background—which was thoroughly theistic, not deistic as Wenley sometimes insists quite inconsistently and with an off eye on the influence of the Enlightenment

---

[8] Wenley, pages 177, 187; also 109.

—and it was this pietism which led him ultimately to a Hegelian organicism, rather than to a purely rationalistic system. In other words, Morris' final thinking is rooted in Hegel, but not in Germany or England. His ultimate view did not arise from the resolution of doubt on a critical or Humean-Kantian pattern, but rather as an intellectualization of a highly personal and integrated love of both science and religion. This personalization of the universe in theistic fashion is the basis of the voluntarism of Morris, to which Wenley remained entirely insensitive. Wenley's mind accepted the mechanical models for the philosophy of science which were current in 1915, and he raised the conventional question of the incompatibility of religious actuality and a scientific comprehension of the world, attributing this problem to Morris. "A real order of existence, the product of concentrated reflection, has been elicited from the apparent order of sensuous things, thus giving ampler import to the plain affairs of the work-a-day world. No doubt, the youthful Morris passes from the one to the other, unaware of the leap for the most part, because he accepts the transcendental order as innocently as he perceives objects that appeal to the senses." [9] There is, of course, no question of the fact that Morris makes this leap, simply because it is no appreciable leap at all in the organic view, and John Dewey gives a more accurate statement of how Morris made it when he said, "But we do him wrong to speak of his religious faith and his philosophic knowledge as if they were two separate things capable of reacting upon each other." [10]

[9] *Ibid.*, page 188.
[10] *The Palladium; An Annual Edited by College Fraternities at the University of Michigan*, 1889, Vol. 31, page 115.

Here is the greatest point of cleavage between Morris and Wenley. Morris never departed from an uncompromising experientialism—as will be brought out in the chapters to follow—and at the end he gave it its greatest and final scope in his own particular Hegelianism, whereas Wenley could never comprehend the organic unity in all time and space conditioning, and so needed the Cartesian dualism as a basis for reasoning about the matter. Hence Wenley starts his exposition with the Calvinism of New England which was "bred in the bone with Morris," and which "held that 'the Bible is the *history* of the redemption, in form of a covenant between God and man after the Fall,'" and affirms that Calvin's reformed theology "made room for a rational account of the development of religion, thus prefiguring the Hegelian system. A series of stages, each higher than its predecessor, *had* occurred in history, until, at length, an 'absolute' stage was reached, thanks to the revelation through Jesus Christ. . . . This stream of tendency," or purely mechanical philosophy of historical development, "lay hidden from him [Morris] for many years. Moreover, I think that, in his ignorance of technical theology, which he came to deplore, he never saw the connection clearly. At the same time, it is unquestionable that the temper and outlook induced by his early norms served but to direct his step afterwards, and to confirm him finally in the convictions that marked his later philosophy." [11]

To say that Morris was ignorant of technical theological doctrines, in any area of rational speculation, is altogether too strong a statement. He had no difficulty handling the

---

[11] Wenley, page 192.

theological points arising in connection with the Ely Lectures, although leaning on Biblical quotations rather than references to the Apologists and ecclesiastical authorities. Dewey explained in 1889 that Morris had "a dislike which never left him" for "what is often miscalled metaphysics, the partly verbal, partly arbitrary treatment of various recondite notions." [12] The Morris presented by Wenley—apart from the external facts and personal record of Morris' life, as already pointed out—is distorted to an extent that calls for considerable reconstruction in the pages to come. Thus Wenley's observations that "it has never occurred to him that the methods proper to treatment of determinate physical phenomena avail us nothing to reach ultimate reality" and that "he is guiltless of philosophical system, and without clear appreciation of the aims of science," causing "no doubt, the confusion and pain he was destined to endure afterwards," [13] show a complete innocence of the major principles coming to formulation in Morris' thought.

In consequence of his basic and serious misapprehensions of Morris' over-all views and criteria, Wenley finds it necessary to say that "no direct clue exists to the reasons for Morris's spiritual unrest as it showed itself in the second year of his seminary course particularly." Hence Wenley's interpretation proceeds, of necessity, on the basis of conjecture. Morris' "previous mental history supports the conclusion, that his extensive and most varied reading, over a term of more than six years, had asserted its effect at length. The youth had been led to admit at least a possible attitude towards the meaning of life in violent

---

[12] *The Palladium*, page 112.   [13] Wenley, page 201.

contrast to the doctrines of his nurture. We should remember that these were the days of that great intellectual awakening, revolutionary in character, now known as the method of science, critical and natural. And many indications, pointing as if by concerted plan in the same direction, must have led an acute youth to observe that some cherished convictions, central to his home-made creed, were under serious fire. Moreover, he had not come by the newer views through the discipline of the laboratory, with its sober restriction to objects that can be weighed, measured or numbered. He had stumbled upon them in works, often semi-popular and of general interest, where much metaphysic, indifferent or bad, was mixed crudely with valuable matter of no metaphysical import. In short, he found himself, almost unarmed, amid the onrush of the battalions of half-truths and half-absurdities that marked the fifteen years after *The Origin of Species;* when the eighteenth century apologetic, attacked on its own ground with modern weapons, went down to utter disaster." [14]

The exposition of Morris' European period by Wenley continues on exactly the same basis. "So far as I am able to infer, after careful inquiry, European study affected him in two ways principally—a positive and a negative. Positively, he learned the necessity for scholarship, and set himself to master the history of philosophy *gründlich.* Building upon an excellent preparation in the New England schools, he came to possess a fund of philosophical information equalled by few, if any, of his countrymen at that time. The humane spirit of Ulrici, ranging with admirable catholicity the field of literature, law and natural

---

[14] *Ibid.,* pages 206–7.

science, and the thorough, methodical, historical accuracy
of Trendelenburg gave him a lead, which he followed up
to the utmost advantage when engaged upon the translation of Ueberweg. Negatively, he obtained no system from
his German masters. His later struggle with scepticism is
traceable, in part, to this, while his evident affiliation with
the British Hegelians, after 1880, attests his own consciousness of the need to bridge the gap. Thus, his German residence was of the utmost importance in that it enabled him,
a decade later, to revert to the great Idealists at first hand,
and with definite knowledge of the issues. Yet, it was an
element in his preparation only. For, at the moment, so far
from easing his doubts, it merely punctuated his years of
transition." [15] This is the George Sylvester Morris of Wenley, given in enough preliminary detail to show the nature
of the portrait and to suggest its complete unreliability as
far as the philosophical achievement is concerned. In order
to get at Morris' actual contribution, it is necessary to start
from the beginning.

[15] *Ibid.*, page 217.

THE MORRIS CHRONOLOGY

1840, November 15, born at Norwich, Vermont.

1854, Autumn, entered Kimball Union Academy.

1857, Autumn, entered Dartmouth College.

1861, Autumn, became principal of Royalton Academy.

1862, October 16, enlisted in the army.

1863, Autumn, returned to Dartmouth as tutor.

1864, Entered Union Theological Seminary.

1866, February 8, sailed for Europe.
(See chronology of European activities on page 133)

1868, August 28, sailed for New York from Havre.
Autumn, resident tutor for the Seligman family, in New York City.

1870, September, Professor of Modern Languages and Literature at Michigan.

1876, June 29, married at Ann Arbor.

1878, January, began philosophical work at Johns Hopkins, dividing time with Michigan.

1885, January, began full time philosophical teaching at Michigan.
Summer, second trip abroad, visiting Great Britain and the Continent.

1889, March 23, died at Ann Arbor.

PART ONE

THE EDUCATION OF THE PHILOSOPHER

CHAPTER ONE

THE NEW ENGLAND CONTRIBUTION

GEORGE SYLVESTER MORRIS was born in a Vermont village, Norwich, situated immediately across the Connecticut River from Dartmouth College at Hanover, in New Hampshire. This was fifteen miles from the Kimball Union Academy at Meriden in the latter state, where he prepared for Dartmouth, and within twenty miles of the academy at Royalton in the former, where he was principal for the year intervening between his graduation from college and his enlistment in the Union army. His birthplace was the center of a town (i.e., a township) with some two thousand inhabitants in the year of his birth. The population of the county was forty thousand, and diminishing slowly under the drain of emigration to the West. The area was agricultural, but there were modest manufactures. The people were predominantly Congregationalist, with some other Protestants (including the Unitarians). Roman Catholics, foreigners and Negroes were seldom encountered. Few sections in the world could be found equally homogeneous on both intellectual and economic counts.[1]

Quite the most important factor in the background of Morris in the 1840's was the essentially frontier nature of the country. Sylvester Morris, father of George, was seven years old when the grandfather, Ephraim, migrated two hundred miles into what then was a mountain wilderness,

---

[1] Wenley, pages 34-5.

settled only recently by its scattered families. There was no
regular communication with the outside world, and as
yet no established church. Eight years later the grandfather
moved again, purchasing a two-story house at Bethel, Vermont, some five miles to the west of Royalton. This he
proceeded to improve and it became the old homestead
known to Ephraim's children and grandchildren. Here
young George is early reported as "playing hide and seek
with his younger cousins all over the house, and seeming to
like it as well as they." Ephraim Morris was a successful
tanner, and in politics a Federalist and Whig.[2]

Sylvester Morris was a tanner by trade, like his father
Ephraim, but also a shrewd businessman involved in many
enterprises. Exceptionally generous, and often violently
exercised over religious and social problems, he frequently
neglected his own financial interests and never accumu-
lated any appreciable means. He gave full expression to
the dominant Puritan traits by which his own son, George,
was to be conditioned. Thus he made his Christian decision and joined the church at the age of twelve. He is
described as "a man to whom the sole realities were God's
providence and the responsibility of man to God, and who
tried everything, great and small, in the absolute balance
of right and wrong. . . . He was afraid of nobody, he
courted opposition, and, serious and severe as he was, he
had a kind of rough humour and a keenness of insight into
the weaknesses of others which he used without mercy.
Intellectual toleration, gentle breeding, and the amenities
of life he neither possessed nor regarded. A radical by the
very constitution of his mind, he appeared to some as a

---

[2] *Ibid.*, pages 8, 12.

Philistine, a fanatic, an impossible absolutist in this sphere of mixed relations; yet in a far truer light he was a hero . . . with the temper of the martyr."

In consequence Sylvester Morris was very active in all religious affairs at Norwich, the birthplace of George. He attended the revivals and spoke up in prayer meetings. However, his greatest interest seemed to center in an active stand on what he saw as the two great social questions of his day. He "was the local apostle of anti-slavery and temperance in the towns in which he lived. . . . On both subjects he took extreme and absolute ground, regarding total abstinence as the solution of the temperance question and slavery as a crime against the inherent rights of man." He maintained a room for fugitive slaves in the famous underground railroad, and exercised varying degrees of antagonism towards the professors at Dartmouth, across the river. He finally came into bitter conflict with the ambitiously named Norwich University in the town to which he had moved (the original American Literary, Scientific, and Military Academy as re-established by Captain Alden Partridge in 1836), since certain convivial times were taken to be the natural prerogative of education on the college level. The students ruined his garden, cut down his trees, even burned him in effigy.[3] Here was the heritage of intense individualism which would have an entirely different expression in the life and character of his youngest child.

Wenley emphasizes in connection with George Sylvester Morris what John Dewey, born seventy miles to the north and west at Burlington only nineteen years later, has brought out similarly in respect to himself. "New England

---

[3] *Ibid.*, pages 13, 15–6, 35–6.

was a relentless school of compulsory labour—a land of
'chores.' A society whose economic foundation was the
small holding, whose commerce hummed in home indus-
tries, promised work, and to spare for all. Children did not
appear 'encumbrances,' there; on the contrary, they were a
'heritage of the Lord.' The six New England generations
of the Morris line are quite typical here. There were sixty-
one children, an average of 10.3 for each succeeding family. In due time they would take their places alongside
father and mother, valiant recruits for the common prosperity. When it was not tilth that cried for hands, it would
be a modest industry—a tannery, perhaps, or a saw mill,
a grist mill, a cooperage where dairy and sugar-sap utensils
were fashioned, a harness shop, or a general store. And,
round the hearth, the womenkind carded and spun,
knitted and did needle-work; churned, saved the wood
ashes; salted the pork for domestic consumption or with
an eye to a fine barter, when the pedlar appeared on his
rounds." [4] This frontier development of individual re-
sourcefulness, and of a highly efficient group integration,
was the first of four important elements in the background
of George Sylvester Morris.

Second of these important shaping influences in his general background was the intense religious or Puritan spirit
already given a brief outline in connection with Sylvester
Morris. "The Sabbath was observed with a strictness which
scrupled at even the picking of a flower; and the head of
the family [i.e., Sylvester Morris] had all a Puritan's objection against games, from authors and checkers down-

---

[4] *Ibid.*, page 27; *cf. The Philosophy of John Dewey*, Paul Arthur Schilpp,
editor, Evanston, Northwestern University, 1929, page 9.

wards. According to the temperament of the different members of the family, this plain living and high thinking produced its impression. It had its dark side, in which are combined memories of the lack of beauty and grace in life, occasional sharp words and rebukes from the mother, the father's seasons of mental depression and fits of the blues, the stern punishments in which whippings followed prayer, and a general distaste for the family radicalism which mortification at the father's loud, long prayers, and great hands stained in the tanyard, went far towards fostering. Yet, on the other hand, one cannot forget on how high a plane the family life ran, or how rich it was in spiritual suggestion and religious aspiration." [5] To be noted here is the opposite face on the coin of individualism, or the sense of self-responsibility and social stewardship as in contrast with self-reliance and the uncritical instinct for social exploitation. The boy, George, was inescapably conditioned by this atmosphere of the home as described from firsthand recollections by his favorite niece,[6] and particularly to be marked is the tendency to depression and an internal seething of the spirit which the last of Sylvester Morris' children inherited in full measure, and upon which Wenley in time builds quite a superstructure of supposition.

Third of the important background elements in the development of young George Morris was music. This became a personal interest paralleling his philosophy throughout his life, perhaps even exerting as large a claim on his basic allegiances of the spirit. It remained supernumerary in the terms of an everyday living, however, and

---

[5] Wenley, pages 14-5. [6] Wenley is quoting Kate Morris Cone.

Morris himself never wrote on the subject other than noting times and places of enjoyment, or reporting casually upon his participation in musical activity or upon his desire to do so. He was largely self-taught, but the family loved music. Except for the sort which would be banned by the Puritan conscience, singing and its accompaniment were welcomed as a proper enrichment for the religious services both at church and in home worship, and so were accepted in train as a means for legitimate self-expression. Lucy Morris, five years the senior of George and his favorite sister, studied music at St. Johnsbury, Vermont, where she taught school fifty miles to the north, and she shared what she learned with him. The family sang together often, first using a tuning fork for the pitch, and then with piano accompaniment when Lucy learned to play. Popular songs, such as were found in various collections, seemed to have been quite acceptable, and were enjoyed by the entire household.

Later, when George was home after the war and a tutor across the river at Dartmouth, he gave piano instruction to two of his nieces in the home where he had first mastered the instrument. It was Kate Morris Cone, one of these, who wrote more than fifty years afterwards that her "earliest recollection of him is as playing the piano, and in a manner that thrilled and educated us all . . . He would play by the hour, completely expressing himself through that medium in a sympathetic environment." In his graduation from preparatory school (Kimball Union Academy) he took the tenor part in the quartette. At Dartmouth College he participated in musical activities and during vacations he practiced on the piano, taught the Sunday-

School children to sing hymns and was one of the organizers of a singing school at the Young Men's Christian Association. When he became principal of the academy at Royalton, on graduation from Dartmouth, he taught some music in addition to his regular subjects. In considering various theological seminaries, he inquired whether an organ was available. On his trip to Europe he gave almost as much primacy to music as philosophy, and on first going to Michigan University he found music the initial open-sesame to the Ann Arbor home consciousness which held him for the rest of his life. Indeed, his early public appearances at Michigan were as a musical performer, and he presided at the organ when a new instrument was dedicated at the Congregational Church in 1876.[7]

The fourth of the important factors which helped condition the intellectual development of George Sylvester Morris was the literary tradition brought into the family by Susanne Weston Morris, his mother. She was no less the Puritan than her more vigorously religious husband, but the strain in her took form in her desire to have at least one son in the ministry. Only George was left to be educated to this end—or appeared to have any special aptitude for the type of study leading to theology—and his sister Lucy added her weight in giving every encouragement to the young scholar. Susanne Morris' father had been educated as a lawyer. Her brother had a college degree, and also practiced law. One uncle was a minister. A sister and a cousin had married into the ministry. George's family, in the male line, had contrariwise been farmers, tanners, pioneers, small businessmen, selectmen and dea-

---

[7] Wenley, pages 38–9, 58, 63, 79, 109, 112, 114, 125.

cons, so that George, insofar as he was a Morris, was a distinct sport or psychological mutation. This is a point which must be emphasized strongly in connection with the analysis of his philosophical contribution. A quotation from a letter written to him by his sister Lucy, while he was serving in the Union army, is revealing. "It is one of the most difficult things for a person of almost purely literary and intellectual tastes," she writes, "to estimate duly the practical side of life." The oblique characterization is by a discerning young lady who had been exceptionally close to him for his entire twenty-two and a fraction years.[8]

His literary inclinations are revealed in his somewhat frequent expressions of himself in verse. These were of the occasional variety, and of no merit except as an additional clue to his own strongly emotional nature. Here was something he was never able to open up and bring into any usual contact with others. The two boys of the New York banker's family whom Morris came to know most intimately as resident tutor—through his twenty-ninth and thirtieth years—report that he "was a gentleman very reserved in his nature and undemonstrative, but . . . with a strong underlying wealth of affection for those he cherished" and that "he kept in touch with us for some years, and . . . his letters were always of an affectionate tone." Literature per se never appealed to him in consequence of this suppression. He could not bare his own soul in words, and by the same token he could not quite quicken his fine critical talents for an understanding of those who did so publicly through the verbal medium. While delightfully witty at times, he was as devoid of true

---

[8] *Ibid.*, pages 9, 37–8, 40, 50, 77.

humor as anyone of real Puritan heritage. As early as in his Dartmouth days his approach to literary subjects was through moralizing dark glasses, as Wenley points out. Even the reading of Shakespeare by the little group away at war in 1862–3, engineered by Morris, reflects the same moralized perspective, as is shown by a paper written at the time and surviving to give the firsthand testimony.[9] His style from the beginning was competent, but to present tastes will seem florid, shaped however instinctively after the New England sermon and the prevailing types of oratory. His range of reference is wide and often very illuminating, but he was always supersensitive to the opposition and as a result his writing is apt to appear cluttered to the reader unfamiliar with the generation in which he wrote and to which he appealed.

These four factors provide the general frame of reality in which the thinking of George Sylvester Morris took form and at length became articulate, and it is in terms of (1) American individuality, (2) religious intensity, (3) an emotional retreat or haven in music, and (4) a scholarly equipment and temperament as a marked deviate in his own family line, that his contribution to the philosophical tradition in America must ultimately be understood.

---

[9] *Ibid.*, pages 53, 72–3, 119.

CHAPTER TWO

THE EDUCATIONAL FOUNDATION

THE education of George Sylvester Morris followed a wholly conventional pattern at the beginning, and fairly full details are preserved. He attended the Norwich District School and then, not quite fourteen, went to the Kimball Union Academy to prepare for Dartmouth College. The academy was far enough from home so that he had to live on the grounds, but the general atmosphere probably differed in little essential respect from that familiar to him throughout his childhood. It was an excellent school which at the time had been in existence for forty years and which, as reported upon sixty years afterwards in Wenley's account, ranked as one of the most successful institutions in New Hampshire.[1] It had been founded to help promising Christian young men, without financial resources, to fit themselves for the ministry. By Morris' day it was a co-educational school, but the boys outnumbered the girls by better than two to one and there was practically no contact between the two sexes. Life on the Meriden hilltop was marked by its strict discipline and a highly religious tone. It was here that the young man made his decision as a Christian and united with the Norwich Congregational Church. He graduated in 1857 with a thorough grounding in Latin and Greek, algebra

---

[1] Indeed, it was still prominent in 1946, through its aggressive headmaster, William Brewster. *Cf. Time,* December 30th, page 44.

through equations of the first degree, English grammar, prosody and prose composition, and of course ancient and modern geography.[2]

He entered Dartmouth that fall as one of sixty freshmen, of whom he was next to the youngest. Until he was a junior he lived at home again, walking the mile between Norwich and Hanover twice each school day. William J. Tucker, his classmate and afterwards president of the college, explains that, as a result of this fact, Morris "did not share as much as some others in the give and take of college life." Any enlargement of horizons was gradual, therefore, and the lack of autobiographical analysis by Morris himself means that any conclusions must remain speculative. College life was a wonderfully warm experience, then as now, but a century ago there was little if any emphasis on creative self-discovery, and the course was prescribed as rigidly as in preparatory school. Latin and Greek were continued for three years, and French through four. Science was represented by mathematics and physics, with physiology added in the senior year. Philosophy was introduced to the sophomores and became the principal subject for the attention of the seniors. Literary and social studies were minimal. Every effort was made to provide the student with adequate tools for an intellectual competence and an enduring appreciation of the culture, but nothing at all was done to help his individual maturity in terms of its own characteristic potentials. The world outside the college community was in political turmoil, with war between the states breaking out in the final months of Morris' undergraduate experience, but his own attitude on social

---

[2] Wenley, pages 37, 39-45, 47.

problems had been crystallized early in his home environment, and the developments were probably more stimulating to prejudice than thought. Thus there is no evidence of any impact on the student body of the great storm brewing over the Dartmouth administration. Under the wise guidance of President Nathan Lord since 1828, the institution had grown from its humble and unpromising situation until it had become one of the leading colleges in the land. But in 1854–5 Lord had published his two *Letters to Ministers of the Gospel of All Denominations on Slavery*, defending the ownership of slaves in principle, and during the Civil War his attitude towards the Union made it necessary for him to resign, although protesting against the rights of the trustees.[3]

There is no sharp point of transition marking the change, from the ministry to teaching, in Morris' choice of a life work. The process may have been quite imperceptible, with many and varying factors contributing to it. However, his qualities as a teacher began to be evident even before he entered Dartmouth. Thus he took the Latin classes at Kimball Academy in February, 1857, when the principal was absent. In January, 1859, during the long vacation between college terms in his sophomore year, he taught four hours a day at a private school in Norwich. He tutored the brother of a faculty member while a junior, and from December through February, 1860–1, taught for twelve weeks in the district school at Medbury, Massachusetts. Out of all this came the opportunity to go to Royalton to become headmaster of the academy there. It seemed a very happy opening. He had his favorite sister,

---

[3] *Ibid.*, pages 45–7, 49–50.

Lucy, to assist him, and in addition to his administrative duties he supervised the study of the classics and mathematics, and also taught German and music when necessary. Thus his second modern language appears in the record, but with no clue to any prior interest in it on his part. Lucy was preceptress, and gave instruction in French.[4] Nonetheless, through all these developments he still looked to the church as a career.

The most important early evidence of the religious stirring or moral urge characteristic of George Sylvester Morris comes out of his enlistment in the Union army. He left his position at Royalton after one year, with the intention of entering theological seminary, but he was torn between this course and a desire to play his part in the military struggle. Patriotism prevailed, with a consciously spiritual motivation. He was just short of twenty-two years old when he joined his regiment at Brattleboro, Vermont, on October 9, 1862. Thirty of the hundred men in his company were from his home town, including the captain. He rose to the rank of corporal, and apparently acquitted himself to everybody's satisfaction. Yet he had no flair for soldiering. In the words of a fellow volunteer, he handled his gun as awkwardly as a woman does an ax. When he marched, he "was out of gear with the rank and file." Hence the colonel, a Dartmouth graduate, "when he found that Morris had enlisted purely out of patriotism and duty" made him postmaster to the regiment and "kept him off the firing line." Life in camp proceeded to break down some of the austerities with which he had been endowed, and the experience probably helped greatly in

---

[4] *Ibid.*, pages 60–3.

bringing him to maturity, despite the degree to which military life was cushioned for him in the bitter days ranging from the disasters of the Peninsular campaign on through the battle at Gettysburg. There was a general prejudice against college people among the soldiers, but they learned to like him, and he never repented his enlistment although to him it remained a duty performed rather than any contribution to his maturing.[5]

After his return from the nine months' term in the army, for which he had volunteered, he attempted to carry out his plan of preparation for the ministry. He was offered the most valuable scholarship given by Auburn Seminary, at Auburn, New York, but this apparently was not financial help enough to enable him to accept. Instead he joined the Dartmouth staff as a tutor in Greek and mathematics, and for the academic year 1863–4 was in residence at Hanover. Here, as at Royalton, his work was excellent. It must be remembered that his proficiency in mathematics was high, a fact not to be lost to sight when examining the later dichotomy he emphasized between a purely mathematical and a more directly phychological point of view, i.e., the contrast between mechanism and organicism which remains the central consideration throughout this study. In July, 1864, he received his M.A. degree, and autumn found him in a position to enter Union Theological Seminary, in New York City. Probably drawn to that institution by the presence there of Henry Boynton Smith, he was thus enabled to make the personal tie which not only unwittingly directed the later course of his career, but in particular encouraged him to look to

---

[5] *Ibid.*, pages 66–78.

philosophy rather than the pulpit for his own intellectual destiny.[6]

He was a student at the seminary for half the three-year course, or until February, 1886, and he found its routine little more than a repetition of his prior educational experience. The studies were prescribed and there was no stimulus to original thought. He was introduced to Hebrew, but did not like it because the personality of the teacher was irritating. Technical theology did not appeal to him, although in later years he came to wish himself better posted in the field (according to a remark made in 1888). The surviving record of his extraordinarily wide reading during the period on philosophy, history, literature and even science is suggestive indication of the extent to which the conventional subject matter in the theological classroom failed to hold his interest. There is no record of any impact by New York City as a metropolis. Union Seminary had been started in reaction from the "high-toned ecclesiasticism" in the Presbyterian denomination. It was thoroughly evangelical, "a hot-bed of temperance and anti-slavery teaching," and Morris probably was coming to realize that the educational foundation he was getting was not meeting his intellectual needs. One of his classmates testified that he "appeared to be somewhat unsettled in his views regarding . . . certain interpretations or explanations of Bible truth," although he was recognized as the superior of his classmates in scholarship, and identified as "the young philosopher." Henry B. Smith, who had ample occasion to test the mettle of Morris' mind and who himself was a brilliant thinker well able to recog-

[6] *Ibid.*, pages 78–82, 88.

nize the potentialities of his student, advised Morris to forego the ministry and proceed to Europe, there to equip himself for a philosophical professorship. William G. T. Shedd of the seminary faculty concurred in this advice, and was in a position—through recent association at Vermont University with James Marsh, one of the pioneers in bringing Hegelianism to America—to explain the particular advantages of German study. Smith's own high reputation in philosophy and theology gave great weight to this counsel. Morris began to consider ways and means, and the trip became possible by the middle of the academic year 1865–6, through the kindness of a friend.[7]

---

[7] *Ibid.*, pages 88–92, 97–103, 107, 174–5.

CHAPTER THREE

FIRST FORMATIVE INFLUENCES

THE best available clue to the conditioning or shaping of
Morris' thought in its earlier phases, or under the impact
of the philosophy current in his milieu, is provided by the
courses of study at Dartmouth and the textbooks used,
together with the collateral reading. Wenley lists the texts
covered by the young student, but his suggestion that
Haven's *Mental Philosophy* had displaced Paley's *"Evidences"* is confusing in the light of a reference from Morris'
journal (presumably to Paley's *Natural Theology*) which
Wenley gives a hundred and fifty pages later. According to
this particular entry Paley "was not made the basis of operations so much as some 'topics' given out by Prof. Noyes."
Morris then provides considerable insight into the operation of his own mind at this undergraduate stage, reporting that the topics, while having some reference to Paley,
"consisted mostly of arguments for the Divine Existence
. . . fully stated and drawn out in various works, such as
Hitchcock's 'Religion of Geology.' . . .

"Through the kindness of Prof. Noyes," Morris writes,
"I obtained a copy of the 'Religion of Geology' a few days
before the examination took place, and found it to be a
most *profitable* and *interesting* work. If people would only
study, and know how things *are,* having a right disposition
and a useful aim, I am sure there would not need to be
so much ignorance and doubt in regard to the truth of

great doctrines, and such as are of vital importance. 'Ignorance is bliss,' you say, perhaps; but hard-earned knowledge is much more than that; and, without doubt, one of the chief delights of glorified spirits is derived from the fact of their vast increase of knowledge. And yet we do not say that the possession of knowledge, in itself considered, is the realisation of the blessedness of heaven. Far from it. For, in that case, the most godless man, provided he be one of great knowledge, would necessarily be supposed to have in the present life a 'foretaste' of eternal bliss. But there is a satisfaction and a pleasure in the possession of knowledge, although it may be lost to some extent, in this life, through the effects of sin, and a diseased heart and blinded conscience." [1]

Edward Hitchcock, therefore, represents a formative influence of importance in the early maturing of Morris' mind.[2] Wenley contrasts the comment of Morris on Hitchcock with a quotation from an early paper written by Morris on "Truth," dated some six weeks later, and re-

---

[1] Wenley, pages 48, 199.

[2] Herbert W. Schneider points out that "during the early part of the nineteenth century the theologians had been kept busy trying to interpret the religious significance of the discoveries of geology. These discoveries were at first attacked as speculative adventures by impious imaginations, but as the concrete verifications kept pouring in and when Sir Charles Lyell finally crowned the science with the philosophical principle of uniformitarianism, doubt vanished, and the only question that remained was one of adapting the Biblical version to the truth as revealed by science. Two theologically gifted geologists led the way in adapting the Biblical story of creation to the evolutionary story of geological epochs . . ." Hitchcock was one of these, professor of natural history and chemistry at Amherst from 1825, and president of the college from 1845 until 1854. "In *The Religion of Geology* (1851) he produced an influential pioneer work of theological reconstruction and paved the way for the general acceptance of his thesis that 'the exclusive object of revelation is of a moral character.' His genial sophistication was remarkably effective in reconciling theists to the general idea of evolution." *A History of American Philosophy*, New York, Columbia University Press, 1946, pages 365–6.

marks,[3] "Evidently, Morris harbours not the faintest suspicion of the lurking contradiction between the two pronouncements. It has never occurred to him that the methods proper to treatment of determinate physical phenomena avail us nothing to reach ultimate reality. In other words, he is guiltless of philosophical system, and without clear appreciation of the aims of science. Hence, no doubt, the confusion and pain he was destined to endure afterwards." [4] However, the assumption that philosophical system is necessary for clear thinking is what might be termed an orthodox Hegelian notion and, in the light of the present study, one which can clearly be dismissed as a *non sequitur* as far as Morris was concerned. The idea that one method is necessary for physical science, and another for spiritual truth, is a fallacy against which Morris protested at every point in his developing conception of a scientifically philosophic method. Meanwhile the effective impact of Hitchcock is to be seen as distilled through the alembic of Morris' mind in an address given by the young preceptor at Royalton Academy in the year following his graduation from Dartmouth.[5]

Wenley preserves evidence from two sources to show that the men at Dartmouth who had the most direct influence on Morris did not include Professor Noyes but rather were Clement Long, and J. N. Putnam, and to them Wenley himself adds Professor Patterson of mathematics. A letter to Wenley from President Tucker in 1912 reports that "the stimulus from Professor Long was that of a perfectly lucid mind governed by inflexible logic. There

---

[3] As already quoted, page 11.   [4] Wenley, page 201.
[5] To which further attention will be given in Chapter Five.

were no evasions or mental excursions in his class room. What was the fact and, if outside the realm of natural things, what was the truth, was the question in many forms which a class had to face before him for an hour a day. Of a different type of mind, Professor Putnam, in the Chair of Greek, was equally stimulating, and perhaps responsible more than any other instructor for the fineness of Morris's scholarship." The dichotomy of fact and truth is to be noted here particularly as not so much a Cartesian dualism but rather a tacit recognition of sensational as versus rational evidence. Morris' niece, Mrs. Cone, reports that "of the professors, Clement Long, as professor of Intellectual Science and Political Economy, had much influence on his pupils, and great strength as an exact thinker. He was very tall and thin and had a high voice. 'You don't happen to remember what the author says on that point?' was a favourite method of address with him. Prof. Putnam taught Greek. He was a charming scholar, a very handsome man of a spiritual type, and possessed of a fine sense of humour." [6]

Of the texts used by Professor Long, Thomas Reid's *Essays on the Intellectual Powers of Man* was Morris' introduction to the dominant academic philosophy by the actual founder of the so-called Scottish school of philosophy. Whether William Paley's *Evidences of Christianity* was used or not, his *Natural Theology* was treated lightly by Professor Noyes. Under Professor Long, Bishop Joseph Butler, represented by *Analogy* and *Ethical Discourses,* and Jonathan Edwards, whose *The Freedom of the Will* was taken up in the senior year, presented the general

---

[6] Wenley, pages 49–51, 60.

theological background of the period in the New England colleges.[7] How far Edwards was expounded, or used as a whipping boy, by the Dartmouth professors in 1860–1 is perhaps beyond demonstration, but the general influence of Asa Burton at Dartmouth must still have been vigorous during Morris' day, and have given theological coloring to disputes on psychological doctrine. Morris in his early thinking held to the argument from design, in terms of final cause, as will be seen through his Victoria Institute papers, but there is not a suggestion of predestination, or any form of Calvinist theology, in any surviving line of his writing. Hence any impact of Edwards—however presented to him—must have been in reverse, as was the common case during the period.

The other texts used by Professor Long are of varying importance to the present analysis. Say's *Political Economy* and *The Federalist* do not seem to have had special significance, in the light of Morris' later interest. He was attracted to the history of ideas, not of institutions. Items such as Campbell's *Rhetoric,* Whately's *Rhetoric* and Schlegel's *Dramatic Art and Literature* (and possibly Trench's *English Language*) naturally added to what President Tucker suggested was "a pretty strong diet for a boy of twenty." They were only incidentally philosophical, but it is important to remember that the rhetoric of these days contained sections on logic, so that Morris probably received his introduction to logic in connection with his

---

[7] At this time, Herbert Schneider explains, "the more philosophical clergymen discovered a new way with Edwards and developed a new psychology to serve their new orthodoxy," so that "the important outcome for philosophy" resulting from the criticism of Edwards was "the founding of a faculty psychology and of an appeal to introspection." *Op. cit.,* pages 232, 237.

study of rhetoric. One book covered in Professor Long's department during the junior year warrants special attention, namely, Whately's *Logic,* and any consideration of the more fundamental intellectual influences in Morris' time at Dartmouth must also include Haven's *Mental Philosophy,* only just published, and the Bampton Lectures by Mansel, to which Morris is known to have given a very careful reading in his senior year.

Richard Whately, professor of political economy at Oxford and archbishop of Dublin, published his *Elements of Logic* in 1826, a work which had gone through numerous editions by the time Morris studied it. Noah Porter reports that this "did more than any book of its day to revive and make practical the study of logic in the universities and elsewhere," adding that "Whately rendered the most important service to free thought in his generation and contributed largely in ways direct and indirect to the promotion of speculative activity." [8] Actually Morris does not seem to have been drawn to formal logic as such, but rather was inclined to speak derisively of it when opportunity offered, and some prefatory remarks by Whately, in view of this, may have significance. "On the utility of Logic many writers have said much in which I cannot coincide, and which has tended to bring the study into unmerited disrepute. By representing Logic as furnishing the sole instrument for the *discovery of truth* in all subjects, and as teaching the use of the *intellectual faculties* in general, they raised expectations which could not be re-

---

[8] Appendix on English and American philosophy, added to Morris' translation of Friedrich Ueberweg's *History of Philosophy,* New York, Scribner, Armstrong, 1871-3, Vol. II, pages 436-7.

alized, and which naturally led to a reaction. The whole system, whose unfounded pretensions had been thus blazoned forth, came to be commonly regarded as utterly futile and empty." [9]

Obviously Whately felt that an entirely new approach to logic was needed, and he provided this by the stress on science which not only reflected the prevailing American and British intellectual climate but which also may well have encouraged Morris in a tendency to emphasize scientific methods in rational no less than in physical areas of judgment. Whately developed a parallel to mathematics, suggesting that "there is in fact a striking analogy . . . between the two sciences. All Numbers (which are the subject of Arithmetic) must be numbers of *some things,* whether coins, persons, measures, or any thing else; but to introduce into the science any notice of the *things* respecting which calculations are made, would be evidently irrelevant, and would destroy its scientific character; we proceed therefore with arbitrary signs representing numbers in the abstract." This is a convenience of reasoning, not a discovery of a truth which lies beyond concrete measurement, and so Whately objects to the fact that "many professed logical writers, not attending to the circumstances which have been just mentioned, have wandered into disquisitions on various branches of knowledge; disquisitions which must evidently be as boundless as human knowledge itself, since there is no subject on which reasoning is not employed, and to which, consequently, Logic may not be *applied.* The error lies in regarding every thing as the *proper province* of Logic to which it

---

[9] *Op. cit.,* pages xv–xvii.

is *applicable.*" He adds that even Aristotle complains of this fallacy of a purely verbal reasoning.

However, many "who do not fall altogether into that error, yet censure any logical treatise which, like the present, professes to be wholly conversant about *Language;* and speak of the science as treating, properly, of the comparison of 'abstract *Ideas,*' of which, Language, they say, merely supplies the *names.* It may be sufficient at present to reply, that, supposing there really exist in the mind— or in some minds—certain 'abstract ideas,' by means of which *a train of reasoning may be carried on independently of Common-terms (or Signs* of any kind)—for this is the real point at issue—and that a system of Logic may be devised, having reference to such reasoning . . . still, as I profess not to know any thing of these 'abstract ideas,' or of any 'Universals' except *Signs,* or to be conscious of any such reasoning-process, I at least must confine myself to the attempt to teach the only Logic I do pretend to understand. Many, again, who speak slightingly of Logic altogether, on the ground of its being 'conversant only about words,' entertain fundamentally the same views as the above; that is, they take for granted that Reasoning may be carried on *altogether independently of Language;* which they regard (as was above remarked) merely as a means of *communicating* it to others. And a Science or Art which they suppose to be confined to *this* office, they accordingly rank very low.

"Such a view I believe to be very prevalent. The majority of men would probably say, if asked, that the use of Language is peculiar to *Man;* and that its office is to express to one another our thoughts and feelings. But neither of these is strictly true. Brutes do possess in some degree the power of being taught to understand what is said to them, and some of them even to utter sounds expressive of what is passing within them. But they all seem to be incapable of another, very important use of language, which does characterize Man; viz. the employment of 'Common-terms' ('general-terms') formed by Abstraction, as *instruments of thought;* by which alone *a train of Reasoning* may be carried on." He continues to demonstrate his point by citing what may be learned from the deaf-mute, and then refers to the case of Laura Bridgman in America, "who has been, from birth, not only Deaf-and-Dumb, but also Blind. She has however been taught the finger-language, and even to read what is printed in raised characters, and also to write. The remarkable circumstance in reference to the present subject, is, that when she is alone, her *fingers are generally observed to be moving,* though the signs are so slight and imperfect that others cannot make out what she is thinking of. But if they inquire of her, she will tell them. It seems that, having once learnt the use of *Signs,* she finds the necessity of them as an *Instrument of thought,* when thinking of any thing beyond mere individual objects of sense." [10] Whately does not carry this objective psychology to an extreme, but he makes language a functional or living phase of mind rather than a mechanical or wholly external process. Here are certain distinct characteristics of Morris in embryo.

Haven's *Mental Philosophy; Including the Intellect, Sensibilities, and Will* was published in 1857, the year that

---

[10] *Ibid.,* pages 18–22.

Morris entered Dartmouth.[11] As Haven uses the designation mental philosophy, it is exactly synonymous with psychology, which was in his generation, he explains, coming into favor as a substitute for the more general term. In view of Morris' later ideas, the point of importance made by this author in his book is the role of the will as the dynamic factor in all psychological reality. Without presenting any philosophical or metaphysical notions as such, Haven outlines a definitely voluntaristic psychology. There is no direct evidence that Morris studied this text, but every presumption that he read it. Moreover, its existence with its marked voluntaristic slant suggests at least a possible direct American source for Morris' otherwise Fichtean voluntarism. Haven acknowledges the dominance of the Scottish philosophy in America, remarking that Hamilton, "by general consent, stands at the head of mod-

---

[11] Herbert Schneider points out that "until about 1820 it has been customary to divide philosophy into natural and moral . . . Logic, metaphysics, and natural theology, like rhetoric and criticism, were usually taught as independent subjects and seldom included under philosophy . . . About 1820, however, there occurred a significant revolution in the very idea of what constitutes philosophy, as well as in its instruction. The Scottish philosophy invaded the country and rapidly crowded out the older eighteenth-century texts. Thomas Reid's *Intellectual and Active Powers* (as his two works were usually called for short) and Dugald Stewart's *Elements of the Philosophy of the Human Mind* (often referred to as *Intellectual Philosophy*) and *The Active and Moral Powers* set the pattern for the new division of philosophy into mental and moral. The study of Locke, Berkeley, and Hume was now absorbed into a course called mental or intellectual philosophy or science of the human mind. . . . In the center of attention was the new faculty psychology or theory of the powers of the mind, so that it is not a great exaggeration to say that for academic purposes philosophy became mental philosophy, subdivided into . intellectual and moral. Though the Scottish texts furnished the models and inspiration for the new American academic orthodoxy, a flood of American texts appeared all on the same general pattern." Of their authors, Schneider identifies Professor Joseph Haven, of Amherst College, as "next to McCosh the most persistent exponent of the Scottish tradition." *A History of American Philosophy*, pages 238–9, 256.

ern philosophers," but then goes on to point out that while Hamilton accepted the doctrine of liberty as a fact (that is, the freedom of the will to act apart from and in divergence from its conditioning) he was at the same time unable to accept the possibility that anything of the sort could happen. In other words, Haven says, Hamilton could not "conceive an absolute commencement." [12] This, by indirection, was no difficulty to Haven, and never at any point a difficulty for Morris.

The strong emphasis by Haven on science as such shows again how little conflict was felt at this time, in New England, between scientific thinking and religious faith. Haven's reason for writing this book was that the texts available in his day confined themselves "for the most part, to the *Intellectual* Faculties, to the exclusion of the *Sensibilities* and the *Will*." Pointing out that the science of nature is physics, while the science of mind is metaphysics, and that these sciences of matter and mind are analogous, he explains that mental science, or psychology, embraces more than metaphysics. The fact that the mind is involved in the analysis of itself is "a great advantage" rather than a handicap because it "can be known with greater certainty." This, of course, is a roundabout assertion of the naïve experientialism characteristic later of Morris and dynamic idealism in general, but in its own generation the exposition was a buttress for intuitionalism. Haven affirms that the observation of mental phenomena is not limited to consciousness and that the relation of mental to other phenomena is a matter of scaling, remarking that "we find in nature a gradual ascending series." Here is sound

---

[12] *Op. cit.*, page 581.

Aristotelian recognition of the continuity of nature, and it is to be noted that Haven rejects the more literal aspects of Locke's faculty psychology when he says that "the mind is not a complex substance, composed of parts, but single and one." Though its "modes of action vary" and are assigned "different names," until "so distinguished and named, they present themselves as so many distinct powers or faculties of the mind, . . ." it is still one "indivisible spiritual principle" which is "acting." [13] Haven thus anticipated the biological or functional psychology which had a marked development in Morris and the young physiological psychologists coming out of Johns Hopkins in the years when Morris was on the staff as professor of philosophy.

The first American edition of the Bampton Lectures by Henry Longueville Mansel (*The Limits of Religious Thought Examined*) had just appeared in Morris' senior year, and a note in his diary reports that he was studying this volume by himself.[14] It was included in a wide range of reading outside class requirements, and the notation in the journal certainly suggests some degree of particularly responsive interest on Morris' part. The American publication incorporated the preface to the third London edition, in which Mansel replies to his critics, and some of his remarks in that connection are especially pertinent. "What, then, is the practical lesson which these Lectures are designed to teach concerning the right use of reason in religious questions? and what are the just claims of a reasonable faith, as distinguished from a blind credulity?

---

[13] *Ibid.*, pages iv, 15, 17ff., 29.   [14] Wenley, page 59.

In the first place, it is obvious that, if there is any object whatever of which the human mind is unable to form a clear and distinct conception, the inability equally disqualifies us for proving or disproving a given doctrine, in all cases in which such a conception is an indispensable condition of the argument. If, for example, we can form no positive notion of the Nature of God as an Infinite Being, we are not entitled either to demonstrate the mystery of the Trinity as a necessary property of that Nature, or to reject it as necessarily inconsistent therewith. Such mysteries clearly belong, not to Reason, but to Faith; and the preliminary inquiry which distinguishes a reasonable from an unreasonable belief, must be directed, not to the premises by which the doctrine can be proved or disproved as reasonable or unreasonable, but to the nature of the authority on which it rests, as revealed or unrevealed. The brief summary of Christian Evidences contained in my concluding Lecture, and others which might be added to them, are surely sufficient to form an ample field for the use of Reason, even in regard to those mysteries which it cannot directly examine." Thus reason is not opposed to faith but made a servant of belief, much in line with the stand later found in Morris.

The role of Mansel in the reviving study of Aristotle at Oxford, dating from 1849, was somewhat parallel to that of Trendelenburg in Germany, and his acceptance of the functional duality of consciousness, throughout his work, can well have contributed to the preliminary shaping of Morris' mind. His indirect criticism of Hegel in the preface may be significant at one point, as a matter of impact on the young senior at Dartmouth. "It is thus manifest that, even granting that all our positive consciousness is of the Finite only, it may still be possible for men to speculate and reason concerning the Infinite, without being aware that their language represents, not thought, but its negation. They attempt to separate the condition of finiteness from their conception of a given object; and it is not till criticism has detected the self-contradiction involved in the attempt, that we learn at last that all human efforts to conceive the infinite are derived from the consciousness, not of what it is, but only of what it is not." He continues, to show that the task of scientifically ordered thinking is neither the proof of absolute hypotheses nor the determination of final insights but rather a verification of values and an evolution of guiding principles. His appeal to experience, for an ordering of any thought about transcendental reality, again can well have had a part in molding the later thinking of Morris.

"If human thought cannot be traced up to an absolutely first principle of all knowledge and all existence; if our highest attainable truths bear the marks of subordination to something higher and unattainable, it follows, if we are to act or believe at all, that our practice and belief must be based on principles which do not satisfy all the requirements of the speculative reason. But it should be remembered that this distinction is not peculiar to the evidences of religion. It is shown that in all departments of human knowledge alike, in the laws of thought, in the movement of our limbs, in the perception of our senses, the truths which guide our practice cannot be reduced to principles which satisfy our reason; and that, if religious thought is placed under the same restrictions, this is but in strict analogy to the general conditions to which God has subjected man in his search after truth. One half of the rationalist's objections against revealed religion would fall to the ground, if men would not commit the very irrational error of expecting clearer conceptions and more rigid demonstrations of the invisible things of God, than those which they are content to accept and act upon in all the concerns of their earthly life." [15]

[15] *Op. cit.*, pages 15. 25. 27.

Chapter Four

FIRST SELF-EXPRESSION

Young Morris had little opportunity to develop any particularly original views of his own, under the crowded and rigid regimen at Dartmouth, but the themes or papers written by him show his thinking in the light of his background, intellectual resources and reading. Of the surviving compositions the earliest was read at the Theological Society on November 6, 1857. Here the young freshman discusses the text, "The serpent beguiled me, and I did eat" in a completely naïve fashion. A real insight into the nascent intellectual powers is provided, however, in a theme dated only ten days later, equally theological in its reference but using a subject matter of philosophical import. It is entitled *"Mens immortalis: corpus mortal."*

In these few words is contained all—for the most part—that is known of the difference between mind and matter—between the living, actuating principle and the gross perishable dust of which we are formed. So limited is our knowledge of that "mysterious instrument" which is so awfully grand in its faculties— so lasting in its nature! For the mind is something so constituted that it cannot be handled or touched— that it cannot be seen, or examined by physical operations: it is a piece of mechanism, godlike in its origin, intelligent in its nature, able to be influenced by outward actions either for better or for worse—and eternal in its destinies.

Of the mind, then, or soul (the two words being synonymous) little can be known except what we may ascertain by reasoning from some of the ways in which it manifests itself upon our actions and consequently upon our characters—and from what is revealed concerning it in the Divine Word. The mind has been made the subject of profound thought and speculation by many of the wise men of earth—and however inadequate may have been the results attained, ill would it become me to enter into any new theory upon the subject. But it is possible to relate some of those things which have been ascertained and are known to be true concerning it from manifest tokens, and from Divine revelation.

The mind, then, is a reasoning and inventive power. This is very evident from the fact that while the action of brutes ever run on in one unchanging and prescribed course the movements of man are continually changing, accordingly as his mind suggests to him an easier or more direct mode of gaining his desired end. . . . The mind is a governing power. This is strikingly exemplified in the evident influence of that inward thinking part of our nature which controls our actions . . . Again, the mind is susceptible of receiving impressions. This is an assertion, too, which has been found to rest upon the best of authority and to need little demonstration. . . .

The ostensible purpose of each one of us in coming to this place of learning is to benefit the mind by the

superior advantages here offered—and we should
doubtless see to it that we do attain that mental and
moral culture to which we should all aim. . . . The
mind may . . . be acted upon, and hence arises the
necessity of looking well to the right cultivation of it
—for there is such a thing as mental culture—and of
giving the proper direction to all its proclivities.
Much in proportion as we form right habits of mind,
are we forming right character, and as are our characters—such shall we be as men—as citizens—as
brothers.

As far as the record goes, here is the initial self-expression of the philosopher, seventeen years and one day by
age, and an undergraduate in college by some weeks. What
is to be identified, in terms of distinctive presuppositions?
The soul or mind (this identification is significant) is
eternal because its potentialities are illimitable, but it
only knows through its works, and any knowledge comes
from an observation of these. Morris defers to the Bible as
a source of information, but does not quote it and apparently considers its testimony as a challenge to personal
investigation or verification. Actually "it is the lofty literary and scientific productions" of mind which "attest its
divine origin and nature." The soul is to be known
through man's actions and his character. Morris' pattern
of analysis thus identifies the functional or psychological
approach, reflecting the new scientific ferment much more
than the pietistic background, and showing the extent to
which he was ready for the impact to be made by other
thinkers of his day. He recognizes the influence of the

mind on external realities, and their corresponding compulsion on its reactions. While it is a "governing power" it is also "susceptible of receiving impressions," and the conception of psychological interaction is complete, whether this generalization was yet a conscious achievement or not. He makes a two-way proposition of the interactive relation, so that a free will and a social conditioning exist together in a close and real partnership. Whatever unusual situation may develop in life, man's unique possession of mind or soul enables him to escape the purely external limitation. Morris had no philosophical language or critical understanding for developing the organic voluntarism involved in his naïve insight here, namely, that free will cannot be absolute, but its foreshadowing is interesting.

His first real philosophical awakening seems to begin with another paper written in the spring of 1858, or towards the end of his freshman year. Entitled "Ideality versus Reality," it shows the full extent of his naïveté relative to the history of philosophy, but it also gives an intimation of the underlying intellectual competence of his own reflection.

That which we commonly call the ideal is the result of the imagination, aided, perhaps, by an intuitive perception of right and wrong, of what is proper and improper—which exists in the human mind. It is that notion which we form with regard to any particular subject, and which is our standard of judgment as well as our point of ambition, with respect to it. It is that in connection with some things, which forms our model of perfection—with others, that which becomes our standpoint of deficiency and imperfection.

That which we term *ideal* is visionary, existing to a great degree in the realms of fancy. In the real are comprised all the occurrences of everyday life and of a surrounding and engrossing world: the ideal springs from the mind, the hidden seat of imagination—the real presses itself upon our attention with renewed energy and force so long as we inhabit the earth. Every one has his *ideal*—his *beau idéal*—and all men have an impressive knowledge of the *real*.

In imagination one's fancy soars at times beyond the cognizance of actual events and fixes itself on things beyond the common scope of thought. It is in these dreamy flights that one gains an idea of what man might be, were he not restrained by any untoward and unfortunate propensities. Then, frequently the powers of the intellect are brought into freer and more copious action, and results are produced which amaze the mass of men, whose thoughts ever flow in the same lifeless channel. But from these imaginary heights how great the descent to the actual and real! How does man almost regret his existence when he considers that his mind is in a measure bound down, and kept from making those upward risings, those advancements in intellectual and moral greatness, to which his whole being aspires!

How, also, does the lack of sympathy and appreciation among his fellow-men grieve his heart, and impress him anew with a knowledge of the unpleasant fact that most men care not for those things to which his soul aims, but are content to remain in a low and unproportionate realization of the things which are truly noble and eternal!

But it is much easier, frequently, for persons to be what they desire to be, *mentally* than it is to be such *really*. *In imagination,* one can be a true gentleman, an accomplished scholar, a profound logician or a wise statesman—but when he attempts actually to be such a gentleman, scholar or statesman he finds a thousand natural or self-imposed obstructions in his way, so that it is only by oft-repeated attempts and perhaps, after successive failures, that he attains the object of his desire. A man is thus taught his own weakness, and sometimes learns to take more humble and correct views of himself.

The ideal has a practical bearing upon the real. For there *is* a *reality.* However man may ignore even his own existence (for such a thing is not unheard of)— and the existence of duties which he owes to himself, to his fellow-men and to God—still these things do exist, and must remain in the future what they ever have been—*stern* and *fixed realities.*

The mind, floating among the realms of the ideal finds a new range of thought, more elevated than that which is common to it, and thus becomes enlarged— the views of its possessor are enlightened and an apparent effect is produced upon the course of his real life. Our treatment of the real thus varies with, and depends somewhat upon, the range of our imagination. One whose ideal is high, and lofty and noble, will be apt to conform his life in a great measure to an elevated standard of action—while those whose ideal is base, or who have none at all, will be found low down in the misty depths of careless ignorance and moral inexistence.

How, then, shall we cause our ideal to be what it should be?

1st, by governing and chastening the fountains of the mind and imagination with a deep sense of moral and religious things. Nothing else will purify our thought, and therefore it is a positive duty to make use of this means. The stream must partake of the nature of its source and if the intellectual font be thus cleansed from all infecting things, the results upon our ideal and real natures must be beneficial.

2dly, by fixing our thoughts upon such things as are right and pure and noble. Such a course must evidently be conducive to the desired end. But if, on the contrary, we allow our imagination to be filled with such things as are low and debasing, its powers will either be weakened, or its tendencies and effects pernicious.

Let us then, Brothers of the Fraternity, thus elevate our thoughts and our natures. Let us have our ideal noble and good in order that whatever talents we may chance to possess may be consecrated to the cause of truth and humanity, and that we may the more satisfactorily accomplish life's great good.

The dichotomy of mind and matter is even less an ontological distinction here than in the paper of the preceding autumn, not because the philosophical problem of the difference had disappeared but because the necessity for a proper psychological interaction between the imagined and the actual has moved forward and become of much more fundamental importance. The young man has grown in his first year at Dartmouth—quite naturally, it may be presumed—and his mental philosophy has come to the foreground. What exists in a world of ideas is of no significance by that fact alone, since the ideal per se is "visionary, existing to a great degree in the realms of fancy." Things of mind are not necessarily worth while. They can be visionary or "filled with such things as are low and debasing," and hence the intelligent person is called on to put his thinking capacities to work to a better end than before, and to train them so that they can achieve this more effectively. Morris has not as yet even begun to free himself from the various limiting presuppositions embedded in his intellectual milieu, but his sharpening sense that ideas have a tool function is an indication of his incipient voluntarism.

There are extant a total of forty-three papers belonging to this general period, and all of them demonstrate his complete lack of literary flair. At the same time they are consistent, showing his philosophical and linguistic inclinations in everything he does. Thus in writing about "James on Art," he is impatient with "metaphysical grubbing." However, the instincts of the careful scholar have not yet been developed, and he reveals a tendency to the uncritical generalizations that betray his conditioning. In a paper on "Slavery" probably written as late as some six weeks before his enlistment in the army—or while he was at Royalton—he remarks that "the hand of God is seen in

the election of Mr. Lincoln." He is often unaware of the
philosophical implications of the literature he is studying,
as markedly evident in a composition on "Bancroft and
Prescott."

His scattered but unorganized scientific observations in
his class-notes under Professor Noyes may represent no
more than that instructor's comments, but it is interesting
to observe what catches Morris' attention. Thus he puts
down that the nebular hypothesis establishes God as final
cause, which is an anticipation of his own later stand. He
reports that "a modern view considers life to be 'electrical
energy' " and that "the fundamental form of organic being
is a globule," the latter notation in probable reference to
the theory that cells arise only from the fission of other
cells, enunciated in Europe just three years before. In his
handwriting is the statement that "man was once a
monkey," indicating the lack of any sharp anti-evolution-
ary religious thinking or dogmatism in these Dartmouth
classes. The development of the organic view, rising with
the developments in biological science and punctuated by
the appearance of Darwin's *Origin of Species* almost at the
time this class was in session, intensified the intellectual
ferment at work. Morris records that "monads have been
shown to be distinct animals," and adds to this that "all experimental evidence is against the development theory," [1]
which means that the young man or those about him were
certainly seeking to think things through in a genuinely
scientific fashion.

It is not surprising, in the light of all these indications of
his intellectual maturing at Dartmouth, that he should

---

[1] The current form of emergent evolution.

subject some of the religious presuppositions of his earlier
upbringing to the rational criteria he is now developing
for himself. In the year of his graduation with the A.B.
degree he writes, concerning the nature of the Bible's inspiration, "The fact is that the Scriptures . . . are all inspired as is taught to the eye of faith by the internal evidence in relation to some parts, and to the eye of the intellect in relation to all its parts. I refer in the latter case to
the direct declarations of Scripture in favor of this position.
Yet a belief in their entire and plenary inspiration is not
necessary . . . to the . . . production of saving faith in
the heart by the working of the Spirit. After this faith has
been wrought in the heart, those facts of the Bible which
are of spiritual significance will be regarded as inspired, as
the word of God, that is to say, we may look for this result,
though I do not assert it to be inconceivable that one
should be a Christian and deny the inspiration of the
Scriptures *in toto*. To the sound intellect and unbiased
judgment, the inspiration of the whole Scriptures should
be evident." However, "no belief in the inspiration of the
Bible is, therefore, pre-essential to saving faith. Subsequently to the possession of saving faith, belief, at least in
their partial inspiration will almost invariably be found,
and if the mental powers be unimpaired in their total inspiration."

Morris has nothing but disgust for the rational sub-
stitutes offered in place of orthodox Christianity. In his
undated "Extracts and Abstracts from Review of Bushnell's
Nature and the Supernatural," he comments on Theodore
Parker who "believes in what is called absolute religion
. . . making reason to be everything in religion, as it is in

philosophy. . . . Accordingly, all that he would call religion, distinctively, consists in sentiment and aesthetics, in
admiration of the true and the beautiful." And, in reference to the opinion expressed by Dr. Bushnell "in one
passage . . . that we need more miracles . . . our Re-
viewer justly remarks, that we rather need grace to accept
what we have. . . . We need to accept more willingly and
so to receive more lovingly, those gifts of the Spirit which
are offered us." However, along with his active concern
over his religious interests—and his free expression of
theistic concepts—Morris was making exceptional progress
towards an excellence on the scientific side of his education, continually re-emphasizing the fact that there was no
important conflict between the theological and secular
aspects of knowledge in the case either of himself or the
Dartmouth milieu as a whole. Then, early in his junior
year, when the undergraduates were coming to spend an
increasing amount of time on philosophy, Morris wrote
his one paper of a technically philosophical nature, entitled "Philosophy Previous to the Time of Bacon."

Beginning with a discussion of "Its Aim," he points out
that among the ancient philosophers the chief object "was
the discovery of some ultimate principle, whether spiritual,
material or theoretical, in accordance with which all the
known phenomena of natural existence might be explained," and that "pre-Baconian philosophy was variously
theoretical, as aspiring after absolute truth; practical, as
designed to influence the life; or political, as contending
for ends and beliefs," adding that "in some cases two of
these characteristics existed together." He turns to "Its
Results" as a second subheading and explains that "the

product of the theoretic or ideal philosophy was substantially an abortion. It neither satisfied the universal reason of mankind, nor afforded a gratification to their curiosity. It never quenched one spiritual longing, or calmed the inward raging of one unenlightened soul, trembling before the startling mystery of its own existence. Instead of an adequate and intelligible explanation of all cognizable phenomena, men caused the original Chaos of Mythology to be succeeded by theories purely conjectural, or at best, having little foundation in recognized truth, but, almost solely, the fruit of pure intellection." Sketching in various examples, he goes on to say that "Socrates rebuked this abusive misapplication of the highest truth, and taught that not the individual man, but humanity was to judge or be the measure of things," and identifies Plato as the "real successor of Socrates."

Plato is summarized with little understanding. "To him belongs the celebrated 'theory of ideas,' or archetypes of things, between which, however, and their material representations, there existed an inseparable gulf. . . . There lacked a moving principle, superior to the ideas and the thing, which should cause them to participate with each other," a remark quite significant in the light of Morris' later insights. "This want was noticed by Aristotle," he continues, "but not supplied." Stoicism and Epicureanism, Neo-Platonism, and Scholasticism alike were unable to meet the need. "Thus did philosophy fail to afford a rational solution of those insensible questions relating to being, its origin and end, which it had proposed to itself. Its range was, however, widely extended, and much that was of importance and utility to man was included within

its domain." But "at best, its results were only partial, and
it frequently ran into absurdities. Philosophy never ascertained for man his origin, or pointed out his destiny."
With this Morris is ready for his third and final subheading, "The means by which these Results were arrived at."

Pre-Baconian Philosophy was, for the most part,
synthetic. It started with some principle, usually attained by pure intellection with little aid from analysis. In accordance with this principle or theory it
was attempted to explain all phenomena—to it all
things were expected to conform. As contradistin-
guished from that method of philosophizing which
was insisted on by Bacon, it was *deductive* rather than
inductive. From a given principle, in the first place, a
material one, as we have seen, afterwards, a spiritual,
men endeavored to deduce the phenomenal world.
The finite sought to apprehend the incomprehensible
and the infinite. This, however, was not a fault peculiar to ancient philosophy, as all are aware, who have
any acquaintance with the attempts of modern philosophers. In the ancients, too, it is a fault that might
well be pardoned, however objectionable might be
the methods with which they sought to compass their
ends, for they are merely engaged in the blind contest
of humanity, obscurely conscious of being a "Connection exquisite of distant worlds!"

"Dim miniature of greatness absolute!" endeavor-
ing to realize the hitherto unknown side of that
wonderful paradox—mortal and yet immortal—human yet divine!

Morris' first philosophical self-expression ends with no intimation of the sources from which he obtained the ideas in his paper, nor is it possible to tell how seriously he took them. Wenley notes that "undergraduates were not only left free to read what they pleased, but encouraged to acquaint themselves with the works of the great writers, past and present, irrespective of the views urged." However, there is no detailed information concerning their availability at Dartmouth. Moreover the letter to Wenley from President Tucker shows that there was very little time for much collateral reading of a technical sort. Morris would have encountered Plato directly in the Greek through the *Phaedo* or *Gorgias* before the end of this junior year, but it is not known to what general texts in the history of philosophy he had access.[2] George Henry Lewes' *Biographical History of Philosophy* had appeared in 1846 at London, and Albert Schwegler's history—which Morris read later at Union Seminary—had been available in an American translation of the abridged German edition since 1856, the latter obviously not read by him at Dartmouth. It is quite probable that he was familiar with Gottlieb Tannenberg.[8] Neither Ueberweg's work nor that of Johann Eduard Erdmann had appeared when Morris was an undergraduate. The preface to the American edition of Ueberweg surveys the situation in this field as it stood only a short ten years later, and the remarks by Ueberweg himself in his introduction show the difficulties faced by the student who sought any competent overview of develop-

[2] Wenley, pages 47, 49, 198.
[8] Revised in German by Amadeus Wendt, translated into English by A. Johnson, and issued at London in 1852 as revised and enlarged by J. R. Morell.

ments in the field of speculative thinking.[4] There was un-limited material on which to draw, but little of it in English or available in the average college library. Any study of the history of thought as an integrated and living process was yet to come.

The precise origin of the opinions expressed by Morris in this composition is of no consequence to the present study except as permitting a more exact reconstruction of the intellectual milieu in which his thought began to mature. The ideas as such are not significant, in other words, but rather the use made of them by the young college student. From this latter point of view the paper is invaluable. The desire to ascertain absolute truth is not repudiated by him, but instead the attempt to get at this by a purely synthetic means. The denial of any possible absolute of a rational nature affords an important anticipation of a very basic principle in his mature thinking. At this time Morris, reflecting his Scottish sources and their preaching of inductive method, is far more Baconian than at any point in his later life. His scorn for the attempt of "the finite . . . to apprehend the incomprehensible and the infinite" is of a piece with his ultimate standpoint, nonetheless, giving early testimony to the fidelity with which he holds to an empirical form of theism, and revealing the underlying direction of his interest from the beginning. Man needs intellect for any mastery of the world, but the reason must look out to more than objective reality, almost as though Morris was thinking of Aristotle's criteria of ordered knowledge as not alone characterized by "accuracy" but also by its continual relationship to "higher

---

[4] *Op. cit.*, pages vii–ix, 8–13.

and more wonderful things." [5] Purely secular philosophy to Morris will ever be a "dim miniature of greatness absolute," and he demands that everyone realize "the hitherto unknown side of that wonderful paradox, mortal and yet immortal, human and yet divine."

---

[5] *De Anima*, 402a, 1–5.

CHAPTER FIVE

EARLY MATURITY

THE exact circumstances which took Morris to Royalton as headmaster for the school year of 1861–2—just before his twenty-first birthday—are not on record. The academy was only twenty miles from Norwich, but intimate touch with his home was as impractical as it had been when he was at Meriden, preparing for Dartmouth. The surroundings must have been much more familiar, however, since he was within some four miles of his grandfather's place at Bethel. The appointment was a happy one in every respect, as has been explained.[1] A very close friendship ripened with the Denison family, long settled at Royalton. Miss Alice Denison taught drawing and painting at the academy, and Professor Charles Simeon Denison was later a fellow-member of the Ann Arbor faculty. Morris' first romantic attachment, apparently developing towards the end of 1865, drew him to Miss Susan Denison, seven years his junior and here not only his pupil but known in the intimacy of New England home life.

This romance ended in disappointment, and the young lady's defection had an unfortunate psychological impact on Morris' spirits while in Europe. Indeed, he did not marry until eight years afterwards, in June, 1876, when he was nearly thirty-seven and was attracted to Miss Victoria Celle, of New York, introduced to him by a colleague on

---

[1] *Cf.* above, pages 28–9.

the University of Michigan medical staff. Then "a home life, singularly bright and happy, grew up." Morris and his wife enjoyed nearly thirteen years of happiness before his sudden death, as the result of exposure to rough weather at North Lake, near Ann Arbor. They had a son, Roger S. Morris, and a daughter, Ethel Morris. His earlier engagement to Susan Denison was entirely an affair of correspondence, however, since he proposed by mail from abroad, and it lasted only a little over a year, or until she broke it, also by letter. She felt he had "grown so learned and had changed so much in his religious opinions," that she "was afraid of him." He was given no chance "to right matters by a personal interview." Her observation that he had changed in his religious opinions is indication to Wenley that Morris had swung away from his early evangelical faith, but the comment of a nineteen-year-old girl could equally well reflect her common reaction to the unfamiliar in the form of his increasingly intellectual and highly erudite interest in the Christian doctrines, as well as a simple but quite reasonable misapprehension of the meaning behind his abandonment of the ministry in favor of a philosophical professorship. Rather than changing, he was holding firmly to the plan of life he had put down for himself at the end of the Royalton year. "What time I do teach, I must make it profitable, that I may earn money to bear further educational expenses, and to assist me in the prosecution of certain designs of travel and study." [2]

Morris reached his early maturity at Royalton, gaining confidence in himself and learning how far he could lean on his own skills in actual practice. It was an experience

---

[2] Wenley, pages 63, 67, 104, 116, 118, 143, 175.

of particular value because he came to realize where he fell short of his own ideals for himself, and perhaps also came to suspect that the course he had laid out was not as simple as it appeared. Preparation for life had given way to the responsibilities of living, and hence the intellectual growth —as a formal educative process—gave way to self-expression of a different sort. Morris was called on to put his knowledge and faith to work, and this he proceeded to do. Much less than at Dartmouth, by the nature of the case, he leaned away from any critical examination of his beliefs or theories, and began to give full articulation to the theistic concepts in which he had been raised. Six addresses or lectures, surviving from this period, show his exposition of his ideas at the climax of his uncritical orthodoxy, and it is significant that even here the philosopher is evident. Five of the talks were delivered to the pupils, but the sixth was prepared for a more mature audience at East Barnard, a town about five miles to the south. The subject of this last was astronomy, and the presentation is interesting in showing Morris' acceptance of the early Bible stories as possibly historical material.

"It is regarded as historically certain, that astronomical observations were made, with considerable success at least, soon after the fall of the tower of Babel." For all his basic intellectual competence, and for all of what in his day was exceptionally fine training at Dartmouth, he as yet was quite devoid of historical sensitiveness. Only German scholarship will break this insular New England tendency to think in a logical vacuum. The theistic background is seen strong and unshaken despite the impact of the new scientific ferment to which he was exposed in his college years, but his intellectual isolationism is as evident in secular as in Biblical perspective. "The visible universe constitutes a standing argument to demonstrate the glory and power of the Creator. A correct appreciation of its vastness and undisturbed order, together with its marks of exquisite design, strengthens in the mind the belief in the Deity." Thus, in common with the Puritan generation from which he has sprung, Morris sees science substantiating the claims made for Scripture, and for the moment he revels in the evangelistic opportunity provided by his preceptorship. This was the enthusiasm marking the momentary stage in his growth, and was probably the attitude which Susan Denison expected him to develop even further.

When it comes to the talks given the hundred odd students at the academy, the one which was the most elaborately developed presentation of the five, on the subject of geology, reflected the obvious inspiration provided at Dartmouth by Hitchcock's *Religion of Geology*. Morris opened with wide and imaginative generalizations, such as would be fascinating to the Susans of any era. "The limits of attainable knowledge are practically infinite. The profusion of objects, suited to gratify the desires of the intelligent mind, is truly wonderful. The material world, however insignificant or unsatisfactory when considered apart from its uses, and from the marks of intelligence which it bears, furnishes ample food for the most rapacious intellect. He who desires to exercise himself in the comprehension of the profoundest truths, singly, or the greatest number of interesting facts, collectively, may have his most boundless wishes satisfied in the contemplation of the broad Universe of God." Morris then goes on to explain that geology is a science of comparatively modern date, and he makes a comparison with astronomy, which is as old as man's organized knowledge. However, "the recency of its development . . . is no argument against the correctness of the deductions of Geology, or the cogency of its facts." Relative to the latter, he then reveals the equal rank in his mind of deductions or verification by tangible and physical measurement, on the one hand, and the insights of such sort as are represented by religion and the inspired writings, on the other, so that validation becomes social and is accomplished through the course of history and the gradual refinement of the race in the terms of ethical and esthetic ideas.

His sketching in of the scientific outlines is clear and competent, and at the end he asks, what all this may imply. "First, it is proved that the earth is not 6000 years of age, merely—but has existed for myriads of centuries. Man may not have seen light till the period indicated by Mosaic record—but the earth must have existed, and been the abode of organized existences ages before the noble thought of God gave itself expression in the creation of man. I have referred to the fossil remains found in the depths of the earth: distinct classes of fossils being found invariably in the different strata. . . . The proof thus furnished as to the age of the globe is decisive and leads to the conclusion I have mentioned. If any one is disposed to inquire how this can harmonize with the account of the creation furnished in Genesis, I have only to say that the facts of Geology do not conflict with a fair and an intelligent interpretation of the sacred canon. Nor do they diminish in the least the respect and reverence due to the word of God, or the authority of its teachings."

The philosophical stand of Morris was already well defined in some important particulars. Thus science does not exist primarily to challenge Scripture—which the older American orthodoxy took for granted—or even to confirm divine revelation—which the new Puritan generation affirmed in a contrary overemphasis—but rather, as was to become the particular credo of Morris, to provide man with tools for a better living. In his lecture on the "Elements of Perfect Manhood," another of the five surviving papers read to his Royalton pupils, he takes up the matter of the interaction between the individual and the environment, and gives a particular stress to this dynamic or tool function of ideas. "It is a principle demonstrated in Natural Philosophy, that *action* and *reaction* are equal. It is upon this principle that all motion over the surface of the earth depends. Just as the application of the lever to any one of its important uses would be impossible, if the support of the fulcrum should give way, as the power is applied—so, for a similar reason, all movements upon the face of the earth would be, to a certain degree, irregular and unequal, were not the principle, to which I have referred, an universal one. Now, human life proceeds upon a principle analogous to this. It is measured by its results. Any life but one of activity would be meaningless. But no efficient activity is possible without self-reliance. If one puts forth his hand, half doubting whether he have the physical ability to do it, his exertions lack energy and effect. So if one engage in any work, without confidence in his ability to perform it, his endeavours are practically ineffectual and valueless. However intense be his desires, or however agonizing his fears, he will fail to produce any decided results. He lacks a fulcrum, sure and steady, without which his efforts are a mockery. He acts, but acts nervelessly, and without spirit. He accomplishes nothing."

What is the answer to human deficiency here? How does the individual gain such a fulcrum by his own act? "Another element of the perfect man is . . . an enthusiastic temperament. Man possesses no natural gift of greater value than the capacity of enthusiasm. Enthusiasm is identical, in nature, with that spirit which appreciates the beautiful, and admires the good. The proper development of this faculty refines the heart. Flowers, statuary, painting, educate the mind only as they incite activity in this principle. If one were of so indifferent a nature as to perceive no beauty in a flower, no harmony in music, no proportion in a work of art, then would all be without significance or value to him. The life of such an one must be passed in the outer court of cold calculating utility, or bare necessity. Even his notions of utility and necessity would be inadequate and base. The worth of things would be measured by their adaptation to supply the grossest wants of the body. If any notions of right and wrong should exist, they would impress the mind with little force. Where, then, would be the zest of living? Objects of beauty are valuable to us, because the ardent apprehension of their beauty is associated, by nature, with elevated and refining ideas." Here is Morris at the threshold of his esthetic conception, a phase of his maturing thought which will have a thorough consideration in the following chapter.

CHAPTER SIX

THE CONCEPT OF SPIRITUALIZATION

THE two years following Morris' preceptorship at the Royalton Academy—or until he went to New York City in the autumn of 1864 to enter Union Theological Seminary —constitute a second phase of his initial maturation. This had its beginning in the nine months of army experience in 1863, since it was in Virginia that he was called on to adjust himself, for the first time in his life, to a social environment totally different from anything he had ever known before. The return to Dartmouth for the academic year 1863–4 was, by contrast, an adjustment consisting primarily of an intellectual regathering and re-expression of the characteristic ideas and convictions with which he had come to manhood, and so preparation for the real change in life plan which would follow shortly.

Dr. Gardner Cox, who served in the 16th Vermont Regiment with Morris and provided Wenley with a firsthand account of the events in Virginia, writes that "As I was an orderly sergeant, I had the privilege of keeping a light burning in my humble tent after all the rest were out. Morris, ever true to his impulses, came into my little tent, where lived four others. He had five copies of Hamlet, little, cheap, paper-covered Hamlets, but Shakespeare's own Hamlet. He said to one Bowman, who belonged to another tent, but who was a fine scholar with me at Royalton, 'Now scholars, I want to introduce you to the best intellectual entertainment in all literature,' and he gave us each a copy. I never had read a word of Shakespeare, and did not suppose ordinary mortals could understand, and I was shocked that he should think that we country chumps could read Shakespeare and understand it . . . We were made to love those evenings with the greatest profit and enthusiasm. Each read a part assigned to him and, in the course of a few months, we had pretty well studied Shakespeare, and had gone over all of the best plays. It whiled away so many of those long, weary, lonesome nights to us poor homesick boys, scarcely acquainted with the world enough to speak for ourselves." [1]

Morris wrote a paper on Shakespeare at Fairfax Station in Virginia—in the spring of 1863, while the regiment was picketing the outer defenses of Washington—and in this he says that the drama "must owe its origin to the existence of some normal and virtuous, or unnatural and vicious want of humanity, and since humanity, the world over, is essentially the same, the same want or desire would not improbably lead to the same concrete result in different places, at the same time. The drama has its original warrant in a real and therefore sacred want of human nature —the want of an actual, perceptible, and comprehensive representation (necessarily a representation of human life) by which individual life should be dignified and elevated, something that would stimulate self-penetration and self-knowledge, and that, by stimulating thought, deepening feeling and imparting knowledge on one's higher capacities, should serve to educate the man. To educate, I mean, in the highest sense . . ." He then suggests that the stage

---

[1] Wenley, page 72.

had degenerated through the rise of comedy in which
serious things were ridiculed, as well as through the be-
littling of public figures and the making of immorality and
indecency a virtue. He explains that Shakespeare's plays
were chiefly tragedies, and that in the Elizabethan age the
stage was "countenanced by the most virtuous, and tended
to the improvement of the people."

The literary criticism is naïve, and amusingly inaccurate
in some of its broad generalizations, but the point of view
—thus clearly stated at the time of Morris' army experience
—is expanded in the fullness of his thinking and presented
in his first book, *British Thought and Thinkers, Introductory Studies, Critical, Biographical and Philosophical* [2]
as a key doctrine of his mature philosophy. After the introductory exposition in this later volume, and a discussion
of medieval anticipations of the modern English mind, he
turns to the Renaissance. "The revival of learning and the
religious reformation reached their fulfillment in England
in the sixteenth century. The tree of human life blossomed
anew, and what magnificent and abundant fruit it bore in
England is known to every student of the Elizabethan period of English literature. It is a matter of the deepest significance to note the precise nature of the nourishment,
which quickened and supported this new and masterly life,
and of the ways in which it actively, spontaneously, power-
fully successfully manifested itself.

"The revival of learning meant, so far as it concerns the
history of philosophy, the revival, and restoration to honor,
of Platonism. And what was that, in distinction from Aristotelianism, which had been so completely absorbed, in

[2] Chicago, S. C. Griggs, 1880.

form and substance, into the Scholastic philosophy? I admit—every careful student admits—no absolute contrast between Platonism and Aristotelianism. Aristotle was the true disciple, though a critical one, of Plato. Aristotle was the real continuator of Plato, more than the members of the Academic school, in which the tradition of his teaching was guarded. Both Plato and Aristotle held to the same fundamental truth of Idealism. For both, essential reality was not material, but spiritual; the material, as such, or absolutely considered, was non-essential, non-real. For both, life (*i.e.*, being) was, in Aristotle's phrase, 'energy of mind.' Nor were it true to say that the way in which Aristotle conceived the same ultimate philosophical truth to be reached and apprehended, was inherently different from Plato's way. If for Plato this result was only reached through a dialectic of definition, and division, and hypothesis, by which the clouds of mere sensuous opinion were scattered, and the soul permitted either directly or through vivid reminiscence to behold the absolute reality, it is a similar work which, in Aristotle's view, is accomplished through analysis and reasoning; these simply clear the mental vision so that it may perceive, and directly know, what cannot be demonstrated. The difference between Plato and Aristotle is the difference between poetry and unimpassioned prose." [3]

Morris feels that there has been a falling away from the basis of the former's vision, which he identifies as the *"vital knowledge* of Plato" and makes the very core of his own philosophical conceptions, saying that without this "vital knowledge" he "cannot admit that philosophy has

---

[3] *Op. cit.*, pages 53–4.

any existence except in name." [4] By this phrase Morris meant an empirical type of knowing which, far from any insight of the senses alone—as in the Scottish intuitionalism —is rather the extension of reason from a mere analysis of what is observed to a full account of the observer as well. Thus he suggests that if Socrates, "Plato's revered master, had made the maxim 'Know thyself' the corner-stone of his teaching, the sum and substance of Platonism was that deeper and more accurate self-knowledge, which is the first direct *way* to the recognition of the divine. True self-knowledge was the priestess of divinity. In like manner the purer Christian doctrine made man at once the rightful son, and heir, and image of God," i.e., knower no less than known. "Obviously the renewed knowledge and love of Platonism could not but work to intensify and deepen the sense of the reality of the Christian idea, held always, in the majority of cases, more or less as an arbitrary and peremptory, but not clearly intelligible, truth of revelation. An inward light would come to meet the light supposed to be purely external and simply authoritative." [5]

Such a statement taken out of context would appear to be an expression of pure subjectivism, indeed Platonistic doctrines have generally been interpreted in that fashion from the beginning. Morris explains, however—continuing his discussion of the Renaissance in his 1880 text— that the religious reformation was not significant because of "changes effected in the forms of worship or the wording of dogmas" alone. This was merely its extremism on the empirical side of things. Its "iconoclasm" was negative, accidental. "Its positive side, its strength and life, lay in the

---

[4] *Ibid.*, page 243.   [5] *Ibid.*, page 56.

new and better life in morality and religion, of which living man felt the possibility, for which his deepest aspirations were stirred, and of which, with something of a sense of creative power to will and to do (while God wrought in him), he was resolved to secure the realization." Here was a stirring which began to express itself "both in poetry and in theology." [6]

The assignment of a common role to poetry and philosophy was, of course, a strange idea to the American mind, as Morris himself recognizes in his opening paragraph of the chapter on William Shakespeare in this first of his books. "Once, when I was instructing, with a German textbook as guide, a class in the history of German literature, we came across the statement that a certain man, of great note in his time, held at one of the German Universities a professorship of 'philosophy and poetry.' The combination of subjects was sufficiently uncommon to be striking, and I asked one of my most thoughtful pupils the question, whether in his view such a combination was not incongruous; is there anything in common between philosophy and poetry, so that these two may legitimately be brought together as constituting one homogeneous topic of study and contemplation? The answer which I received was the same which, I doubt not, would be given, at first thought, and without deeper reflection, by ninety-nine of any hundred persons. . . . To mention philosophy and poetry in the same breath was regarded as a ludicrous anomaly."

This suggests another dichotomy which the Morris of the eighties feels to be equally confused in common thought. "Need I remind the reader that there are two

---

[6] *Ibid.*, page 70.

things which, although absolutely distinct, and even contrasted, in their immediate aim, subject-matter, point of view, and method, are yet so closely related (being indeed correlates, complementary subdivisions of the whole of human knowledge) that they have, to the greatest extent, in the history of human thought, been confounded with each other? I refer to physics and metaphysics, or to physical science (with all its subdivisions, exact and descriptive, or both combined) and philosophy—the former having to do with sensibly verifiable *phenomena*, their classification, their mechanical explanation, and their perfect expression in mathematical formulæ, and the latter with rationally apprehensible *realities*, with the living causes of phenomena and their rational explanation; the one dealing with apparent form, the other with vital substance, the one with sensible fact, the other with rational, ideal, spiritual truth, the one content simply to take the measure of the sensibly actual, however imperfect, the other testing all by the standard of the ideally perfect and so prescribing to the imperfect the law of its progress to perfection; and, finally, the one—Science—tending to the present material utilities and, in certain branches, humanities of life, the other to that still higher, sacred utility, the present and eternal development and conservation of humanity itself—the actual realization of the ideal Man, in feeling and in reason. These two, I say, philosophy and physical science (in which I include constantly mathematics, the special organon and methodological ideal of physical science), are complementary to each other, having each its peculiar province and inner justification, and yet so organically related that each leads to, implies, demands the other.

But the time has never yet been when the distinction, or at least the true relation, between the two was clearly and universally perceived and respected. . . .

"My present point is this: Philosophy is a positive thing, as positive as existence itself. But it is not a mere knowledge of details and minute relations. Its characteristic function is not numbering or measuring. It is not anatomy. It does not, if true to itself and its aim, place the objects of its investigation in a vacuum of abstraction fatal to life (which physical science really does). . . . Now, philosophy proper being *theory of life,* in the broadest and highest sense of this term, I affirm that poetry is the *exposition of life,* whether life of man or of nature. On the side of their insight the philosopher and the poet are brothers, with somewhat of the difference which Plato puts between them, namely, that the former is explicitly conscious of the theoretic sense and import of the vision, and the latter not, though this difference is only relative. Both bring the same message, for both report the same simplicities of being, the same eternities of truth—only, the one in forms of demonstration, calculated to produce a reasoned conviction; the other in forms of living fancy, adapted to enhance the fascination of the message." With this functional distinction in mind he says, "I would fain exhibit now, though briefly, William Shakespeare as a poet in the sense just explained. For, within the limitations fixed by the definition given of the poet's nature and function, I see in him the supreme exponent of the philosophic thought of his age and nation; indeed, a true prophet of mankind in all ages and all nations." [7]

---

[7] *Ibid.,* pages 80–2, 84, 86.

The technically exact manner in which the idealism of Morris is dynamic should begin to be evident, and its roots may be recognized at the time of his return to the Dartmouth campus. Not only is the ideal (1) voluntaristic but also (2) evangelistic in the strict terms of theism, that is, poetic in the more philosophical sense of a living prophecy and stimulus to better living. This is the teleology of a curiously individual sort which perhaps could arise only in late Puritan New England. In any case, Morris in 1864 already was able to express his over-all conception in the title of his master thesis, "Spiritualization the Law and Goal of Human Progress." This was presented as an address at the Dartmouth commencement in July of that year, and it shows the impact of his military service on his thinking.

Learning history retrogressively we find an increasing subjection of man to sense. Society in its infinite condition presents him chiefly occupied in providing for his grossest and most palpable wants, and in the search for sensual gratification. Thought as abstraction and generalization scarcely exists, or is confined to the few whose superior natural endowments have led them to the acquisition of more than usual wealth and power. This oligarchy of intellect and strength exerts its energies mainly for the perfection and perpetuation of its authority. The race is still savage—controlled it may be more or less by reason, but not vivified and spontaneously directed by its happy and incomparable impulses. But with advancing time and enlarging experience, in spite of all obstacles, the thoughts of men are widened, social and political affairs are removed gradually from arbitrary control, and there is developed a broad and intelligent facility in all modes of physical application.

Such is a general and perhaps truismatic exhibition of the historic fact that, with the advance of the race in years, there is a progressive redemption of the same from the dominion of material necessity, and an elevation even, where at present partial, indeed, and in too many cases scarcely begun into the sphere of immaterial forces. That is undergoing development which is alone susceptible of it. For the purely material is dead. The material physiologically vitalized is still brutish. The material intellectualized and rendered moral, i.e. under the control of a spiritual force, is alone of creatures upon earth capable of evidencing rational progress.

We base therefore on admitted facts of history and a liberal analogy the following three-fold division into stages of the passage of the human race from its nudist condition to that now ideal goal to which refined art and religious expectation unite in pointing:

1st: Animal lawlessness.

2d: Reason partially developed and the animal nature more or less arbitrarily controlled by it.

3d: Reason waiting against the bounds which it has itself established, in the interest of its own development, and the spiritual in man finally predominant.

The race then, in its beginnings, is unspiritual. . . . In the earliest state of things, each man, having the germs of reason but without their development,

is a law unto himself, guided by his original un-
chastened instincts to self-preservation and sensual
indulgence. . . .

At the next step in the general progress, the chaos
of pristine unsophisticated license is transformed into
external order by the iron rule of force. To this
men are brought by their native convictions of right,
which exist in greater or less distinctness in every
one according to the distance, be it more or less, by
which he is removed from a primitive and sensual
state, and by considerations of interest and ambition
operating in the few of superior power and endowments. The despotic nature of mere form, with reference to which men are *compelled* to adjust their
actions while reason is the object neither of appeal
nor reliance, now manifests itself in public tyranny.
Of morality at this stage, which is however necessary
in the normal order of development, many laudable
things may be predicated, yet chiefly negative. There
may be most complete absence of disorder and common lawlessness, but there is no positive public life
advancing with generous rivalry and mutual help to
any national end. There still exists the immunity of
the one—the tyrant to whose irresponsible dictum
all remain in mechanical subjection. . . .

We rightly look for the characteristics of the age
and the signs of the times, to that land when the
theory and practice of politics and society least conflict with liberal and correct views of truth and right.
Our own country now illustrates the double opposition just named. The worst elements of our nation,

under able guidance, have excited and wonderfully
energized an armed opposition to the just authority
of government. This is the lower nature lusting for
unshackled license. Its ends are infernal, and if se-
cured, minister to barbarism. It is unreasoning and
passionate and can be met only by force. It is destined
to complete suppression, unless truth is to be branded
with insult, God seemingly banished from history and
the bestial in man to dominate the rational. But there
is also that general uneasiness under the restraints
of law which is to be extensively accounted for on
principles already enunciated. It is reactionary in
character, and of no permanently dangerous tendency.
It is to be regarded as no sign of degeneracy. It is not
to be opposed by brute force but guided and modified
by reason. It manifests itself in irreverence for pa-
rental and public authority and apparent disrespect
for religion. Young America, it is said, shows an increasing disregard for his superiors. But, since progress is by successive overthrows of the old and it may
be violent establishment of the new, the relation of
the child to the parent is passing, perhaps by a road
of reaction that involves something offensive, from
abject dependence to loving communion, spiritual
equality and willing obedience. The shortsighted com-
plain of increasing irreligion. True, there is not that
respect for the ritual observances of religion, which
these received in a less questioning and intelligent
age. The progress of refined intelligence forbids one
to regard with genuine esteem aught in organized
religion except its substantial verities.

Increasing apprehension of these verities and advancing spiritual culture, however things may seem for the time to foster irreverence, it were truly irreverent to regard as tending to anything other than an ultimate establishment on an inexpugnable basis of a generally diffused and authentic religious spirit. One of tolerably unfettered spiritual apprehension can but feel, and know by daily observation, that the religious consciousness of the race is enlarging, that any apparently irreverent elements now manifested in it are largely factitious and transient, and that men are coming to know (however distant be the day of perfect knowledge) how much and what must be submissively and may be honorably received—Truths whose denial contradicts the deliverances of consciousness or revelation, though themselves too high for the present mastery of human understanding—and how much, too, of personal responsibility attaches to every man. If any person, therefore, asserts the progressive degeneracy of the race, we meet him with direct contradiction. The belief in God is growing and having practical effect. Philosophy in its most authoritative utterances is now intensely theistic. Science not merely acknowledges but unites with Religion in affirming the substantial character and credibility of those verities transcending human comprehension to which religious faith so warmly clings, and both Philosophy and Science work with renewed vigor and firmness in paths newly defined and discriminated from the confines of faith. They relinquish naught of their spirit, independence or usefulness.

Literature is marked by those humanities which are anything but a sign of coarse disbelief. Infidelity is not denial of God and duty. Renan, its more recent apostle, is obliged to humanize—which in the last analysis is to spiritualize—as will be seen when the absurd notion of a normal conflict between the finite and the infinite shall have been supplanted by the better conception of their harmony and mutual aid. The variety of sects and schools only marks a transitional phase of progress from the formal old to the new and freer. From the homogeneous society passes to the heterogeneous, to be unified again in the general acceptance and practice of absolute truth—in one common life and faith.

> "Lofty as is the love of God
> And ample as the wants of man,
> Let knowledge grow from more to more,
> But more of reverence in us dwell,
> That mind and soul, according well,
> May make one music as before."

In the realization of this prayer is the travailing race proceeding from a divine origin to a divine end —not to oriental mysticism, but to manly acceptation of essential truth. We hail heterodoxy, therefore, not on its own account, but as evidencing the reverse of mental and moral stagnation and as the highway to those modifications in religious and philosophical statement which inevitably attend their development into absolute perfection. We name the general spiritualization of the race as the supreme goal of human progress, because none higher can be conceived. All genuine philosophy, which regards not less the primal instincts of our best nature than the teachings of history, forces us to this belief, under penalty of forfeiting an absolute *sine qua non* to general progress.

Indispensable to the most successful cultivation of all art is the artist's profound conception of a certain perfect ideal. . . . Similarly essential to the best advancement of the race is the general diffusion among its constituents of a genuine and hearty conviction of exalted earthly destiny of humanity. . . .

Perish then the grovelling opinion, so palseying to the hearts and destructive of one's best impulses and capacities, that the actual tendency of all things human is through Divinity directed, downward, and that the nations shall not yet know God and obtain a rational mastery of themselves! The hand that traced on canvas the divine glories of the Transfiguration was guided by an ethereal soul, thoroughly inspired with faith and power to conceive and reproduce the fine realities of the subject. Like inspiration rest upon the human race, to realize in thought and believingly aspire after those nobler possibilities of its own no less divine forthcoming—nay progressive transfiguration out of the uncomeliness of natural deformity and weakness into heavenly beauty and power.

> "That one far-off divine event
> To which the whole creation moves!"

Here the idealism of George Sylvester Morris at twenty-three and a half years of age has achieved the evangelical form to which it will unswervingly conform, and this is perhaps the principal result of his first two years of adult self-discovery, standing as yet unrefined by European study and without the later dissipation of the naïveté which has nourished his marked originality. His magistral address presents the basic organicism of his thought, such as must be kept in mind through every consideration of his subsequently more formalized and detailed exposition. First, in the light of history, he sees a threefold process of human development, namely, (1) disorder, (2) order externally imposed, and (3) order voluntarily created or accepted for administration. Law therefore may be as much the agent of tyranny as the organic reality of a perfect society. "Spiritual liberty disdains its control as far as it is merely enforced." Inspiration has its roots in man, not some *deus ex machina* of the philosophers, so that the world's literature will be at once the record of and the means for the growing spiritual insights which in their turn can only arise out of experience. A true personal liberty is a "manly acceptance of essential truth." The older theism, holding to a rigorous Calvinistic predestination and seeing ugliness where beauty is to be found, is of no piece with this fine New England voluntarism. God is final cause, in any possible philosophizing about deity, and human reason is man's tool for the discovery of his own divine nature at the best, precisely as it may be the agency administrating the enslaving dictates of his senses at the worst.

PART TWO

TOWARDS THE REFINEMENT
OF A PHILOSOPHY

CHAPTER SEVEN

THE INFLUENCE OF HENRY B. SMITH

HENRY BOYNTON SMITH, who had occupied the chair of Systematic Theology at Union Theological Seminary in New York since 1854 and was the most outstanding member of its faculty, was just approaching his forty-ninth birthday when Morris, on the threshold of twenty-four, arrived on University Place. Smith was born and educated a New Englander, but had gone to France and Germany for three years of post-graduate work. He was well acquainted personally with a number of European thinkers whom Morris would also come to know in the flesh, and Smith's point of view had been shaped very largely by Schleiermacher's disciple, Johann August Wilhelm Neander, with whom he had studied in Berlin. He had returned to America in the year of Morris' birth, had taught part time at the Andover theological seminary, and before accepting the call to the New York school in 1850 had been professor of moral philosophy at Amherst for three years, while Edward Hitchcock was president. Originally a Congregationalist, he had moved over into the Presbyterian denomination, where he became a widely acknowledged leader of the "new school" group which had founded Union Seminary in 1835–6. Smith's judgment of the situation at his new post in 1850 is preserved in a letter in which he says, "I go to New York in full view of all the uncertainties and difficulties of the position. . . .

There are many unfavorable things. . . . A teacher is not felt as he would be in a quieter place. . . . The literary character of the Seminary is slight, its zeal in theological science is little, the need of a comprehensive range of theological studies and of books thereto has got to be created." [1] While great improvement certainly had been effected in the fourteen years following 1850, there was nothing as yet to meet the real needs of the young Morris. His experience as a student for the three semesters has already been described.[2]

While Smith played a vital role in launching George Sylvester Morris on a philosophical career—most importantly by suggesting European study, and engaging him to translate Ueberweg—the older man's intellectual impact was slight to a degree which seems rather remarkable under the circumstances of their relationship. Classroom interchange was stimulating, so that Morris impressed his fellow students as fond of philosophical debate, but the "school of conciliation" had nothing to offer the "earnest searcher after truth" who here was led to shy away from formal theology and all its works. For intellectual stimulus Morris apparently came to rely more and more on his range of reading, but this widening of his interest was yet part of the intellectual climate which Smith probably dominated far more than Morris realized. "By a happy accident," as Wenley puts the matter, "records are preserved of the books bought or read by him between August, 1864, and January, 1866. These lists intimate not a little. Technical theology failed to attract him. . . . On the other hand he read

[1] *Henry Boynton Smith, His Life and Works*, New York, Armstrong, 1881, page 159.
[2] *Cf.* above, pages 30–2.

widely in philosophy, history and literature, and made occasional excursions into science. The entries contain no less than one hundred and fifty titles." [3] An analysis of the more evident potentials of philosophical impact—out of the examination and at least partial digestion of what in normal case must have been two to three volumes weekly—yields a fairly clear if somewhat hypothetical picture of his development during this period of transition, immediately preceding his European studies. Moreover, an illuminating frame of reference is provided for such an analysis of his reading, since two short compositions of the period have survived. They are both dated in February, 1865, when a first semester had run its course, and they are strikingly significant in the light of points brought out in the preceding chapter. Morris' range of experience is widening, but his faith remains one-pointed and his underlying practical sense is very evident.

The titles—"The Practice of Preaching among Theological Students while still in the Seminary" and "Artist, Poet, Preacher . . . the Greatest of These is Which?"— show the evangelistic phase of this thinking in the foreground of his interest, and suggest that his forward view on the practical side of philosophizing had remained unchanged. He evidently had come to realize the characteristic barrenness of a seminary training, indeed Wenley comments on his "vein of irony." [4] Something other than a mere manipulation of words is necessary to achieve the vital knowledge of Plato. Here may well be the beginning of the great gnawing in the depths of Morris' own soul. A need is seen, but not how to meet it. He is in definite

---

[3] Wenley, pages 91-3, 97.   [4] *Ibid.*, page 93

and articulate protest against mere rational or verbalized
theology when he says, in reference to student preachers,
that "with no proper conception of the magnitude and
vital import of the truths which they are to vindicate and
apply, with nothing in many cases of fixed and hearty belief arising from independent investigation, they suppose
the mere formal mastery by the memory of a set of prescribed doctrines to be a sufficient outfit for their life's
work, as though the course of study and training in the
Theological Seminary were like an apprenticeship for the
practice of a mechanical art. No amount of emotional
piety can meet the want of thorough and thoughtful mental culture in one who proposes to unfold and enforce
truths which the angels desire to look into."

The great truths of understanding arise out of actual
life, but this does not mean that it is possible, or that it
would be desirable, for everyone to have every requisite
experience. There must be a transmission, a sharing. This
seems to be the social and ethical view of Morris as it
began to take an organized form in his philosophy, and as
it was now revealed particularly by his teleological interest
in literature. It is a phase sharpened by his Shakespeare
sessions in army days, and especially articulate in his magistral address at Dartmouth. Hence he could say, at Union
Seminary, that "the practice of preaching while yet students in the Seminary implies too low an estimate of liberal studies. Not to speak of their influence upon the
preacher as an antidote for narrowness of views and illiberal dogmatism in opinion (on which, alas, experience
shows the most sincere religious character to have no pre-
ventive and but little palliative influence), these studies

are increasingly common among the masses. Their influence is growing with amazing rapidity."

Quite obvious was the fact that liberal studies could direct the reason as easily towards disbelief as the contrary. Morris unquestionably had observed the process, realizing that a broadening of secular knowledge had proved to be an additional and continual confirmation of his own faith, while at the same time having quite the opposite effect on any number of intelligent people around him. Hence he says that "as things are now" the liberal studies are "likely to be misinterpreted so as to furnish the short-sighted, and many sincere men who have not time or ability to examine them, with arguments for infidelity. Now religion, in its commonest present acceptation, involves the support of certain dogmas in the form of verbal propositions which constitute a great part of our real or supposed knowledge. The belief in them . . . is likely to be affected by such generally accredited and well substantiated facts as do really, or may seem to, invalidate them. In either case, the defender of religion from the pulpit, who is not familiar with the facts and their proper explanation, deserves not, and will not receive, the full respect of the generality of hearers. Nay, he wastes his influence with many, appearing positively ridiculous."

His attack on mere verbal rationalizing is without compromise, and the whole later reformulation of his thoughts is founded very largely upon this conception of a continual necessity for the restatement of truth, that is, meeting every shift in the experience which becomes history and, in doing so, refines language and so controls the implication of any given or once-stated truth. He points out that "the increasing light of accumulating experience and continued reflection varies considerably the verbal expression of the objects of Christian faith. That there is reason for farther change cannot be logically denied on any ground, and is particularly evident to many, since, were this not so, it is incredible with them that certain dogmas should be entertained for a moment in this 19th century. In their view—and I think it is just—nothing but the inconsiderateness with which theological students found themselves on a prescriptive faith . . . prevents theology from a considerable and speedy enfranchisement from the puerilities and mistakes of darker ages."

In the second Union Seminary paper he reaffirms the point of view here, and puts his over-all attitude on record as it undoubtedly dictated his reactions and movements on arriving in Europe just a short year later. "Art, poetry and religion are the actual and representative expression of humanity—the one sentimental and ocularly discerned; the next imaginative, the exponent of creative power; the last moral, and the preëminent index of character. . . . Let divine power accomplish its utmost for the religious life of man, it still transcends Omnipotence to do more for him in this respect than develop his underived potential spiritual possessions without making him præter-human— a thing which no one, since the days of apotheosis, has a right to look for. . . . History most amply justifies our implied allegation of what may be called the spontaneity of the trio under consideration. Their universality, the absence of special external causes which could be supposed to account for them by force, and the conscious free-will of man, combine to show conclusively that art, poetry and religion are ultimate facts among men. *Nascitur, non fit,* truly describes man regarded as the living subject of each. . . .

"The consideration of more recent times is unnecessary to furnish testimony to the universality, spontaneousness, and alliance of religion and, as they may now be called, its servants, poetry and art. This only has almost without exception been peculiar to the case thus far, that, while the poet and artist, except when the subserviency of their functions to religion degenerated into servility, have wrought largely under the mastery of passion, with a dominant sentiment of love for their work, the religious functionary and the devotee have lacked this vivifying element. Religious love was rare indeed previous to the incarnate revelation of God as Love, and since, even to this day, we know too well how seldom and feeble its manifestation. Moral ruin, for obvious reasons, affects the religious side of man more destructively than any other. What marvel that its restoration be more slowly effected, and that the contrast between the bright and healthful inspirations of all untrammeled art and poetry, and the gloomy and really burlesque human developments of religion, should embolden scoffers and the short-sighted, to suspect the essentially human and divine character of true religion. Here art and poetry are the faithful allies and renovators of religion."

With this frame of reference, the wide reading of Morris at Union Seminary may be approached, both for an analysis of its possible influence on his thinking at the time when he lifted his eyes to the promised land of European scholarship, and for some appreciation of his immediate intellectual orientation. To be noted, at the outset, are the basic texts in the common philosophical tradition, which included (among those that need mention only) works by Coleridge, Hamilton, Hegel, Kant, Lewes, John Stuart Mill, Pascal and Spencer. A great deal of similar reading may be presumed, and perhaps rereading. There is a record, for the first time, of a particular history of philosophy, namely, that of Albert Schwegler, which probably was of general service to Morris.[5] Then there are four other writers to whom consideration should be given, in some detail, relative to their impact on him during his seminary days, namely, Chalybäus, Pressensé, Buckle and Draper. As for general history, Edward Gibbon is in the list of the books Morris perused, as is Thomas Arnold, who prepared an English edition of Thucydides and wrote a three-volume account of Rome, and also Charles Merivale, the publication of whose seven volumes on Roman history had just been completed. Henry Hallam, who became famous as the "philosophical historian," is represented, as are Henry Hart Milman, whose *History of the Jews* had been memorable on its appearance in 1829 for its somewhat secular but highly sociological outlook, and Arthur Penrhyn Stanley, whose two-volume *History of the Jewish Church* had appeared in 1863 and 1865.

Morris himself suggests, by quoting Erdmann's reference to Heinrich Moritz Chalybäus in the sketch of Ulrici

---

[5] The American translation of Schwegler's *Geschichte der Philosophie im Umriss, ein Leitfaden zur Uebersicht* (Stuttgart, 1848) was by J. H. Seelye (New York, 1856; third edition, 1864), preceding the English translation of J. H. Stirling (Edinburgh, 1867).

which he prepared some four years later for his translation of Ueberweg,[6] the degree of stimulus the Kiel professor (that is, Chalybäus) may have given to his thought as a Union Seminary student when he read the *Historical Survey of Speculative Philosophy from Kant to Hegel*.[7] Chalybäus was identified by Ueberweg himself as one who, while also under the influence of Schelling and more particularly of Herbart, belonged to the post-Hegelian group which sought "by critical modification to reconcile speculation on the one hand with theology, and on the other with empirical science."[8] What probably appealed to Morris—in the light of his later thought—was the stress upon scientific method, the emphasis of a basic experientialism and the insistence that philosophy be pursued as a science rather than an art or a mere rational speculation. In his introduction Chalybäus insists that philosophy is not opposed to the healthy common sense of humanity, though it continually transcends the ordinary powers of the latter. Common sense alone has the right to judge, and it must not believe anything which it has not experienced. "Nothing is to be taken as a matter of faith, but all and every thing, which we admit, is to be admitted only because we have attained to an internal conviction upon the subject, or because we *know* it." This is the unqualified appeal to experience already marked in Morris.

"Theoretical philosophy," Chalybäus continues, "is nothing more than the self-acquired insight into the method by which we may attain to a certain knowledge of

---

[6] *Op. cit.*, Vol. II, page 299.
[7] Completed by Chalybäus in 1837, with the English translation published at London in 1854.
[8] *Op. cit.*, page 298.

any thing; hence it is *science* or knowledge pre-eminently so called. . . . In what this special kind of knowledge consists, whether it has any necessary limits, and what these may be, cannot be indicated beforehand. . . . As yet philosophy has not attained to perfect knowledge; 'it is not yet the ἐπιστήμη, after which Plato strove; and it must still content itself with the modest name of a longing endeavour after, or love of wisdom. . . . The judge, the teacher, the physician—must each act according to his own convictions; this is not only allowed them, but has become a matter of conscience, and in so far as they ground this conviction upon certain ultimate fixed principles, they are philosophers, and move within the sphere of that science which, properly speaking, is the scientifick of all disciplines." Thus a true or scientific philosophy is conceived to be the scholar's sacred duty. Such a philosophy must be indomitably individual or subjective in its roots, but must culminate in objective verification. Here is idealism, but neither a Platonic absolutism nor a purely mechanical rationalism.

Chalybäus' skillful analyses in order of Kant, Jacobi, Herbart, Fichte, Schleiermacher, Schelling and Hegel— philosophical material with little direct translation into English in 1864—at least familiarized Morris with the salient features of German romanticism, but more particularly they gave him a peculiar evaluation of Hegel's system. "Whoever has succeeded in surveying the Hegelian system in its totality," Chalybäus remarks, "will now have presented to his intuitive faculty the revolving epicycloid of its categories as universal mind, and this ultimately in the absolute idea (*Idee*), as the eternally self-thinking truth.

Philosophy, now perfected, stands no longer without and prior to the universe, but is the real being itself which has arrived in it at perfect self-consciousness. The antitheses of ideality and reality are only internal self-distinctions of the Absolute framed within itself; we may call the *whole* system just as well Absolute Idealism as Realism, and in this very way is attained what should be attained, the all-pervading self-cognition of the universe in itself, which has this point of penetration of itself in the consciousness of the human species, and knows itself in the science of the latter, so that the human being knows or becomes cognisant of itself in its science as the all-pervading absolute knowledge. Arrived at this point then, it was asked, what more can possibly be left for us to attain, what higher standing-point for philosophy can be thought of? The absolutely highest point seemed to be gained, philosophy, at least upon the whole, to be perfected, and what remained to be a mere matter having reference only to details. Accordingly, the Hegelian workmen gathered themselves together, in order that they might celebrate the final erection of an edifice which it had taken thousands of years to build.

"The voice of the exoterics was then—now fifteen years ago—scoffed at, when they called to mind, that the same festival had been so often celebrated before, and the same cry of exultation raised successively in each school of philosophy by the heralds of her universal wisdom; for the founder of every new system must of necessity feel convinced that he it is who to the building has affixed the key-stone. As regards, however, this the most recent or Hegelian system, if it makes the idea of absolute progress the direct principle and law of the universe, it does but

deal ironically with itself, in hoping for the absolute per-
sistence of such a scheme; for this new and pretended
key-stone will but share the fate of the stone of Sisyphus.
That which was not acknowledged at the time, soon, however, declared itself to be a fact, for in the school itself a
schism took place concerning the authentic interpretation
of Hegel's doctrine and opinions. His followers divided
into a Right and Left, into Hegelians and Young Hegel-
ites, and in the middle remained a feeble centre, which was
in good truth only the εἴδωλον of Hegel, the body of his
posthumous and collective works. For as has happened
hitherto with each philosopher of repute, that while im-
bodying in his writings a deep amount of truth, he has but
partially elaborated, fashioned, and systematically evolved
this, or else left it behind him ill-shaped or moulded in
itself, so also, in our opinion, was the same the case with
Hegel.

"The immediate problem of philosophy subsequent to
Kant, was to overcome the subjectivism of his stand-point,
and advance to an actual knowledge and willing of objective truth. Fichte, Schelling, and Hegel have grappled with
this problem, and the latter has methodically carried it
out. While, however, it might seem as though the whole
matter was in this way completed, it is evident at once that
that direct passage from subjectivity to objectivity has been
effected *at the cost* of the subjectivity, and thus a third
problem presents itself as left for solution, namely, the
concrete union of the two sides, in which the objectivity
is not, as in Kant and Fichte, extinguished, nor the subjectivity demolished, as with Schelling and Hegel, in the
objectivity, but both arrive at their just claims—a point

this which was, doubtless, by Hegel *wished* and *intended* also. If now, we were to abide by this deeper intention, why then we must, in order to bring it into the light, as it were, of day, complete the form also; but if we abide by that form of the Hegelian philosophy, which is represented by the disciples of the Left, it follows that we must separate from it all that, strictly speaking, does not appear therein, and so must depart from Hegel's intention, nay more, as a direct consequence, from his very principle and standing-point also: there will come out, as has been already proved in fact, a one-sided objective Neo-Spinozism, utterly opposed to the deeper subjectivity, which Hegel strove to attain; and this of necessity, on account of its one-sidedness, may at the same time be just as well regarded as a subjectivism, which ends anew in empiricism or scepticism, and in this very way completes before the eyes of contemporaries the true critick of the original system as such."

This leads, according to Chalybäus, to the consequence for religious conviction which became central in Morris' interest. "In the beginning the system, as being opposed to the Kantian rationalism, held good as orthodox, especially since it reassumed the doctrine of the Trinity, which had been set aside; and pretended to commemorate the mysteries of Christianity from behind the veil of its terminology in a clearer or glorified light. Criticism, however, speedily dispelled this cloud, and the community of initiated followers, divided partly into such as openly confessed that they were no Christians at all, and levied war against the church with downright zeal and abuse; partly into those who, being undeceived as to the system, renounced Hegelianism altogether, and cither sought, as has

recently occurred, for satisfaction in Schelling, or else returned, in far greater number, back to the standing-point
of Kant; and, finally, into those whose intention was to
stop where Hegel did, and who recognised in his system,
as its true content, a theism that could be retained in con-
junction with Christianity." [9]

In view of Morris' study under Trendelenburg (to whom
reference is made here by the Kiel professor) [10] some of the
further observations of Chalybäus are significant, especially his reliance upon an Aristotelian method. "If the
natural categories thought of as truly objective, and as
holding true relations with each other, corresponding to
the reality, do not, as Hegel himself confesses, lead of
necessity from below upwards, how, then, could this take
place in that very part of the logic which bears the name of
objective, and busies itself with these natural categories?
We are of opinion that the apparently objective progress
is here also no true or genuinely objective one, but a hidden phenomenological one, which results only from the
ultimate design known and willed beforehand, namely,
the absolute subjectivity, although Hegel does not admit
this, but aims at going to work in a purely objective,
genetic manner. If, upon the one hand, we take away this
ultimate design, *i.e.* the ready-prepared subject of the
philosopher with its fundamental activity, and then, without, upon the other hand, letting ourselves be blinded by
the potentialising aspect of the dialectick, abide only by
the objectivity, it follows, that we must necessarily seek
for the progress of the thinking process from one category

---

[9] *Op. cit.*, pages 364–6.
[10] *Logische Untersuchungen*, Vol. 1, section 3.

to another by the empirical route, and arrive also at the conviction that, without experience, there will be no such progress or advance.

"In this light Schelling, also, among others, appears to regard the present question, and in this way to indulge a hope that experience itself may be strengthened into becoming a necessary postulate for philosophy as a system. The very same notion was also present to Aristotle with more or less distinctness, for even he does not discover and furnish any necessary transition and connection of the categories from below upwards, but takes them up singly as empirical, and then arranges them. Hegel reproaches him for this, and finds therein, as a result, a want of organic unity in the whole system, declaring that Aristotle was not acquainted with the principle of absolute negativity, as being that alone which could dialectically mediate this progress. From genus to genus, however, we are impelled by no immanent necessity: each principle (or generic idea) gives forth and lives out what resides in it; for it continues to reproduce its genus, and produces nothing better than it was itself. There lies no absolute contradiction in the lower special ideas in themselves, for such would involve the *impossibility* of these ideas themselves; so that, as such, they would not exist even a moment, setting aside the fact of their being able to form a concrete system of nature. Thus much will suffice in order to explain the motives for affirming that the dialectick, just as Hegel has elevated it to the method of philosophy, is not the *whole*, but only a part or moment of the speculative method. No dialectick can *originally* posite and begin; it can only originate from behind the positing, and point out what must be posited simultaneously and together with the first position, or what, if not simultaneously posited, would suppress the posited itself: it has, in truth, a critical value; but for itself alone, without a positive moment, it degenerates into a negative action, which has been already pointed out, by Aristotle, with a perfectly clear insight into the matter, to be sophistic." [11]

There is nothing to indicate how carefully Morris studied this book but it is clear that the young theological student was introduced to Hegel's philosophy in terms of a criticism which ended Hegelianism as a school in Germany, however much it also reflected the spirit of Hegel. On arrival in Berlin, Morris went out of his way to get help for the study of Hegel in German, [12] a fact which is more than sufficient indication that he was interested in Hegel's doctrine, but one which does not imply any tendency towards an orthodox Hegelianism. However, it must be noted that Morris had a well-defined interpretation of Hegel long before he encountered the British Hegelians, and by them was less brought to a discipleship than to perhaps a more mature appreciation of Hegel's value.

A second major theological influence on Morris was Edmond de Pressensé, [13] an ecclesiastical writer who could remain uncompromisingly pious while yet setting the framework of his thought in a valid scientific analysis. Pressensé accomplishes this by accepting a process of natural growth

---

[11] *Op. cit.,* pages 375–6.   [12] Wenley, page 113.
[13] The major work of this historian, in four volumes, *The History of the First Three Centuries of the Church,* was not available in English, but the introduction, which would appeal to the young student in the light of the other clues to his tastes at the time, had just been published in translation with a special preface by the author, namely, *The Religions Before Christ,* Edinburgh, T. and T. Clark, 1862.

or development as the basic explanation for Christianity. He sees Christian ideas arising from a cultural evolution. "It is impossible to retrace the triumph of Christianity in the first ages of our history, without referring to that ancient world which it came to destroy. If it found that old world armed at all points for the combat, and ready to turn against it the vast resources of a refined civilisation, without neglecting the employment of material force— this last resort of waning faiths—it was not wanting in points of contact with the society of the time. The new religion did not break upon the earth as a sudden, abrupt event, unconnected with the past. It was, to a certain degree, the outcome of the whole religious history of humanity. Christianity was the answer of Heaven to the aspirations of earth. It brought to the wearied world the solution that the Zoroasters and Platos had sought after and caught glimpses of. It was at once divine and human —profoundly human, precisely because it was divine: that is to say, adapted by God Himself to man's real necessities.

"It will not, therefore, suffice to contemplate the heaven from which it came. We must also consider the earth on which it took footing. Without in the smallest degree sacrificing its divine origin, we may acknowledge the harmony existing between it and human nature. It was made for human nature, as human nature was made for it: so much so, that while rejecting it, and often cursing it, human nature proves, even by its agitation, that it cannot dispense with it. The history of the religions of human origin is the most striking proof of the agreement of revealed religion with the soul of man; for, on the one side, each of these forms of worship is the expression of the wants of conscience, its eternal thirst after pardon and restoration—rather, let us say, its thirst after God. On the other hand, their succession proves their insufficiency, and the necessity of a higher religious form, which would supersede them, and in which humanity might find rest. To isolate it, then, completely from the past, would be to voluntarily refuse to comprehend the nature of Christianity, and the extent of its triumph." [14]

Looking back upon the ancient world, or before the advent of Christianity, Pressensé realizes that the great distinction between the pagan and the modern world is a matter of respect for personality, that is, the recognition of the individual's spiritual integrity which Morris had begun to demand. The transition from the earlier view was made possible by the Greek philosophers. "Adopting what was best in Paganism," philosophy as they developed it became "an instrument to destroy Paganism, and thus cleared the way for definite religion." Hence philosophy, "above all . . . effectively contributed to purify the idea of divinity, though this purification was but an approximation. If at times it caught glimpses of the highest spiritualism, yet it was unable to guard against the return and reaction of Oriental dualism. In spite of this imperfection, which in its way served the cause of Christianity by demonstrating the necessity of revelation, men like Socrates and Plato fulfilled amongst their people a really sublime mission. They were to the pagan world the great prophets of the human conscience, which woke up at their call. And the awakening of the moral sense was at once the glory and ruin of their philosophy; for conscience, once roused,

---

[14] *The Religions Before Christ*, pages 5–6.

could only be satisfied by One greater than they, and must necessarily reject all systems which proved themselves impotent to realize the moral ideal which they had evoked." [15]

Pressensé's summary of his position may well have encouraged Morris in his own functional reconciliation of higher and lower realities through the normal or everyday interactions of experience. "We shall not enter here into the metaphysical subtleties which time and the disputations of the schools have gathered round the person of Christ, nor discuss scholastic distinctions concerning the two natures—their relation or penetration. We confine ourselves to the simple, grand declarations of the Scriptures: 'The Word was made flesh.' 'In Him dwells all the fulness of the Godhead bodily.' The humble Christian, who, taking his stand on these promises, and receiving daily the precious earnest of their accomplishment, growing up into Christ as the branch does into the vine, partaking of His substance, receiving His sap, His life, His warmth, carries in his own heart an invincible demonstration of the divinity of Christ." Today's reader who is unfamiliar with the theological nuances may question the descriptive validity of the dogmas here, but yet should note that the reason is discounted even as the reason is used or as there is appeal to its powers of comprehension, since metaphysical subtleties are made quite subordinate to the main act-of-being at issue—which ultimately affords the only possible definition of the Word made flesh, and so on—namely, the daily earnest of a personal experience.

The metaphysical dualism is rejected, despite what might seem to be its rational necessity, because a complete

---

[15] *Ibid.*, pages 99–102.

or perfect interaction of higher and lower has been achieved in history. "Jesus Christ came not only to bring the most signal proof of divine love, but also that He might enter into communion and partake of the sufferings of humanity, to the end that He might represent humanity, and in its name offer the atoning sacrifice. It was not possible that the fallen, guilty race could be restored to its privileges, so long as it continued stiff-necked, proud, and rebellious. God's love, immense though it be, cannot save a being who refuses to respond to it, who even rejects it with disdain." The theological language is somewhat absurd out of context, but the portrayal of the recalcitrant separations in unspiritualized experience are clear enough. And how is the dualism resolved? "Let us not forget that love is another name for holiness, since it presents the highest form of good. It is at once the supreme benediction and the supreme law. It demands reciprocity." [16] Here, of course, is encouragement for Morris' idea that experience is not a continuum in which man's participation is passive —the observational, fundamentally sensational view which underlay not only British empiricism and Scottish realism but much of the German speculation as well—but is a dynamic and ideal reality which can act eventually for good or evil depending on the quality of man's participation, i.e., a dynamic, voluntaristic and theistic idealism.

The appearance of Henry Thomas Buckle's *History of Civilization in England* in 1857, or the year Morris entered Dartmouth as a freshman, had a breadth of intellectual impact in the English-speaking world which made the au-

---

[16] *Ibid.*, page 251.

thor famous and gave his work a significance obscured only by the considerably more important event of two years later, the publication of Charles Darwin's *Origin of Species*. Whether Buckle made any contribution to Morris in the young student's undergraduate days is not known and is probably beyond more than pure conjecture. The stir created by the initial volume of the *History*, and Morris' presence in a milieu as sensitive to the new books as the New England campus of the period, are facts that suggest at least an acquaintance on his part with Buckle's grandiose scheme and so with the point of view on which it was based. In any case, immediately after Buckle's *Essays* was issued in America,[17] Morris was at Union Seminary and this new volume provided him with a critical evaluation not only of John Stuart Mill, whom he read also in this period and might have been inclined to regard favorably, but of British philosophy and character in general. Later Morris remarked that Buckle's ideal thinker—i.e., John Stuart Mill—"possessed a considerable degree of heat, with little or no light" and that—perhaps as a species of recognition by Morris of his very great potentiality—he had had the "personal misfortune" to have been born "the son of James Mill and not Johann Gottlieb Fichte."[18]

What Morris may well have derived from Buckle was an articulate criticism of the dichotomy of the objective and subjective sides of experience, the functional interpretation becoming for Morris an intellectual corrective for the more naïve but entrenched conception of an ontological distinction between mind and matter. Buckle, of course,

[17] By Appleton in 1863.
[18] *British Thought and Thinkers,* pages 327, 336.

remains at heart the British psychologist, in no sense ex-
tricating himself from what the idealists regarded as the
fallacies of England's empiricism. Indeed, Morris moves
far from Buckle's position in arriving at his ultimate organic view, which was grounded almost entirely in German rather than British sources, but yet the idea in English thought that there is a free interaction of the psychological and the practical, as developed by Buckle, might
have been of real service to Morris in shaping his early
and groping speculation, despite his quickening prejudice
against the British empiricism.

In the first of Buckle's two essays read by Morris at
Union Seminary—which is at once an exposition of the
author's own views on the general subject of the advancement of knowledge, and an introductory review of John
Stuart Mill's *On Liberty*[19]—Buckle suggests that the
younger Mill among all living European writers has made
the greatest contribution to the enlargement of human
understanding. This he feels to be true because, in accordance with a proper philosophy of history, Mill *fils* has investigated questions which concern "on the one hand, the
practical interests of every member of society, and, on the
other hand, the subtlest and most hidden operations of the
human mind." This indeed was a rare gift. And when
Buckle says, "to a philosophic mind the actions of an individual count for little; to a practical mind they are everything,"[20] he gives point to the conclusion to which the
youthful Morris was brought. The conflicting generalizations which have comprised philosophy and theology
through every age have been altogether barren, as far as

---

[19] London, John W. Parker and Son, 1859   [20] *Op. cit.*, pages 39, 43.

giving any insight into the nature and potentiality of personality as such is concerned, just as the more recent humanistic attempt to arrive at wisdom by a tabulation of instances has been no more fruitful. A very possible contribution of Buckle to Morris, therefore, was the realization that deductive and inductive reasoning only complement each other, and that neither alone is competent for the needs of good thinking.

The impact of Buckle may also be marked in another area of the young student's thinking when, in stressing the point that a perfect intellect would unite both views— that is, thinking from the perspective of the most general as well as the most special—he says that "such a feat is of the greatest possible rarity. It may in fact be doubted if more than one instance is recorded of its being performed without a single failure," and thereupon cites Shakespeare as the case in question. In view of Morris' interest in Shakespeare during his army days, and his emphasis on Shakespeare as a philosopher in his subsequent *British Thought and Thinkers,* it is interesting to realize that he read, while at Union Seminary, "No other mind has thoroughly interwoven the remote with the proximate, the general with the special, the abstract with the concrete. No other mind has so completely incorporated the speculations of the highest philosophy with the meanest details of the lowest life. Shakespeare mastered both extremes, and covered all the intermediate field. He knew both man and men. He thought as deeply as Plato or Kant. He observed as closely as Dickens or Thackeray. Of whom else can this be said? Other philosophers have, for the most part, overlooked the surface in their haste to reach the summit. Hence the anomaly of many of the most profound thinkers having been ignorant of what it was shameful for them not to know, and having been unable to manage with success even their own affairs." [21]

It is more than possible that Buckle contributed, as Chalybäus did, to preparing Morris in advance against an overliteral conditioning by German thinking, such as could have made him the second-rate disciple rather than one of the true heirs of German idealism at its best. Buckle on the whole came fairly close to giving Morris a foreshadowing of the organic view that Morris ultimately would derive from Hegel, and in addition to this he also approximated Morris' fundamental experientialism in approving Mill's dictum that the logical process is from particulars to particulars. Morris would interpret this latter proposition by affirming that all reality must be approached from a perspective which fundamentally is in the here and now, or in a convergence of the remote in the immediate, whether this be a matter of time, space or anything else. However, any direct contribution of Buckle or Mill to Morris is hardly to be traced beyond an early stimulus for Morris' efforts towards a more adequate realism of the common-sense variety.

There remains for consideration, of Morris' reading at the seminary, the more recent developments in scientific philosophy, which reinforced the earlier impact of evolutional theology upon him in undergraduate days through Edward Hitchcock.[22] The work of unquestioned importance in this connection was the two-volume *History of the*

---

[21] *Ibid.*, pages 46–7.   [22] *Cf.* above, pages 33–5.

Intellectual Development of Europe, which had only just been published.[23] John William Draper, its author, was one of America's outstanding scientists—a chemist, physiologist and a pioneer photo-chemist. In his preface he explains that his new work is intended to complement his former one on human physiology, in which man was treated as an individual, and that now man is to be considered in his social relations. "The life of an individual is a miniature of the life of a nation. . . ." Society is organic, that is, evolving from potentials within itself and developing by an "orderly process of civilization," so that history, seen "through the medium of physiology . . . presents a new aspect to us. We gain a more just and thorough appreciation of the thoughts and motives of men in successive ages of the world."

The biologizing of reality is then carried to the point where time itself becomes organic, Draper agreeing with Pascal that "the entire succession of men, through the whole course of ages, must be regarded as one man, always living and incessantly learning" and adding that "since events are springing as consequences of preceding events, and ideas from preceding ideas—in the midst of the most violent intellectual oscillations—a discerning observer will never fail to detect that there exists a law of continuous variation of human opinions." There is continuity, but not in objects or ideas as such. Man persists, but not changelessly in any measurable particular. Thus the turn to faith is in response to actual evidence of an immutable factor in all the kaleidoscopic transformations of the empirical world. "Then forms are in their nature transitory, law is

---

[23] New York, Harper, 1862.

everlasting. If from visible forms we turn to directing law, how vast is the difference. We pass from the finite, the momentary, the incidental, the conditioned, to the illimitable, the eternal, the necessary, the unshackled. It is of law that I am to speak in this book." [24] Here is the basic type of organicism which Morris refines at the end, but not in the form presented by Draper, who destroyed rather than exalted personality or the individual spirit.

The conception coming to slow formulation in modern terms, through these many converging strands of contemporary thinking, is perhaps the most central of all realizations in Morris' philosophy. What now begins to fit in place is the notion that man is the microcosm, and the best of all possible clues to the nature and privileges of the macrocosm, a concept which of course is found in Greek thought, long before Draper. Thus Ueberweg explains, interpreting Heraclitus, that "the λόγος or the eternal, all-embracing order . . . is . . . immanent as the ξυνόν (κοινόν), or universal principle, in change itself, and he [Heraclitus] calls upon each individual to follow in his thought and action this universal reason. . . . Without knowledge of the universal reason, the senses are untrustworthy witnesses," since eternal reason is "immanent in the world of individuality and change." [25] This Heraclitean hylozoism, identifying the individual with the eternal potential of the world around him, was a marked anticipation of dynamic idealism, but it was not the complete subordination of the individual to the whole as in the new scientific thinking. The classical notion of organic interaction between man and his universe may have filtered to

[24] Op. cit., pages 13-4, 16.   [25] Op. cit., Vol. I, page 42.

Morris through Henry B. Smith from Schleiermacher—
the great eclectic for whom man as the unity of the real and
the ideal was the presence or actuality of God in experience, and who could say "No god without a world, and no
world without a God" as a recognition of the tie through
this mutual function of the changeless and change per se
—but Draper's highly naïve stress of immutable law and
personal effectiveness of living, as two facets of a physiological or organic interdependence throughout all manifestation, was point and punctuation for the intellectual
climate at Union Seminary, however superficially realized.

The shaping of Morris' mind, as this continued during
his three semesters at the seminary, has thus been recon-
structed—however hypothetically, as a matter of necessity
—and what will complete the overview of this period in
his development is an examination of the single philosophical writing which comes out of it, actually written in
Europe but prior to any apparent impact upon him of the
Old World's intellectual milieu. Here is final light on his
thinking at the threshold of the intellectual reorientation
which is yet to come in Germany. What seems to be his
initial but instinctive mistrust of German idealism, added
to his native distaste for British empiricism, is important
in revealing the strength of his grounding in wholly indigenous materials for his voluntaristic and theistic concepts.

Henry B. Smith was co-editor of the *American Presbyterian and Theological Review*. He was thoroughly aware
of Morris' exceptionally wide reading and interest in new
books of philosophical moment when he asked his protégé

to prepare a detailed review of Hodgson's *Time and Space; a Metaphysical Essay*. Morris read this work, which had appeared in London some months before, while crossing the Atlantic. Apparently he completed the criticism at Lausanne in the late winter of 1866–7, after possible conferences with Smith during their meeting at Halle in the summer of 1866, and the article was published in April, 1867.[26] It is the only major writing of Morris until his long exposition of Trendelenburg seven years later, excepting of course the tremendous labor of a different sort represented by the translation of Ueberweg. He is only otherwise in print, prior to 1875, through translating Julius Hamburger's "The Theosophy of Franz Baader" without comment [27] and preparing three articles or circulars in connection with the teaching of French at Michigan.[28]

Shadworth Holloway Hodgson was eight years older than Morris, a Rugby and Oxford man who devoted himself to the study of philosophy as a private scholar from his middle twenties. He is generally known in America as a friend of William James in person and by correspondence, and this was the first of three books written by him at rather considerable intervals and so the earliest formal presentation of his ideas. His classification in the philosophical tradition is difficult, primarily because his originality has called forth many varying opinions. Wenley particularly clouds the issue with his comment that "Hodgson was a pragmatist long before the first pragmatist in the

26 *Op. cit.*, Vol. V, pages 217–308.
27 *American Presbyterian Review*, 1869, Vol. I, pages 171–185.
28 Wenley, pages xi–xii, 110–1.

United States." [29] As far as pragmatism is an identifiable movement, its British representation hardly goes beyond F. C. S. Schiller, whose article in the Fourteenth Edition of the *Encyclopædia Britannica* does not mention Hodgson, and Hodgson's name does not appear at all in Ralph Barton Perry's *Philosophy of the Recent Past, An Outline of European and American Philosophy Since 1860,* although quite a few pages are devoted to James and others classified as pragmatists.[30] Much more suggestive of Hodgson's basic orientation in philosophy is the fact that he founded the Aristotelian Society, some fifteen years later in London, and served as its president for more than a decade. This does not make Hodgson an Aristotelian in any literal sense, but Wenley fails to realize that the best of all possible clues to the thinking of Hodgson is the Stagirite's prejudice against absolute disjunction and any regression to infinity, and also to note that Morris felt it necessary to saturate himself in Aristotle's *Metaphysics* at the time he wrote his review, reading it in both Greek and French, together with Ravaisson's *Essai sur la Métaphysique d'Aristotle,* Zeller's *Philosophie der Griechen* and the pertinent *La Métaphysique et la Science* of Etienne Vacherot (who stressed the necessary separation of scientific reality and the ideality known inwardly by man).[31]

Wenley, seeking to classify Hodgson, leaned rather heavily on Hodgson's dedication of the *Philosophy of Reflection* to Coleridge, "my father in philosophy, not seen but beloved," but this remark was made thirteen years after the publication of *Time and Space.* The only possibly

---

[29] *Ibid.*, page 216.   [30] New York, Scribner's, 1926, pages 186–96.
[31] Wenley, pages 111, 215.

significant reference to Coleridge in the earlier volume seems to be in Hodgson's discussion of a "distinction . . . often made between understanding and Reason," which he explains is a "distinction, as a difference in kind," which "comes recommended to Englishmen by the honoured name of Coleridge." Hodgson goes on to stress his own idea that the difference between understanding and reason is one of degree "expressed by or consisting in the fact that the object, on which they are employed, assumes a new aspect when the higher degree has been reached. Phenomena assume the character of objects in presence of a Subject." [32] Here is no intellectual heir of Coleridge in the romantic movement of which Hegel in general and Schelling in particular are the high priests. Wenley's identification of Hodgson with James Frederick Ferrier and Scottish Intuitionalism is equally somewhat wide of the mark. The Scot's *Institutes of Metaphysic,* published in 1854, unquestionably was significant in emphasizing the problems involved in any distinction between thought and material objectivity. Hodgson quite possibly was influenced by Ferrier in method, as Ferrier in turn has been said to follow the method of Spinoza or the Schoolmen, namely, a strictly logical or rational demonstration. Ferrier, however, would be no encouragement to Hodgson in developing a new phenomenalism. Hodgson builds on Kant, as Wenley says much more correctly, and as Hodgson himself admitted when he affirmed that Kant's distinction of matter and form is still the basis of philosophy, but this is a generalization of relatively little meaning since the dichotomy parallels ordinary and uncritical observation.

---

[32] *Op. cit.,* page 509.

The statement of Wenley that Morris "still under the sway of Deistic rationalism, accepts the medieval notion of causation, which Hodgson dismisses for scientific reasons" and that he "also postulates an Absolute—making this identical with the God of theology, however—while Hodgson excludes this entity for ethical reasons," is a case of reading elements into Morris which in actuality were never present by any fair or careful definition. Morris' voluntaristic and evangelistic approach to the problems of life, in a universe which he has come increasingly to accept as organic or a matter of functional interactions, is not even remotely an acceptance either of medieval causation or the rational system-building of the Schoolmen. The claim that he postulates an Absolute as an entity is simple misrepresentation of his theism. Wenley probably speaks truly enough when he goes on to say that Morris was "impervious to the bearing of an argument of this kind," that is, was unaware of what Wenley identifies as Hodgson's "palpitating ethicism," but Wenley himself is blind to the fact that Morris could hardly see anything other than a pure manipulation of words in the assumption that "perfect love, perfect power, and perfect knowledge . . . as united in one Subject . . ." because "modes of its consciousness . . ." could thereupon establish such a unity in an "ideal person" and identify God. This ethical apotheosis only outraged Morris, to whom God was a definitely personal participant in normal objective experience.[33]

Hodgson demands the rational conception of deity, but explains that all this is "the concrete and total content of the abstract idea, the subjective feeling of happiness," and

---

[33] Wenley, pages 215–6.

so something that "belongs more properly to ethic than to metaphysic; belongs to the practical branch of human knowledge rather than to the purely theoretical." Wenley fails to observe that Hodgson, in his final summary immediately following, says that "analysis of the ideal of God here proposed is proposed as an analysis of the Christian ideal of God, that is, as an analysis of that ideal of God which is implicitly adopted by true Christians. And if the Christian ideal is capable of being so analyzed, it follows that it shares the truth of that analysis. . . . Figurative expressions best convey, and have always been found the best to convey, to human consciousness the idea and the ideal of God, inasmuch as they best signify the unapproachableness and the infinity involved in the idea. . . . It is another thing altogether to analyze the object meant by these expressions, the emotions which prompt them, and the ground and nature of these emotions. The emotions themselves are the phenomena from which we start, and the facts which have to be explained." [34] It is Hodgson and not Morris, if anyone here, who is "under the sway of Deistic rationalism," or a purely mechanical accounting for God and His works.

When Wenley expands his criticism of Morris, suggesting that Morris retains "one trait distinctive of his youthful outlook—a tendency to stamp intellectual opponents as sources of moral corruption," he does not seem to realize how morally corrupting the theist would find a reduction of the ideal of God to a dependence on the emotions, or on what Hodgson called the faith of an individual. Wenley's suggestion that Morris was "whistling in the dark, to

---

[34] *Op. cit.*, pages 574–5, 586–7.

keep his courage up," is a wild shot in the same dark which seems to exist only in Wenley's mind. He takes Morris at the age of twenty-seven, as quite sophomoric in contrast with Hodgson, who wrote *Time and Space* as "a mature man of thirty-three," and explains that Morris, moreover, was not "drawn to philosophy by overpowering domestic sorrow," forgetting that, before the lapse of the six years more which apparently add up to philosophical maturity in Wenley's mind, Morris would have the double sorrow of his mother's death while he was away from home, and the defection of his fiancée before he has once held her in his arms as his promised love, indeed, Wenley over-looked Morris' subsequent lifelong dyspepsia as testimony to quite as effective an inner brood of devils as Hodgson may ever have had for this supposedly necessary intellectual stimulus.

Morris begins his review of *Time and Space* with full recognition of the fact that man and his environment are integrated at all points, or that the relation of the individual and his world is organic. This was the general framework of the so-called school of conciliation in which his thinking then was set, and it is also and more importantly the largely indigenous American functionalism or organic perspective to which primary attention has been given in the first section of this chapter. If a book such as that of Hodgson appears, it does not begin to exist suddenly in a vacuum. It emerges in an intellectual milieu, and serves some sort of purpose. Its specific usefulness does not have to be elevated into a metaphysics, however, creating a utilitarian or behavioristic philosophy, nor does its appearance have to be accepted as the out-working of things according to the plan of some cosmic mind or intelligence, establishing a determinism or absolute idealism. Morris declines to follow Hodgson's example, that is, approaching his criticism on verbal grounds, but proceeds rather along lines suggested by the Aristotelian differentiations of knowledge according to subject matter and general frame of reference. He calls attention to the fact that Hodgson had separated metaphysics from psychology and philosophical science, and yet had made it of the same nature, i.e., its subject is their relations. Hence the "investigation is empirical," and since empiricism restricts itself to that of which it has immediate evidence, it cannot project itself beyond its own milieu, however valid or invalid any purely speculative thinking may be. Hodgson seeks to extricate reason from the limitations inherent in experience by making a distinction between experience and experience (i.e., subjective or potential versus objective and actual) but such a disjunction is in the mind and hence a part of experience. Morris can find nothing but the mere verbalization of a completely nondynamic philosophy. This is his over-all view of Hodgson.

Hence he points out first that *Time and Space* is "one product of that increasing metaphysical activity which has expressed itself in England, within the last two years, in the publication of many philosophical works. Though not written, like most of these treatises, in the professed personal interest of either of those two great parties, whose strife has of late mainly occupied the energies of English philosophers, it is easy to assign it its place with reference to the subject of that strife. It contains, in fact, sensationalism, newly worded and newly formalized. Its intellectual parentage is, however, not so much to be traced to such men as Hume and Helvetius as to Bacon and Locke." This of course is a reversal of what Hodgson himself held, and so Morris explains that the exposition was not designed to do all over again what Hume had done—that is, teach skepticism—but that nonetheless it restricted "to excess the sphere of knowledge, denying to it an absolute character." Presumably Wenley saw Morris positing an absolute at this point, but the context shows that Morris only had rational reliability or certainty in mind. "If the remark of M. Taine, the French critic, on Mr. Mill, that 'he has described the English mind, while thinking to describe the human mind,' is a fair criticism, we think it would be still more àpropos to a work like this of Mr. Hodgson's. As an empiricist, he represents that phase of character which makes an Englishman delight above all things in facts of experience. As a theist and Christian, he marks the sturdy adherence of this nation, proud of its material prosperity, to at least the traditions of its religion. It is such a combination of elements rationally unallied and even repugnant to one another as can hardly be found anywhere but in England."

Morris goes on to make his point that Hodgson's metaphysics is empirical because it fitted into that basic experiential and sensational cast which British philosophy has brought down from John Locke. Properly "metaphysic . . . deals with the foundation and possibilities of knowledge regarded as a qualitative product, wholly unrelated in nature to the conditions of material existence." Quantity and relation are empirical measures, as is even modal-ity once it enters into experience, but quality always has a subjective reference. The quality of anything is its dynamic constitution, unconditioned because self-determining at root. Hence the notion that metaphysics is no more than what Hodgson, in his chapter titles, designates as metalogical thought, or as an extra logic, is a pure verbal subterfuge that ignores any subjective reality as such. The one-remove in reason merely constitutes an ontology (a *deus ex machina*), showing Hodgson to be doing the very thing he claims to be avoiding. Hodgson's rejectiòn of any philosophic method based on history, or developmental sequences—the criterion accepted by Morris as the most valuable or trustworthy—means that the Englishman by his own choice is abstracting himself from time (history) and space (logic) in one sense as a means for ordering them in another—that is, as phenomena per se—and hence Morris, unwilling to reason except within some functional context—since thought and action are the same thing, and since both are interactive—finds him merely toying with terms.

"It is obvious that Mr. Hodgson's identification, by correlation, of the necessary and universal, is a radical error . . . It shows him to be rather a counter than a thinker. We may liken him to a tree sprung up in a valley into which a river's current has been turned, that, only because it is rooted in the firm earth beneath, is able to breast the current, and arrest the straws floating on its surface. For so it goes with every empiricist whose formula is: Necessity-Universality, and no more. By his own acknowledgment, if we fairly interpret the formula, he can only catch at disconnected straws of phenomena, and enumerate them, and measure them, and, after recording his estimates throw them aside for others it may be to reject and disgrace, or to modify and confirm—every thing being a product in which uncertain sense is one of the factors; while if he could but know it, it is only by his being rooted in his intellectual nature in the solid ground of rationality and *real* necessity, that he is able to accomplish the least of his labors. Empiricism has no bottom. It can not be consistent and live. On its own principles it can affirm nothing. It may not even affirm the contingent except contingently, and that again only contingently, and so on *in absurdum.* All is opinion; and even to that, its supreme treasure, it has no right, for it does not acknowledge, as absolutely necessary, those grounds of thought and knowledge which make opinion possible. It defies refutation, for it recognizes no principles of consistency."

Instead of offering a philosophy which deals with "the rational conditions of phenomena (i.e. with consciousness and the nature and purport of its deliverances)" and which has "its end in itself" as Hodgson claimed, Morris sees his presentation as no more than "an empirical investigation prior to the consideration of the real questions of philosophy," and explains that Hodgson contradicted his own claim. "Let us read passages in section five of his book . . . First, p. 13: 'Metaphysic is, properly speaking, not a science but a philosophy; that is, it is a science whose end is in itself, in the gratification and education of the minds which carry it on,' etc. 'Philosophy is a pleasurable and noble emotion no less than knowledge.' 'Philosophy is carried on for the sake of the knowing and learning which it involves.' Metaphysic deals with the ultimate grounds and ends of life, knowledge and being, lying beyond experience, as he approvingly quotes from Kant. It deals with the last questions man can propose, such as 'whence [man] and the world came; whither they go; what is the meaning of the whole scene of existence,' etc. But Mr. H. proceeds to declare (p. 14) that 'the very condition of prosecuting the inquiry is metaphysic' (the condition of metaphysic is metaphysic!) 'that is the analysis of the phenomena whose *history* (!) and import are to be studied.' From this we learn that metaphysic, expressly or impliedly alleged to be the final science based on the necessities of things, unriddling and setting forth the rationale of thought and the universe, is after all but a compendium of the universal in experience as a sine qua non to the inquiries proper to metaphysic!"

Morris offers his own positive stand on a metaphysics which cannot be divorced from ontology—such as Hodgson attempts to establish by a rational circularity—and explains that "the true doctrine" is that "all actual knowledge arises *in* experience (i.e., in the course of a life conditioned on a physical organism in time and space), but is, among other things, and this by its very nature, of the everlasting conditions of being and knowledge—is so perfect that we may make important affirmations with absolute assurance—reveals categories of thought and existence within which all is disjunctive and indifferent—asserts, not that the sheep must be white or the stone black, or, in general, that the material universe *must* have its present constitution by eternal necessity, but that there are known laws and limits of actual, intellectual and moral existence which may not and can not be transgressed. This implies no 'transformation of abstractions into complete objects or complete existences,' which Mr. Hodgson alleges as the essence and defect of ontology." Hodgson was "influenced by his indignation at that notorious and frivolous distinction between things and things-in-themselves," and so dropped the latter "for deserved reasons," but then he came to the conclusion that "nothing remains knowable or conceivable except what is revealed to passive experience," which was a direct regression to John Locke's *tabula rasa* and a naïve sensationalism.

The most important approach to the criticism of Hodgson's essay is on logical grounds. Hodgson has said that analysis was his only instrument, and Morris remarks that analysis is "incompetent to any real or proper metaphysic," since it is only half the mental process, i.e., a screening out or discrimination of factors for separate examination with a full realization, properly, that any consideration of objects in their discrete state is altogether inadequate for real understanding. He explains that Hodgson found "all synthesis to be a natural spontaneous product of the physiologico-mental nature" which, of course, is not only rank sensationalism but also an extreme rationalistic monism. Because Hodgson rejects the notion of efficient agency, no problem of productive dynamics could be considered, and this would be his principal defect in Morris' eyes. Hodgson projects a truncated world in which reality is known only in fragmentation and where the only law of intelligence is one of infinite division and particularization. Hodgson himself is undisturbed by the instability of his phenominalistic universe because to him experience holds everything in order. As long as he remains the naïve experientialist his contribution has a potential value, but when he seeks to deduce universal principles he promptly reaccepts a principle of necessity, as Morris observes very quickly, and so defeats his case by begging the question.

Hodgson is simply illogical when he accepts the subjective-objective dichotomy, and rejects all other dualisms, because the one he selects no less than the others requires a synthesis in the mind. Morris sees that this particular dichotomy is especially inclined to disappear. Indeed, the tendency of subject and object to merge at all points is a keystone of the philosophy that came to fruition in Morris and Dewey, both of whom have seen the distinction to be wholly functional. This development might reflect, in the later Morris, a transition from the Kantian and Fichtean stage of a nonbiological type of activity, with thought and force seen to be an ultimate duality, on to the functional idea of Ulrici and Trendelenburg, but its germ is here in the criticism of Hodgson. "We willingly admit," Morris writes, "that the last analysis of the sum of things, including consciousness, must, likely enough, be expressed in a duality, as of thought and force—the former dominating the latter. But these terms are equally objective, distinct from each other and separate from human consciousness. Of Mr. H's correlatives, the subjective and objective aspects of phenomena, the one is individual consciousness, and the two are substantially identical. We hesitate not further to affirm as absolute the union of thought and force—not their parity or commensurability—in the synthesis of existence. We believe all sound rational activity to be driven to this result."

Although Hodgson "pretends to avoid this step," actually "we know not what he means by the term phenomena, unless it be a single category to express the whole of consciousness and the universe. To use the term phenomena, instead of existence, is to employ an exactly equivalent synonym, unless it be desired to contest the reality of every thing testified in consciousness, in which case we leave him to enjoyment of his doubts. We know Mr. H. pretends that phenomena mean more than existence, but we shall soon see how little that more is. But were even this pretension valid, it would still hold good, that our author's own practice illustrates the view, that philosophy must start from and end in a single term, whether that term expresses something supposed or real." The difficulties encountered by Hodgson are largely a result of this effort to escape recourse to a synthesis and so, presumably an infinite regression. When he comes to define the subject, he has to do so "in the only way by which an absolute correlative for existence could possibly be constituted. What this subject is, we shall state more fully further on. It is however related to existence as potentiality to actuality, or as nonentity to entity. As potentiality it is only the material conditions of consciousness *without time* for their development into an actual product. This subject, to be entitled to the least regard, ought to have some share in being. So far as it *is*, it is a part of existence, not a second term by which to unriddle it; so far as it is not, why, it is not, and 'there's the end on't.' "

Thus Hodgson, as Morris explains, was ready to swamp his subjective distinction in the objective, despite his overall subjectivism, since it remains no more than potentiality in reference to the actual. His doctrine is "worse than

Kant's" since time and space are made indispensable to all consciousness, whereas Kant leaves pure reason independent of time and space. Hodgson's theory is "a sort of extreme physiological subjectivism," and its "guarantee . . . is the 'individual consciousness' of the author. He has given his testimony, we doubt not honestly, on fundamental problems in philosophy. He lays no claim to infallibility. He has merely contributed his witness to the elucidation of a part of science which he regards as not yet fixed, and which must be decided according to the general consciousness of the reflective portion of the race. For one, we think he has egregiously erred, by persistently regarding consciousness in its physical dependencies, to the exclusion of its more important rational contents. This latter element seems to us so clearly unrelated to any of the sensible conditions of life, as to be only an associate of such life, not at all identical with it."

Morris thus shows how little interest he has in the psychological perspective of the British. Again he affirms his own idealism, but not as a variant subjectivism or spiritualistic rationalism. Meanwhile he continues with his criticism. "If Mr. Hodgson's analysis were as complete as he desires and believes it to be, all phenomena, rational or sensible, could be explained upon it. But no phenomena of rationality have been found in the supposed exhaustive analysis of consciousness—and as that is the only source of knowledge and existence, it only remains to show for what sensible phenomena, facts of rationality have been mistaken. This, however, will remain impossible until it can be shown that quality and quantity are not two categories, but one, and that two objects may be absolutely identical. When this shall have been done, the prediction of Mr. Hodgson's exordium will have been realized, and 'what is called mind, and what are called existences, and that which Kant calls *der transcendentale Gegenstand*, will have melted into phenomena, out of which they indeed originally grew.' Then will 'men have lost their reason.' " As for the idealistic view, standing at the opposite extreme in philosophy, "it is alleged, against the postulation of an absolute and the ascription of existence to it, that this course labors 'under the fallacy of *obscurum per obscurius.*' Is it not possible that Mr. H. misunderstands here those whom he combats? Those who call existence a mode of the absolute, do not necessarily 'add to the phenomena of existence another imagined phenomenon which needs to be explained.' They rather find existence to be the absolute, all-inclusive category, covering therefore the ground of the absolute—hence also of the relative, which depends on it." Here is Morris' actual absolute, not an ideal entity.

Morris then proceeds to deny that "making existence the mode of the absolute" presumes an infinitely regressive absolute behind it, which perhaps is the most incisive point made by Hodgson. Morris sees the possibility of an absolute in knowing, or a certainty which in scientific terms is the possibility of complete validation for human wisdom. Both Morris and Hodgson find an inclusive inexhaustibility in the universe, and this the one approaches through scientific verification in a material world of every day, and the other through a logical confirmation in an intellectual realm of no less everyday experience. The latter denies the absolute in any sense of German idealism, in order to exalt the relative, but the former realizes that the relative can reveal and delimit the absolute. Morris does not posit an absolute as a *deus ex machina,* and denies that the "absolute is . . . a super-additive existence, invented to explain existence. It is rather something which exists and is known to exist, not merely through the categorical fact of existence, but also on other and decisive grounds. It is *the* fact *in* existence, most supremely demanded and authenticated by our rational nature, leaving aside objective proofs." [35]

[35] *Op. cit.,* pages 217–24, 227–9, 231–2, 236–7.

CHRONOLOGY OF EUROPEAN ACTIVITIES

February 8th:
(1866)
Morris left Norwich, Vermont; sailed from Hoboken on the 10th aboard the North German Lloyd steamer *New York.*

February 24th:
Arrived at Bremen; moved to Kassel, one hundred and fifty miles to the south, where he concentrated on improving his German.

April 2d:
Arrived at Halle, in Saxony, a hundred miles to the east of Kassel, where he met Ulrici, took in concerts at nearby Leipzig, and attended Ulrici's lectures for the semester on logic and history of philosophy.

Late June:
Went to Dresden for three weeks of recreation.

Early August:
Frankfort on the Main and varied sight-seeing.

Late August:
Moved to Lausanne, on the Lake of Geneva, where he settled down for five months, perfected his French, wrote his Hodgson article and made his most intimate European friendships.

January 30th:
(1867)
Met Trendelenburg in Berlin, arriving in that city by way of Halle, but was restless and not yet ready to attend philosophical lectures.

March 2d:
Back at Lausanne for another five months' stay, traveling by way of Nuremberg, Munich and Zurich among other points; learned of mother's death here, and again was restless, visited Paris, etc.

November:
To Berlin, by way of Cologne, and in residence for the first semester of 1867–8, attending two lectures a day under Trendelenburg, Meyer and Hause; worked on **Aristotle's** *Ethics* in Trendelenburg's seminar; planned private study in Hegel.

March:
(1868)
Visited Dresden again; then brief stays in Prague, Vienna, Venice, Bologna and Florence on way to Rome for Easter, followed by visits to Naples, Pisa, Florence again and Milan on way to Lausanne.

May 4th:
Lausanne until August 20th.

August 27th:
Arrived at Southampton via Paris and Havre, sailed aboard the *Allemania* on the 28th, arrived in America the second week of September.

CHAPTER EIGHT

A REORIENTATION IN GERMAN THOUGHT

MORRIS kept a diary covering his European sojourn in considerable detail until the final three months in Lausanne, when the increasing uncertainty of his future was bearing more and more heavily upon him, and it is from this source and some surviving letters that his activities abroad are known. Wenley remarks that these materials provide "little, if any, light upon the course of his intellectual development" because "Europe was a panorama, and Morris was ever reticent in the extreme," hence "the drama of the soul, whatever it may have been, never obtrudes itself." However, "we may infer, from numerous pious expressions, that he preserved his evangelical traditions substantially for two years at least," or through the time when the diary entries are really informative. This would be a year after the vocation of the ministry had been abandoned definitely in or around December, 1866, and it must be remembered that the trip was planned originally as preparation for a philosophical chair instead of the pulpit—and also that even Sylvester Morris had applauded this change in plans in a letter written in January, 1866— so that the piety was not at all linked up with a life work in professional religious channels. One significant entry in the diary is probably a real clue to Morris' own innermost motivation in looking across the Atlantic for further training and inspiration. He had arrived in Bremen on a Saturday evening, and the Sunday morning service in the cathedral "was an altogether new sight, strangely affecting me; so different was it from anything I had seen or could see in America in style and arrangement, and so various and profound were the emotions excited at the architectural, pictorial and commemorative expressions of Christian faith and reverence which it contained. . . . It gave me for the moment a kind of inspiration, and yet set me again desperately at work over the problems of Christianity."

Just exactly what Morris meant by the problems of Christianity is actually the key to any proper analysis of his life and writings. Wenley's over-all hypothesis is that the young student had come to doubt his basic faith, and was looking either for new ideas and explanations which would buttress it, or else for some substitute anchorage in rational realms which would take the place of theology altogether. This point of view approaches the whole proposition as an issue of subject matter, and sees Morris' need as an adjustment in the content of his thought. The supposition, if the known record be examined carefully enough, proves rather superficial, indeed, altogether too easy. Morris has been the consistent deviate from the beginning, ever inclined to go his own way and to do his thinking for himself, and one who, according to Wenley himself, "never called any man master." There is a steadiness of on-going in the young man's intellectual progress which has just been suggested again through the "pious expressions" of the European diary. The move to Europe does not represent nearly as sharp a break in events as suggested by Wenley when he explains that Morris "could not have foreseen the enormous changes of standpoint, method and general atmosphere, that awaited him over the water. The Germany of 1866 was nigh two generations ahead of the English-speaking world in treatment of philosophical and theological problems, and even farther removed from the United States than from England. Hegel, who, in this very year, was just beginning to be noised abroad in Scotland . . . had run his course in his native land. The Hegelian school had fallen to pieces long since; the fever of materialism had passed its crisis and the Neo-Kantian movement had set in. . . . On the contrary, the Protestant preachers, who filled American chairs of philosophy, were still winning bubble reputations in the 'free will' controversy." Wenley's judgment arises out of the Hegelian presuppositions which must be taken into account in connection with any philosophical opinion he might express. This does not imply, of course, that Wenley was an orthodox disciple of Hegel, only that he held to an experientialistic absolute as the denial, on the one hand, of any revealed truth such as theism might present and, on the other, of any metaphysically barren theories which a purely empirical science might offer.[1]

_____

[1] Wenley, pages 102–4, 106–9, 206. Schneider, in the *History of American Philosophy*, page 191, quotes a statement made by Wenley in the year following his call to the chair of Morris at Michigan, and so one which probably provides a very fair epitome of Wenley's personal stand. "We need not exclaim 'Lord, Lord,' to Hegel, yet we cannot but acknowledge the reasons for his sway. The absolutism, out of which so many fashion a convenient body, has after all little to do with man's making himself in God's image. Rather, it relates to certain contributions to the conditions of philosophic and theological progress, in the absence of which a theory of things would be incoherent or impossible. Experience must be its own judge. This, in a word, is Hegel's epoch-making discovery." And it is

What must not be lost to sight is that Morris, while still at Union Seminary, had not only read Kant's *Critique of Pure Reason* and Hegel's *Philosophy of History*, but also the competently critical *Historical Survey of Speculative Philosophy* by Chalybäus. He arrived in Europe, not as a neophyte about to enter some Greater Mysteries with becoming modesty, but as a young scholar who was thoroughly saturated in the current literature through which the most recent theological developments in Germany had had their refining influence on a current American theology. This, in its turn, was no less linked intellectually with Old World speculation. He himself had accepted the general opinion that science tended to prove the traditional assumptions of Protestantism rather than the reverse, in conformity with the characteristic American reaction, but he also realized—as the European philosophers were more inclined to do—that scientific discovery was unquestionably rectifying the theological interpretations at a host of unsuspected points. What he probably saw most clearly was that the problems of Christianity were not intellectual ones in the sense of a straining to retain the basic faith— or perhaps to regain it—on purely rational grounds. Morris represented the practical spirit of America. The task faced by the devout Christian, for the evangelism of his neighbors no less than the world at large, was no different than it ever had been. Rational satisfaction was not the goal, but rather was the implementation—through the reason—of a religious dynamic. It was the necessity of

---

this absolutistic or intellectual experientialism which is Wenley's basis for considering American biologically-ordered thinking, with its verification in sensual experience, quite inferior to the Neo-Hegelian rationalisms.

bringing the testimony of an inner conviction into intellectual harmony with a practical validation for the same spiritual insights that made the philosophical clarification so difficult for the youthful thinker.

Morris had come through what probably had been an altogether disconcerting experience some four and a half years before, when he had been the headmaster at Royalton Academy. According to his own written statement, he had "failed." Despite his high achievement as the foremost member of his class at Dartmouth, and his own personal fervor as a Christian, his influence upon the boys and girls under his care had fallen disappointingly short of his expectation. Perhaps for the first time in his life he had observed the inadequacy of purely intellectual tools—or of an idealism which was not dynamic in direct and personal experience—for the accomplishment of a moral purpose in an everyday milieu. This unquestionably is the meaning, in the mind of Morris himself, of the "problems of Christianity" noted in the diary. The first impression in Europe, after his initial night on foreign soil, was apparently the feeling that often may have swept in upon him at home, namely, the need for inspirational power which a spiritual insight must have if it is to be translated into the act and living of another individual, i.e., if it actually is to be communicated. Here is preview of the present chapter's basic consideration. Morris' reorientation was on the side of logic, not as a formal discipline of the mind but as a realization that the fundamental emphasis in philosophy is functional. Hence the turn in basic interest—to express the matter in the light of the later developments through both Morris and his students, Dewey in particular—is away from ontology, as an idle or futile metaphysics content to dwell in its ivory tower, to epistemology, that is, to ideas at work through human lives in an organic society.

The continuity of intellectual climate between America and Europe was particularly emphasized for Morris through the theological school of conciliation. This represented the continuing influence of Schleiermacher, Fichte and Schelling upon a group of French and German theologians with whom Henry B. Smith had very close ties. Smith had gone abroad in his early twenties, shortly after the death of Schleiermacher, but he was not himself a disciple of the latter in any direct sense. His own summary of the developments in Germany, "from about 1817 to the present time," is given in his *Introduction to Christian Theology*. "A new basis for investigation was presented in the philosophy of Fichte, Schelling, etc. A more deeply-awakened religious spirit appeared. There arose a more thorough and philosophical view of the history of the church and of doctrines. The general aim has been: to reconcile Christianity with philosophy, putting Christianity on independent grounds. . . . The aid has been sought of (a) a profounder view of the real nature of Christianity . . . (b) a profounder view of human reason than Rationalism had possessed . . . (c) the reconciliation of scriptural and historical with speculative theology. Among the orthodox Germans, there are several noticeable peculiarities . . . a more thorough grasping of the nature of Christianity . . . a greater, though not blind, regard for the past theologies and confessions of faith, and also, a defense of these, on philosophical as well as scriptural grounds. Schleiermacher (with excellences and great defects) begins this movement, then follow Neander, Tholuck, Müller, Nitzsch, Twesten, etc., to Dorner." [2]

Smith was not recognized by his contemporaries as a spokesman for the European thinkers,[3] but he was responsible for introducing considerable German material to America in translation, not only through his sponsorship with Philip Schaff—also on the Union Theological Seminary faculty—of Ueberweg's *History of Philosophy* (which as translated had its publication in 1871–3) but also rather significantly in 1864—when Morris entered the seminary as a student—through his editorship of the American edition of *A Text-Book of the History of Doctrines* by the German theologian, K. R. Hagenbach. This work was first published abroad in 1841, or shortly after the time of Smith's student days in Germany, but Smith's edition was based upon the Edinburgh translation of C. W. Buch, which he revised "with large additions from the fourth German edition, and other sources." Smith's special regard for this work is a useful indication of his own theological standpoint, that is, his fundamental orientation in the Neo-Schleiermacher developments. Pointing out that "the value of Dr. Hagenbach's work is attested by the constant de-

---

[2] *Op. cit.*, New York, A. C. Armstrong & Sons, 1882, pages 68–9.

[3] Thus Robert Hastings Nichols, in the *Dictionary of American Biography* (New York, Scribners, 1935, Vol. XVII, page 278), summarizes Smith's work by explaining that "in theology he was of the school of Jonathan Edwards." Frank Hugh Foster, in *The Modern Movement in American Theology* (New York, Fleming H. Revell Company, 1939, pages 139ff.), pointing out that "the German theological writers only began to influence American developments" directly in any degree "in the latter decades of the nineteenth century," makes no mention of Henry B. Smith's part in furthering the process, but identifies Lewis F. Stearns, Smith's biographer, as one continuing the emphasis by Schleiermacher, Albrecht Ritschl and Frank of Erlangen on Christian experience as the only possible source of theology.

mand for new editions in Germany, in the midst of much competition," he gives expression to its merits as he sees these and then adds that "the theological position of the author is on the middle ground between the destructive criticism of the school of Tübingen, and the literal orthodoxy of the extreme Lutherans, while he also sympathises with the Reformed rather than with the Lutheran type of theology." Smith then concludes with the remark that Hagenbach's work "is still perhaps the one best adapted to general consultation and profitable use." [4]

Dr. Hagenbach gives a clear explanation and identification of the school of conciliation, explaining that "though the speculative philosophy of Fichte and Schelling seemed to have brought about a certain reconciliation between the two extremes above mentioned [i.e., rationalism and supernaturalism], it was still to be seen whether that reconciliation was a real one. Herder, in the spirit of a poet, pointed out the historical nature of the Christian doctrines, as well as the distinction between religion and doctrinal opinions, and opened the way, in connection with modern culture, to a new and living treatment of Scriptural subjects, founded on more accurate views of oriental and biblical modes of thought. On the other hand, the philosophy of the Absolute was combated by Frederic Jacobi, with pious wisdom. In opposition to this philosophy, he endeavoured to show that faith, which he distinguished from knowledge, must have its quiet home in the human heart. Though he did not mean by faith either the orthodox faith of the church, or strict Scriptural faith (in the supernaturalistic sense), his more profound and prophetic theory was wel-

---

[4] *Op. cit.*, New York, Sheldon & Company, Vol. I, pages iii–iv.

comed, even by those who felt the necessity of a more positive system. The philosophical system of Jacobi, designed to meet the religious feelings of men, served as the basis of a new school, the adherents of which are also disposed to adopt the principles of modern philosophy in general. They endeavoured to bring about a reconciliation between the extremes, by historico-critical, as well as philosophical researches, by psychologico-anthropological rather than by speculative investigations." [5]

When Smith was studying abroad in the late thirties he had found his greatest personal intimacy with Friedrich August Gottreau Tholuck, who then and for better than a decade had been Professor of Theology at Halle, and who had come to be ranked among the foremost preachers of his time. This university had been the real center of German rationalism, and it was almost entirely due to Tholuck's influence and efforts that the overemphasis on a pure intellectualism had given way to the reconciling spirit or basic experientialism of the new movement. Dr. Smith's own comment on the characteristically middle-of-the-road view is found in the Hagenbach text, as an editorial addition. "The theology of Schleiermacher made an epoch, in consequence of its peculiar relation to the two opposite systems of rationalism and supernaturalism, in the midst of whose conflicts it appeared. It 'combines the elements of both, in representing the essence of Christianity to be the immediate utterance of the religious consciousness, which in its inmost spirit, it says, is Christian.' This Christian consciousness 'has, on the one hand, whatever is essential in Christianity; while, on the other hand, it is viewed as only

---

[5] *Ibid.*, Vol. II, page 401.

the more definite explication and concrete expression of what is inherent in man's religious nature.' The same general tendency of thought represented by Kant is also developed in Schleiermacher's system; but this is only one of its aspects. The other aspect is 'that what makes the substance of the Christian consciousness is not something which it produces, by and of itself, but something imparted and received. The Christian consciousness is the reflex and expression of the Christian fellowship.' " [6]

The original reconciliation between the opposing claims of rationalism and supernaturalism came to take its new form, in the generation of George Sylvester Morris, as a fusion of science and theology, reflecting the tremendous developments of the scientific materialism stimulated by such events as the promulgation of the cell theory by Schleiden and Schwann in 1839, the appearance of Darwin's *Origin of Species* in 1859, and so on. This transition is particularly evident in the work of Hermann Ulrici, with whom Smith had lived for a considerable part of his time while a student in Germany and who had been the first of the European associates of Smith in this school to give Morris, three decades later, the measure of personal welcome that stemmed from Smith's earlier friendship. Ulrici was of great assistance to Morris when it came to proceeding intelligently with the German studies, as well as helping him to know at first hand the full hospitality of these old-school philosophers. The delightful camaraderie of the Ulrici home, which once had been a haven for the youthful Smith in times of illness and financial stringency, is revealed in the letters written by Smith from Europe,

---

[6] *Ibid.*, page 404.

and preserved by his wife, and apparently it was offered as freely to Smith's protégé.[7]

Ulrici was thirty-four years older than Morris, that is, just sixty and, while he had two decades more to live, he was at the height of his powers and was completing his most significant work at the time Morris met and knew him in 1866. Because of this latter fact, Ulrici's final views and perspective may well have had an appreciable impact upon the younger man's thinking, ultimately if not at once. In this particular book, *Gott und der Mensch*, Ulrici explains that in his earlier work, starting out from Schleiermacher, he had tried to show the methodological continuity between natural science and a theism based on feeling and religious experience, arguing that God was a necessary postulate for the objectivity of this religious feeling, as well as for all other forms of sensitivity. This was the chief theme of his earlier view and the basis of his *Gott und die Natur*, published at Leipzig only five years previously. In other words, the new development in Ulrici's thinking was recent enough to suggest a vitality of interest which would be apt to communicate itself to Morris. The transition is a shift from a Schleiermacher formulation of religious experience to a Neo-Fichtean emphasis on fact (*Tatsache*) and self activity (*Tätigkeit*), that is, to the experience fundamentally self-activated or voluntaristic as against a stirring in response to the fructifying divine impulse, such as would remain essentially an exterior stimulus. The conflict is no longer between the rational and irrational, but rather between the measurable and that which claims it cannot be subjected to scientific criteria.

[7] *Henry Boynton Smith, His Life and Works*, pages 47–52.

Ulrici was quite familiar with Trendelenburg, Lotze and other philosophers of his time, and he shared with them the rather general aim to reconcile material science and theistic speculation. However, he thought that Trendelenburg's method was too analytical-critical, and that Lotze was too idealistic. He rested his case on what he called a logical reconstruction. In his logic he emphasized two basic ideas. The first of these is that the Fichtean self-activity is an activity of making discriminations, and that this capacity to discriminate self—within the general milieu of all that has existence—is the absolute presupposition of all natural being, and so necessarily of all human thinking. The second of his basic ideas is that any adequate scientific logic must accommodate teleology, that is, purpose as the naïve fact or only possible recognizable result of discrimination as known or knowable, both to the particular discriminator and to any other discriminating existent to which the existence of anything in question is significant.[8]

Here is the logic of voluntarism, and it is based almost entirely on Fichte as Ulrici himself shows. Thus he states that "only by strength of will does it [the soul] sustain itself as a self because it is defended and protected only through it [will] against the counterefforts and desires which attack it, and [against] the power of the exterior sense impressions and the act stirred up by them threatening its self-sufficiency. Without the strength of the will it [the soul] would be like the animal, a plaything of these drives and efforts. Thus no self has being without complete self-sufficiency. Let will and self-consciousness be the factors

[8] *Op. cit., Zweiter Theil: Grundzuge der Praktischen Philosophie Naturrecht Ethik und Aesthetik, Erster Band,* Leipzig, 1866, page vii.

of its selfness in this sense, then one can assert correctly that the soul through its own activity as self, as ego, postulates itself. This very famous and much ridiculed (Fichtean) postulate only insists: the human soul is, originally and as such, only a self according to the potential, the drifting, the determining; the selfness is not given to man prepared and finished; rather he must and should make himself first into a self. The ability for this he possesses in his discrimination and will power. Through the activity of this discrimination-of-self-as-itself he grasps and *recognizes* himself as self; through the will he himself *acts* and makes his *place* as self. Through this act alone does he become and remain a *reality* which originally he was only potentially (*potentia*)." [9] From this point of view, Ulrici ridicules both Schopenhauer and Von Hartmann. He goes on to emphasize the fact that the self engaged in reflection is the same self as that which acts voluntaristically. Thus thinking and acting are essentially identical. A freedom of the will over external stimuli must be achieved, however, which means that self-control has to be developed. This, of course, is discrimination as it becomes more than the basic or simple fact of mere identity. Ulrici explains that man, through the activity of the self—or the conscious ego —achieves a self-reliance. This he feels is a much better basis for asserting self-reliance than Schleiermacher's reversed emphasis on a dependence directed outwardly, albeit to a higher power.[10]

Morris attended Ulrici's lectures in the spring of 1866, but not much direct influence at this time can be assumed in any but the most general terms. The sessions came a

[9] *Ibid.*, pages 29–30, translated from the German.   [10] *Ibid.*, pages 31–2.

bare two months after his arrival from America, and Morris' mind was busy on the creative side with the analysis of Hodgson, which remained the immediate intellectual work to be done. He may have listened to Ulrici in part as a courtesy and—probably in much greater part— as a means for improving his German. Indeed at Kassel, in the five weeks preceding, he had concentrated on that task. As far as Henry B. Smith's much more intimate German tie with Professor Tholuck is concerned, there is little indication that Morris had anything but the most casual contact with the theologian. Widely known and greatly loved throughout the Protestant world, Tholuck was certainly the outstanding individual on the theological side to whom Morris could be introduced with advantage. The diary reports that Morris was taken to dinner at the Tholuck home by Smith during the latter's European visit in the summer of 1866, but there is not the slightest intimation of intellectual or theological sympathy between Morris and the aging professor, who was then nearly seventy.

A further indication of the relatively slight importance given to his experiences at Halle by Morris himself, in after perspective, is to be seen in the fact that, contrasting sharply with the detailed analysis of Trendelenburg and incisive criticism of the Berlin professor's work and role, which he published on his return to America, Morris treats Ulrici very lightly, referring to him in the Ueberweg text only, and there merely (1) summarizing the events of his life in a few lines, (2) listing the numerous works he had published—including his extended contributions to the *Zeitschrift für Philosophie* and speaking of his "abun-

dant literary activity" as "very important contributions to
the philosophical science of his times"—and (3) dismissing
him otherwise with two sentences, of which one is almost
entirely a quotation of Ulrici's own words. Thus Ulrici's
"position in philosophy is independent," and "he seeks to
mediate between realism and idealism, but to show that
'to the soul in distinction from the body and to the [divine]
mind in distinction from nature, not only independent
existence, but also supremacy, both belong and are actually
given.' " [11] Hence it is entirely possible that the Fichtean
impact through Ulrici was something to which Morris
was not actually sensitive at the time he was working on
the Ueberweg translation in 1868–70. For his further account of Ulrici's system Morris quotes Erdmann without
comment, and as for Tholuck—probably considering Tholuck wholly the theologian—Morris does not add him to
Ueberweg's account nor give him consideration elsewhere.

While later developments show Morris' mature thinking almost wholly ordered by the German philosophy
which he studied in its own milieu during his two and a
half years of European sojourn, it is yet very evident that
he felt much more drawn, temperamentally, to the French
mind, as in (1) the apparent warmth of his living contact
with Jean Frederic Astié, who was only eighteen years his
senior, a professor of philosophy but certainly more eminent as the theologian aligned with the school of conciliation, (2) his three considerable stays at Lausanne which,
with travels in France and Italy, aggregated better than
half the total time abroad, and (3) the predominant read-
ings in French during the early part of 1867 when he was

[11] Op. cit., Vol. II, page 299.

at work on his first published article, on Hodgson, to which attention was given in the preceding chapter. Astié, however, did not have the originality of Ulrici nor the over-all significance of Trendelenburg. Moreover, Astié at the time Morris knew him seems to have been much more interested in the fresh impulse given to Protestantism by Alexandre Rodolphe Vinet [12] than in any development of philosophy or theology on his own account. Thus Astié puts a quotation from Vinet, ridiculing the current intellectualism, on the title page of his book, *Les Deux Théologies Nouvelles*: [13] "Intelligence having to do solely with ideas, abstract and nonsentient things, has no need for charity. Charity in its case would be suicide. Intelligence, which lives on truth, cannot refuse this nourishment without dying, and who, pray, would profit from her death? It is of *man* that charity is demanded. It is he who in attacking the error must deal thriftily with the lost sheep." [14]

The hallmark of the school of conciliation was a demand that truth or understanding be grounded not only rationally, on the scientific side, but also experientially and much more importantly in the individual's own experience. Vinet built everything on conscience. Hence a true intelligence would require a conservation of experience as such, or a very appreciable respect for human personality as the final source in any practical validation for truth, no matter how imperfectly the individual may be struggling. In his *Les Deux Théologies Nouvelles* Astié concerns himself very largely with the intellectual conflicts

[12] Vinet, a French Protestant of Swiss birth, had died as a relatively young man twenty years before.
[13] Paris, Librairie de Ch. Mayrueis et Cᶦᵉ, Éditeurs, 1862.
[14] Translated from the French.

which stand in the way of a more full and direct spiritual experience for man. His attack upon a self-sufficient intellectualism or all-resolving rationalism is very sharp. "What better can one hope from the present conditions of human nature? But, you will say, what can you expect of a man who wants to be a Christian and a philosopher at the same time. It is a burning problem for him. What shall I make of this? I demand of him that he do not go outside the common right, that he accept frankly the conditions of the present life. There are but three possibilities. In one case, his philosophy and his Christianity will be in accord, in which case there is no problem, no need of prescriptions for a patient so remarkable and in such good health. Or, in the second case, perhaps unconsciously, the philosopher would be more important than the Christian, or the Christian than the philosopher. In such a case let this be at his risk and peril. If that which prevails with him is within the truth, he will become one of those rare geniuses who advance the chariot of truth; if not, in spite of his talents he will fall back into the great mass of those who apply the brakes. There is still a third case, even more tragic. What would you think of the man feeling his philosophy and his Christianity in disaccord, not willing to abandon either one or the other because he believes that both are true? Is such a dualism to be tolerated?

"Behold, the great word is spoken, the magic term which is able to drive back into the darkness the most constant facts and to plunge us into the thick fog which recalls those happy days when our acorn-eating ancestors were making their way from the high plateau of Asia towards the dark countries of Europe still covered with forests! If one listens to certain friends of progress, who nevertheless pride themselves on their respect for history, one would think that we had recovered those ancient days of Greece, that period before Socrates when philosophy in the cradle had not yet arrived at a distinction between subject and object, between mind and the world. The intellectualism of certain people goes so far that one would take them from their language for pure spirits. The dualism of body and soul does not exist for them any more. Time and eternity run together. Nothing has struck them to the heart. They no longer understand this antagonism between the moral ideal and the sad reality, between liberty and the nature within us. Everything is resolved for them into a grandiose and glorious synthesis." [15]

The ontological synthesis of this sort, as achieved by a purely rationalistic idealism, is attacked further by Astié in his criticism of the dialectic, and he complains that "unfortunately in our own day under the influence of idealistic schools, formal logic is coming to devour all the other branches and to absorb the whole of philosophy." This attitude is significant in the light of Morris' later sharp prejudice against both formal logic and historical dialectic. Astié does not lean to the opposite extreme at any point, but regards supernaturalism as no less an intemperance, and considers it "more vague and untenable than that of rationalism, reconciling itself only that much more easily with the mystic tendency." [16] Thus the school of conciliation sees that if a philosopher is to be a pure rationalist, dialectician or formal logician, and if a Christian is to be

---

[15] *Op. cit.*, pages 300–1, translated from the French.
[16] *Ibid.*, pages 305, 330.

entirely the supernaturalist and mystic, there obviously is no practical way by which any one man can be both. Moreover, the individual cannot get out of the world in which he finds himself, and around him are plentiful evidences of both mechanically ordered and subjectively distributed experience. Science and religion actually exist, side by side. If any person attempts a synthesis on the basis of subordinating either one of these extremes to the other, he is in difficulties, as no one saw more clearly than Morris himself. Rare indeed will be the genius who discovers the truth by this means. The person who divides himself, recognizing both realms of experience as valid but knowing no effective co-operation between them, is of course in the worst case of all.

Perfect health in philosophy and theology is based upon the agreement which is not the sort of synthesis which attempts to eliminate the differences but rather the one which is essentially functional or organic, revealing a division of labor rather than a fragmented reality. Here is the conception of intelligence achieved by Morris, and foreshadowed in the school of conciliation. The efforts of Vinet to gain a complete freedom of religious belief—reflected for Morris in the impact of Astié—were closer to Schleiermacher, constituting a basic reference of moral criteria to conscience and a form of externalism which is not to be found in the thinking of Morris at any point. It seems rather probable that what Morris gained immediately, from his European studies, was not a pattern or model for the ordering of his thinking, which at the end found its instrumentation in a reinterpretation of Hegel, but rather was (1) a growing familiarization with the ma-

terials and climate of philosophy and theology and (2) a
training in the use of scientific modes of interpretation.
Consequently the contribution of Friedrich Adolf Trendelenburg was more significant, providing the momentary
stimulus he needed, even if later he held to few of Trendelenburg's formulations. Curiously enough, he was not
drawn to the Berlin professor at all, nor to German
philosophy itself in any appreciable degree at the beginning. Thus he postponed any intention he may have had to
study in Berlin when he met Trendelenburg himself early
in 1867.

Henry B. Smith was familiar with Trendelenburg's
work, respected him as teacher and probably recommended
him, but Smith was not situated either temperamentally
or in content of interest to profit from the type of Neo-
Kantian movement for which Trendelenburg was responsible. Smith had listened to Trendelenburg in 1839, on
"Criticism of Hegelian Philosophy," and had heard him
again when he made his 1866 visit, stating at the latter time
that Trendelenburg was "the best Aristotelian in Germany" and one of the men whom he had heard in his youth
"still reading their courses with unabated zeal," indeed,
actually not now seeming "older than when I formerly
heard him expounding the philosophy of the great Stagirite, or analyzing and refuting the logic of Hegel, the
great German counterpart of Aristotle." [17] This typifying
of Hegel as Aristotle's German counterpart, although by
Smith probably meant only in connection with logic, is
particularly significant in the light of what John Dewey has
termed Morris' fusion of Aristotle and Hegel and in con-

---

[17] *Henry Boynton Smith, His Life and Works,* pages 65, 258, 269.

nection with Morris' unpublished introduction to *Hegel's Philosophy of the State and of History,* to which attention will be given later.[18]

The fusion of Aristotle and Hegel is, of course, the development of the purely functional approach in both psychology and philosophy, ending in the case of Morris with the Hegelian organicism of his final thinking. At the root of this point of view is what seems to have been an almost instinctive distaste for rational system-building, possibly resulting in part from the critical materials through which he had worked in his undergraduate and graduate days, and in part from the philosophical and theological expositions which failed to hold him at Union Seminary. It is a distaste perhaps coming to a focus in the latter milieu through a sense that the school of conciliation, whether so identified or not, failed to touch reality because of a tendency to run with the hare and hunt with the hounds. What emerges, after the European sojourn, appears to be a strengthened confidence in the characteristically American approach to metaphysical problems through the mediation of tool-ideas or functional concepts. And it is with some support for the notion of an operational role of ideas in Ulrici's doctrines—perhaps emphasized originally in the lectures on logic and on history of philosophy attended by Morris—that the great logical dichotomy, so characteristic of Morris' later thinking, begins to take identifiable form.

Rejecting all idealistic dualism, as ever ontologically absolute, it is yet possible to see the necessary movement in existence and experience towards law on the one hand,

---

[18] *Cf.* below, pages 246–8.

and towards experiment on the other, as the response in man to final cause in the first instance and efficient cause in the second. The interpretation of God as final cause becomes an important initial phase of Morris' positive thinking, to which consideration will be given in the following chapter. It is at this point that Trendelenburg contributes very specifically to the organum which at length will emerge through the young man's mind as the very core of dynamic idealism, identifying primal motion as efficient cause or means, and purpose or motion in its rational aspect as final cause and the basis of necessity and so the starting point in any science of ethics. Morris himself outlined this voluntaristic logic of his Berlin mentor in the long article to be discussed shortly.

The attempt of Hodgson in his *Time and Space* to separate metaphysics from ontology has been criticized by Morris as actually a case of ontological system-building,[19] that is, an effort to establish a species of rational absolutism that can be known independently of conditions in the everyday world. The impossibility of any such a complete metaphysical separation of the things of mind from those of sense is therefore almost a cardinal principle in Morris' critical view, and hence at no time acceptable in German lineaments. The logical distinction of a parallel sort, by contrast, is the effective unification of material and intellectual components of being, but neither as a synthesis in mind nor as the end result of a genetic process in the cosmos, since both of these devices really provide a *deus ex machina* for the subordination of the one type of reality to the other, and so definitely deny the validity of their dis-

---

[19] *Cf.* above, page 123ff.

tinction *ad absurdum.* Instead the functional interaction of thought and objective actuality is something which is encountered naïvely in normal life, requiring no acceptance by special rationalistic skills. Therefore philosophy does not properly speculate relative to the world at large in order to know what it is—that is, how it is to be defined in terms of something other than itself, or through mental ramifications that can only regress from the practical reality—but to provide an intelligent organization of man's approach to himself and to his world as a means for his conscious manipulation or control of his experience. This is logic, not as a formalization of verbal patterns but as a development of the tool functions of the mind.

Thus the criticism of Hodgson was made, for the major part, on logical grounds, and it was completed before Morris had attended the lectures of Trendelenburg, whose principal stimulus to the younger man was in this field of logic. The ensuing line of continuity in his thinking may be traced out, perhaps most significantly, through the firsthand testimony of John Dewey, whose daughters, writing with his direct co-operation, have said that "the influence of Professor Morris was undoubtedly one source of Dewey's later interest in logical theory. Morris was given to contrasting what he called 'real' logic, and associated with Aristotle and Hegel, with formal logic of which he had a low opinion." This has followed on their explanation that it was "from the idealism of Hegel, as interpreted by Morris," that Dewey "obtained in his late adolescence that fusion of emotions and intellect for which he had sought unsuccessfully in his boyhood religious experience." [20]

---

[20] *The Philosophy of John Dewey,* pages 17–8.

Thus Morris had been quite able, fifteen years after his wrestling with the problems of Christianity in the European milieu—at least in the case of Dewey—to communicate his own evangelical conviction, indirectly if not directly. This must have been something of the ferment which he had identified as the vital knowledge of Plato, and to which Chalybäus had referred as the love of wisdom or as the attitude of living. Any lack of orthodox Christian orientation or conciliation would not affect the basic temper of this philosophy, nor discourage its truly religious enthusiasms.

Dewey's special testimony to the evangelical impact of Morris is given at the time of his seventieth birthday, in a first-person autobiographical sketch. "In philosophy, at least, the influence of Johns Hopkins was not due to the size of the provision that was made. There was a half-year of lecturing and seminar work given by Professor George Sylvester Morris, of the University of Michigan; belief in the 'demonstrated' (a favorite word of his) truth of the substance of German idealism, and of belief in its competency to give direction to a life of aspiring thought, emotion, and action. I have never known a more single-hearted and whole-souled man—a man of a single piece all the way through; while I long since deviated from his philosophic faith, I should be happy to believe that the influence of the spirit of his teaching has been an enduring influence. While it was impossible that a young and impressionable student, unacquainted with any system of thought that satisfied his head and heart, should not have been deeply affected, to the point of at least a temporary conversion, by the enthusiastic and scholarly devotion of

Mr. Morris, this effect was far from being the only source of my own 'Hegelianism.' " [21]

The identification of Morris as "Hegelian" enters the consideration at this point, and it is perhaps necessary, in the light of Dewey's comments on Morris, to see just what the term means to the younger and better known of these two men. In 1930 Dewey explains that Hegel had left a permanent deposit in his thinking, and in 1939 he clarifies the matter in a carefully written paragraph. "Hegel's idea of cultural institutions as an 'objective mind' upon which individuals were dependent in the formation of their mental life fell in with the influence of Comte and of Condorcet and Bacon. The metaphysical idea that an absolute mind is manifested in social institutions dropped out; the idea, upon an empirical basis, of the power exercised by cultural environment in shaping the ideas, beliefs, and intellectual attitudes of individuals remained. It was a factor in producing my belief that the not uncommon assumption in both psychology and philosophy of a ready-made mind over against a physical world as an object has no empirical support. It was a factor in producing my belief that the only possible psychology, as distinct from a biological account of behavior, is a social psychology. With respect to more technically philosophical matters, the Hegelian emphasis upon continuity and the function of conflict persisted on empirical grounds after my earlier confidence in dialectic had given way to scepticism. There was a period extending into my earlier years

----

[21] "From Absolutism to Experimentalism," in *Contemporary American Philosophy*, edited by George Plimton Adams and William Pepperell Montague, New York, Macmillan, 1930, Vol. II, page 18.

at Chicago when, in connection with a seminar in Hegel's Logic I tried reinterpreting his categories in terms of 'readjustment' and 'reconstruction.' Gradually I came to realize that what the principles actually stood for could be better understood and stated when completely emancipated from Hegelian garb." [22] What Dewey had caught as the functional interaction of the universal and the specific— the macrocosmic-microcosmic type of logic which Morris quite probably acquired in general outline while at Union Seminary and took to Europe—is quite a different matter from the ontological derivation of all things from the contradiction in unity of being and negation, or Hegelianism as a metaphysics of pure thought.

Dewey in his day, as Morris before him, was in rebellion against what to him was the senseless fragmentation of reality, with the resulting conflicts and human unhappiness, and what to Morris was the lack of a personal dynamic able and eager to idealize its world. Dewey, in his 1930 autobiographical narrative, sketches in the situation as he encountered it when studying under Morris at Johns Hopkins. "The 'eighties and 'nineties were a time of new ferment in English thought; the reaction against atomic individualism and sensationalistic empiricism was in full swing. It was the time of Thomas Hill Green, of the two Cairds, of Wallace, of the appearance of the *Essays in Philosophical Criticism*, co-operatively produced by a younger group under the leadership of the late Lord Haldane. This movement was at the time the vital and constructive one in philosophy. Naturally its influence fell in with and reinforced that of Professor Morris. There was but one marked

---

[22] *The Philosophy of John Dewey*, pages 17–8.

difference, and that, I think, was in favour of Mr. Morris. He came to Kant through Hegel instead of to Hegel by way of Kant, so that his attitude toward Kant was the critical one expressed by Hegel himself. Moreover, he retained something of his early Scotch philosophical training in a common-sense belief in the existence of the external world. He used to make merry over those who thought the *existence* of this world and of matter were things to be proved by philosophy. To him the only philosophical question was as to the *meaning* of this existence; his idealism was wholly of the objective type. Like his contemporary, Professor John Watson, of Kingston, he combined a logical and idealistic metaphysics with a realistic epistemology. Through his teacher at Berlin, Trendelenburg, he had acquired a great reverence for Aristotle, and he had no difficulty in uniting Aristotelianism with Hegelianism." [23] Thus Hegelianism is a very general term, identifying in Dewey's mind a Neo-Kantianism comprising Hegel as a critic of Kant and also including a vital infusion of Aristotle. In Morris' thinking it would largely consist of his European reorientation as grounded in his analysis of Trendelenburg and his accompanying reworking of Neo-Kantianism for his own purposes. It is a step beyond the school of conciliation in a sharpening of epistemology and hence a further turn from speculative ontology.

Although stressing the fact that Morris was an omnivorous reader, Wenley yet presents him as thoroughly insulated from any but the one major strand of thought while in Europe—that is, the school of conciliation, or the

----

[23] *Op. cit.*, page 19.

Neo-Fichtean group in somewhat broader identification—
thanks of course to the contacts arranged for him in advance by Henry B. Smith. The question whether the long
developing and underlying voluntarism of Morris gained
any direct moral support from Fichte is probably beyond
competent analysis, with little to lean on other than the
material reported upon by Wenley or preserved in the
Michigan historical collection. Wenley's approach to the
proposition is important, however, since his volume remains the major source of information concerning the
events in Morris' life, and since the correctness of Wenley's
judgments relative to his predecessor has gone unchal-
lenged for thirty years. The point of view employed by
Wenley, however—which seeks understanding genetically,
or by assuming the nature of anything best exhibited by
its source or origin, and thus thinks in terms of a purely
behavioristic transmission of impacts—is at root no more
than the essentially empirical point of view against which
all Morris' more strongly held opinions are a protest, indeed, this latter attitude of Morris, when exhibited in the
Wenley framework, takes on at least the appearance of a
highly emotional or temperamental animus.

Hence Morton G. White, whose principal source of information concerning Morris was Wenley (and of course
the Dewey reminiscences, supplementarily), sees only a
highly prejudiced individual. "Morris, the idealist, . . .
had nothing but contempt for . . . the philosophy of
science. . . . This apathy towards the more progressive,
scientific tendencies on the campus seems to have brought
Morris into conflict with Gilman and to have led to his
ultimately leaving Johns Hopkins. . . . Morris has a

deep-seated preference for German thought and a rabid dislike of British thought before Green." The net result of elevating the method of physical science by British philosophers, "according to Morris, was a degenerate neglect of Absolute Spirit. The British refused to study its nature, contenting themselves with religion and science as the only forms of speculation. The result of this, in turn, was a conception of philosophy as worthless metaphysical jargon. . . ." And so it is that, "With the greatest of scorn Morris gives the British their philosophical due by calling Shakespeare, Wordsworth, Coleridge, and Tennyson their greatest philosophers." [24]

Wenley was far from the empiricist, but his absolutism which he believed contributed to "conditions of philosophic and theological progress, in the absence of which a theory of things would be incoherent or impossible" [25] was a thoroughgoing expression of the genetic approach, paralleling the basic defect in Hegel which Trendelenburg noted and made the basis for a major demolition of the earlier Hegelianism.[26] Wenley fundamentally reflects the naïveté of the observational theory of knowledge in which he came to maturity, and so discounts the newer functional and psychological conceptions with no apparent sensitiveness to this blind spot in his own outlook. "For better or worse," he writes, with excellent historical perspective, otherwise, "Morris found German thought well started upon that long period of transition which, beginning about 1840, still continues. But the *personnel* of his teachers and friends was such that the anti-philosophical implications of

[24] *The Origin of Dewey's Instrumentalism,* New York, Columbia University Press, 1943, pages 9, 12, 14.
[25] *Cf.* above, page 136 (footnote).   [26] *Cf.* below, page 175.

the movement, destined to gain ground steadily after 1870, were concealed from him. On the other hand, probably without realization of the fact, he was wafted back to the pre-scientific stage, when humanistic problems—critical, literary and theological—predominated, but when, at the same time, confusion had succeeded confident system-making. Although the epithet fails to cover all the factors, we approach the truth if we say that he fell into the Neo-Fichtean circle; and this was eclectic, except in so far as it developed too soon for due appreciation of the rigour and vigour of modern natural-scientific methods, with their attendant presuppositions. . . . While the activities of Liebig about 1826, and those of A. von Humboldt immediately afterwards, gave natural science a position unparalleled in Germany since the Wars of Religion, it was not till the discoveries of Schleiden and Schwann (1838–9), and especially of Virchow and Helmholtz ten years later, that the realistic reaction gathered irresistible force. . . . The early votaries of biological inquiry, misled by the mechanical generalizations of the seventeenth and eighteenth centuries, rushed headlong into a popular philosophy . . ." and "instead of appraisal of the logical methods of science, or of sober examination of its necessary metaphysical assumptions, philosophical activity took the shape of an attack upon materialism, no formidable enemy."

Then Wenley, far less happily or accurately, proceeds to frame the young student from America in this philosophical chaos. "Tossed about by many winds of doctrine as Morris must have been, one solid plank, floating amid the wreckage, afforded him temporary refuge at least . . ." namely, the discovery of Aristotle through Trendelenburg.

Wenley thereupon repeated the "often quoted" and "memorable" passage from Trendelenburg's *Logical Investigations*. "The prejudice of the Germans must be abandoned that, for the philosophy of the future, a new principle had to be discovered. The new principle has been found; it lies in that organic conception of the universe which has its foundation in Plato and Aristotle, and which, continuing from them, will have to complete itself in a profounder examination of fundamental ideas, and through an interchange with the science of reality." This leads Wenley to the consideration of pre-Darwinian science, together with the arrival of Darwin and the *"fermentum cognitionis"* which he suggests to be as significant an impact as that of Newton, Kant and Hegel, but one by which he presumes Morris to be little touched, although probably unable to "escape the drift . . . of the popular Darwinian movement." By the same token Wenley decides that F. A. Lange —whose *History of Materialism* was published in German the year before Morris' arrival and was, according to Wenley, the volume which marked the end of the most productive period in German thinking—was also of no intellectual service to Morris. Rather he sees the young man, surrounded by all these varying influences, left in a personal state of uncertainty and transition, with his German residence to prove "of the utmost importance" only because "it enabled him, a decade later, to revert to the great Idealists at first hand, and with definite knowledge of the issues." [27]

Except for its biographical material and a few summary remarks quoted from it, Wenley curiously ignores Morris'

---

[27] Wenley, pages 217–28.

best known and ultimately most significant writing—perhaps not even excepting the four published books—namely the article on "Friedrich Adolf Trendelenburg." [28] Practically every other appearance of Morris in print is given detailed attention, but not this twenty-thousand-word analysis of the Berlin thinker and its exposition of Trendelenburg's devastating and historically most successful attack on the basic notion of an absolute. The probable reason is his belief that "the leadership of the . . . group to which Ulrici, Trendelenburg and Ueberweg belonged, in a mediating type of thought, foot-loose from thoroughgoing system, had been challenged successfully, because with a system, by a greater than they —in the person of Lotze." [29]

As for Rudolph Hermann Lotze, who was fifteen years younger than Trendelenburg,[30] Ueberweg postpones the consideration of Trendelenburg until after a discussion of Lotze, then stating that "in the midst of the struggles of philosophical parties, a common basis of philosophical knowledge is found partly in the history of philosophy, partly in single philosophical doctrines which are no longer disputed (mostly in the province of logic), and partly in those results of the positive sciences, and especially of natural science, which are intimately connected with philosophy. It is the essential merit of Adolf Trendelenburg, the Aristotelian, as a philosophical investigator and instructor, to have gone back to these common starting-

---

[28] *The New Englander*, April 1874, Vol. 33, pages 287–336, reprinted in full as an appendix in the present text, pages 370–433.

[29] Wenley, page 218.

[30] Lotze was born at Bautzen in Saxony, graduated at Leipzig, where he gained his extraordinary professorship in 1842, preceding his call to Göttingen in 1844 as ordinary professor.

points of philosophical inquiry, to have criticised one-sided doctrines, and to have undertaken to reconstruct philosophy upon well-assured bases." Morris, as translator, followed the same policy with Lotze as with Ulrici, quoting Erdmann's account of Lotze's philosophy, through eight and a half pages of very small type as against five and a half on Ulrici. Morris' own exceedingly brief estimate of Lotze is to the effect that "the wide range of his information in physical (especially in physiological) science, and his familiarity with metaphysical speculation, the independence and discretion of his own philosophical investigations —a discretion which, but for its foundation in knowledge, might well be termed skepticism—and the brilliancy of his style as an author and lecturer, have combined to secure him a high eminence among living German thinkers."

This indicates both the slightness of any possible influence of Lotze on Morris and also suggests the agreement of Morris with Ueberweg, who in his summary paragraph says that Lotze's doctrine "is similar to that of Herbart, and still more so to the philosophy of Leibnitz, although Lotze justly protests against being termed a Herbartian, since he accounts for the possibility of the co-existence and the phenomenal interaction of the numerous essences (monads) by reference to the necessary unity of a substantial cause of the world, to the activity of an original, essential unity in all real things. The Infinite, says Lotze, is the One Power, which has given itself, in the whole world of spirits, numberless accordant modes of existence. All monads are but modifications of the Absolute. Mechanism is the form of finite existence, the form which the one real essence gives to itself." Lotze thus is almost of necessity as uninteresting to Morris as Herbart, although Lotze stands at the idealistic rather than the empirical extreme of lean upon mechanism which is shared by both these thinkers. The particular extremism of the former, of course, would be precisely the reason that Wenley might be expected to applaud his system per se. As for Johann Friedrich Herbart, Ueberweg remarks most importantly—in the light of the present analysis, and from the general point of view of the school of conciliation—that his "philosophy . . . has signally promoted the genetic comprehension of nature and mind," i.e., has accepted the naturalistic assumption of mechanism against which Morris at all points is struggling, whether this takes idealistic or realistic form in Germany and whether it turns up as empirical or subjectivistic philosophizing in England and America.[31]

Trendelenburg was born in 1802, four years before Ulrici, and was given a very thorough educational groundwork in the gymnasium of the small North German free city of his birth. He studied under a number of exceptionally able teachers, and heard lectures by Hegel, Schleiermacher, Neander, Ritter and others. He taught philosophy at Berlin from 1833; became a member of the Berlin Academy in 1846, and was secretary for the section of history of philosophy from 1847, until his death in 1872. He described his own attitude when, entering upon the rectorship of the University of Berlin in 1857, he said that "the ancient languages and the mathematics are the way to the heights of humanity and into the innermost nature of things." He had found that the reading of the

---

[31] *Op. cit.*, Vol. II, pages 280, 312ff., 324.

classics in the gymnasium had led him "to seek for the spirit of the ancients in their writings, to strive to learn how to think after the model of the great thinkers, and to clothe his thoughts in similar beautiful form." This was the major characteristic of his philosophical view. Hence Morris, for the opening sentence of his article, quotes Fichte in the statement that philosophy is the history of philosophy. The individual fits into the general scheme because, as Trendelenburg early wrote, "one must have a philosophical system, just as one must have a house, and this house each must build for himself; it must be almost moveable, like a tent, and susceptible of enlargement."

Here is Morris' concept of social interaction, or a functional rather than merely external or mechanical ordering of man and his world. He suggests that the working out of the principle is well illustrated in the life of Trendelenburg, and it is no less demonstrated by the drift of circumstances in his own career. His own greatest achievement, at least in terms of any common or widespread recognition in his day, was the translation of Ueberweg's history of philosophy. The task consisted of much more than rendering the German into English. It was a very remarkable editorial job. The amplifications, explicatory notes and corrections—in co-operation with the author by correspondence—made it, according to a report by John Dewey in 1889, a better work in English than in German.[32] Thus Trendelenburg as his principal intellectual mentor, on the one hand, and the economic need which the assignment helped to meet on his return to New York, on the

---

[32] Wenley, page 121.

other, combined to anchor Morris very solidly in the formal philosophical tradition on the historical side. However, his tastes were evangelical, not critical. His criticism tended to run off with itself emotionally, as has been seen. He needed, rather, an outlet where emotional or evangelized ideas would be put to work in a human society, but his own spirit of intellectual inquiry had deflected him from his original goal of the ministry.

The derivation of philosophy from language—the Trendelenburg version of social-personal interactivity which does not become very explicit in Morris' report—would attract the young scholar. However, Morris actually found his point of sympathetic contact in the emphasis on creative personality, which is the less rational or more voluntaristic facet of the same logical perspective. "It were easy, by reference to the history of philosophy and the biographies of its representatives, to show how, universally, the personalities of the leading philosophers have found expression in their systems. The aristocratic Plato has a more than wholesome horror of the so-called pollutions of matter, and identified true reality with the ideal. And, for the rest, modern philosophy has not found it easy, as yet, to determine what reality, if any, belongs in fact to the material as such—that is, what matter truly is. Aristotle, more involved in the practical problems of life, plants his theory more cautiously on the palpable earth. In modern times, the calm and consequent spirit of Spinoza gives birth to the all-comprehensive system known by his name, in which God is all, and tranquil, unfretful submission to the necessary laws of the universe (of God) is deduced as the corollary, and is exemplified in the philosopher's life.

The pietistic training of Kant's youth leaves its traces in the well-known, life-long conscientiousness of this founder of modern critical philosophy, and re-appears still more conspicuously in the notion of duty, on which his moral philosophy is founded, and in the categorical imperative, in which its fundamental requirement is formulated."

What an individual *is* has a compulsion on what he *does*, in terms of a categorical imperative Morris himself acknowledges, hence there is that in anyone which may be called to the ideal no less than depressed to a lower potential. Thus the unchanging or evangelistic Morris is consistently articulate. "From facts like these, what is to be inferred? That philosophy is simply a system of beliefs, the expression of personal traits, and that it moves hence, eternally round in the vicious circle of the ever-varying but substantially unchanging opinions and characters of mankind? This was not the view of Trendelenburg, who sought in the systems of the past for the elements of permanent value, and sought to add to these and to build upon them, as upon a basis of historically demonstrated solidity." What then was the bottom realization in Trendelenburg? In Trendelenburg's dissertation, when he took his degree at Berlin in 1825, he developed his primary roots in Aristotle and—although declining a number of advantageous openings because he did not feel himself sufficiently prepared for the demands the positions would make on his knowledge—he demonstrated the extent of his scholarship at this time by preparing and annotating an edition of Aristotle's *De Anima*. Its publication "marked an epoch in the careful study and correct interpretation of the Greek author." In many respects, therefore, the Back-to-

Kant movement was paralleled by a return to Aristotle. This was the bottom, the potential of growth out of experience, and a continual reference back to that which has been verified in a living actuality.

Trendelenburg gained the widest notice during his life —in the form of a rather considerable and unfortunate notoriety—as a result of his acrimonious debate with Kuno Fischer on the interpretation of Kant. This is treated very gently by Morris, who said that "after a tolerably careful review of the arguments and proofs on both sides" he could only "express his agreement with many whom he believes to be among the most impartial of philosophical judges in Germany, that Trendelenburg was triumphantly in the right, as he was far superior to his opponent in point of temper." What Trendelenburg demonstrated very effectively was "the incompleteness of Kant's proof of the exclusive ideality of time and space," and Morris pointed out that this had cut away the ground "from beneath the feet of the whole subsequent development of German idealism." Aristotle thus speaks through Trendelenburg and Morris, affirming again the unbroken or completely functional continuity of nature. This Aristotelian ordering is evident when Morris proceeds to summarize the basic character of philosophy in Germany, saying that it "had ever been and still is prevailingly idealistic. Its founder, Leibnitz, an Aristotle by his encyclopædic knowledge and his thoughtful union of the theoretical and the practical, had identified matter with active force and had conceived the latter after the analogy of spiritual, conscious existence. The life of the monads was ideal; it consisted in the possession of more or less distinct perceptions."

However, with Kant "the cardinal point in philosophy became, under the influence of the English philosophers, Locke and Hume, anthropological and, if it may be thus termed, cognitional, rather than ontological or cosmological; the question of first importance was, what can man know? and not, as it had been before, what is the nature of things? The skeptical conclusion, by which theoretical knowledge was confined within the limits of the subjectively phenomenal and relative, and the moral conclusion, resting in the postulates of God's existence, of human freedom, and of the immortality of the soul, led, as is known, in the system of Fichte to the doctrine of complete subjective idealism; since, of the two factors, by the coöperation of which Kant accounted for the facts of human knowledge, namely, the mind with its innate forms and functions, and the unknown and unknowable 'things-in-themselves,' the latter had inconsequently had ascribed to them by Kant a causative agency in the production of impressions and ideas in the human mind (inconsequently, for Kant had elsewhere sought to demonstrate that the range of causality was confined absolutely to the sphere of phenomena, in distinction from 'things-in-themselves')."

It was then that Fichte, "with characteristic logical boldness and recklessness, resolved to derive the whole universe from the subject alone, i.e., from the *Me*, and hence was obliged also to identify God, the Absolute, with the absolute subject. Philosophy, thus fairly launched on the sea of pure speculation, with no acknowledged guidance but that of a purely *a priori* or dialectic method, did not delay, with the aid of Schelling and Hegel, to run to the very end of the idealistic tether, landing in the system of absolute idealism. In this system the absolute, apprehended in pure thought as identity of thought and being, figured as the source whence the dialectic method was to trace the development of the whole universe of reality. The real was to be construed—ideally constructed—*a priori*. Rich in grand conceptions and suggestive thoughts, this philosophy, nevertheless, did such insolent—had it not been ludicrous—violence to established facts of positive science and of history, that, while the crowd of men aspiring to be accounted the possessors of philosophical opinions, but too indolent or impotent to form them for themselves, were sunning themselves in the light of the new intellectual luminary, others, more suspicious of appearances, could not but inquire whether the original source of all this glow were perhaps, after all, but the phosphorescence of unsound materials. . . . This philosophy wrenched by its demands and claims too violently the fibres of average human belief, not to be followed by reaction and resistance. Criticism would naturally seek to detect flaws in the principle and method of the new philosophy, and when these had been discovered and set forth with sufficient evidence to shake the convictions of unprejudiced believers, the query would naturally arise: what philosophy shall we fall back upon?—or, what does the history of philosophy teach us to rest upon as solid ground of theory?"

The appeal here was in no respect to the genetic view which—in its extremism, at least—had left German thinking in the awkward situation of Mohammed's coffin. Morris saw very clearly—however correctly or incorrectly he interpreted the German idealists—that the price of excluding the empirical skepticism from such system-building—when it came to scientific knowledge, or demonstrable knowledge in Aristotle's terms—was the loss of all demonstration in actuality, and so an inevitable uncertainty on the side of everyday experience. Metaphysics could not be abstracted from life completely and become anything but affirmation in a vacuum, a point he had stressed in his criticism of Hodgson.[33] Hence "Trendelenburg's positive aim was the establishment of a philosophical theory which could stand the test of comparison with the results of modern science, nay, more, which should be confirmed by and, so far as practicable, founded on those results. Recognizing fully the necessity of experience for all concrete knowledge, respecting the various positive sciences as sovereign within their respective spheres, he sought in philosophy the common band which should unite these sciences, and not a speculative principle which should produce them *a priori*. Philosophy was to be, in some sense, the one eye overseeing them all, the one mind comprehending them in their mutual relations and as parts of one ideal whole; it was to recognize in the case of each science, whether concrete or abstract, its place and use in the whole *organism* of knowledge; it was to be consummated in an 'organic conception of the universe' of thought and being."

For Trendelenburg the grounding of philosophy in science meant an epistemological emphasis, altogether different from the increasing attempts to build a naturalistic metaphysics out of observed phenomena in a field of reality which was limited in all respects to physical measurement and sensational criteria. Scientific thinking as an

[33] *Cf.* above, pages 125f.

organization of speculative ideas is a method of mind, not
a subject matter set apart in rational realms, and hence
it is primarily a criticism of logical procedures. Morris explains that German philosophy "had partly developed,
partly adopted two views of logic." Trendelenburg attacked both (1) the formal conception of which Kant had
been the exponent and Hamilton the contemporary representative, and which would have its later if somewhat indirect fruits in mathematical logic and various forms of
positivism, and (2) the dialectic method, developed through
Fichte, Schelling and Hegel as an adaptation of Plato's
method of division. Trendelenburg insisted that the
thought process cannot be divorced from the thought
content, or vice versa for that matter. His criticism of
Hegel's derivation of the universe from an absolute is given
by Morris at great length, building on the very dramatic
but essential realization that "felt presence and influence"
of "the shadowy forms of banished objects" is present in
any conception of the supposed "pure thought" out of
which Hegel makes his beginning. Morris quotes Eduard
Zeller to the effect that Trendelenburg's criticism was
"sharp and successful," and himself adds that "the breaking up of the Hegelian school simultaneously with the
publication of the 'Logical Investigations' and with the
public discussion which they stimulated, was by no means
accidental."

Trendelenburg identified "the true source of modern
philosophy" through Aristotle, and in consequence, Morris
reports, "it was his custom to spend two hours in each
week in the public explanation of some portion of Aristotle's writings to a voluntary class of students. . . . He

was not blind to the indefinite and fantastic in Plato's philosophy, in whose theory of ideas and of the cognition of ideas he discerned the ancient prototype or beginning of the modern notion of pure, unimaged thought. The Platonic Idea was true and real, but not such, nor cognizable, apart from 'things'—the reality and cognoscibility of which were . . . not to be contested. In Aristotle he found a more discreet, because more realistic theory of cognition, a conception of nature which so commended itself . . . that he made it the ground-work of his own theory . . ." Morris then goes on, not only continuing to sketch in the positive exposition of Trendelenburg but also obviously speaking for himself to a considerable degree. "Philosophy, as Trendelenburg loves to repeat after Plato, is the sentinel on the boundaries of the other sciences, fixing and preserving limits, uniting, demonstrating, and in all this morally purifying. 'Philosophy is the religion of science.' The special sciences point to the universal; philosophy seeks to realize this universal. She 'furnishes principles for the beginnings of the special sciences, establishes harmony among their results, and maintains a living *rapport* among them; she is thus at once *a priori* and *a posteriori;* the latter because it is in the other sciences that she finds her material, and the former, since she must go beyond and above the material thus furnished in order to seize and exhibit the living band that unites the whole.' Philosophy must then bear a due relation to the real and the ideal; she can be neither purely empirical nor purely *a priori*. Ideal-realism will be her proper name."

Philosophy is logical method, whatever else it may become or cease to be in passing. "In every act of knowing is involved the antithesis of being and thought. The former is taken up into the latter; the latter penetrates the former. How is this possible? It was a saying of the ancients that like is known by like. Knowledge, as the union of thought and being, can be possible only in virtue of something which belongs equally to these two factors, something in which each resembles the other. And since thought is essentially active, this element common to thought and being must be some form of activity. The first mark, then, of that active principle which shall mediate between thought and being, must be that it shall be common to both. It must, secondly, be primitive and therefore need and admit no explanation, and hence, thirdly, simple, for the complex is not, logically, primitive." The criteria here, of course, are Aristotle's. Morris adds, "It will be evident how, in the view of Trendelenburg, motion, as a physical and ideal (theoretical) activity, is to be regarded as the *prius* of experience," and this leads to the discussion of categories, to which Trendelenburg gave considerable attention and which Morris analyzes at length. For present purposes, however, the complete swing away from the Fichtean union of thought and being in a wholly ontological assimilation, in favor of the functional or purely epistemological synthesis, is the point of pertinent emphasis.

Motion is the manifestation of efficient cause in a primary sense, and thought is represented in the organic or function view by purpose as the complementary final cause. "The notion of purpose, inherent end, as manifested in organic existence, is for Trendelenburg the second fundamental notion in philosophy. Motion—the efficient cause

—forms the basis and becomes in the organic sphere the material of purpose—the final cause—and thus philosophy and nature are carried up above the purely mathematical and physical realm into the organic and ethical. There is differentiation, but not opposition. The real categories receive a new and profounder significance, but do not disappear, when permeated by and in the realm of the organic. . . . The fundamental emphasis which is laid upon finality in nature, is calculated to shock the prejudices of positive philosophers and of some scientists. But the legitimacy of their seeking only for the efficient cause or the mechanics of the phenomena which they investigate, is fully admitted. Since intelligence, if it rule at all in nature, can rule only through the agency of physical causes and on the basis of physical laws, every organism presents a problem in mechanics, which science has to solve. If by usage or courtesy the realm of efficient causation, and that alone, is set apart for science, yet philosophy, whose glance is more comprehensive, must regard phenomena in all their aspects, and if an aspect of them is found which, though not contradictory to the scientific aspect, is yet decidedly different and seemingly higher, the truly scientific spirit will be the last to object to anything being inferred from that aspect, which the facts may warrant or the analogies of thought may necessitate."

This brings the consideration to the realm of ethics, and the consideration of values and norms as "a higher state or potency of the organic." The ethical is "the organic become free," but "the founding of the ethical in the organic may strike some strict constructionists among our intuitional moralists as bringing the theory of morals too near to the realm of empirical philosophy, and theologians may reproach it with naturalism. The former objection will tend to disappear when it is recalled that for Trendelenburg the organic is the expression of thought, the illustration of an Idea; not, however, of an idea known apart from experience, but of an *a priori* revealed and confirmed in experience. Nor is the theologian's objection more substantial, for the theory expressly admits and claims that the Idea and its requirements (e.g., the idea, end, of man, and the duties following from it) are the revelation in human nature of the will of the infinite, unconditioned God." Here Morris spoke, but Trendelenburg himself no less. Morris had already pointed out, in a footnote, that while not in position to speak of Trendelenburg's "dogmatic views in theology" in detail, since with him as "with German philosophers, generally, who are not professed theologians, philosophy was an independent science, which was, if any thing, to confirm, and not to be confirmed by, religion . . ." yet Trendelenburg "could be termed a 'Christian philosopher.' " However, nothing is offered at this point of any better theological straw in the brick than the equally verbalized affirmations on the secular side of idealism, offered by more naïve proponents of an undefinable absolute whom Trendelenburg had attacked most devastatingly. There was no solution here for the problems of Christianity which had vexed Morris and taken him to Europe for a reorientation in German thought.

At the best Morris has encouragement for the identification of God in final cause, and for endowing the universe with a rational explanation through finality or purpose. The next chapter will be devoted to his outgropings in this

180   GEORGE SYLVESTER MORRIS

direction. In the meanwhile he has, within his grasp, a better recourse in a logic of truth, or a meeting of the evangelistic spirit of the quickened understanding with a self-
discovery in the realms of free inquiry, which at least is
the vital knowledge of Plato in general potentiality. Perhaps Morris himself failed most signally in avoiding the
partisanship which he now sees to be destructive to a
genuine philosophical spirit. He yet is able to put the
vision in words, as he begins to close his account of Trendelenburg and to complete his most significant magazine
article. "It is a peculiarity of truth," he writes, "resulting
from its organic nature, that, just as, for example, in the
human organism, no member can be understood out of
relation to the whole organism, and the complete comprehension of any member involves a general comprehension
of the whole, so the complete consideration of any part of
truth leads, when correctly carried out, to the consideration and knowledge of the whole. And since truth is multifarious and many-sided, the approaches to it are correspondingly numerous. The philosophy of Trendelenburg
is an approach to truth and an attempt to comprehend it,
from one direction. Equally possible were it, however,
conceivably to make the approach, as others have done,
from other directions and to arrive at substantially the
same results.

"A philosophical system conceived in this way does not
admit of partisans, since a system thus conceived does not
and can not claim to be the only true avenue to truth.
Only a system, which pretends to take its stand *a priori* at
the centre of absolute knowledge and thence to derive by
necessary deduction all truth of fact, must have one-sided

partisans for its disciples. But it is hoped that all who shall read the first division of this Article, will be disposed to allow that such a system is impossible for man. Nothing hinders, then, our conceding the general truth of Trendelenburg's doctrine, without, however, granting that his theory is the only one which a true philosophy may adopt. Nor in accepting conditionally his doctrine is it necessary to accept all the minor statements, although we believe that remarkably few just grounds of criticism will be found in them. . . . This only must we say by way of criticism, namely, that the reduction of force, as a physical category, to motion, does not seem to us to have been properly supplemented by Trendelenburg in the part devoted to the treatment of the organic sphere. Here force appears as . . . we know it in consciousness—not separate from motion, it is true, but with a significance which includes much more than motion. To find this pointed out we have sought in vain in Trendelenburg's works." [34] Moral power or the dynamic ideal is omitted from the schematism, and this is the most vital factor in all human existence. German criticism has given Morris new tools of thought, perhaps, but not what he sought most eagerly: an instrumentation for his deep-seated evangelistic fervor.

---

[34] Cf. below, pages 336–7, 339, 341–2, 346–7, 350, 358–9, 363–4, 367, 369–70, 372, 381–3.

NINE YEARS OF PERSONAL ADJUSTMENT

The program of European study might have worked out altogether differently for Morris, had he obtained the continued financial backing he had expected from the friend who had made the trip possible in the first place, but there is no indication of the plans he may have had in mind.[1] The death of his mother, together with the breaking of their engagement by Miss Susan Denison, were depressing psychological factors which did not help when added to his uncertainty concerning money matters towards the close of his stay abroad. Furthermore, there was no promise of a position at home worthy of the intensive preparation, and so he explained, in a letter from Lausanne, that he would "take whatever may offer." As a result of this attitude he found himself resident tutor in the home of a prominent New York banker, Mr. Albert J. Seligman.[2] A measure of considerable intellectual compensation, however, was his commission to translate Ueberweg's history of philosophy, an opportunity which came to him within

---

[1] He wrote in his diary, on August 22, 1867, that "Mr. Larrowe's . . . conduct is very enigmatic, to say the least," but neither here nor elsewhere is there any clue to the conditions under which the original three thousand dollars were advanced. Mrs. Morris could only say that this altogether mysterious M. D. Larrowe "later in life . . . defrauded Mr. Morris of considerable money." *Cf.* Wenley, pages 101ff., 116.

[2] At 2 West Forty-sixth Street according to Wenley, at Gramercy Park, according to G. Stanley Hall as quoted by Wenley, pages 119, 153.

a month of his return to America.[3] The appearance of the first volume exactly three years later had been preceded, of materials from his pen, only by his article on Hodgson, published while he was still in Europe, together with the inconsequential item of translation in 1869. The excellence of his work with the Ueberweg text had an almost immediate recognition, however, and it was inevitable that a major appearance in print such as this would open a university position for him.

While Morris' own contacts were not very great, and his temperament was not at all adapted for self-promotion, Henry B. Smith, who admired him very greatly,[4] had already obtained very serious consideration for him at Smith's own alma mater, Bowdoin College, in Brunswick, Maine. A circumstance that may possibly have led to Morris' start as a teacher on the college level was his meeting and long talk in Europe with Professor L. D. Chapin of the Michigan University faculty. The new post at Ann Arbor was in the field of modern languages, however, not in philosophy, but the opportunity at Michigan was unusual, and Morris' achievement was close to spectacular. Henry Simmons Frieze, professor of Latin since 1854, was acting president when Morris joined the staff, holding that place until the accession of his pupil, James Burrill Angell, a New Englander under whose administration (1871–1909) the institution in many respects became the outstanding American state university. A very intimate friendship grew up between Frieze and Morris, thanks to their common interest in music, and the younger man not only

---

[3] *Henry Boynton Smith, His Life and Works,* page 190.
[4] According to G. Stanley Hall.

found himself in congenial circumstances but free at last
from economic uncertainty. Timid or temperamentally
aloof at the beginning, he soon responded to the general
congeniality of his situation. His marriage took place at
the same time he found himself able to return to his fundamental concern over philosophy, however much a side interest, and to write the articles with which this chapter is
concerned. He established his permanent home, and created the personal ties that held for the rest of his life.[5]

It was generally realized that Morris desired a philosophical appointment, but this was impossible at Ann
Arbor. The situation in the philosophy department was
somewhat unique, due to the personality of B. F. Cocker,
who held the chair. Cocker was a clergyman, possessing exceptional talents as a speaker, and was of very great service
to the university's public relations. He was almost completely devoid of training or resources in philosophical
scholarship, however, so that a transfer of Morris to his
department would have put him in eclipse, a circumstance
he was able to anticipate clearly enough. When he needed
help with his classes, a little later, Morris was absent for
half the year at Johns Hopkins University, and a chair
could then be created for the younger man, since it was
only occupied for the one semester. As a part-time professor Morris offered less occasion for academic jealousy.
When Cocker died in 1883, and the expected opening for
Morris as a full-time department head at Baltimore had
not materialized, the trustees at Ann Arbor established
Morris as head of the Michigan department—in January,
1885—and he held the position (with one change in title)

---

[5] Wenley, pages 122ff., 131f., 153.

until his death four years later. Thus the period from his return to America in the autumn of 1868, until he obtained this position worthy of his philosophical training and talents, represents the great hiatus between the practical completion of his preparation and his actual start in the life work of his choice. Of these more than sixteen years, the first two—when he was resident tutor for the two Seligman boys, and concurrently engaged on the Ueberweg translation—embraced the initial and sharp period of uncertainty which had had its beginning in Europe, and the following seven—or until December, 1877, when he received an invitation to become lecturer on history of philosophy and ethics in the new graduate school at Baltimore—constituted a happy enough time on the personal side, although he was pursuing a course quite tangent to his own deeper interests. Probably he chafed inwardly, but there was much employment and a real recognition for his scholarship, and his later ideas must have been germinating.

As for the next and additional seven years, covering the desultory association with Johns Hopkins University—but a creative period, represented by three of his four books— the broadening and creative outlet for Morris' thinking was still handicapped because at Michigan the dominance of Cocker's superficiality required many adjustments and at Baltimore his point of view was subordinated to the equally superficial experimentalism represented by G. Stanley Hall, and encouraged by President Gilman. It is probably in view of this latter fact that neither Morris nor Dewey gave attention to the mathematical logic under its very original and concurrent development at Johns Hopkins by Charles Sanders Peirce.[6] The final productive period in the life of Morris, supported as it was by (1) actual classwork in philosophy at Baltimore, (2) concurrent work under Cocker at Ann Arbor, and (3) at length his own fully organized department of top rank at the latter place, was preceded by a continuity of philosophical interest which saw the appearance of the Trendelenburg article immediately following the completion of the Ueberweg translation, and then a series of papers that seem to have their stimulus from the fact that Morris was persuaded, "by an English friend," to join the Victoria Institute of London as an associate member.[7]

Morris was seeking, as a result of his European orientation, to establish a continuity of method or scientific criteria between spiritual and material knowledge. This functional unity of a whole-world of experience would provide a true intellectualization of faith, and so give real power

----

[6] The philosophical staff at Michigan during this general period (1869–94) consisted of Cocker, alone until 1881, then assisted by and in 1883 succeeded by Morris (officially in January, 1885). Associated with Morris was George H. Howison, from November, 1883, followed by John Dewey when Howison went to California a year later. Williston S. Hough replaced Dewey when Dewey obtained the chair of philosophy at the University of Minnesota in 1888. Dewey, called back on the death of Morris in 1889, to head the department, left in 1894 for his post at the University of Chicago, whereupon Wenley was called to the chair, five years after Morris' death. Cf. Wenley, pages 122–76.

[7] This was one of the more obscure learned societies, founded through the efforts of James Reddie and E. Gardiner Fishbourne, British naval men, with an initial meeting on May 24, 1866, or shortly after Morris' arrival in Germany. Morris seems to have remained a member until 1883, or for some seven years after his second paper was read. The society was "a body of highly respectable gentlemen, quite innocent of philosophy after Kant and of theology after Schleiermacher, almost as innocent of science after Lyell, Helmholtz and Darwin, who, stung by the 'scandals' of the moment . . . proposed to save the fabric of *religion* by reverting to eighteenth century apologetics with all its brood of pitiful misconceptions." Cf. Wenley, pages 229–38.

to the neglected spiritualizing influences in a highly scientific age. He had ended his Trendelenburg article on a note of criticism, pointing out that philosophy must recognize a moral or organic dynamic in life, no less than a basic and perhaps wholly physical motion, and now he proceeded, on the positive side, to attempt the meeting of this necessity. Here was the first phase in his own mature thought. His initial Victoria paper was entitled, "The Final Cause, As Principle of Cognition and Principle in Nature" and it was read for him at the ordinary meeting of the society on May 18, 1874.[8] He starts out by citing the number of times the subject has been discussed by the Institute, but explains that his approach is different in that he seeks to "establish the definite presence of the idea in the world of reality" and the consequent necessity that any thinking about the world of reality be framed in this concept. Settling down to his task of analysis, he then quotes Trendelenburg's essay, "The Ultimate Ground of Distinction Among Philosophical Systems," as a means for general or logical orientation, and at once gives the clue to the over-all path on which his own reflections are proceeding.

"In all systems of philosophy, either force is conceived as superior to thought, so that thought is not primary, but rather the result, product, and accident of blind forces; or thought is made superior to force, so that blind force alone is not primary, but is the outcome of thought; or, finally, thought and force are represented as at bottom the same, and only distinguished in human opinion." Morris re-

[8] *Journal of the Transactions of the Victoria Institute or Philosophical Society of Great Britain*, Volume IX, 1875, pages 176–204.

marks that the disjunction put down by Trendelenburg "seems exhaustive, and there can be no doubt under which member of it we are to range ourselves. Not the first alternative, which is espoused by materialism, nor the third, which corresponds to Spinozism, but the second covers the ground of our Christian idealism. We hold that primacy in rank and in power belongs in this universe to thought, or intelligence. This is our philosophical attitude, which becomes further differentiated and illuminated by the addition to it of Christian faith."

What is this orientation, ontologically? The real distinction here is implicit rather than explicit, although obvious enough. The dichotomy of materialism is genetic—since thought becomes a product of matter—and that of Spinoza is illusory, so that both of these are infinitely regressive, while that of a true Christian philosophy alone maintains the continuity of nature because thought and intelligence are not made ontologically distinct from physical reality but rather are given "primacy in rank and in power," i.e., they are effective and consequently evident in the voluntaristic self-expression of man. Hence, towards the end of his paper, Morris definitely dismisses Kant's theory of final cause as merely regulative in nature, or not constitutive, and himself identifies final cause with idea as such. In other words, although hailing the revival of Platonism, he does not defend transcendental archetypes, or formal cause, but rather describes "a principle working immanently in nature," and preserving an over-all continuity as quite independent of time and space. He rejects absolute idealism when he demands a scientific verification of knowledge through a world of reality. His point of view is essentially his own, not a mere German importation. Obviously he is at all points not only the scholar—neither the mystic nor the dogmatist—but also the rationalist, with a full faith in the competency of human thinking whenever it operates according to its own principles. What he exhibits, however, is a dynamic or voluntaristic rationalism, not a species of positivism or the materialistic speculation based on a purely naïve view of mind and its powers.

Immediately after quoting Trendelenburg, Morris proceeds to defend his position, which he identifies as "scientific." He points out that validation may be not only by the use of hypothesis and verification, but by entirely rational criteria or through "metaphysical argumentation," and also by the results of "philosophical and psychological observation." He is very explicit on the point that "what is true in thought, we claim, can not be false in nature, but must find in the world of natural reality its confirmation and realization. If the ideal controls the real, if intelligence governs force, there must exist in the world of real forces indications of this control and government." He goes on to claim that because man is a part of nature—evidently meaning this in the Darwinian sense—it is possible to assume, a priori, a fundamental likeness or other relation between what is essential in man's nature and what is essential in the world about man. He rejects the notion that it is human opinion which makes the distinction between thought and force when he affirms that "all concrete relations . . . can not be said to be introduced into nature by the intelligence of the observer," and expands his point of view by saying "all that is, appears," which of course means that "in this sense it may be said that all our knowledge is of the phenomenal," or established in the everyday world of reality, "but the (conscious or unconscious) employment of the appropriate logical processes leads us nevertheless to distinguish between the real and phenomenal," i.e., logically.

Here is Platonic realism, as quite distinct from subjective idealism or a thoroughgoing otherworldliness. "By knowledge of the real I mean . . . metaphysical knowledge," he writes, and then makes his statement more specific by adding that "pre-eminently, and in the first place, our knowledge of reality is knowledge of ourselves, furnished in direct consciousness." This is not in either rational or psychological discreteness, however—which would mean that he was coming around to agree with Hodgson on the one hand or with Protagoras and the concept of man as the measure of all things on the other—but instead is in a realization of the continuity enabling any individual to find the world patterned in himself.[9] The point of view is dynamic idealism per se, affirming a voluntaristic integrity and establishing the moral incentive as a necessity of nature rather than as an ideal expression of reason. Man is two things, so to speak, both the world and himself. Experience is the basis of knowledge, willy nilly, bringing the objective and subjective into mutual focus, and it can be generalized successfully or correctly only as it is universal in its own roots. Hence "if any representatives of science lend their countenance to philosophical materialism, they favour, in so doing, a *metaphysical* theory," i.e., they are giving the primacy in rank and power

---

[9] Through a microcosmic-macrocosmic type of interactivity, as already suggested. *Cf*. above, page 114f.

to thought or intelligence despite themselves, and defeating their own insights by utilizing the very duality they deny.

Man's actions always characterize him as a rational animal—that is, he moves to an end or in accordance with ideas embodied in his own nature—and in consequence only final cause can be a *"true principle of cognition . . . for the sphere of rational life,"* since this constitutes *"the only sphere of which we have direct knowledge,"* i.e., of unmediated consequences of choice or self-affirmation. But when Morris points out that "the marks of the action of final causes are . . . order, orderly movement, combination and convergence of forces," he is rejecting both the ontological discreteness of a spiritual world and the supposed original passivity of the human mind, and so again, however indirectly, is affirming the continuity of nature. In rejecting also the correlative supposition that the material world *qua* material can be taken by itself alone, he is emphasizing the fact that what he has identified as the marks of final cause cannot be identified alternately as the efficient causes known through physical science and a purely phenomenal world. Thus the notion of chance never explains phenomena, but only shows an inadequate grasp of causal relations. Chance is merely a regression to nonorder.

Morris' title for the second of his papers for the Victoria Institute, read two years later at the ordinary meeting of June 19, 1876, was "The Theory of Unconscious Intelligence, as Opposed to Theism." [10] Here he seeks to show that final cause involves far more than a mere generaliza-

10 *Transactions*, Vol. XI, 1876, pages 247–91.

tion of purpose or order out of phenomena. Intelligence does not create the structure of the universe in a vacuum. Hence the idea of pure mechanism, when given a metaphysical actuality by such thinkers as Karl Robert Eduard von Hartmann, is never anything but a *deus ex machina,* representing a roundabout attempt to comprise the realm of thought within a materialistic reality. The attack upon the world by the mind which would understand it must at all times be a matter of experience in continuity. Therefore Morris points out that new knowledge must arise out of the old, or be fundamentally "of a piece" with it. Intellectual validation is a consensus ultimately, and this unalloyed experientialism of Morris is his point of most thorough break with both the rational system-building of the German idealists and the metaphysical fragmentation of British empiricism. His affirmation of complete reliance on the scientific method, when it comes to things of a nonmaterial nature, is his mode of rejection for all intuitionalism or subjectivism on the one hand, and all dogmatic theology or rationalistic authoritarianism on the other. "Guided by the same principles, the philosopher whose work differs from that of the man of 'exact science' only in that it is less directly susceptible of sensible verification, seeks to arrive at the formulation of the most fundamental truths of being—truths which must be apprehended rather with the eye of the mind than with the eye of the body." He then states what he will be repeating, over and over again in various forms. "It ought to be, but is not, ridiculously superfluous to add, that the results sought by a true philosophy will not disagree with the facts of internal and external experience, since, the rather, the former must be an expression of the underlying truth of experience, what experienced fact should suggest and in its measure illustrate, and in which the various experimental sciences should find their connecting link and the element of their life."

Summarizing the whole course of philosophical development as the gradual perfection of a purely rational science of sciences, or an intellectual statement of the over-all ordering of verified knowledge per se, Morris suggests that the foundation of this rational achievement is in recognizing that the order becoming manifest through the more material side of reality is always a contribution of a more immaterial mind. Any theory of unconscious intelligence must therefore be ruled out as inadequate, or as representative of earlier and fumbling stages of metaphysical thinking, since the abstraction of the power of thought from the thinker who is thinking it is a manifest absurdity. This is not widely realized, since "all the systems of strict pantheism or naturalism must necessarily contain, virtually, the doctrine of unconscious reason," that is, they attempt to comprise mind within what normally would be developed as matter, along the lines already suggested. Philosophy requires mind for any ordering of the world—no matter how it may choose to account for mental phenomena—and at the beginning of speculative thought the most significant or enduring analysis has begun with an acceptance of mind as somehow implicit in nature as such. "The absolute being of the Vedas is reported to be pure cognition, which yet neither knows nor is known," and so constitutes mind as ultimate reference—much as in the later and Western parallel provided by absolute idealism—while

Plato perhaps spoke for all the ancients when he held, according to Morris, "that the universe is the product and exhibition of mind." This would be the more primitive view according to a subjective type of efficient cause with a universal scope, man not as yet dissociating himself rationally from the world about him.

To the rationalist—and Morris is ever the rationalist, if never the positivist—all reality is an exhibition of purpose originating in the mind, hence Aristotle, the virtual creator of Western rationalism, "never tires of affirming that nature does nothing in vain. The controlling element in all natural causation, according to him, is the end in view, and if the end is sometimes not attained, this is owing to change or to material obstacles. . . . It is evident that in his separation of the divine thought from the world, and in his practical treatment of reason (the ideal 'form') as an agency independent of any clear relation to a conscious subject possessing and directly or indirectly controlling it, Aristotle early paved the way for the vague modern theories of pantheism or atheism concerning a so-called unconscious intelligence." The dichotomy of thought and thinker—by which alone any generalization or scientific knowledge is possible—seems more actual than functional, positive than tentative, because of a common and faulty interpretation. Secular naturalism, as all speculation caught in the pseudoactuality of the dualism here, needs an entelechy to hold its world together and accepts a cosmic intelligence or natural orderliness without realizing that to abstract either consciousness or over-all order from it is merely to match a logical fallacy with another one, and to end up with the *deus ex machina*. Descartes got involved in the difficulties at this point and was responsible for "the modern theories of pure materialism, in which God, the divine thinker, is dispensed with, and thought is swallowed up in mechanism," and "Spinoza follows along in this." Morris then turns to criticize, on this basis, several philosophical writers of current importance in the seventies, particularly Von Hartmann whose *The Philosophy of the Unconscious* had been published in 1869.

Morris never appears to lose sight of what he has termed the problems of Christianity, as shown by his critical sensitiveness to theological fallacies. He realizes that the theory of theism must not duplicate the errors of a materialistic or mechanistic view in a different form or aspect, and so he asks, towards the close of his paper, "Do we then identify God and the world?" Is God, in other words, a universal intelligence only rationally distinct from nature? "By no means. The world has its being in God, but is not God; it is of divine origin and nature, but not of divine essence." There is absolute continuity of world and God, but a complete rational distinctiveness. This is not a case of producer and product in any mechanical sense. Creation is continuous, as Morris had explained in the first Victoria Institute paper, saying that "final cause is a principle working immanently in nature" and on the spiritual side God thereupon comprises nature within Himself. What this means is brought out through the reverse microcosmic-macrocosmic perspective, or the recognition of God as actually knowable in discrete experience. That is, God cannot be reduced to the mechanical function of world totality. God is universality as logically discrete or personal in any individual situation—the basic tenet of theism—so that "God is a perfect, personal spirit. We can have no conception, and we are not justified by the logical laws of scientific inquiry in attempting to form one of a spirit which is not a self, a person."

This would mean that the race goes forward through the development of individual personality and its Godlike potentiality, and that not only literary masterpieces but all the artistic and esthetic achievements of men are the record in experience of what some have done and what all can do, at least in essence, to further such a potentiality. The material side of life reveals and supports no less than it limits or betrays the higher spirit in the human mind, and reason makes it possible for all people to know the universal quickening of an immortal realization in the here and now. With this point of view constituting the very fiber of Morris, it is not surprising that a group of undergraduate students under him should read such a text as *La Philosophie de L'Art* by Hippolyte Adolphe Taine. It had been published in 1865 and it represented at once that author's misanthropic estimate of the human species together with his high admiration for the virility and sense of grandeur to be found in Shakespeare, Titian and anyone else able by art to bring life to an exaggerated if false promise. Morris probably had every respect for the Frenchman as a critic and scholar, but considered his philosophical gifts of slight value, and so was led to give a lecture on "The Philosophy of Art" which was then published as an article by William Torrey Harris in the *Journal of Speculative Philosophy.*[11]

"Being and Thought are one," Morris explains, quoting

---

[11] January, 1876, Vol. X, Number 1.

Parmenides as "the grand old poet-philosopher" who "sang before the classical epoch in the history of Greek philosophy," and it is in thought, as God-touched, that man transcends simple being and becomes more than the *bête humaine* of Taine. "Philosophy is the demonstration of the ideal as the living truth of real things, as underlying, determining, constituting what is figuratively but vaguely termed their blind necessity, as furnishing the origin of their true existence, and the end towards which they tend." This ideal philosophy "can alone account for art and the artist" since otherwise any concept of true creativeness would be only a matter of words, or a description of a mechanical conditioning. Indeed, "I may remark, parenthetically, that it is not only those who admit the existence of a personal God who adopt a theory of art like the one here advocated. The whole army of modern pantheists admit more or less explicitly the spiritual or ideal nature and substance of all things" although denying that "the source of this nature is a personal, self-conscious being." The ideal side of life participates in the universal immediacy which establishes the phenomenon of a person in the lower or strictly phenomenal world, hence "genius, the true artist . . . works under the guidance of the higher life of the soul, in its true ideal element" whereas talent as a mere conditioned excellency "works according to the laws of the lower everyday consciousness." The Godlike freedom or immortal potential of the ideal is shown because "reflective science does not discover the laws of genius until *after* genius, proceeding without any formal or scientific consciousness of them, has already illustrated them in its works."

The great service of the artist, Morris then remarks, was that he gave a true representation of a higher reality in realms where the senses could function. Thus Morris denies any essential evil in the lower world, reversing the superficial Platonism that found material substance and all its works inherently vile by nature, and in another article published almost simultaneously [12] he emphasizes the fact that it is on the plane of common and social experience that the more exalted realizations of man are substantiated. The immortal continuity of man and nature simply loses all meaning if the functional dichotomy of thought and being is made an actual division of the cosmos. "We need to remind ourselves at the outset that, whatever conclusion we may arrive at, it must not, and cannot if it be true, conflict with anything which science strictly demonstrates. It is a part of that beautiful harmony and unity of all truth that its parts all belong to one symmetrical, ideal structure."

Here is a construct of reason for which "the realism of material science furnishes the basis, while the idealism of faith, hope, reason, completes the superstructure." When it comes to a consideration of the latter, aspects of the former must be kept in their proper sphere. "The cappingstones of a building are not to be laid side by side with the stones of the foundation. Thus placed, they will evidently not all fit into each other, will seem incongruous, and perhaps mutually contradictory. But each in its place, viewed in its relation to the whole building, will be seen equally to be justified in its existence, and to contribute

---

[12] "The Immortality of the Human Soul," *Bibliotheca Sacra*, October, 1876, Vol. 33, pages 695–715.

to the due proportion and completeness of the whole." It is the attempt to deal with the elements of experience out of their logical context that is responsible for so much absurdity in philosophical speculation. Purely subjective relations are individual, and so beyond much social rectification and perhaps all scientific measure. Yet they cannot be dismissed altogether, even if useless for a cold logical analysis. Hence Morris continues, explaining that he leaves out of consideration "all forms, real or fancied, of direct knowledge by which it might be claimed that we have an immediate experience of the great truths in question," but yet asking "how many may there not be of the pure in heart who see God now, who know him by the life of God in the soul? And who shall term illegitimate the ecstatic fervor of conviction of those who, having such an experience, affirm that they feel their immortality as an actual fact already begun, the future contained in the present— their eternity, following the thought of the great German theologian [i.e., Schleiermacher], included in every instant, since they have become consciously one with the infinite?"

Here once more is the microcosmic-macrocosmic interactivity on which dynamic idealism rests. God is manifest through man—or as a self or a person, in Morris' terms— and man finds or completes himself through a direct and perhaps mystical assimilation into the universal total as a personal immortality. The concept is theism per se. And then, in parallel, there is the psychological side of the matter, or the evidence of the senses and the possibility of direct intuitive knowing as of like value, provided only that both modes of realization supplement and confirm each other in and through all experience. Morris explains that the immortality of the soul may be inferred from (1) its intrinsic nature, which presents itself as scientifically measurable through the phenomena of its conscious life and its social existence, (2) the very clear evidence of a transcendental capacity shown by human beings, when contrasted with other creatures in an evolutionary scale of existence, and (3) the moral dynamic of man, whereby he is capable of responding to final cause or personal motivation on ideal levels of experience. It is this last, of course, that is of the most general interest to Morris, since the fundamental problem of Christianity is its quickening and the consequent call to an individual salvation. The conception is the basis of all evangelism as such. Morris proceeds to develop his arguments, but he realizes that there is no rational conviction to be gained beyond direct experience, so that the article at the end reflects the dilemma of his very earliest thinking. He can appeal to the experience of those who have been touched by a sense of divinity but theirs is not the real need. To the scoffer on the one hand, and the unawakened understanding on the other, his words either are meaningless or ridiculous. He is no further along the path of a universal evangelism in 1876 than he had been when he set foot in Bremen ten years before.

There is one more paper in print during this period, and it suggests that Morris after all might end up as the critic and the unusually competent expositor in the history of philosophy, rather than as a truly creative philosopher in his own right. Holding uncompromisingly to his attack upon all purely mechanical interpretations—whether of man or God, the world or reason—he prepared an article on "Spinoza—A Summary Account of his Life and Teaching," commemorating the two hundredth anniversary of Spinoza's death.[18] Quoting Leibnitz, Spinoza's contemporary, and identifying the latter as a Cartesian and as the one who carried ontological dualism to its extreme, Morris then points out that "with Descartes, God is recognized, theoretically, as the creator and preserver of all things. The continued existence of things is due to the constant agency of God. In this agency, the agency of an *intelligent power,* is found the true and universal type of genuine causation." Indeed, "Descartes recognizes, also, the absolute liberty of God," so that the ideal originates and sustains all reality at root, as Morris himself believed. But "on the other hand, Descartes as a physicist showed himself completely under the domination of the 'scientific' conception of mechanism or automatism—a conception which, as experience shows, inevitably leads in the direction of atheistic conclusions, unless kept in due subjection to, and not allowed for an instant to usurp the place of, the true idea of causation."

Descartes pursued goals in two different contexts and bequeathed a legacy of confusion to all who followed in the train of his contribution. The world of common experience was dichotomized with an absurd literalness, leading Morris to point out that "the still unresolved problem for many of our dilettante but not uninfluential philosophers of to-day, is to reconcile mechanism with idealism, necessity with freedom; to see how *mechanism* is, as the word implies, but the use or operation of means for ends, and that the ends are set and the means directed by ideal causes

---

[18] *Journal of Speculative Philosophy,* July, 1877, Vol. II, Number 3, pages 278ff.

—i.e., as above expressed, by *intelligent power;* and, finally, that the 'necessity' of things is the necessity of wisdom and not of unyielding fate or of a mechanism which, of itself, can do nothing." Morris is not merely following Ulrici in a bare intellectual synthesis, nor attempting to resolve the dualism by paralleling Trendelenburg's return to a naïve Aristotelianism, but he sees the whole issue as superficial, or a matter of logical confusion. "Descartes may be said to have handed over to Spinoza the two conceptions, the mechanistic and the idealistic or theistic, in unreconciled dualism, but with a marked tendency on the part of the former to supplant the latter. Spinoza takes them up, and instead of assigning distinctly to each its due place, seeks to blend them" with the result that "the mechanical conception gains the upper hand and is made virtually primary, while the idealistic mostly fades out of sight or is treated as a derivative result of the former. Thus, the prevailing idea of God in the first part of the Ethics turns out substantially identical with the pseudo idea of a universal force, the blind 'cause' (?) of all things, which pervades so much of the philosophical writing of to-day. The duality of thought and extension, in Descartes' philosophy, reappears in the form of two attributes (and the only two of the 'infinite number,' which Spinoza mentions) of the one divine substance; identical in fact, but differing in manifestation."

On the evangelistic side the result of the Cartesian development is barren because there is no possibility of personal assimilation to the Godhead. "The God of Spinoza is conspicuous on account of its lack of moral attributes. In this it resembles the God of Aristotle, but for different reasons. Aristotle's God possesses all intrinsic excellence, being inherently perfect. If he is not represented as good, just, tender, loving, etc., this is not because Aristotle considered these qualities as mere 'modes of thought,' denoting nothing real, but because they were not included in his ideal of perfection. But the God of Spinoza is left without them, because the words good, perfect, and the like, taken in a moral sense, have no absolute significance, but are simply signs of 'prejudices' of the human mind; and, further, because a *force*, abstractly considered, can have no moral character. God's 'love' of himself, and of man in himself, can only be considered as a kind of mechanical consequence, or 'virtue' of the operation of intellect." Morris then suggests that "Spinoza possessed a nature deeply inclined to idealism," but failed to recognize what Morris feels to be the essence of any ideal concept, a wholly personal and highly responsible participation in any eternal reality. Spinoza was an "intrepid seeker after truth," but he sought it rationally, out in the cosmos, in a fatal separation from himself and his own individual experience. This is a particular error in concept against which Morris has struggled from the beginning of his own thinking.

Any intellectual difficulty Morris might encounter would come not from the lack of an ordering principle, which he has always had ready at hand in his theism, but rather would reflect his effort to establish a rational dynamic, such as would enable, every intrepid seeker after truth—not Spinoza and the professional philosophers alone —to experience the wholeness and order of the world about him through an individual, intelligent and conscious act. Here is the end towards which Morris always seems to move in his struggle to solve what to him were the problems of Christianity. This is the primary key to Morris. Never calling any man master, he possessed an unusually open mind, reaching out in all directions for materials he might put to use. Throughout his life he remained the omnivorous reader, always characteristically abreast of the latest publications in the fields of major interest to him. He was also, and perhaps without quite realizing the fact, very much the literary opportunist, utilizing the intellectual goods at hand to an extent particularly noticeable whenever his reading can be checked against his various lectures and articles, indeed, this may be seen to a marked degree throughout these pages as his writings are brought into orientation with the events of his life. As a result of this characteristic he also exhibits an exceptionally stubborn loyalty to the doctrines and principles he had found useful in the development of his own thought. They have constituted his experience, and in logical realms they remain the experiential continuum to which he makes his ultimate rational appeal. This is the secondary key to the man, and it reveals the consistency of his thinking relative to the principles which he evolves, and to which he gives his intellectual allegiance. With these factors in mind it is possible to proceed to his major formulations.

PART THREE

THE PROCESS OF FORMULATION

CHAPTER TEN

THE ATTACK ON BRITISH EMPIRICISM

WHEN Morris went to Europe, in 1866, the great philosophical ferment in the world's thinking was German. The Old World had become a promised land to which any embryonic philosopher would look, almost without second thought or reflection. Henry Boynton Smith, Morris' intellectual mentor, had completed his education abroad, as had G. Stanley Hall, with whom Morris in a sense was competing for a philosophy chair at Johns Hopkins University through the years 1878–85, and no less Morris himself. The impact of Immanuel Kant's *Critique of Pure Reason*, almost an exact century before Morris' first book appeared, had dictated this course of events. Now another epochal milestone had been passed in man's intellectual history, marked by the publication of Charles Darwin's *Origin of Species* in 1859 and *Descent of Man* in 1871. The Darwinian influence had entered into Morris' thinking early through the scientific ferment in New England,[1] but the real consequences of the naturalistic leaven were not evident in philosophy on the idealistic side until the period to which attention now must turn. Darwin's basic contribution had been to reinstate man in the natural order of the world. The correlative step in thought, the assimilation of nature into man which would enable man

---

[1] *Cf.* above, page 56.

to become a rationally competent thinker, was a slow development and one that perhaps has not yet had an adequate formulation.

It was this process of enthroning the world in man—or in his mind, certainly—that has come to be identified, among the English at least, by the term Hegelian. One of the leaders of British Hegelianism, Edward Caird, was well aware of the nature of his own idealism. "The work of Kant and Hegel," Caird writes, "like the work of earlier philosophers, can have no speculative value except for those who are able critically to reproduce it, and so to assist in the sifting process by which its permanent meaning is separated from the accidents of its first expression. And such reproduction, again, is not possible except by those who are impelled by the very teaching they have received to give it a fresh expression and a new application. Valuable as may be the history of thought, the literal importation of Kant and Hegel into another country and time would not be possible if it were desirable, or desirable if it were possible. The mere change of time and place, if there were nothing more, implies new questions and a new attitude of mind in those whom the writer addresses, which would make a bare reproduction unmeaningful." [2] This is a thoroughly organic idealism, anchored in neither rational system-building nor scientific staticism.

Morris studied the gathering strength of the British Hegelians, taking the "keenest interest" in these authors. James Hutchison Stirling published *The Secret of Hegel* in 1865, and his *Textbook to Kant* in 1881; Thomas Hill

---

[2] *Essays in Philosophical Criticism,* edited by Andrew Seth and R. B. Haldane, London, Longmans, Green, 1883.

Green wrote his "epoch-making introduction" to Hume's *Treatise of Human Nature* in 1874, and his *Prolegomena to Ethics* in 1883; William Wallace issued *The Logic of Hegel* with its "admirable prolegomena" in 1874; Francis Herbert Bradley's *Ethical Studies* appeared in 1876; Edward Caird's article on "Cartesianism" for the *Encyclopædia Britannica* was written in 1876, his *A Critical Account of the Philosophy of Kant* in 1878, and his article on "The Social Philosophy and Religion of Comte" for the *Contemporary Review* in 1879; the lectures by Robert Adamson on Kant were given in 1879, and on Fichte in 1881; and John Caird's *An Introduction to the Philosophy of Religion* was published in 1880. Of these items, it is to be noted that only Stirling's book on Hegel is earlier than 1874, when the translation of Ueberweg appeared, and that Stirling is the only one of these authors there mentioned. The development is largely contemporaneous with the appearance of Morris' *British Thought and Thinkers,* and is a movement in which Morris participated in a very real sense, although he was more American and less Hegelian. Indeed, "Mr. Andrew Campbell, who . . . had every opportunity to keep in close touch with him during the period of the philosophical professorship" was able to inform Wenley that "Morris did not undertake exact study of the Kantian succession, Hegel particularly, till after 1877." [3]

Morris' 1877 paper on Spinoza, therefore, marks the beginning of this new development in his philosophy, and the problems sharpened through the discussion of Spinoza unquestionably remained central in the new seminal pe-

---

[3] Wenley, pages 239, 254.

riod, not only during his reading in the British Hegelians as the materials appeared but also through his subsequent personal touch with the men themselves. This was by correspondence initially, but on his second and last European trip some time later—covering three months from June, 1885—he had stimulating visits with both Edward and John Caird, as well as with Bradley and Wallace.[4] The first of the four books written by Morris, and the one which rounds out his point of view up to this point, was his *British Thought and Thinkers*. Its contents comprise the substance of his lectures given at Johns Hopkins University early in 1880, or as a principal part of his work in launching what was then a new or enlarged activity at Baltimore, that is, covering an entire semester of each academic year rather than the month of January only, as had been the case in 1878 and 1879.

The twelve lectures were public in the sense that since "the members of the University rarely require the entire room, the Trustees have great pleasure in inviting other persons, not connected with the University, to attend. As these lectures are not intended for popular entertainment, but for the instruction of students, those persons first receive tickets . . . who are known to be especially interested in a particular course. Preference is thus given, according to the character of the course, to teachers in other institutions, public and private; students of medicine, law, etc. . . . The hall is full when 200 hearers are present; it is uncomfortable if more are admitted. . . . To give the lectures elsewhere would alter their character as a part of the ordinary academic work of the University."

[4] *Ibid.*, pages 165–70.

Morris explains that he spoke to a "mixed audience of ladies and gentlemen" and that "simultaneously with their delivery, another, more extended and technical, course, on the history of British speculation from Bacon to Spencer, was in progress, attended only by university students" and that "to this course" with three weekly sessions "the lectures here in substance reproduced were partly introductory, while in part they were intended to present a general summary of results reached and illustrated in more profuse detail in the special course." Stating that, in the book, there were "slight changes . . . consisting mainly in amplification of the theoretic portions" in several places, he adds that "by the addition of a chapter on Herbert Spencer the main thought of the volume is followed out of the British past into the immediate present." [5]

The book represents an American analogue to Green's work on Hume, and it cannot properly be taken as in any way concerned with the idealist ferment of "the immediate present," despite the some three years of attention Morris had given to the new development. By the same token it cannot be seen as an exposition of an earlier stand which Morris will repudiate later. Wenley views it in this latter light, however, believing Morris to be as yet naïve in respect to any real understanding of Hegel, and proceeds to criticize the exposition from his own Hegelian perspective, that is, the one he has assimilated into the subsequent Hegelian Morris of his private creation. Because of this special coloring in his own mind, Wenley persistently finds Morris overconcerned with a consideration of the dichotomy set up by distinct phenomenal and noumenal worlds.

---

[5] *Ibid.*, pages 138–9; *British Thought and Thinkers*, pages 3–4.

"The empirical and intuitional schools divided the empire between them, splitting the universe in halves. Accordingly, man was either a mere incident in the mechanical order, a beast, sorrowing because he could contemplate his dread fate; or, cut off from this order, he became the exponent of caprice, the master of a lawless will. Morris was quick to seize the former alternative and to expose its hollowness, but the latter still lay in shadow for him, it was almost unsuspected." In other words, Morris "tends to solve the difficulty by ridding himself of one term," i.e., Morris had not yet realized the need Wenley thinks he ought to have for such a synthesizing principle as the Hegelian dialectic would afford and "hence, he has no eye for the third great contribution of British thought to human culture—science—where, after a manner, the age-old opposition between philosophy and poetry is overcome."

What Wenley has in mind, of course, is the continuity throughout nature of which Darwin was perhaps the more true exponent in 1880, and when he remarks that "Morris is weak, and the weakness is a symptomatic commentary upon his own viewpoint just when a fuller light was about to break," he overlooks the fact that Morris, at the very moment, was teaching a class in German esthetics and at least within the year was doing preliminary work on his exposition of Kant and planning the series of philosophical studies of which he was editor and which would bring the idealists of Germany within reach of the average English reader. Forgetting for the moment the theory that Morris was passing through a period of great spiritual doubt, Wenley further proceeds to suggest that Morris was leaning towards a vestigial "Natural Theology" in his opposition to "the subversive speculation affected by rhetoricians of science in the first blush of optimism" which had developed as "atheism under a mask," and therefore as attempting "to vindicate the reasonable character, not of Religion, but of certain dogmas wherein *a* religion had crystallized at a definite state in its history, forgetting that these involved more or less definite philosophical presuppositions. Thus, his attitude was theosophical and mystical, just as that of contemporary science was empirical and mechanical. Accordingly, in so far as philosophy and science shared a mutual rationalism, both came under the same condemnation," that is, Morris was still too narrowly Christian in Wenley's eyes to appreciate the religion of the Absolute. This is not the Morris who speaks for himself in his book, nor is Wenley's view a correct representation either of the intellectual climate for which Morris himself was responsible at Johns Hopkins, or of the general lines of progression in his thought as shown by the interrelations of the man and the general philosophical milieu in which he was functioning.[6]

John Dewey was in residence at the Baltimore graduate school as a student under Morris, was also an assistant under Morris' direction for the two academic years ranging from the autumn of 1882 through the spring of 1884, and was Morris' associate on the Michigan University staff, moreover, for four years afterwards. Dewey, who certainly was in an excellent position to know the elder man's cast of mind and general philosophical attitude, was not impressed by any pre-Hegelian Morris on the one hand, nor by a Morris whose stand was in any way incongruous with

---

[6] Wenley, pages 245-53.

the *British Thought and Thinkers*. What Dewey remembered, rather, was the stimulating intellectual climate centered in the school of thought for which Edward Caird
and Green primarily had been responsible. Morris already
was utilizing the new English texts, as Bradley's *Ethics* for
a principal subject matter in September, 1882. Dewey
characterized the movement as "the vital and constructive
one" with an influence which "fell in with and reinforced
that of Professor Morris," [7] noting the high individualism
of Morris, since "his idealism was of the wholly objective
type," i.e., not a subjective absolutism in any respect. To
Morris—as seen through the ever-appreciative reminiscence of Dewey—the task of philosophy was not the proving of existence and matter but rather a discovery of the
meaning or practical import of whatever existed or had
substance, so that Morris in his turn to a species of Hegelianism was not reversing but fulfilling himself. The attitude was entirely pragmatic, logically empirical rather
than ontologically subjective. Here was a reorientation in
that contemporary frame of reference which might seem
to him to have the most power for quickening minds and
understanding. It was in this milieu that philosophy for
the moment offered a living experience, and hence presented the chance for a moral dynamic which the individual reason could make its own. Morris would never forget
that thought and being are one, that philosophy is the
history of philosophy, and that the present builds on the
past in every aspect of both mental and cultural realms. In
his survey of the pre-Hegelian British thought, therefore,
his approach was entirely functional or a case of thorough-

---

[7] As already quoted above, page 159.

going social relativism, and he was judging English philosophy not in a vacuum but in its own living context.

Since he was an idealist, rather than either a sensationalistic empiricist or a positivistic rationalist, the obvious
start of any inquiry on his part would be with the idea,
and so with the person or self capable of ideation. In a
neat example of his characteristic intellectual strategy, he
begins his exposition by giving it a firm anchorage in the
philosophical tradition, quoting Schopenhauer's *"Die
Welt ist meine Vorstellung"* [8] as a convenient expression
of his own voluntaristic but non-Schopenhauer leanings.
Then he goes on to describe a reflective experience as a
boy which, he believed, represented "a bent common to the
universal mind of man." [9] Here, of course, is the basic
presupposition of all rationalism, namely, that the constructs of the mind provide a reliable representation of
nature, and that order and permanence are introduced by
mind into what he describes as otherwise altogether ka-

---

[8] "The world is for me an idea."

[9] "I can remember how, as a mere boy, more than once, in an evening
reverie, an experience somewhat in this vein came to me. All my boyish
ideas of things seemed, as pure creations of my own fancy, to melt away,
and there remained, as the whole sum and substance of the universe,
only the abstract, but otherwise empty and uninstructive, and, by any
law of sufficient reason, inexplicable, necessity of being, plus a dull,
confused, and yet thoroughly unique, and for this reason indescribable,
sensation, as of a chaos of shapeless elements, moving noiselessly among
each other—a *plenum* of scarcely greater value than an absolute *vacuum*.
Then came the return to what is termed the literal fact of experience, or
better, to the world such as, under the influence of a dawning mental
activity, guided by sensitive experience and by instruction, it had actually
shaped itself in my imagination—the earth, with its green fields and forest-
covered mountains, the world-inhabited heavens, the changing seasons,
man and his past history and unrevealed earthly destiny, not to mention
the myriad little and familiar things which would necessarily crowd the
foreground of such a picture in a boy's mind. The view which a moment
before had demonstrated so signally its capability of dissolving, recovered
its relative consistency and became again a slowly changing panorama of *a*
world, or of 'the world' as it was for me."

leidoscopic, or as no more than pluralistic potentiality. He makes a contrast between the idea which is only "a changing picture in the imagination" or "a *representation*," that is, the impression upon a Lockian *tabula rasa*—and the idea which "shall be a rational type, a self-evidencing law, an all-sufficient, all-explaining, all-necessitating reason," and by this latter he means, not something mysteriously self-sufficient in mental realms, but rather the functional process or activity through which the world that "was 'my idea' (in Schopenhauer's phrase) is to be transformed, in its measure, into the image, or rather into a participation, of the divine idea of the world."

What follows immediately in the text may well be a reference to the British Hegelians, no less than to the German idealistic speculation in a more general way. "I have thus stated, in outline, the grand and comprehensive motive which underlies all finite thought as such, and which therefore reveals itself, clearly or obscurely, in all the thought of man. It were easy to show, in detail, how it governs at once the systematic inquiries of philosophical speculation, the exact inquiries of physical science, and the freer intuitions of poetic fancy, as well as, also, the sober contemplations of history. Nor would it be more difficult to show that in this presupposed ideal of stable Truth—believed to be attainable for man: else why and how strive after it?—moral and aesthetic elements are intrinsically involved. But to attempt this here would be to go aside from the purpose of our present inquiry, as well as to repeat a labor already well performed by others." Instead, holding to his immediate goal, Morris continues, explaining that "my object now is only to direct attention

to the universally observable fact that men, finding themselves in, or in possession of, a mental world, which is at
first (as regards their own *insight*) so largely, or exclusively,
subjective, variable, phenomenal (and so, to use Kant's
metaphor, like a restless ocean), believe in a continent of
objective, stable Truth, think that they have glimpses of
it, seek to approach it, and set up way-marks (in their literature and institutions) of their progress toward it, and by
their notions (or knowledge) of it form their judgments as
to the significance and value of human life and history,
and of the physical universe itself."

Man's thinking is an integral part of his culture. Hence
"it is through the different notions which the men, the
thinkers, of an epoch, a race, a clime, a great nation, form
and express concerning the geography of this continent,
through the spiritual colors of which they profess to have
caught glimpses, the maxims of hope, of conviction, or of
despair, sorrowful, reckless, or even blasphemous, which
they have inscribed upon the guide-posts set up by them;
it is through all these, and through other signs flowing
from, or otherwise necessarily connected with, these that
the peculiar complexion, the special attitude or tendency
of the thought of a particular epoch or nation is known
and judged." Thus philosophy does not exist in a vacuum,
and is not an Absolute overlaid on a world of phenomena,
but is a product of experience. However, the matrix of
experience is not without its potentials of order since all
literature and art, as well as all civil and social institutions
in their fundamental measure are interpretative or ex-
planatory, and like philosophy and science are "simply
. . . familiar signs and products of the idealism innate in

the universal mind of man." This idealism "is no accident, but a constituent and necessary element of human nature; nay, more, is that which essentially constitutes it," because the world, as Morris had just stated, no less exists in man than the reverse, through the "participation" of the divine idea in every aspect of universal reality. Human nature, as ultimately expressing divine idea, makes it manifest through the ideal per se.

"Intelligence is an active function, not simply a passive possession" since "strictly passive, it were no longer intelligence, for then, inactive, it would not have intelligence of itself." Mind "can comprehend no world which is not permeated with its own attributes." Mind is social, hence personal. It does not determine the world but orders it, makes use of it and interacts with it. Rationality is a mode of participation in existence, not a cosmological hyle. The idealism of the mind is a characteristic of being, not a kind of being *a priori* to all characteristics. Therefore, "among the Romans we find a peculiar reverence for law, among the Greeks a passionate love of the beauty of limit and proportion, and among the Hebrews a regard for moral goodness or righteousness." The ideal is not only a cultural pattern but is also an intellectual attitude which may take its social form as "a revealed and accepted religion," with its explanation in a "consecrated language" and with no attempt made to understand it or to render its doctrines rationally intelligible. What is more, the truth of the dogma that the ideal "alone has reality, and that even in the most lifeless stone the measure of reality is proportioned to the ideality typically or intrinsically present" may be accepted without realizing that "ideality is inexplicable apart from living personal mind as its cause and constant supporter. Then we have the various forms of philosophical hybridism—pantheism in its protean forms, intellectual naturalism, certain phases of mysticism, doctrines of an impersonal idea, an unconscious but ideal something, underlying or accounting for the world."

What then of British thought in general? The English mind has a first and most prominent characteristic which "may perhaps be described as consisting in this, namely, that its interest is far more concentrated upon the vital and practical side of truth than upon the abstract or theoretical side. Truth, in its living, effective power, so absorbs its attention that little care is left for inquiries concerning its ultimate grounds and guarantees, or for laborious exactness in the statement of it. . . . Faith in this truth is faith in themselves. To relinquish it would be moral suicide—to doubt it, moral treason. . . . The only other nation known to Occidental history, which has possessed anything like so palpable and consistent a character as the English, namely the Romans, in like manner, and even in a more marked degree, were remarkable for their almost absolute neglect of abstract speculation. Their old-fashioned reverence for law and duty, and their self-respect, were ideal forces which wrought in them and through them, and fitted them for the rough and solid work of world-subjugation. No wonder that they felt a greater interest in the practical solution of living, flesh-and-blood problems, which the progress of events forced upon them, than in their theoretical explanation. If the ideal, which is the only essential side of human nature, has a really sustaining support and source of constant nourishment in a sterling national character, it is by no means an obviously superficial question to ask why human nature should bother itself continually about such subtleties as the ultimate constitution and ground of existence, the abstract conditions and laws of perfect humanity, the sources of moral obligation, the meaning of beauty's charms, the intrinsic value of human life. . . .

"Certain it is that this happy, unbroken wholeness (if not completeness) of the English character has naturally extorted the admiration of other nations, in whom the harmony, or harmonious correspondence, between inward thought and aspiration, and material and historical condition, is, or has been, far less perfect than in the case of the English. . . . How much more fortunate has not the English people been than the French or German! The French, exercising their analytic talent, formed very definite, sharp-cut ideas of the rights of man; but sought with hopeless, unintelligent energy, through, one might almost say, dozens of revolutions, to give them practical realization. The Germans, with unsurpassed penetration and comprehension—as of the problems of universal existence in general, so of the grounds and elements and worth of an organized political life in particular—yet presented till recently the most lamentable spectacle of national disintegration and impotence. . . . It is no wonder that in the midst of all the aspirations and agitations and revolutions through which the continental nations of Europe, during the last century, have sought to improve their political condition, the example of England—its constitution, its vigorous, self-poised life, its *character*—has been the sometimes unacknowledged but, more frequently, openly avowed guiding-star. Such an example is a veritable inspiration, since it is the outcome of ideal forces—the only real ones and the only ones that can act upon man. These forces are, in this case, conscious self-knowledge, self-restraint and self-assertion, the first conditions of strictly human life, whether in individual or in nation."

Warning his readers against any "over-hasty conclusions" that the German speculation is useless, Morris then points to the "concentrated moral and physical power" which he sees transforming Germany as the result of the "intellectual and moral *Gedanken-arbeit,* or travail of thought, which has been going on in German climes for the last two hundred years. During all this time the Germans have been making their character," that is, the one of which Kant and the Kantian succession have been the prophets, and with this in mind Morris then unquestionably referred to the new Hegelian ferment in British thinking when he adds, "Were it not that I perceive in the history of English thought and in the English mind the signs and elements of a far more than ordinary purely intellectual and moral vitality, I should, for one, certainly look for a far less glorious future for the empire of English thought, and consequently for English power and influence in general, than I now anticipate." Recognizing that "the strong or marked sides of the English mind are three, the religious, the scientific and the poetic," but not attempting to coerce these elements into any sort of dialectical relationship, Morris proceeds to the very important statement of his own theological stand—as it had matured just over the threshold of his fortieth year—in a paragraph running to a good four pages in length. British thinking is not dismissed as sterile, but as unquickened to its own more spiritual potentialities.

"On the religious side the English share with their Teutonic ancestors and neighbors in a certain depth and sincerity of spirit, which is opposed to all sham, is never long satisfied with mere appearance, admits no separation of substance from form, and demands, along with a formal assent to the doctrines proposed to faith, an inward experience of the power of truth, accompanied by appropriate works. In other words, the English are genuinely religious." Thus Morris, in passing, is making his fundamentally evangelical concept quite clear, together with his demand for a philosophical rectification of belief through its rational integrity and experiential continuity. He continues to expand his own conception, arising from his New England pietism, as he finds it rooted in the British, whether he stops to contemplate this fact consciously or not. "A genuine religious spirit is necessarily idealistic. It carries with it the habit of referring actions to moral standards of judgment, of seeing in events a providential agency, of regarding the universe as an outcome of the divine will and in some sense a constant manifestation of divine reason." However, at this point, a shadow of Morris' years of struggle with the problems of Christianity may be seen in the background of his exposition. "In the matter of religion, the intensely practical attitude of the English, their sense, perhaps, of the substance of religion as a vital element absolutely essential to individual and national life, and as something already safely in their grasp, in their possession, seems to me to render them impatient of inquiries relative to the ultimate warrant of faith."

Religion may fail to live up to its true potential if its ideality is merely a transcendental empiricism. "The immediate, practical warrant of religious faith may indeed be found in vital experience and in historic power," Morris goes on to say. "Such a faith is not to be stigmatized as absolutely blind and unreasonable. Yet it is far short of *insight*. It is not faith resting on and illuminated by intelligence. If reasonable, it is not wholly rational. It implies a childhood in understanding, against which the Apostle of Christianity to the Gentiles utters an express warning. A consequence of the religious attitude of the English mind to which I am now referring is, or has often been, a disposition to cut short inquiry and to cleave knots of difficulty with the oracular utterance, 'Thus it is written.' . . ." This is a holding to the letter of things which is "precisely such a substitution of mechanism for intelligence and life as, in other fields of explanation, English science-philosophy has sought to effectuate. Another and a related consequence of the same mental attitude has been a disposition to restrict the sphere of human reason by emphasizing the existence of a sphere of mysterious and essentially unintelligible truth, somehow made known to man in terms, but for the rest only to be unquestioningly received by him as an unconditional prerequisite for the restoration and preservation of his soul's health. This is, considered *in se*, no better than the old attempts to attract or exorcise spirits, good or bad, by pronouncing a series of unmeaning syllables. But, then, here again a distinction is to be made. The body cannot flourish unless certain physiological processes are executed in it. . . . In like manner, spiritual life and moral health cannot exist without obedience from a sense of duty to laws and principles, the whole import and rationality of which we may not yet be prepared to perceive or appreciate."

However, "man might have had from the beginning a reasonable confidence that every fact of the physiological process was essentially, not mysterious, but explicable. . ." and so why should men be told, in "matters pertaining to the spiritual life," that " 'this and that formula you must accept as an accurate statement of the facts, laws and principles (or some of them) concerned, but neither you nor I, nor those who come after us, can ever expect to be able to render such an account of them as shall satisfy the reason and intelligence of man.' Yet this is just what the English mind, through the mouth (for instance) of such a typical and genuine representative of it as Francis Bacon . . . has presumed to declare as final truth. It is on spiritual and moral inquiries, according to Bacon, that God has pronounced a curse, upon which therefore man should only venture very daintily, if indeed at all, to enter. The appropriate field of knowledge for man is physical in nature, *i.e.*, that realm of things which 'do appear' to man in sensible experience. Bacon's attitude well illustrates the manner in which English theology and English science, in their philosophical negativism, extend the hand to each other. The same thing is illustrated in a more developed form in recent phases of religious and 'scientific' philosophy in England. Thus, we find, on the one hand, Dean Mansel, as the representative of the religious side . . . with philosophical weapons borrowed, through Sir William Hamilton, from Kant, proving the utter disparateness of the divine spirit and the spirit of man, and of the ways of God and man's ways, so that the former are for human reason absolutely incognoscible."

If the free human spirit has been thwarted on the side of religion, the situation "on the scientific side," as Morris views it, offers no improvement. "We have Mr. Herbert Spencer, as the lineal descendant of the more renowned British philosophizers and as the accredited mouth-piece of the philosophizing science of to-day, quoting Mansel with delighted approval in support of the (gratuitous) conclusions which the scientific (in distinction from the philosophical) method, applied to specifically philosophical problems, necessarily and naturally arrived at, namely, that these problems are inherently insoluble for man. The phenomenal, sensibly observable, is, it is held, (relatively) knowable; the real is absolutely unknowable. The true philosophy is to have no philosophy, to deny the possibility of philosophy, or else to term by that magnificent name the broadest generalizations and the negations of physical science." It is in neither religious nor scientific analysis that the English thinkers have really developed their theoretical talents through an adequate philosophy, but instead they have expressed their greatest genius in "a preëminent gift for poetry, perhaps the most perfect that has ever fallen to the lot of any people." The fundamental appeal of Morris to a voluntaristic or vital knowledge, which he has identified as Platonic, and his unique hypothesis that this has had a markedly outstanding expression through the English poets, has been discussed at length in Chapter Six of the present text, since it is the concept lying at the root of his master thesis at Dartmouth and providing the core of his philosophical thought when this is seen in over-all outline. The goal is spiritualization no less in 1880 than in 1864.[10]

Plato, of course, is the great example of the "close relation between poetic and philosophic endowment." Morris therefore launches his detailed analysis of British thought with only a brief summary of the Schoolmen, and gives next and full consideration to the poets, from Plato's Spenser to England's own Shakespeare. What he recognizes is "rapt thinking," or literature as revelation rather than art, and he uses the distinction between philosophy and poetry to bring out, by analogy, the real difference between a mathematical or mechanical and a metaphysical or organic point of view. This latter dichotomy is the sharpest possible distinction that can be made within a strictly philosophical frame of reference, and it is the differentiation which continues to be the point of major interest in all his thinking. He explains, at the beginning of his chapter on Shakespeare, that the average person sees rational analysis and creative art as utterly discrete, even ridiculously incongruous, but that "there are two things which, although absolutely distinct, and even contrasted, in their immediate aim, subject-matter, point of view, and method, are yet so closely related (being indeed correlates, complementary subdivisions of the whole of human knowledge) that they have, to the greatest extent, in the history of human thought, been confounded with each other. I refer to physics and metaphysics, or to physical science (with all its subdivisions, exact and descriptive, or both combined) and philosophy—the former having to do with sensibly verifiable *phenomena*, their classification, their

---

[10] *Op. cit.*, pages 7–27.

mechanical explanation, and their perfect expression in mathematical formulæ, and the latter with rationally apprehensible *realities,* with the living causes of phenomena and their rational explanation."

He then goes on to repeat that "these two, . . . philosophy and physical science (in which I include constantly mathematics, the special organon and methodological ideal of physical science), are complementary to each other, having each its peculiar province and inner justification, and yet so organically related that each leads to, implies, demands the other. But the time has never yet been when the distinction, or at least the true relation, between the two was clearly and universally perceived and respected. . . . Philosophy is a positive thing, as positive as existence itself. But it is not a mere knowledge of details and minute relations. Its characteristic function is not numbering or measuring. It is not anatomy. It does not, if true to itself and its aim, place the objects of its investigation in a vacuum of abstraction fatal to life (which physical science really does). Its problems are problems of life, because they are problems of essential being and of the active power. Its problems are synthetic and organic, because life is synthesis and organism. They are ideal and rational." [11]

The Schoolmen represented the beginnings of interaction between the developing culture of the British Isles and the continuing rationalistic synthesis of the Medieval Latinists and their essentially legalistic thought. Morris largely dismisses the period, characterizing it as the "early schooltime of our Occidental Christian civilization," pointing out that "Christendom . . . had then but recently

----

[11] *Ibid.,* pages 28, 81–4; and already quoted, *cf.* above, pages 77–8.

emerged from heathendom . . ." and "the Occidental mind was then like an overgrown, undisciplined boy . . ." so that "the first condition of its future mastership was, then, that it should itself be mastered. It could learn to rule both itself and others only by first undergoing a suitable and prolonged training in regulated obedience," and this the Roman church furnished through its schools. However, with a gradual liberation from the ecclesiastical discipline under the Renaissance, even among the Schoolmen who were "strictly English," there were "already distinct evidences of that type or direction of thought which in the last two hundred and fifty years has become so pronounced a characteristic of the English mind." Thus John of Salisbury laid great stress on utilitarian criteria, and was little caught up by the quest for ultimate truth. Roger Bacon, despite a tremendous interest in language and an ability to read the philosophical texts in their originals, was most of all concerned with the book of nature, and anticipated modern physical science by turning to a combination of mathematics and experiment. Duns Scotus viewed the world as a means incidental to man's attainment of eternal life, not as intrinsically a manifestation of divine intelligence or goodness.

But with the conflict between Platonic realism and nominalism, which came to the fore with William of Occam, Morris recognizes the key problem of all philosophy, perhaps seen only imperfectly during the Middle Ages but evident enough, namely, "whether the universe of existence, relative and absolute, is, synthetically, rationally, intrinsically comprehensible, or only analytically, superficially observable. This is tantamount to the query, whether existence is knowable *per se,* or not. . . . If not knowable *per se,* it is then knowable only as it happens to strike, or to be reported by others to, each individual, only in the impressions which each or all receive, namely, in a series of insoluble, but more or less orderly, phenomena, of which we only know that we experience (or, in the language of present psychology, *feel)* them, but of which no real causal or otherwise rational and ultimate account is possible." Since the nominalism of Occam asserted the latter of these alternatives, according to Morris' interpretation, it was of a piece with the general English thought, and he criticized the point of view for making mind as utterly passive as in John Locke. His exposition of Francis Bacon's projected restoration or clarification of philosophy begins with this same issue of the *tabula rasa.* "Just as Descartes cleared the way for his own constructive speculations by first enforcing upon himself a methodical and universal doubt respecting all notions hitherto received, so Bacon requires, of the modern renascent mind, as a condition precedent to the entering upon the possession of the province of 'all knowledge,' that it rid itself of all its previously received ideas (*idola,* false, vain ideas). These are the *Idola* of the Tribe, the Cave, the Marketplace, and the Theatre, as he in his figurative language terms them." [12]

Bacon's method consisted "first, in placing the mind in a purely receptive attitude with reference to nature. We are to 'wait upon nature'—in agreement with the first member of Bacon's favorite (though not original) apothegm, 'Man the servant and interpreter of nature.' We are

---

[12] *Ibid.,* pages 32, 36–47, 130–1.

to receive and record the impressions which she produces
with the unprejudiced simplicity of the little child. And
then, further, our 'interpretation' of her is to consist in our
making ourselves her mouth-piece. She, duly questioned
and listened to, will infallibly disclose to us all that it is
needful or useful, or indeed strictly possible, for us to
know respecting her secrets. . . . 'Starting directly from
the simple sensuous perception' (I cite Bacon), the mind
must 'be from the very outset not left to take its own
course, but guided at every step; and the business be done
as if by machinery. . . . Such a method 'leaves but little to
the acuteness and strength of wits, but places all wits and
understandings nearly on a level. For, as in the drawing of
a straight line, or a perfect circle, much depends on the
steadiness and practice of the hand, if it be done by aim of
hand only, but if with the aid of rule or compass, little or
nothing; so it is exactly with my plan.' This plan, this machine, the use of which was to ensure to all men substantially the same success in prosecuting natural investigation, is 'induction.' 'Our whole hope lies in induction,'
cries Bacon." Here is no employment of man's reasoning
powers, however, but rather an effort to make the philosopher a counter instead of a thinker. "Bacon's place in
the history of philosophy is easily stated. Of philosophy as
such, in distinction from physical science, he had but
slight conception and still slighter opinion. . . ." His
tendency was "to make physical science and its method
coextensive with the realm of all knowledge and all
method," that is, to limit every function of mind to sense-
known phenomena.[18]

---

[18] *Ibid.*, pages 133-7.

Morris explains that Thomas Hobbes "was not a great philosopher," although "he occupies an important place in the history of modern, and especially English, thought. His reduction of all phenomena, including those of mind in their physical relations, to modes of motion, was a rather remarkable declaration of a scientific view, now, at least, universally accredited. In his philosophy of man, the foundation of his political theory, he was the first one to follow the method . . . of purely empirical observation, analysis, and description. If in man a distinction is to be made between man true to himself (*i.e.*, man as he might be and ought to be, but never is, except approximately) and man as he actually appears—between man the *noumenon* and man the *phenomenon*—between man as a free, ideal, spiritual agency apprehended in philosophical self-consciousness, and man as a series of 'mental states' which, however determined, follow each other in time, or a 'bundle' of 'mental processes' or 'perceptions,' it is to the latter exclusively that the attention of Hobbes . . . is directed . . ." thus "identifying philosophy with empirical psychology" and "substantially suppressing philosophy." Here was an intellectual perspective which resulted from "a disposition (historically grounded in and justified by a dread of scholastic subtleties, from which the light and power of reason had fled) to make things easy; in other words, to treat as an affair of sensible demonstration an order of truths which lie back of, and indeed shine through, but are not absorbed in, sensible data. The knowledge of the data is to take the place of the knowledge and the power of that which they, rightly considered, do but reveal. Physical science of phenomena is to take the place of philosophical science of ideal and absolute reality." [14]

It was following along the natural course of this development that John Locke "sought . . . to reduce the intelligible to the sensible, and to explain the former through the analogy or on the basis of the latter. The ontological agnosticism to which he was led was the same which, in the whole history of thought, has resulted—as it must necessarily result—from similar attempts. That Locke did not rigorously deduce and apply all the consequences of this result and proclaim a universal philosophical scepticism, was due to the confusion of his own thought, and to the practical hold which the vital, synthetic truths by which alone man, as man, in the true sense lives, through which the universe subsists, and which all positive, affirmative philosophy depends, had upon him. It remained for David Hume, as the spokesman of a later generation, to complete Locke's destructive work." Meanwhile Locke is also "Berkeley's starting-point," a fact which explains the more "glaring deficiencies" of the latter. Berkeley professed "with his more energetic vision to penetrate the clouds which bounded Locke's mental horizon, and lo! they become for him celestial forms of light. . . . There soon flashed upon him . . . a 'new principle,' as he termed it, a principle which presented itself to him with the clearest light of self-evidence, and which, once generally perceived and accepted, was, according to his unhesitating conviction, destined to be fraught with consequences of incalculable value for the relief of man's intellectual and moral estate." Berkeley was "the truest, acutest philosopher that Great Britain has ever known."

---

[14] *Ibid.*, pages 165–7.

The denial of matter in any literal sense is a philosophical intemperance which of course would be as foreign to Morris' thought as the other idealistic extreme of absolutism, or that complementary rejection of ultimate individuality with which he has refused all commerce. But the conception of sense-known things as unreal in having no direct or immediate compulsion on the human spirit is a species of voluntarism-in-reverse for which he would have considerable sympathy.[15]

Morris is ready now for the philosophical developments in which his own background of thinking has been framed, and he continues, pointing out that "the most influential current of British speculation in the eighteenth century and in the first half of the nineteenth flowed through Scotch minds." The first of these Scots, of course, was David Hume, who was the final one of the "three classic names in the history of British speculation" (i.e., Locke, Berkeley and Hume). Hume was important because he "applies the brakes . . . to the precipitous train of human speculation" and "is the sworn enemy of all enthusiasms," and his contribution can be summarized when it is realized that "the attempts of genuine philosophers are attempts to reduce to logical, intelligible expression" the "truth of living, experimental, essential reality." Morris believes that the destiny of philosophy is "to lift men . . . up to that plane of philosophic insight on which genius stands," and identifies this as the power of Platonism. However, there had been a falling away from the essential core of the Athenian's vision, namely, the *"vital knowledge of Plato."* As already quoted,[16] he affirms that, without this,

---

[15] *Ibid.*, pages 197-8, 204, 212, 233.   [16] *Cf.* above, pages 74-5.

"I cannot admit that philosophy has any existence except in name." Hence Hume was perfectly right in drawing negative conclusions, and in assuming that "no others were to be found," because the premises on which he operated— of a purely sensational nature, thanks to his predecessors— were not "germain to philosophical questions." The "living kernel of real consciousness," not the "inanimate hull," is "dynamic, dramatic, rational." The former is "vital, self-illuminating, rational activity," whereas the latter "must be contemplated essentially as a succession of lifeless images or pictures." [17]

With Hume, and with Thomas Reid after him, "the substantive nature of either mind or matter is beyond knowledge." Immanuel Kant, like Reid in reply to Hume, "makes no attempt to rescue the knowledge of reality. We know, he admits, only phenomena, which are modifications, however determined, of mind." Kant is only able to press on beyond Hume by finding that "the order of the concatenation of phenomena in our knowledge is not arbitrary as Hume had asserted, but fixed and necessary . . . but, like Reid, he shares in the constitutional intellectual infirmity, or scientific prejudice, of his century, in being unable to see in anything but sensible consciousness a possible type or standard of reality. This, however, at once reveals itself to Kant, as it always does, and must do, to all accurate inquirers, as a scene, not of reality, but only of shadow, appearance, or intrinsic unreality," thus making the true thing-in-itself "absolutely unknowable." Explaining what is designated as "the famous law of the Relativity of Knowledge," Morris defines this as "but a

---

[17] *Op. cit.*, pages 234, 242–3, 254–5, 265.

new and unnecessary version of the old story concerning the incompetence of sense to penetrate to, or grasp, reality," and adds that "this alleged logical constraint which we are under, to believe what we cannot conceive, is construed by Hamilton, with some impressiveness, as teaching the 'salutary lesson' of faith in the invisible." Morris' revealing criticism, in his dismissal of Hamilton, can be taken quite fairly as his judgment *en passant* on the intellectual milieu in which he began his thinking. "The 'lesson' is indeed a salutary one, and is the first one to be learned in philosophy, as in religion. But it does not follow from Hamilton's data and arguments. The data are all essentially sensualistic, and the arguments sophistical." [18]

Morris turns next to John Stuart Mill, and his curt dismissal of that gentleman, epitomizing the substance of thirty-five pages in the book, has been quoted in connection with the impact of Henry Thomas Buckle in Morris' Union Seminary days.[19] The following and final chapter on Herbert Spencer comprises material which was not included in the Johns Hopkins lectures, but which was of great importance in the thinking and general attitude of Morris. He sees Spencer as the accredited mouthpiece of the philosophizing science of his day and remarks that "the sceptre so long and effectively wielded by Mill was transferred, without difficulty, into the hands of Mr. Spencer," whose strength "lies in his familiarity with the conceptions of physical science" and who "astonishes his readers through the apparently encyclopedic comprehensiveness of his scientific information. This qualifies him to take up and repeat with an effect of imposing authority the parable

---

[18] *Ibid.*, pages 289–91, 295–6.   [19] *Cf.* above, page 109.

of his British predecessors, to the general effect that such conceptions and such information constitute the impassible limit of all possible human knowledge. . . . The unwelcome verdict which the student of the history of philosophy finds himself compelled to pass upon that line of British thought . . . is that it remains essentially at that stage which is illustrated by the pre-Socratic 'philosophers' of ancient Greece. The earliest of these thinkers directed their attention to the contemplation of the physical universe, and sought to invent and . . . demonstrate by experimental proof some descriptive theory concerning the process of the universe. . . . However heterogeneous and varied the world, in its contents, might at present appear, yet it was held that all things were but diverse modifications of one elementary material nature. . . .

"Then followed other, more reflective, philosophers (or incipient philosophers), who perceived that these physical inquiries concerning the processes of phenomena led to no conclusions concerning the nature of being, but the rather, that if the sensible conceptions on which they were founded were to be regarded as ultimate, human reason was landed in an inextricable maze of contradictions. (Compare, in modern times, Kant's 'Antinomies of Pure Reason,' echoed by Hamilton, and reëchoed by Spencer.) Then arose sophists like Protagoras, who affirmed that nevertheless sensible conceptions—*appearances*—were indeed ultimate and final for man, that beyond them knowledge could not pass, and that consequently the absolutely real and true was unknowable." However, "the parallelism with British philosophy . . . breaks off where Plato begins," and Morris in his final pages remarks that "true philosophy is catholic. It welcomes science as in truth its handmaid. It reveres religion, which is but the faithful love and service of the supreme object of philosophy's demonstrations. But it insists that things distinct shall not be identified with each other." [20] Would another Plato, in the British tradition, carry forward the parallel for another two millennia? Did the British Hegelians give any promise that they might meet the challenge? If Morris considered the possibility, he did not commit himself in print.

---

[20] *Op cit.*, pages 337, 340-2, 387.

CHAPTER ELEVEN

IDEALISTIC RECONSTRUCTION

GEORGE SYLVESTER MORRIS, in his effort to find an adequate intellectualization for his religious faith, was very representative of the devout thinkers in his own generation, as well as of those in the preceding one which had nurtured him. The world-wide development of science and the general technological advances of the nineteenth century had altered the mental outlook of all men in this period, far more than the average individual among them might have realized. While Scottish intuitionalism seemed to have saved the day for orthodoxy in the minds of many, the general revolution in intellectual realms was altogether too complete for the solution provided by Reid, Hamilton and their fellows of the spirit to prove more than a very temporary and limited one. Merle Curti, in his *The Growth of American Thought*,[1] describes the extraordinary scope of the new naturalistic secularism. Morris had received the direct impact of this through the work of such men as Hitchcock and Haven. Not only did the orthodox mind have to meet these new ideas—either by assimilating or combating them—but it also had to face a rather instinctive reaction, under the lush physical conditions of a pioneer country, against "the most repulsive form of Calvinism," as pointed out by Herbert Schneider

---

[1] New York, Harper, 1943, the chapter entitled "The Expanding Enlightenment."

in the special instance of John Fiske.[2] The Protestant Christian theism was, in the New World as in the Old, under attack from almost every possible direction.

Professor Lewis F. Stearns of Bangor Theological Seminary, biographer of Henry Boynton Smith, writes in reference to Smith's studies abroad through the three academic years of 1837–40 that rationalism, while showing "its utter insufficiency to meet the deeper needs of human souls"— so that "its dominion had been overthrown"—yet "still continued to exist and to exert a baneful influence in theology and religion." He goes on to indicate what he means by this, adding that "the meagre and superficial 'popular philosophy' underlying rationalism had given place to the great philosophical systems which followed each other in quick succession from Kant to Hegel. These —at least after Kant—were prevailingly pantheistic, and were dangerous to Christianity just in proportion to the friendliness of the guise in which they approached it. The dominant system was that of Hegel, which knew so well how to express itself in the phraseology of orthodoxy as almost to deceive the elect themselves." Stearns then explains that "a new and startling turn had been given to affairs when, three years before Smith's arrival, D. F. Strauss, a young *Privatdocent* at Tübingen, had published his 'Leben Jesu,' in which he denied the supernatural character of the Gospels, reduced their histories to myths, explained away their doctrines in accordance with the principles of the Hegelian 'Left,' and rejected the Christian view of the Saviour's person." This, Stearns adds, was before the rise to prominence of Baur and the so-called

---

[2] *A History of American Philosophy*, page 321.

"Tubingen School," although the former's work on the Pastoral Epistles had already appeared.[3]

Over and above all these things was the steady encroachment upon Protestant supremacy, within theistic realms themselves, by a Roman Catholicism which had been gaining strength ever since the counter reformation. Henry B. Smith—as quoted by Stearns—gives a typical churchman's estimate of this enemy within the fold. "The Roman Catholic system is the most comprehensive, subtle, self-consistent, flexible and inflexible polity which the mind of man ever wrought out for purposes of spiritual and temporal authority. . . . And its systematic power is rivaled only by its zeal, and its zeal is not greater than its adaptedness to almost all moods and classes of mind. It awes by its power those whom it cannot enchant by its flatteries; it is harmless to the submissive, meek to the inquiring, and intolerant to every adversary. It appeals to all the senses in its varied rites; it charms the understanding by the consistency of its system; and it subdues reason itself by its claim to infallibility. . . . Rome does not know how to reconcile Christianity with popular rights, nor reason with revelation. It cannot do this on the basis of its system. It has said something about these things, but it has not discussed them. It can enforce duties, but it cannot recognize rights. It does not know man as man. Nor does it know, nor is it able to satisfy, the highest spiritual wants of man. It is not fitted to grapple with the great social problems of modern life." As a matter of fact—as Stearns reports—Smith was attracted to the Roman faith, but ultimately had

---

[3] *Henry Boynton Smith*, by Lewis F. Stearns, Boston, Houghton, Mifflin, 1893, pages 55-6.

turned in the general direction of Schleiermacher instead.[4]

Smith was one of many who encouraged the tendency to look abroad for the idea that might buttress the orthodox position. In the five years of his pastorate at West Amesbury, Massachusetts—1842-6—he made a number of translations from the German. "His own studies in German philosophy and theology had led him to believe that the German speculations on the subject were of value in giving these great doctrines a rational basis, and thus not only confirming them to the Christian, but recommending them to the cultivated thought of the age. While far from accepting the positions of Schleiermacher or of Hegel, he believed that both of these men had contributed something to the fuller understanding of these priceless truths."[5] Despite his broad philosophical orientation, Smith was unable to meet the real intellectual needs of the American generation of young men in attendance at Union Seminary in the 1860's—at least those of Morris' intellectual caliber—and now Morris himself was in not dissimilar difficulties, a generation later, as the instructor of the new youthful group comprising John Dewey, Joseph Jastrow and many others of high later significance in American philosophy and psychology at Johns Hopkins, i.e., unable to communicate a true theistic view and fervor.[6]

Morris began his mature thinking under the impact of these widely ramifying influences. He had acquired a new responsibility with the Johns Hopkins opening, and he found the intellectual world considerably changed from the general aspect familiar to him in 1874, when the Ueber-

---

[4] *Ibid.*, page 50.   [5] *Ibid.*, pages 88-9.
[6] However, *cf.*, above, pages, 157-8.

weg translation and the Trendelenburg article were completed. He was confronted now by a revivified Hegelianism, which had come forward to complement the Darwinian ferment and which comprised a fresh and highly alive body of secular thought. This philosophical climate of his Johns Hopkins and later Michigan years offered a marked contrast to the milieu at Dartmouth and Union Seminary, where he had encountered the earlier leaven of the German idealism. Here was an ideal philosophy which to a considerable extent had become characteristically British and American. In the New World there were any number of related and indigenous developments which sought to provide an adequate account of man's rational nature and powers, and to find a way for drawing the two realms of thought and fact—so sharply delimited in man's experience—into a functional unity which the mind could manipulate without dictation by things of the body.

The scientific speculation had marked an advance of understanding in the area of reality known primarily to the senses, but any acceptance of the limitations set up by an intellectual analysis which was held within these sensual boundaries would almost instinctively outrage man as a thinking animal, quite as much as the reverse flouting of sense-known values by a literal Calvinism. Morris' very full and complete expression of rational resentment against the empirical narrowness has been seen, throughout the preceding chapter, in his attack upon the very spirit of sensationalistic naturalism. Thus he remains an important figure in the American idealistic reaction which is coming to a real sense of itself in the eighties and nineties, and it must be realized that the stirring of which he was part was against both the superficial scientism of which Spencer had been an outstanding exponent and the wholly irrational spiritualism entrenched in the churches. Morris exhibited a better balance of interest in both sides of this coin of ethical relationships than most of the more academically conditioned or nontheologically inclined men with whom his efforts came to be linked, and his persisting concern over the problems of Christianity, in the light of this, will have further and detailed exposition in the following chapter.

As he took up his long desired role of professor in philosophy, he obviously sought to organize his materials with the same thoroughness that had characterized his development, a decade before, of the newly constituted department of modern languages at Michigan. The assault upon British empiricism had probably seemed the best means for providing his students with a proper intellectual orientation in American philosophy, since the sensational view was highly entrenched in academic psychology and science, and especially so at Johns Hopkins. This consideration —whether he took it into account consciously, or only instinctively—gives special point to his selection of the pre-Hegelian English thinkers for his first series of lectures and accompanying classes in the early months of 1880 at Baltimore. In the following February and March he gave a correspondingly comprehensive course of lectures and classes on the history of philosophy in Germany from Kant to Hegel. He included biographies of Leibnitz, Fichte and Schelling as well as the two major figures, and presented a comparative view of the theories developed by these philosophers in respect to knowledge, being, nature and man. He also gave attention to the philosophy to be found in German literature. In the previous half-year he had taught German esthetics and ethics in addition to the work on the British thinkers, and in this second season he taught the history of philosophy in general, together with ethics again, now including a seminar in Aristotle's ethics. In 1882 he offered classes in Greek philosophy and again in ethics, and gave a course in Kant's *Critique of Pure Reason*. This last course became the basis of his second book, with which the present chapter is most centrally concerned.[7]

Logic and psychology were now taught, respectively, by Charles Sanders Peirce and G. Stanley Hall, and there was additional undergraduate instruction given by Mr. B. E. Smith from Amherst College. The following academic year, or from September, 1882, through the spring of 1883, Morris presented, in addition to the history of philosophy in Great Britain and a seminar in selective texts from ancient and modern writings relative to the science of knowledge, a course in ethics "with especial reference to F. H. Bradley's *Ethical Studies* and Hegel's *Philosophy of History*." The latter item marks the appearance, in lecture and class form, of the material which constituted one of the two parts in his fourth and last book, or the translations and exposition of Hegel which he put out without critical comment. It is at this time that he repeated the Ely Lectures, given at Union Seminary in New York, as part of his Johns Hopkins program, and it is their substance which makes up his third book and comprises the theological analysis to which the following chapter is devoted. In the academic year 1883–4 he gave courses in both the historical

---

[7] Wenley, pages 144–6.

development of German thought and the general history of philosophy, as well as seminar instruction in Spinoza's ethics. The following and last year of his association with the Baltimore institution his classes were in the history of philosophy and Greek ethics, with new work offered on the philosophy of the state. The last named was his oral presentation of the other section of Hegelian material going into his fourth book. The appearance of the British Hegelians in the general picture here, through the use of Bradley's *Ethical Studies,* should not be overstressed, since there was also a seminar on Spinoza, whose system was not at all acceptable to Morris, and it has been seen that he did not hesitate to study writers who offered illustration for any of the points he was making, even through he might object to their philosophical stand. His organic point of view made him catholic in this respect.

Equally significant with these academic courses and general lectures, in indicating the developing thought of Morris, is his broad-scale attempt to bring the original materials or direct sources to American attention and to permit the various major philosophers to speak for themselves in an adequate translation or exposition. This at least was the expressed motive behind the Griggs series of published and projected books known under the general title, *German Philosophical Classics for English Readers and Students,* of which Morris was general editor. His volumes on Kant and Hegel were included, as was John Dewey's 1888 volume, *Leibnitz' New Essays Concerning the Human Understanding.*[8] In the prospectus for this series, which Wen-

---

[8] Written under Morris' influence while Dewey was associated with him on the Michigan staff.

ley suggests was "undoubtedly written by Morris," it is explained that "each volume will be devoted to the critical exposition of some one masterpiece belonging to the history of German philosophy. The aim in each case will be to furnish a clear and attractive statement of the special substance and purport of the original author's argument, to interpret and elucidate the same by reference to the historic and acknowledged results of philosophic inquiry, to give an independent estimate of merits and deficiencies, and especially to show, as occasion may require, in what way German thought contains the natural complement, or the much-needed corrective, of British speculation."

Thus Morris' intention was to present the German speculation critically, which he does in 1882—since the Kant volume definitely attempts a critical evaluation—but he was himself inconsistent in following out this policy since his Hegel text of five years later is without as much as a line that can be construed fairly as opinion or a personal estimation of the Hegelian system on Morris' part. Wenley says that "the short introduction does indeed defend Hegel's attitude towards ethics, but so succinctly that Morris leaves no place for his own views. The thorough mastery of Hegel's text and meaning makes one regret the more—especially when the date of publication is recalled —that he did not omit the *Philosophy of History,* in order to give fuller treatment to the *Philosophie des Rechts,* then misunderstood sadly in the English countries." [9] Wenley here fails to take into account the point made by Morris himself in an unused introduction which had been written for the Hegelian volume, and which has survived in both

---

[9] Wenley, pages 261, 282.

an original and a corrected draft.[10] The latter version consists of fifty-one pages of typescript, with additional re-
visions by hand and with various notes attached, probably
put aside before Morris had it ready for typesetting, and it
is included in the appendix of the present text as quite
possibly Morris' last appreciable statement of his philosophical view.

"Hegel's Philosophy of History," Morris writes in the
abandoned introduction, "may be termed a continuation
of his Philosophy of the State. . . . The political student
of Hegel, who should confine himself to the *Philosophie
des Rechts,* and neglect the *Philosophie der Geschichte,*
would miss our author's most luminous generalities respecting the universal nature of the state; while, on the
other hand, the historical student, who should confine
himself to the latter of the two works named and neglect
the former," would similarly miss Hegel's conception of
"the very elements of history." Thus the Hegelianism to
which Morris moves in the final formulation of his thinking is not the discipleship which even Wenley has rejected,
at least in principle. What Morris rather is to be seen
taking out of Hegel is the total integration of all the parts
in a universal totality. He is not presenting the letter of a
master's statement, such as the faithful can assimilate
piecemeal and apply entirely out of context. Morris says
of the German philosopher that the contribution of Hegel
at this point, like that of Aristotle, was that he "at once
gathered in and went beyond, or beneath, the results of
brilliant predecessors in political inquiry." The particular

---

[10] In the 'Michigan historical collection consisting of Wenley's source
materials.

type of organicism which characterizes Morris is perhaps
very happily illustrated by Hegel, but certainly not derived exclusively from Hegel's insights. It is given its expression rather than its limitation by the Hegelian development.

The circumstances which led to the preparation of the
shorter introduction found in the published volume, with
the resulting complete absence of any critical approach
such as Morris had promised for each of these German
classics—and had given in the Kantian exposition—are
simply unknown. The preservation of the more critical
introductory remarks is fortuitous because they show that
Morris towards the end of 1886 was not deviating in any
way from the general trend of his thinking throughout
this decade, thus ruling out any assumption that he was
presenting the Hegelian text as a gospel which needed no
evaluation or that, contrariwise, he was here an entirely
impersonal editor without real sympathy for the contents
of his pages. Since he was no actual disciple, in the sense
that he would be content to accept and to pass on what he
believed worked out by another and greater thinker than
himself, his own thought was probably marked by a continual process of refinement through the years, and there
is evidence for the truth of this to the very end of his
career, as in the unsigned comment of Dr. B. F. Burt just
after the death of Morris in the biweekly organ of the
students at Michigan. "The present writer, it should be
said, is fully aware that the published writings do not contain all of their author's best and most fully elaborated
philosophical opinions." [11] Morris was ever growing, and

---

[11] Wenley, page 284.

this was evident to his students and his faculty associates.

Here is the essence of dynamic idealism, or of the genuine voluntarism which is never completion in the form of a staticism at any point in reality, but instead is always an eternal beginning or the spirit of inquiry, investigation, experiment, and so on. In almost the last of Morris' published writings, an essay on "The Philosophy of the State and of History,"[12] he gives another clue to his own species of Hegelianism when he says that "history is not simply (multifarious) events. It is the logic of events. Historic intelligence is not merely information respecting events. It is the comprehension of their logic." Here is no recognition of an absolute off in rational realms somewhere—such as dictates an inevitable course for things—but merely the realization that man no less than God is immanent in his world. Thus "philosophy demonstrates that the essential and all-determining nature of intelligence is to be self-conscious reason. And it also demonstrates that true self-consciousness is something that transcends the individual, being realized only through the 'objective' consciousness and progressive knowledge of the whole universe of dependent existence, and in organic dependence on an universal and absolute self-consciousness." The Hegelian absolute is pictured here, obviously enough, but in no respect as abstracted from life or made inaccessible to the particular person. Organism, not mechanism, is the key to Morris' concept.

Morris then continues with a frank description of his own intellectual opportunism. "If the philosophy that one

---

[12] Written for the volume *Methods of Teaching History* in G. Stanley Hall's *Pedagogical Library*, Boston, Heath, 1886.

have, or that one find current, be unfortunately one-sided, abstract and inhospitable toward certain sides of that whole world of actuality, which it is the sole business of philosophy to comprehend, yet one must accept it, and apply it as far as it will go, and so make the best of it." He is discussing the pertinency of principles learned from empirical investigation, in their application to the more idealistic realms of experience, and implicitly if not actually he is affirming that all nature has a continuity and that either sense or thought has light to throw upon the other mode of experiencing. "The relative truth, and, within its peculiar bounds, the important truth of the mechanical philosophy in its application to the moral world, which includes the world of history . . ." should be "fully recognized. No one can shut his eyes to the mechanical aspect which belongs to all events, whatsoever, that occur within the bounds and under the forms of space and time, including, therefore, the events of history. But the eye of really concrete, catholic, and all-embracing philosophic science, sees that the mechanical aspect of events is only an aspect." [13] The sense world of time and space is not the whole of reality, nor is it wholly excluded from the real. It is participant in the ideal, which in turn is immanent throughout its extensiveness in both extension and duration. Here is the highly organic species of idealistic reconstruction with which Morris is concerned, and which he now designates as Hegelian.

To Morris, apparently, the fundamental tenet of Hegelianism, that the real is the rational, did not have to be

------

[13] Op. cit., pages 150, 154, 157.

interpreted either in pantheistic fashion—that is, as the nonexperienced immanence of spirit in all things—or in an overliteral sort of speculative logic which would suggest so complete an assimilation of nature into mind that all individual experience again would be denied reality. Both these intellectual conclusions would prove as unsatisfactory as the thoroughgoing subjective idealism of Berkeley, whom Morris had adjudged the "truest" of Britain's philosophers, and Morris had only come to find his own way in the midst of the idealistic self-contradictions by a rather long process of rethinking his convictions. Thus, in the summer immediately following the publication of his book on the British thinkers, he read a paper at the Concord Summer School of Philosophy and Literature,[14] and this was published under the title "Kant's Transcendental Deduction of Categories."[15] Here Morris approaches the problem of mechanism. The categories—whether in Aristotle, Kant or Hegel—are the ultimate synthetic capacity of thought. As an agency for the reduction of all things to unity in a single pertinent real on the side of mind—which is the function of any category in logical analysis—they attempt to chart the derivation of all manifold existence from a single source, and merely describe a mechanical process which is empirically conceived and which transforms idealism into materialism in a very literal fashion. Always sensitive to the consequences of this, Morris now sees, as the first problem in idealistic reconstruction, a necessity to turn away from the genetic or

---

[14] A project of considerable significance in the idealistic recrudescence. Cf. Schneider, A History of American Philosophy, pages 289, 456–7.
[15] Journal of Speculative Philosophy, Vol. XV, Number 3, dated July, 1881, pages 253–74.

essentially mechanical approach of rational schematism. Hence he writes that a "determinate knowledge of phenomena in time and space" is possible if the categories are *a priori,* or are the universal and necessary syntheses, or synthetic conceptions, of understanding. Kant's delimitation of durational and spatial boundaries in the world is a contribution of the reason as the representative of order in the universe, but at the same time these boundaries have universality and necessity because they can be generalized out of experience. Morris asks by what right this latter or nonexperimental factor, which originates in the reason through generalization, enters into the experimental realm known to empirical observation, and answers that on no other conceivable condition can the former or rational component enter into the experience of knowledge. The mind cannot come into the relations of objective being without bringing something of itself along with itself. The *tabula rasa* cannot make a contribution out of its nothingness. If the characteristic act of material reality is experiment—Morris' term in this paper for nonrational experience—then the activity of reason must have a corresponding character of ideality which, in any pragmatic view, is the organic phase of experience. "Just, therefore, as mind, working under the guise of imagination, creates in space and time the fixed form and condition or the only intelligible element of sense, so, working under the guise of understanding or intellect, it creates like form and condition, or the truly intelligible element in experimental knowledge—the element by virtue of which it is indeed knowledge."

This is knowledge framed in wholes, or absolute in its

essential ideality, and in consequence quite distinct from the mechanical conception of aggregation, combination and other sequential phenomena of time and space. "The understanding is thus the 'author of experience' and of its objects, in any sense in which these latter are intelligible, are real objects for us. It is thus the author of 'nature, regarded as the sum of all phenomena,' and prescribes to it *a priori* its universal and necessary if not its particular laws; it prescribes to nature the laws to which all its special laws must conform." This organic reality of the idealist is consciousness. An organism by its ideal nature is self-centered, however much its self may assimilate to other self or entertain the assimilation of other self—that is, it is not either exteriorly dependent or in itself a combination of components on the analogy of the discrete objects known to empirical sensation—and therefore Morris points out that Kant was correct in his criticism of Hume's atomism. All consciousness "thus expressed is pure self-consciousness" or is a unity which is "present in and comprehends all other consciousness." There is always a thinker. The "I" always originates in the pure "spontaneity" of mind because the ego is an activity, not a kind of static or fragmented material entity to be identified apart from its function and so reduced to one of its own objects. Kant's reaction to an atomistic naïveté is expressed through a presupposition of *a priori* necessities in understanding, so that "all combination of ideas or of their elements in unities, in wholes, or in 'objects,' is, then a work of the understanding . . . and *a priori.*"

Idealism is in no respects solipsistic when it makes knowledge and existence identical, or takes them as organic and a phenomenon of consciousness, since each man sees the world and knows his fellows through himself. The point, however, is that this is not a mechanical relationship, conditioned by time and space. Morris asks, "On what condition, then, is sensible experience, and the knowledge thus derived, of what we call nature possible? Or, on what condition is 'pure physical science' possible?" And he replies, "It is that our consciousness of nature be, at least in form, strictly a consciousness of self—a *self*-consciousness— or necessarily involved in and determined by that combining activity of the understanding, whose highest and original and essential and universal potency is manifested in the realization of self-consciousness." Man's consciousness, however, is not so much self-aware as object-aware, on the practical plane of everyday experience. "Our ideas of natural objects are considered with reference to their matter and not to their form, sensuous perceptions, containing multitudinous elemental impressions of phenomena in space and time. When the understanding combines them, it exercises what, logically described, is an act or function of judgment. Through this act it puts that perception in one of those determinate but universally synthetic forms which it must have in order to become a part of real consciousness. These forms are, as we have already seen, nothing but forms of synthesis, or combinations and relations, in space and time, wrought by the imagination under the determining influence of the understanding."

This ordering ideality, unless it is to be given a mechanical functioning and an analogy to the empirical world, has a life of its own, hence both Hume and Kant were perfectly correct in seeing that consciousness or mind, in its ultimate or ideal and organic nature, cannot be deduced from material existence. Morris remarks, "We do not perceive substances: we only conceive them." Everything in mind is a phenomenon of mind, however representative this may be of something physical or tangible in any other fashion. The transcendental deduction of categories is actually an impossibility, if by the phrase is meant that the material universe is a proof and demonstration of the immaterial one. In the same way that the British failed in their attempt to show that the mental side of life was a mere reflection of the sensational, so the Germans have failed to show, contrariwise, that the sensational is the proof and demonstration of the other. "The notion of a causal relation as existing between successive phenomena, or between successive aspects of the same phenomenon, is the result, not of our perception, but of our conception." Kant had accomplished much in the way of demonstrating the nature and conditions of physical knowledge, but "his assumption that such also are the nature and conditions of all real knowledge, or of all knowledge of reality, is purely dogmatic, and hence a delusion and a snare, as well as a source of needless confusion." It is only when "the apparent opposition in nature between subject and object" is resolved through their "organic identity" in consciousness that philosophy begins to emerge in its "brighter and truer light." [16]

Another paper was published the following spring in the *Princeton Review* under the title "Philosophy and Its Specific Problems," [17] and Morris restates his familiar

---

[16] *Op. cit.*, pages 254-5, 259, 260-4, 266, 268.
[17] March, 1882, Vol. IX, pages 208-32.

256   GEORGE SYLVESTER MORRIS

thesis in his opening remarks. "There lies before me a work just published in German, the object of which is, like that of Mr. Spencer's 'Data of Ethics,' to build up a 'Rational Ethics' on the basis of the truths of biology. The belief that such a construction is not only possible, but is really possible on no other basis, implies, by a deduction the terms of which may here be omitted, a conviction that no real, exact, unadulterated knowledge exists or can exist for man except in the form of physical science, and that, accordingly, no object of knowledge is accessible to human faculties, except such as physical science can grasp." Hence Morris feels it necessary to redefine the idealist position, explaining that "to knowledge in its most absolute, universal, and final form for man the name philosophy is commonly given in European languages. As matter of historic fact, philosophy in its grandest and most influential forms has not been a thing identical with physical science. The belief above ascribed to the author in question is tantamount to the belief that philosophy, in the true sense of the term, and physical science are nevertheless *per se* identical. This persuasion is expressly enunciated by him in the introduction to his work. It is well known that physical science, as such, is the science of things sensibly observable. There is no physical science that does not 'depend on sensible perception and observation.' Our author now declares that all knowledge whatsoever is dependent upon the same characteristic conditions, and, moved by the conviction, adds: 'It will be the task of a new generation to study philosophy not simply with the aid of the physical sciences, but through and in them alone—in short, to resolve philosophy into physical science.' "

Here are views which Morris feels would "strike one who is acquainted with the history of British speculation in its most conspicuous movements as anything but novel. The rather they will seem like the reappearance of 'old, familiar faces.' " However, the notion that the "redistribution of matter and motion" offers a "final explanation of all that man knows or can know" provides what Morris terms the "spur of denial," and so what he thinks has been the goad to "every historic instance of high philosophic achievement" since it has led the human mind "to the rescue of its most sacred and substantial, i.e., its ideal, possessions." As for Kant, his *Critique of Pure Reason* was "simply a re-examination of the traditional British theory of sensible consciousness," although it had "the result of showing that all consciousness is not merely sensible, but also intelligible." However, Kant 'went only half way in his exploration of conscious experience. Under the influence of early prejudice he was led to treat intelligence only as a logical or formal aspect of sense, which latter was held to be the dominant factor in consciousness and alone the determining factor of real knowledge." Thus Morris believes that Kant had taken over a mechanical view from Hume while attempting to refute Hume's skepticism, and that this was quite as one-sided as the British empiricism from which it sought to separate itself.

Thereupon Morris makes the distinction which—on Wenley's hypothesis—would mark Morris' own breaking into the "brighter and truer light." [18] Kant's successors, Morris writes, "demonstrated, not by far-fetched, roundabout ways of indirect 'proof' or of merely plausible but

[18] Wenley, page 259.

fanciful hypothesis, but by a more complete and unprejudiced scientific examination of the facts of the case itself,
that sense is the rather only an aspect of intelligence; that
intelligence, further, is not merely subjective, a purely
formal mechanism of the intellect, but is also objective,
and stretches out spiritual arms to embrace, not the dark
phantom of the 'unknowable' or of the inaccessible, because non-sensible, *Ding-an-sich,* but an intelligible, rational, self-illuminating, and self-explaining world of living, present, and effective reality." This is the concept of an
organic consciousness which was brought out by Morris
in his paper on Kant's categories, read to the Concord
School of Philosophy the previous summer, and as it now
takes form in his own characteristic and special emphasis
on a whole experience, a thoroughgoing organicism. Much
as psychologists in modern times are increasingly prone to
accept the fact that every part of an organism makes at least
some minor move or co-operative adjustment whenever
any other part acts or reacts in its environment, so Morris,
in perhaps a species of anticipation, held that when man
did something the world also was active in direct concord
with him, and that by the same token the world itself
was only an actor in and through the individual human
being or other discriminated parts of itself in action. This
was an idealistic development on and beyond the original
Kantian criticism, or Morris' own version of the idealistic
reconstruction on which the British Hegelians were engaged.

The second critical contribution of major compass by
Morris is represented by his volume *Kant's Critique of*

Pure Reason, A Critical Exposition.[19] This complements his work on the British thinkers, and rounds out his philosophical formulation as far as it was completed on the logical and epistemological side. Again the new Hegelian orientation goes unmentioned. Once more the analysis is supported out of normal human experience and the general philosophical tradition. Despite Wenley's identification of a final trend in Morris, believing it to have a beginning here, the influence of Trendelenburg is as marked as ever, not only in the approach through social interaction and an essentially historical evaluation, but particularly in Morris' keen sensitiveness to the problems of language, that is, to the fact that scientific knowing must always be grounded in logically consistent definitions. His prefatory remarks draw special attention to the verbal impasse he faced in his task of interpretation. "To the special student of Kant, the difficulties which must attend the attempt to furnish a summary account of the 'special substance and purport' of the 'Critique of Pure Reason' are well known. Not the least of these difficulties arises from the circumstance that Kant's work marks and conspicuously illustrates a stadium of transition in the history of modern thought. It is far more eminently the story of a process of inquiry and demonstration than a didactic exposition of finished results. And with reference to this process the *terminus a quo* and the *terminus ad quem* are widely different." Thus to discuss Kant as in line after Hume, and in reference to the sterility of the empirical position, is one matter, and to approach him in the light of the idealistic reconstruction is quite another.

---

[19] Chicago, Griggs, 1882.

"Hence, as the inquiry proceeds," Morris explains, "words and phrases acquire, and have attached to them, new meanings. This produces an air of variability and uncertainty in the use of words, which Kant, owing, doubtless, in part, to the haste with which his work was written, has not taken care to reduce to a minimum. Add to this the fact that Kant's intellectual attitude, in some of its most essential aspects, remains, to the end, thoroughly confused, and the reader will have some conception of the hindrances which lie in the way of an attempt to produce a 'clear and attractive statement' of what Kant has to say." This situation called for some sort of positive affirmation on which a critical analysis could build, and so Morris proceeds, in the introduction, to give a reasoned statement of his own views in an essentially Aristotelian vein. "All science involves two elements: knowledge of the particular, and knowledge of the universal. A particular fact is not scientifically known until it has been classified with some other fact or facts. This means that it is not an object of scientific knowledge until there is discovered something—a nature or law—which is common to it and to other facts. And that which is thus common to all is the so-called 'universal.' It is the universal quality, or mode of existence, or of activity, of the class of facts or objects in question."

Morris' approach is consistently experiential as he goes on to say, "Now, it is peculiar to all objects of knowledge that, in some form or other, they exist. To all of them Being of some kind is ascribed. This is their universal predicate. The peculiar object of philosophic science is the determination of the meaning of this predicate. What do we mean when we say that an object of knowledge *is*, that the universe *is,* that man *is?* What is it to *be? What is?* What is the universal nature of existence? And if there are more *kinds* of being than one, what is that universal kind which includes and explains them all? Such are the first and cardinal inquiries of philosophy, which, accordingly, was with perfect accuracy defined by Aristotle, more than two thousand years ago, as the 'Science of Being as such.' " Reason can begin properly, in other words, because the mind starts with the postulate which lies at the root of experience. Morris could observe, "That the results of such a science—far from being as is often thoughtlessly supposed, merely 'speculative,' and so unpractical and useless—are of the highest consequence, both for the universal enlightenment of intelligence and for the direction of conduct, becomes upon reflection perfectly obvious. A science so universal in its range as philosophy, by its definition, is, must contribute something to our comprehension of every object of knowledge; and inasmuch as conduct depends on knowledge, it cannot be without its powerful influence upon the practical direction of human affairs."

Philosophy thus charts the universal predicates by which man shapes his culture. Man's rational orientation is the key to his individual interaction with society at large. "Philosophy is the Science of Being. But Being, or the Universe of Reality, is given only in the realm of experience. The Science of Being can therefore be studied only through study of the content of experience. And thus it is studied. Philosophy does not transcend, nor pretend to transcend, the range of experience. And if 'philosophies' have differed in their ostensible results, this has been only because their respective advocates have found, or thought they found, some more, others less, contained in experience." Here is the crux of Kant. Morris goes on to explain that "it is only by a figure that experience can be likened to a vessel, which 'contains' objects or the knowledge of objects. At all events, the relation between experience and its so-called contents is not purely mechanical and accidental, so that the nature of the latter may be studied apart from the former. No, the 'study of the content of experience,' considered absolutely, cannot be carried on without experience itself. Now, experience is nothing other than our real or implicit knowledge, or our real or implicit consciousness. It results, therefore, that the Science of Being and the Science of Knowledge are organically one and inseparable. The study of the one can be prosecuted only through, in, and along with, the study of the other. The recognition of this fact is of capital importance for him who would understand the peculiar nature of philosophy's problems, and comprehend the historic methods and results of philosophic inquiry."

Morris then outlines the development of the new Hegelianism in considerable detail, by a resort to historical perspective, and in passing gives a real insight into the flow of his earlier into his later thinking. "The interdependence of these two, ideally, but not really, distinguishable sciences is illustrated in the whole history of philosophy, and contains the key to the explanation of the apparently conflicting results of philosophic investigation. The germs of the science of knowledge lay scattered—in no great profusion, it is true—in the pre-Socratic 'philosophy' of Greece. Such as they were, they furnished the impulse for that intellectual movement which resulted in the classic philosophy of Greece—the philosophy of Plato and Aristotle. Plato's 'theory of Ideas' is at once science of Knowledge and, through and in it, of Being. The philosophy of Aristotle has its real strength in his science of Knowledge. The great merit of the modern German movement in philosophy, from Kant to Hegel, lay in the new development which it gave to the same science. It was through this science that the final leaders in this movement rehabilitated the science of Being. It was through it that, in the language of a recent German writer, these men rescued the modern mind from the barren heath of purely arbitrary reflection and subjective uncertainty, and brought it back to the green pasture of objective reality, restoring us to rich and concrete knowledge of ourselves and of the world."

The logical approach of Trendelenburg is evident as Morris continues. "The impulse to the modern movement was the same in kind with that which brought forth the ancient one. It consisted in the intense cultivation, on the part of earlier 'philosophers' (Locke, etc.), of certain rootlets, or first beginnings, of the science of Knowledge, with results which were so far from corresponding with human knowledge, or experience, in its actual organic wholeness that they contained a direct challenge to further and more complete inquiry. Outside of the two historic movements of philosophic inquiry which culminated with Aristotle and Hegel, it can hardly be said that the science of Knowledge, organically one with, and absolutely inseparable from, the science of Being, or from philosophy proper, has ever been investigated in such a way as to take complete account of all the elements of the problem as presented in conscious experience. It is certainly true to say that, independently of these two movements and of their influence, the problem in question has never been thus investigated. And it is also true that the result of the modern investigation was confirmatory of the result of the ancient one, but enriched with fuller detail and more copious demonstration."

The psychological orientation of philosophy is highly characteristic of Morris, and is marked as he proceeds to affirm that "the science of knowledge is the key to the science of Being, and the different conceptions respecting the nature of Being, or of absolute Reality, which have been propounded in the guise of philosophy, all result from different conceptions respecting the nature of knowledge. The different views which have been held respecting the nature of knowledge are simply so many views respecting the nature, conditions and range of experience. Further, these differences of view are—if the expression may be allowed—rather differences of more and less, than of contradiction. Knowledge is a complex process, and the different views held concerning it result from the circumstance that some look only at one or two sides of the process, while others—the true philosophers—look at all sides. The former, of course, see in knowledge or experience less, the latter more. Those who see the more see also and recognize the less. There is here no contradiction. Apparent contradiction arises only when those who see only the less declare that the less is all, and so deny the more. Such contradiction, however, is purely dogmatic, and does not arise from the nature of the case itself which is under examination. In other words, the positive, scientific results of inquiry are not contradictory, but complementary."

In explaining what he means by "scientific examination," Morris centers the whole problem in psychological or epistemological criteria. "Knowledge is a conscious process. The question is, What is the nature and true description of this process? and what are the terms or factors involved in the process?" Answering, he goes on to establish another fundamental of his own idealistic position. "The process of knowledge most obviously involves the distinction of two factors, termed subject and object. It is in these factors that Being inheres. The process into which they enter is, in its results, knowledge (knowing) consciousness, experience. What is the relation between the factors as involved in this process? This may be termed the fundamental question, or problem, of the *science of knowledge*. Upon the answer given to this question depends the answer which must follow the further inquiry. What is the nature of the factors themselves?" Mechanism by its manner of functioning cannot be the author of itself, and so Morris asks, "Where in this result are the factors which produced it? They are not contained in the product, but are left behind or without it. By virtue of the very nature of the terms in which they were conceived, and of the relation posited as existing between them, it is impossible that this should be otherwise."

The sensationalist must justify a "practical belief" in these factors external to experience, as Morris is quick to see, although "the belief is confessedly opposed to the results of his theory, and so strictly 'unscientific.' Still, as it cannot be got rid of, it must somehow be made at least to *seem* rational. And thus the need of a new 'science' is made to appear—a science called 'metaphysics,' whose 'great problem' is to prove the 'existence' of something which lies wholly without the range of experience, as 'scientifically' defined, namely, the 'existence of the external world.' Observe, now, that this problem is an artificial one, created by and resulting only from the negative results of a highly artificial and incomplete theory of knowledge. For a broader and complete science of knowledge, or of conscious experience, this problem does not exist. What is called the 'external world' already exists and is given in man's (not merely *sensible*) experience, and the problem of philosophy, or of the Science of Being, in this regard is not to 'prove' its existence, but to comprehend it as it exists. The 'metaphysical' problem, which sensationalism thus creates for itself, is of course really insoluble on the basis of the sensational theory of knowledge. And so the 'metaphysics,' which seeks to solve the problem, can really only consist in covering it up with a cloud of meaningless words and hair-splitting, but wholly nugatory, distinctions." Once more Morris has affirmed his basic disinterest in a merely metaphysical ontology.

Morris then raises "the first and main question," asking if it is "experimentally true that the sole relation between subject and object in knowledge is a mechanical one; and, if not, what other relation do the facts disclose? What are the facts? The facts are that subject and object are distinguished within consciousness, or knowledge, and not simply outside of it. This means that, while numerically different, they are, in some real and effective sense, one. And this, again, means—'discloses,' demonstrates, shows—

that the relation between them is not simply mechanical. Things which are only mechanically different can in no real sense be one. They can at most be one only in the sense in which we say that stones thrown together form one heap, or aggregate, of stones. But this unity, the unity of mere aggregation, is not of the kind which is revealed in conscious knowledge. Subject and object are not indifferent to each other. It is not pure matter of accident whether they come together or not. The rather, they are inseparable from each other. Each implies and is most intimately one with the other. The object becomes object only as it becomes a part of the subject—all consciousness is *self*-consciousness. On the other hand, the subject becomes subject only as it merges itself in its object—all consciousness is objective consciousness. These *facts* of conscious experience cannot, without contradiction, be stated in terms of mere mechanism, or conceived with the aid of its categories alone." This is Hegel's contribution, the realization that genuine contradiction implies a connection and not a disjunction, and that the resulting unity is the result of an organic reality implicit in the discrete terms.

Morris has rejected an ontological Hegel in the sixties only to embrace a rediscovered and epistemological Hegel in the eighties, and this is the synthesis of his rational consistency implicit in his thinking at the beginning. Hence he is able to point out, through the ordering provided by his own experience, that "the 'steps' which Kant, Fichte, Schelling and Hegel took, mark a progress. . . . It is perfectly true to say that Hegel is the true interpreter of Kant, and that the cry now prevalent in philosophical circles, 'back to Kant,' means and can only mean, when logically

interpreted, 'back also to Kant's successors.' " For Morris
this is the expansion of Trendelenburg in the new Hegelianism, but is not a matter of changing masters. "Because
one recognizes and insists upon what a given philosopher,
or set of philosophers, has positively achieved, it does not
therefore follow that one must have a partisan's blindness
to all the possible defects or incompletenesses of the
achievement, or to the possibly erroneous inferences
which the philosophers themselves, or their admirers, may
have drawn from their achievement." And so he summarizes what, in the newer view, better expresses his original insight. "The relation between subject and object is
. . . a relation which can only be called organic, or the relation of particular to particular through the organic
identity of both in the universal."

Morris completes his Introduction to the Kant volume
with a terminal outline of his general view as a philosopher, written at the high tide of his intellectual ministry
at Johns Hopkins University. "Philosophy has, with reference to physical science, nothing to do but to acknowledge
and confirm the justness of her results, as far as they go.
But she supplements them by showing what they mean.
She shows that sensible phenomena point to and *manifest*
a reality which is within, and not without, experience.
The physical or so-called material universe is real—real
not only in the abstract and ontologically shadowy sense
in which physical science, or the 'philosophy' reared in its
name, depicts it, but in a concreter and more vital sense.
It is real, not simply as the subjective conscious product
of assumed forces, but as the objective scene of the action
of real forces, which, being true *forces,* are of spiritual

origin, subject to laws of perfect purpose, and consequently of invariable order, and which work together for the production, not simply of 'one far-off divine event,' but of myriads of present and ever-continuing divine events. The whole truth, such as it is, of materialism is not only recognized by philosophy; it is also explained, and that, too, in agreement with the essential nature of human experience. But the characteristic side of human experience is not materialistic, mechanical, sensible. Man has a life, and this his characteristic life, in religion, art, society, and even in communion with and mastery of nature herself."

Ever the evangelistic voluntarist, Morris affirms that man's experience in all these relations "confirms and is explicable only by that organic-spiritual theory of experience which results from the completed science of knowledge, and which philosophy adopts. In all of them the individual, while retaining all his individuality, is yet organically one with a larger life, which imparts to his own individual life its true substance, giving it a fixed and inspiring purpose, and a character founded in the universal, the abiding, the true. . . . The fundamental relation in all conscious experience is a relation of members which are in organic unity, which exists only as terms of a living process, in and through each other, or in and through a universal, a *power* and life of spirit, which (as God) indeed transcends them both, but still does not exclude them; the rather, in agreement with its essential nature as Love, includes them in its own embrace, and so gives light and being to everything that 'cometh into the world.' Such, in general and all too vague outline, is the only ontology known to philosophy. It is the only ontology which has in its positive, nay, universal and all-comprehensive substance, being founded on the whole of experience and mutilating or cutting off no members thereof. It alone makes the universe to be, for intelligence, not merely a universe of brute fact, (and so in truth not a universe for intelligence!) but of overflowing meaning and of absolute, because spiritual, and so effective and self-illuminating, reality. And of such order is the truth demonstrated in the classic philosophy of Greece, and in German philosophy from Leibnitz and Kant to Hegel." [20]

---

[20] *Op. cit.*, pages 1–28.

CHAPTER TWELVE

THE THEISTIC CULMINATION

THE Ely Lectures on the relation of philosophy to Christianity, delivered by Morris in 1883, are criticized by Wenley in terms which provide an excellent summary of the *Weltanschauung* with which Morris' thought has culminated. Wenley holds that Morris, thanks in Wenley's view to inhibitions surviving from the New England background, had failed to "go more than a mile with an adequate metaphysic"—i.e., to accept a genetic ontology such as Wenley's own nonvoluntaristic Hegelianism—but yet had gone "all the way with an adequate view of religion," so that, in consequence, "moralism rears its head still, as if current convictions in conduct were the sole pathway to heaven. Individualism still has its say, as if *the* ideal could not be realized except on the plan native to New England. The appeal to coercive emotion is still magistral, as if chosen objects or values, themselves characteristically temporal, could furnish all-sufficient predicates for the universal. In short, forgetting the paradox central to religion, in his anxiety to affirm Christian truth, Morris tends to take the kingdom of heaven by merit, little recking that, in the nature of the case, human 'perfection' is as filthy rags. Being too righteous, he is not religious enough. For, he would fain reduce his faith to a form of knowledge, if not to a species of activity." Here indeed, although stated in disapprobation, are the basic and positive ele-

271

ments in Morris, who consistently—from at least the time of his master thesis at Dartmouth nearly twenty years before—has held to the idea that the goal in human living is spiritualization. His appeal to the vital knowledge of Plato and his insistence on looking at all life and phenomena through an ethical perspective—giving him his moralizing dark glasses when it comes to literature—has already been discussed at some length in Chapter Six. His magistral address in many respects set the scene for the intellectual drama to which he devoted the rest of his life.

He is ever speaking and writing in a theological climate that has been outlined in the light of the widespread and increasing demand for an intellectualization, such as would meet the competition if not the direct or indirect attack of a rising secularism, and this rational need of his faith is unquestionably what Morris meant in his reference to the problems of Christianity on the morning of his first day in Europe, seventeen years before this return to Union Seminary as a guest speaker. The theistic conception of a personal deity is one which *ipso facto* calls for an immediateness of participation in any possible reality, holding that man enters completely into nature and that God flows fully into and through human individuality. The philosophical problem involved in this functional absolutism is one for which Morris has gained a measure of answer through the new Hegelian organicism. Wenley misses the point completely when he explains that Morris "in the stage at which he had now arrived . . . could never compass a consistent philosophy of religion," and then proceeds to add, finding an analogy in the transformer of an electrical power circuit, "it scarcely occurred to him that religious experience always 'steps down' the Absolute." [1] Contrariwise, it is against this very type of conception that Morris is most in rebellion. He would have said to Wenley that such a notion was entirely "mechanistic," that it assumed causal sequence as a metaphysic in a fashion wholly characteristic of materialistic thinking, and that it failed to take into account the nature of organism.

Before proceeding to a consideration of the Ely Lectures, as the most important single expression as well as climactic exposition by Morris of his own positive views, the general setting must be sketched in sufficiently to give any analysis a clear frame of reference. Three factors have to be taken into particular account, namely, the philosophical perspective which Morris has rather well refined for himself by this time, the personal acceptance and reconstruction of Hegel which determined the language he used for the communication of his ideas, and the theological situation which was reflected in the occasion of the lectures themselves. Turning first to the orientation in philosophy on the academic rather than religious side, what seems to lie at the foreground of Morris' thinking is his consistent stress on a species of whole knowledge. Thinking and being are identical, says the functional logician. Taken together, therefore, they are an activity of organism or wholesomeness which can only be known—in experience, or in language which of necessity arises out of experience—as spiritual, i.e., as involving a continuous immediate, a total of assimilation of the particular and the general in each other at any and all points of knowing. This is the spiritualistic idealism identified by Morris in his criticism of Kant,

---

[1] Wenley, pages 280–1.

or what subsequently has come to be known as voluntaristic or dynamic idealism.

Not the least of the enrichment in intellectual and educative opportunity which came to Morris at Johns Hopkins was through a discussion group known as the Metaphysical Club, conducted at first under the leadership of Charles Sanders Peirce and then, later, of Morris himself. Abstracts of the talks presented before this group were published in the *Johns Hopkins Circulars,* including three by Morris. He spoke on "English Deism and the Philosophy of Religion" in November, 1881, and pointed out that "religion subsists—if at all—only in the form of a relation between God as a *spirit* and man as a *spirit.* There will therefore be no philosophy, or absolute science, of religion, unless the functions of human thought are adapted to the cognition of *spiritual* objects and relations. As a matter of historic fact, it may be said that all philosophy proper, (opposed to agnostic negation of philosophy, on the one hand, and to pure dogmatism, on the other,) has consisted, whether in ancient or modern times, in the demonstration that all knowing is a spiritual activity; that it is a process, the subject of which is a spirit, and which implies, and, in the universe of Being, finds an object or objects cognate with the subject. On the basis of a truly philosophical and objective science of knowledge, therefore, a philosophy of religion seems to be, and is, indeed, possible. It is not possible on any other basis. For the want of such a basis, the movement known in history under the name of English Deism, was crowned with none but negative results. Its principal leaders took the commonplaces of their 'philosophy' from Locke, who saw in knowledge nothing but a mechanical relation between a subject and an object, both of which *per se* were unknowable. The final result of the Deistic movement was therefore necessarily, not knowledge, but scepticism. Or else God was imagined merely as an extramundane *Deus ex machina,* a mechanical 'first Cause,' between whom and man none but mechanical—i.e., non living, spiritual, and truly religious—relations could exist."

The organic view of the universe which is accepted by theism—and which ranges Morris on the Hegelian Extreme Right, in Wenley's analysis [2]—places man and God in continuous and intimate fellowship, and makes the destiny of the world in consequence dependent upon the success of both the human and divine mind in building the world into themselves. It is the theological parallel to the whole view of philosophy which Morris brought out in speaking before the Metaphysical Club a year later, in December, 1882. His title was "The Fundamental Conceptions of University and Philosophy" and, according to the abstract printed in the *Circulars,* "it was pointed out that the very conception of the University is a philosophical conception. This is suggested by the name University. The *Universitas literarum et scientiarum* is not merely mechanical aggregation of all 'letters and sciences,' each of which is to be treated as ideally complete in itself and to be prosecuted in total disregard of aught but itself. On the contrary, the phrase in question points to the truth that 'all letters and sciences' must be regarded as members of one organic whole, having, in spite of their specific differences, a common life and a common nature; so that no one

---

[2] Wenley, page 272.

of them can be truly or perfectly pursued—or, at all events, none of them can be pursued in the true 'University' spirit —unless such pursuit be accompanied by an appropriate knowledge of the whole, of which, rightly conceived, it is an organic living member. This, the necessary and essential conception of the University, is specifically a philosophical one. For philosophy is peculiarly the 'science of wholes.' It is, in particular, the science of the whole of experience, or of experience considered, subjectively, with reference to its whole or universal nature and, objectively, with reference to its whole or universal content." i.e., its illimitable potential of assimilation to itself in an organic universality.

Philosophy is this, "in its two inseparable parts, as Theory of Knowledge and Theory of Being, the Science of Sciences itself. Or, it is the science, whose subject-matter is all the sciences, considered, not separately, but as members of one living whole. Thus philosophy is—in the words which constitute the motto of the University of Kiel—the 'bond of sciences.' The relation thus recognized, between the University idea and the idea of philosophy, is recognized in Germany by the name 'Philosophical Faculty,' which is given to the general Faculty in all or most of the Universities. The relation being admitted, the necessary place of philosophy in the life and work of the University may at once be inferred. Philosophy represents the catholicity of science, as it was argued accordingly, that one of the special functions of philosophy in the University is to act as a liberalizing agency, anticipating and so preventing the confessedly illiberal and narrowing tendencies of extreme specialization. . . . The attempt was further made

to show the connection of philosophy with the promotion
of the more comprehensive and public aims of the University, which include the development of its members—along
with symmetrical and catholic culture—of intellectual
self-mastery, and the contribution to church and state, to
science, literature and religion, of leaders capable of recognizing the true ideals, of intelligently directing the nature's
energies to their accomplishment."

When Morris became head of the Department of Philosophy at Michigan, in January, 1885, he planned his
program with the same care he had exhibited twice before,
first in connection with modern languages at Ann Arbor
fourteen years earlier, and then with his philosophical instruction when he launched his full-scale schedule at Baltimore in the spring of 1880. What obviously would suggest
itself to him would be the formation of a discussion group,
such as had proved its value at Johns Hopkins, and so the
Philosophical Society of the University of Michigan was
organized, and given its blessing by Morris with an address
on "University Education." He quotes Plato's *Republic*
on what constitutes a real university—"the detached
sciences in which they were educated as children must be
brought within the compass of a single survey, to show
the co-relation which exists between them, and the nature
of real existence"—and interprets this synthetic ideal as
ethical and an approach to a personal knowing of world
wholeness as over against the recognition of atomistic and
fragmented components of an aggregate having no life of
its own, i.e., an approach quite contrary to that of secular
scientism. The philosophical faculty and its over-all view
of life, taken in contrast with law, medicine and theology

as specific preparation for the learned professions, is the true university idea, and this organic function of philosophy must be given proper attention to counteract the growing overemphasis of the special sciences in American educational institutions. The method of exact science keeps that description formal and superficial, and so what must not be lost to sight is "the essential unity of all truth" or the inclusion of "all sciences in that higher unity . . . in the knowledge and comprehension of which true science consists." [3]

Morris closes his Michigan talk on a religious note, a fact which is important as an indication that his theistic orientation has been consistent throughout the later and Hegelian period in his thinking, and also that his primary interest has remained centered, on the philosophical side, in a whole or organic knowledge. When he spoke some two years earlier before the Metaphysical Club at Johns Hopkins, on October 9, 1883, his subject was "The Philosophical Conception of Life," and it again is preserved in outline through the abstract in the *Circulars*. The Ely Lectures were given in this same year, so that a theological emphasis may be expected to predominate—with its special pointing to the goal of spiritualization for the individual—but the central interest is the same as in the other informal talks of the period, namely, the revelation of the real nature of each other by both man and nature, and the mutual contribution of their act-of-being to a whole or ideal existence. "The writer first briefly substantiated the view that all attempted explanations of life in terms of

---

[3] *University of Michigan Philosophical Papers*, Series 1, Ann Arbor, 1886, pages 1, 21, 25.

what is considered 'mere matter' and motion, or of mere 'force,' have always been and must ever remain fruitless, so far as it is a question of recognizing and demonstrating the characteristic and essential nature of life itself, and not simply the laws of certain of its sensible manifestations. Matter, motion, and force presuppose life; or, life is their logical and ontological *prius*, and is not, therefore, to be conceived as their mechanical product."

Morris then argues "(1) that all life is an activity. (2) This activity has in every case a definite and specific character, law or direction. It is typical, or conforms to a specific type, which is to it as its *idée directrice*. (3) The activity of life is thus teleological. The type, by which it is defined, is realized in and through the activity; it is the 'end,' in which the activity is completed. (4) The activity in question is thus also ideally determined, at least in form; and, what is more important to notice, the *form* of any, even the lowest, process of life is one of self-determination, or of self-realization; the type, the law, the idea, has the air of giving to itself its own concrete realization. It is this appearance of spontaneous, independent, and ideally directed activity, that gives to nature its true poetic charm for human intelligence; and it is indeed this, also, that renders nature, in the exact and complete sense of the expression, an intelligible object for man. (5) To the *form* of *self*-realization the proper corresponding *substance* is self-conscious will, or will permeated by, and organically one with, conscious intelligence. This, of which the life of nature, as above characterized, must be held to be prophetic, is found in man, who, in his character as a consciously self-determining and self-realizing spirit, is to be viewed as illustrating in greater fulness and completeness than any other created being known to man, the true and concrete nature of life. In all life that which truly lives and is, is something ideal, some truth—in the lower grades some law, idea or type—working itself out into reality, and sustaining itself therein, by an apparently independent and self-directed, active process. In man this 'something ideal,' this truth, has consciousness of itself, and its independence and self-direction subsist, or are to subsist, not only in form, but also in substance and in full reality."

Thus Morris affirms the living or organic nature of the universe in terms of the Hegelianism which he has adapted for himself. The abstract of his talk continues, explaining that "attention was then called to the fact that the truth, of which the higher life of man is to be the expression and (in its measure) the realization, is not merely single and particular, like the 'idea' of the tree, or of the human body. It is not simply some truth, some ideal, but the truth, the ideal, universally, that in some way and essential measure he must realize or actively share in, in order that he may lead the truer life of the spirit. Its center is therefore not in the individual, but outside of him; and it realizes and manifests itself, first of all, as an organizing principle of society—in family, in civil relations, in the state, and in the great movements of history—in and through which the spiritual personality of the individual lives and thrives, and separated from which, he would run the risk of speedy decay. But in none of these shapes does the truth manifest itself in an absolutely independent life. This life it must be held to lead in God, as Absolute spirit, in which, accordingly, all the dependent life of nature—

but especially the self-conscious life of the human spirit
—finds its true centre; so that the perfect life of man is
to know God, as the living Truth, and by doing his will,
('walking in the truth,') to share in his life." The center
is re-established in the self, as a self-activity, and the logical
circularity again is a certification of the ideal wholeness.

The personal or psychological set with which Morris
approached the Ely Lectures has been sketched in by
Wenley correctly enough—although obliquely and very
much out of Wenley's own presuppositions—as a "straining in the interests of faith." If Morris' contribution at
this climactic moment in his career is to be accepted as
representing "a transition stage in philosophy of religion,"
Wenley believes it to be then "in one sense . . . too theological, in another . . . not theological enough," because,
as Wenley's own thinking requires, the relation between
personality, as attributed to God, and the Absolute per se,
"is scarcely faced." Thus to Wenley, while "the personality
of God is strongly affirmed" by Morris, the divine person
yet remains a "pictorial declaration of the religious consciousness" or "an 'appearance' rather than the Reality."
There is neither the rationally unconditioned independence of individual experience which a full-blown absolutism requires for its presupposition regarding a discrete
integrity of thought, nor that complete immanence of the
divine in all being which—by the same point of view—is
the necessary form of any ultimate or totality from which
there can be no exception, that is, no mechanical separation in any possible identity or spiritualistic individuality.
Hence Morris "reposed too little confidence in the 'finite'
and, therefore, did not penetrate it sufficiently . . . in

short, he had not contrived to divest himself completely of Deistic influences and, to this extent, failed to come to close quarters with the methods of Theism." This misinterpretation of Morris' unswerving experientialism creates the illusion of a view on Morris' part which is incomplete only under the assumptions of a mechanistic Absolute. Wenley admits, however, that there is "no sort of vacillation" in Morris. In seeing a "drift towards speculative idealism," represented by the Hegelian organicism, Wenley also discerns what he terms "lapses" into the "ethical theism" which is what actually characterizes Morris throughout. Utterly unable to comprehend Morris' point of view, Wenley can recognize only a shading off into "intuitionalism, or mysticism, or an emotional theism, as the case may be." [4]

The Ely Lectures were delivered at Union Seminary, repeated at Johns Hopkins University and published as the third of Morris' books.[5] Morris must have been very pleased at the invitation coming to him to succeed J. W. Dawson, James McCosh, A. P. Peabody and Henry Calderwood as lecturer on this foundation. The deed of gift providing the funds had specified that "the course of lectures . . . is to comprise any topics that serve to establish the proposition that Christianity is a religion from God, or that it is the perfect and final form of religion for man," and suggested a number of subjects that might be discussed, such as "The Nature and Need of a Revelation" or "The Character and Influence of Christ and His Apostles" and ending up with the one selected by Morris, "The Phi-

---

[4] Wenley, pages 276–7.
[5] *Philosophy and Christianity*, New York, Robert Carter and Brothers, 1883.

losophy of Religion in its Relation to the Christian System." Wenley remarks that the Ely Lectures alone exhibit Morris "in a role other than that of a commentator," not only giving him full scope for the development of his own ideas but also facilitating the true climax of his philosophical contribution in the field of his greatest personal interest. Less than six years before his life would be cut short most unexpectedly, he was called on to give a complete account of his conclusions relative to the problems of Christianity. He had a free rein to present the evangelistic necessity which he saw laid upon the hearts of all men who had any intimation of the ways of God and the life of the spirit. He probably felt a challenge to give his voluntaristic leanings a spiritual instrumentation, and to stress, in formal religious exposition, the organic theism which had held him from his earliest student days and which now had come to have some degree of real philosophical description in the Hegelian concepts. Wenley could well remark that Morris "buckles to his task *con amore*." [6]

When Morris, in his opening remarks, says that the foundations of "the most sacred and purest interests of humanity"—i.e., religion and intelligence as the subject of his first lecture—are deeper and more impregnable than anything else, constituting the "rock of the ages," he is affirming his basic and naïve experientialism. When he goes on to say that both religion and intelligence rest on this foundation "in harmonious union and to the complete satisfaction of man's highest, spiritual and intellectual needs," he is stressing his concept of whole knowledge and giving full allegiance to his matured idealistic posi-

---

[6] Wenley, pages 145, 255, 270-1.

tion. But he then turns at once to logical and psychological considerations far more reminiscent of his earlier Trendelenburg than his more recent Hegel orientation. "First we note," he explains, "that religion, even if it should be held to involve, in itself, no function of intelligence—nay, even though it were regarded as involving the complete subjection or abrogation of intelligence in the religious subject —cannot withdraw itself from the liability of being made an object of intelligence, *i.e.*, of what is called intelligent or scientific inquiry and examination. To this liability it is subject in common with every other conceivable phase, phenomenon, or incident of the world of reality in which we are placed." Nothing can be withdrawn from experience, or function in some exclusive realm of ideality or spirit, and so become exempt from scientific inquiry.

The plain psychological fact is that "intelligence, thought, knowledge, consciousness, must have its object. This object may be intelligence itself, or anything whatever that enters within the realm of man's conscious knowledge or experience. Its relation to intelligence may be purely, or, at all events, predominantly mechanical, external, accidental. Objects in such relation are, for example, stocks and stones, in which, as first perceived, intelligence does not, in any especial degree, find itself reflected, or through the mere taking cognizance of which it does not find itself specially strengthened or built up. They are *there*, the intelligent subject is *here*—mechanically separate from and independent of them. They are viewed as casual, not necessary objects of his [man's] intelligence. He takes note of them and observes that they 'are there,' that they exist; perhaps, if he belong to a learned society or, for any other reason, be disposed to cultivate the scientific habit of mind, he enters into a more minute examination of them; he subjects them to the test of fire and of hammer, and, after taking copious notes of all that he observes, is ready to inform the world respecting the phenomena of stocks and stones. He has met the first requirement of intelligence respecting stocks and stones. He has ascertained and knows the immediate, sensibly demonstrable facts about them. But, I repeat, his relation to them is, so far, relatively and characteristically mechanical and accidental. Certain 'objects,' 'facts,' or 'phenomena' are brought—it may be either wholly fortuitously, or in consequence of a systematic intention on the part of the inquirer—within the range of his observation, and he simply observes and records the first and direct result of his observation."

Thus Morris has described the realm in which empiricism or secularism functions, and has sketched in the observational theory of knowledge in bare outline, in order to proceed beyond it. He continues, explaining, "Now, religion 'is there,' exists in history and among men, nations, and tribes at the present day. Nay, what are called 'religions' exist, with characteristic, visible marks of agreement or of disagreement among themselves. Upon them, as objects in purely mechanical relation to intelligence, the latter may fix its attention. It may do this in the same unbiased way, or with the same absolute freedom from presuppositions, with which it addresses itself to the analytic observation and description of rocks and trees. Looking at religion in its manifestations as one among the many different objects *presented to* intelligence, its first work will

be to take accurate note of all these manifestations, whatever they may be, whether existing in the form of myth
or fable, of sacred legend or story, of dogma or of practice,
of rites, ceremonies, etc. The result of all this praiseworthy
and indispensable industry will be what is called the
'Science of Religions.' From such mechanical relation to
intelligence, religion—or, rather, religion viewed with
reference to its visible or historic phenomena—cannot
withdraw itself."

Intelligence must move beyond the merely mechanistic
or materialistic stage, however, and hence "the aforemen-
tioned industry—an industry like that of the ant, being
devoted to the amassing and orderly arranging of multitudinous items of information respecting particular facts
or classes of facts—is only the beginning of, or, better, the
mere scaffolding for, the true and complete work of intelligence. It is the first step leading to complete or absolute
intelligence, or *comprehension;* but it is only that. I may,
for example know the names of all the classes, orders,
families, genera, species, or what not, of living existences
. . . and yet I may not know what life is. What I know is
precisely the special *modes,* the phenomena, of life, these
alone—but not *what* it is to *live.* The *essence* of life may
still be to me a profound mystery. . . . And so, too, with
regard to stocks and stones, I am far from having absolute
intelligence respecting them. . . . These objects have this
distinction, viz., that they *exist,* that they *are,* that they in
some way possess *being.* In what way or sense do they *exist?*
Wherein does their *being* consist? They are, by common
repute, material objects. But *what* is it to be material? Is
material existence absolute and independent existence? Is

there such a thing as absolute matter, wholly independent of and unrelated to spirit? Or is what we call material existence only a dependent function of Absolute Mind. . . . These are questions to which intelligence must find an answer . . . imposed upon intelligence by virtue of its own nature. And questions such as these, relating to absolute *essence* and *cause,* are precisely those which form the special subject-matter of *philosophy.*"

Religion is not only subject to examination by a scientific approach on the secular side—its objective manifestations measured and counted under a superficial observation —but "the science of *religions* must be followed by the philosophy of *religion.* After learning what are the phenomena of religion, intelligent man must ask, *What* is *religion?* Is it an hallucination, or a well-founded reality? Is it a mirage, or do those who breathe its atmosphere constitute the true city of God on earth? The question must and will be asked. Nay, it is asked, and has again and again been asked. Religion has been and is sure, over and over again, to be placed in the crucible of philosophic intelligence, and its votaries cannot with indifference look upon the result of this test. Shall this result be, in the language of a recent foreign writer,[7] that religion 'is nothing more nor less than a belief in conflict with experience, and resting on the most exaggerated fancies,' or that—in the words of him who may be regarded as the profoundest and most deeply experimental philosopher of modern times [8]— religion, in the territory of human consciousness, is 'that

---

[7] L. Oscar, *Die Religion zurückgeführt auf ihren Ursprung,* Basel, 1874, page 2.

[8] Hegel, *Vorlesungen uber die Philosophie der Religion, Werke,* Bd. XI, Berlin, 1840, page 3.

region, in which all riddles of the world are solved, all the contradictions of speculative thought are reconciled, all agonies of the feeling heart are allayed—the region of eternal truth, of eternal rest, of eternal peace?' If any doubt exists as to the answer which real philosophy, real intelligence, real and complete experimental inquiry, gives and must give to this question, this state of things cannot but be looked upon by religion with the greatest concern."

Thus Morris identifies religion with philosophy in a very complete sense, making it the whole view of experience which he has been developing in his own philosophical thought. He then turns to the rising agnosticism, but dismisses the entire attack of materialistic naturalism on conventional Christianity as one from which "religion may consider herself essentially safe. She may do this, because history has demonstrated that she is, with reference to such attack, invulnerable, and also because, in the matter of resistance to it, the cause of religion is, from the very nature of the case, identical with the cause of philosophy; and philosophy is, among other things, and first of all, the demonstrative, experimental refutation of Agnosticism." This statement, in the best spirit of Trendelenburg and Aristotle, prepares the way for his exposition of philosophy's nature and value in its historic perspective. He explains that, like religion, it has a "perennial existence. It exists as demonstrative and in the highest and most preeminent degree experimental science. Indeed, philosophy may well be defined, in distinction from all other sciences, as the science of experience as such." Here, in a one-sentence summary, is Morris' total doctrine. "It determines —finds out and declares—what is the absolute nature of experience, and what is that nature of being, of reality, which is given in and is organically one with experience." Hence the organic nature of the universe is experiential, or experimental in Morris' terminology. In logical delimitations this means the continual reconstruction of all reality, or the phase of Morris best developed by John Dewey, and ontologically or metaphysically it implies the continual assimilation of man and his world into each other as a continuing and living rather than a time-and-space-conditioned or mechanical being.

Morris then reaffirms his basic historical hypothesis. "Twice, in the history of occidental thought, has philosophic science reached its flood-tide, first in the classic philosophy of Greece, with Plato and Aristotle, and again in the now classic philosophy of Germany. *Results* were reached in both cases—not disparate and opposed, but confirming and complementing each other. How should this be otherwise?—since the subject-matter of inquiry, viz., the world of man's conscious experience, or what we call the world of reality, and the agent of inquiry, viz., human intelligence, were in both cases the same." This means that "the results of philosophic inquiry exist, then, and are embodied in literary monuments accessible to the world. These results, too, have been wrought or assimilated into the intellectual life-blood of the western world. . . . The classic philosophy of Greece was the intellectual rudder of a score of centuries. With its aid Christianity itself . . . first took its bearings in the world of intelligence, found and further made itself at home in this world, and so was the better able to commend itself successfully to a pagan world, waiting to receive its light. . . .

Nor has the positive substance of the classic philosophy of Greece, essentially, been displaced to-day—any more than Homer and Sophocles and Phidias have been displaced. Men no longer write Homeric epics, or Sophoclean dramas, nor do they longer seek to honor 'the gods' through new statues, of Phidian conception." The same situation holds in respect to "the fundamental philosophical conceptions of the Greek masters in philosophy, their conceptions respecting intelligence and respecting that nature of Being which alone intelligence can, must, and does recognize." It is not a succession of fragmented ideas that makes up philosophy, but a continuum of realization in which progress is a regathering of the better or more thoroughly demonstrated insights. To Morris philosophy is still the history of philosophy.

In consequence the "final result of that modern philosophic movement, beginning immediately with Kant, which has now become classic, was an essential reaffirmation of the best Greek conceptions respecting the universal, necessary, and eternal nature and content of human experience. But it was not mere reaffirmation, not mere verbal repetition. It was a new demonstration, the outcome of the labor of the modern mind through centuries of struggle. It was therefore peculiarly relative to the needs, the difficulties, and the peculiar lights of the modern world." Here is the social interaction of Morris, not a lapse into empirical utilitarianism. Hence he could say that it is "more complete than the ancient one" because of "the new light of experimental fact . . . owing to its possession of which modern philosophy was able, on the one hand, to correct and, on the other, to render more com-

plete the demonstration begun in Greek philosophy," and
add that the "new light" has been "notably and especially"
gained through "the fundamental facts of Christianity."
Nothing is more important to Morris than the realization
that "philosophy has an historic existence. . . . Philosophic intelligence does not consist in repeating the words
of others who have gone before," but "the past is not to
be ignored," that is, man's experience is to be taken into
account in its wholeness. This brings Morris to a consideration of the ill results that follow from any intellectual
isolation.

The insulation of the philosophic mind from many areas
invaded by man's experience, under the dogmatic canons
of a superficial scientism, has been a very great concern of
Morris from at least as early as his Hodgson paper. In his
own self-development, if not in modern intellectual history, religion has been the prime corrective of the rational
fragmentation, and so Morris returns to his basic theme in
the Ely Lectures by asking "What then, is the verdict that
philosophy pronounces on religion, when, having accomplished the preliminary task of demolishing its natural
adversary, sensational Agnosticism, it proceeds to its positive work of sounding to its lowest depths the sea of our
conscious experience?" Morris explains that "religion, as
presupposing and requiring knowledge of the Absolute,
and philosophy, as the pure, unbiased search for and demonstration of it, occupy like ground. Each implies (1) a
process, way, or means of intelligence, by which (2) the
Absolute Object of intelligence is reached." This functional identity has suggested his course of procedure in the
lectures. "Our purpose and method will require us, ac-

cordingly, first succinctly to indicate the general nature and results of the philosophic theory of knowledge and of the absolute or final object of knowledge; and then to seek to state, in part with greater fulness, the conceptions respecting the same topics, which are presupposed or proclaimed by Christianity; with a view to showing that the Christian conceptions are not repugnant to the conceptions of philosophy, that the former are, rather, the fulfilment and enrichment of the latter," indeed, in the light of Morris' total contribution, they are the dynamic or ethical corrective needed in any philosophical speculation. " 'True religion' finds itself, not disgraced, but justified" by philosophy.[9]

The second lecture, on the philosophical theory of knowledge, is an exposition of Morris' own basic epistemology. "Intelligence in its fundamental nature is an organic process." Hence "whenever intelligence comes to know *itself in* its instrument (sensation), and hence also in its distinction from and superiority to the same, its conception of reality is corrected accordingly, and becomes that which is set forth in the great philosophies—the philosophies of Aristotle, Leibnitz, Hegel, etc.—and which, as we shall see, Christianity at once presupposes and proclaims. . . . Intelligence and reality, like father and son, or like subject and object in consciousness, are strict correlates. There is no science of the one, without science of the other. In this sense Parmenides spoke truly, 'Thought and Being are one.' The science of being *per se* is but the demonstrative interpretation of intelligence, or experience *per se*. Wherever, therefore, philosophy has a positive existence, there

[9] *Op. cit.*, pages 1–7, 11–5, 19.

you may look for more or less complete developments of the science of knowledge. I need scarcely add that in modern philosophy these are found in greater extent than in ancient philosophy. The difference, however, is only one of completeness and extent, but not of kind." Here Morris makes clear that his own development as a philosopher cannot be marked by a later rejection of an earlier inadequacy, but only by a fulfillment in better form of insights which must have had some verity in the beginning if they conducted the way—even negatively or critically—to a truth in the end. As he proceeds he continues to reaffirm his basic tenets. Thus, the "relation of so-called subjective, mind-generated, synthetic *form*, to so-called objective, sense-generated, discrete *matter* of sensible consciousness, is not merely mechanical."

Indeed, "only in a superficial sense can it be thus styled. In essence it is organic. It is, in kind, not a dead, but a living relation. Space and time are not merely receivers or containers of physical objects, such that the former and the latter might and would still remain all the same—and wholly unchanged, even though separated from each other. Nor are the categories merely a dress, which, sensible objects may—but need not necessarily—put on, and which serves, like all dress, rather to conceal than to reveal the immediate, true, and characteristic nature of its wearers. Time and space without sensible objects, and sensible objects without time and space, are purely mechanical, forced, and unreal abstractions. . . . The science of knowledge has nothing to do with unknowable objects. It has no ground on which to posit their existence. It has positive ground for absolutely denying their existence, for *know-*

ing that they do not exist, since the very conception of them is a pseudo-conception, *i.e.*, a false and impossible one, like that of a square circle or a piece of wooden iron. The science of knowledge is the science of experience. . . . Knowledge, then, is of the concrete universal. The true universal alone is concrete. The particular, to which only this name ('concrete') is so often given, is, as such, indeed abstract." Here is the epistemological germ of Morris' ultimate organicism. The abstract—which is only a mental construct, even in actual experience—is that which is fragmented or atomized, whereas the concrete, rather than that which by abstraction is capable of aggregation and combination, is whatever stands or comes whole in experience.[10]

In his third lecture, on the philosophical theory of reality, Morris points out that "in the largest generalizations of physical science, no attempt is made to reach an absolute unity, but only a relative one—the unity, namely, of the sensibly phenomenal or material universe. Thus the earliest Greek inquirers, turning their attention only to questions of speculative physics, only presupposed and attempted to demonstrate the unity of the physical universe in its proximate or sensible essence, as consisting of water, air, fire, or the like. Of precisely similar nature, or scientific quality, is our modern nebular hypothesis, with its accompanying theory of cosmical evolution. The unity which is sought in such theories is, we may say, not the unity of essential being, but of its sensible form or appearance." Actually physical science "finds, and, in truth, seeks, no absolute" and yet, seen within its peculiar and limited

---

[10] *Ibid.*, pages 20, 31-2, 43-5, 48.

sphere, it "illustrates the truth that being is one, and that the unity of being is the presupposition upon which alone any science is possible," because "real *science,* all real *knowledge,* consists in a reduction of the particular to the universal or in a comprehension of the many in the one. . . . The science of knowledge shows us subject and object, or intelligence and being, in organic unity. It follows . . . that the distinction made between intelligence and being is a purely formal or logical one, not real. . . . When I say *one,* I do not mean *mechanically single* or *simple,* as though the activity in question were like the motion of a point in a straight line" which "is in no true or fundamental sense an *activity,* but at most only the sign and effect of one" and so "is not simple, but complex. And not complex, again, in the sense in which a so-called system of motions . . . is complex . . . for . . . the unity of such a system is not organic, internal, and essential, but mechanical, external, and superficial; it is only the apparent and perishable unity of parts which are *per se* indifferent to each other and may conceivably be separated without losing their identity. No, the unity in question is a *living* one. It is a unity, not simply in spite of, but by very virtue of complexity, an *identity,* the very condition of whose existence is *diversity,*" i.e. an unconditioned capacity for ramification in experience.

Here is the ideal rather than the empirical unity, the "*one* and indivisible ego, self, or spirit, whose function is intelligence," and which possesses unity because it is "*one in, through,* and *by virtue* of its self-intelligence." This "same permanent reality—variously styled 'subject,' 'spirit,' 'self,' etc.—*distinguishes* itself as subject and object (*it*, as subject, knows itself as object), and this as the very condition upon which alone it can know itself to be *one*, and can in fact be one. Here we have an *ideal activity* which (paradoxical as this may sound) constitutes the *agent*: the agent *is* only through its *activity*." Hence "being, like knowledge, is thus primarily revealed as a spiritual *activity*. Almost the first lesson which the beginner in philosophy has to learn is this, that nought essentially exists by mere *inertia*. Existence, *as such*, or absolutely and truly considered, is in no sense whatever *passive*, but is absolutely and only *active*. . . . The difficulty of learning it arises only from the force of a prejudice or habit, precisely like that which stood in the way of the acceptance of the Copernican astronomy." What philosophy demonstrates is the "ideal-real—*i.e.*, the spiritual—nature (the spiritual derivation) of space and time. It shows them to be equally subjective and objective, hence *in their sphere*, universal, or at once independent and inclusive of the particular (individual) subject and objects of our sensible consciousness. They are, therefore, living, constantly-maintained products of an absolute activity, which transcends and includes all subjects and objects—the activity (in the last resort) or absolute spirit, or, rather, of *the* Absolute Spirit, of God."

When it comes to the nature of this "absolute activity," as in contrast with the motion in spheres of causation which material science measures, Morris leans rather heavily on Aristotle, whom he says "saw clearly, and pointed out, how every thing that exists 'by nature,' exists only as it actively *realizes* its existence, and realizes its existence only as it fulfils a law, or process, which is the law or process of its existence. It performs a 'work'—or, a work is performed in it—and this work is none other than the realization of its peculiar type or idea, its good, or purpose. Indeed, Aristotle perceived . . . that the genus of motion is not change of place, but fulfilment of purpose. . . . The activities of organic nature present to us a scene, in which not only the 'fittest'—which is nothing other than that which is best adapted to its purpose—'survives,' but also . . . in which the law, type, and nature of intelligence are visibly reproduced, in a magnificent 'object-lesson,' before our very eyes." Intelligence or self-consciousness, Morris explains, is "a process in which the one subject identifies with itself its many objects. It goes out among its objects and never loses itself. It makes them at once instrumental to, and also integrant portions of, its own life and being. This process we have already termed 'organic.' " This means that man as a subject, therefore, is "primarily, fundamentally and essentially a spirit," and that "the recognition of the principles is nothing other than the recognition of theism itself," and i.e. what "for philosophy" is "none other than the Unity of Absolute Spirit."

The theistic foundation in Morris lies in his recognition of personality as an expression of the "unity of Absolute Spirit," whether this is identified in God or man. "It is a concrete unity—a unity through and by virtue of difference, and hence active and living. It is, in virtue of the principles of the concretely experimental *science of knowledge,* a unity of intelligence and power. It is a unity which is centered in personality and self-consciousness. It is the unity of God." However, "from the ascription to the absolute being of self-conscious personality, many persons have in modern times professed to find themselves deterred by what seem to them insuperable scientific difficulties. Personality appears to them to be a special mark of finitude and hence something which must not be attributed to the Infinite Being." They "identify personality, which is essentially a spiritual category, and so transcends and conditions space and time and their relations, with sensible, numerical individuality, which is an affair merely of limitation in and by space and time. By such *individuality*, one is *pro tanto* cut off from connection with all the rest of existence, and is indeed pre-eminently finite. But by his *self-conscious* personality, on the contrary, man finds himself, not cut off from, but indissolubly bound up with, all the rest of existence, including the Absolute (God) itself. It is thus precisely by his personality that man finds himself taking hold upon the infinite, joined to it, and capable of becoming organically one with it . . ." i.e., the microcosmic-macrocosmic interrelationship. "This view is the only one, which does not necessarily lead to the errors of atheism and pantheism. . . . If God is a spirit, and if man is a spirit, and if the root of all existence whatsoever is spiritual, then, and only then, can unity—organic, living unity, namely— consist with real difference and plurality, and the independent absolute with the dependent relative." [11]

With his fourth lecture, on the Biblical theory of knowledge, Morris comes to the question of truth, and falls back at once upon his own spiritual experience, and the necessity—in the light of the organic or nonmechanical ontology to which he had just given attention—that any revelation be an entirely personal affirmation in word or attitude.

---

[11] *Ibid.*, pages 61–3, 71–4, 81–8.

He explains that "in planning and preparing the present course of lectures," he felt "an irresistible tendency to go back in thought to the time, years ago, when, for a limited period" he too was registered at Union Seminary, and to "reflect on the intellectual experiences" through which he had passed and to judge the needs of these students by what his own had been. "The position of one disposed to thoughtful and thorough study of 'the faith delivered to the saints,' or of what currently and worthily passes for theological truth, was then, and is still, beset with many difficulties and perplexities." This was not doubt, but rational transition. Each student properly "must argue to himself on contemplating the body of doctrine which he is beginning to study, and which he has already nominally accepted," that it "claims to be the truth, the truth *par excellence*. . . . But what is truth? . . . Is the truth which I accept as 'revealed' indeed truth for my intelligence? Is it really an object of knowledge to me? Has my intelligence passed, with reference to the alleged facts of 'revelation,' from the state of mere information respecting the facts as reported or alleged, to the state of knowledge that the facts are indeed facts, or that they contain indeed the truth which they are reputed to contain?"

The whole basis of spiritual knowing, according to theism, is a continuous and personal realization. "Religion and, hence, religious truth are an absolute illusion, unless man be really a spirit and unless God, the universal and eternal source of all existence, be also, and be known to be, a spirit. But, now, if man is a spirit, and if he is the subject of spiritual—which are vital, organic, and substantial or essential—relations (not dead, mechanical, and purely phenomenal or insubstantial ones,) he may be expected in some way to be aware or assured of the fact. For of what should man have knowledge, if not of himself and of that which stands in vital and essential relation to himself? And so, indeed, the sense, either clear, conscious, and explicit, or, more usually, obscure, more or less unconscious, and inexplicit, of man's spiritual nature furnishes the inexpugnable and indestructible root, from and upon which, in the universal consciousness of mankind, religion imperishably thrives. So long as his spiritual nature is to man not an object of clear, explicit, reflective and scientific knowledge, it takes for him the less hardy, but scarcely less persistent form of a 'faith,' on which he dares to found all his hopes and by which he is more than content to be guided in all his conduct. But faith is only inexplicit knowledge. If it be any thing other than this, it is worse than worthless." The statement probably has autobiographical reference, since some such sort of inner assurance certainly held Morris steady during his long intellectual pilgrimage.

As in his own case, the rational side of understanding, quite properly, demands more than an inner or subjective assurance. Therefore he returns to the dichotomy of his opening lecture, between religion and intelligence, and points out that the student of theology "has a right and it is his duty, to ask whether religion is scientific, is philosophical, is in agreement with the results of science and philosophy, and, consequently, to inquire what science and philosophy, as such, are, what results, relevant to the subject-matter of faith, they have reached, and how and on what grounds they have reached them. . . . If religion

is a domain, not of pure fancy, error, or illusion, but of
solid and everlasting truth and reality—if the fact which
it presupposes and proclaims is, not in discontinuity, but
in continuity with the fact which philosophic science, with
its strictly experimental and unbiased method, discovers
and declares—then religion is surely entitled, and theological students are entitled, to be assured of the fact, and
that, too, in the name of science and philosophy themselves." Therefore Morris desires "to point out how Christianity, as the most spiritual of all religions, is also, and for
that reason, the most philosophical, and to show, in particular, that Christianity, in its Scriptures, either directly
contains, or else immediately and obviously presupposes, a
theory of knowledge and of the objects of knowledge—of
the Absolute (or God), of the finite world, and of man—
which is not only confirmed by the results of philosophic
inquiry, but also has positively contributed, in the most
marked way, to the enrichment of philosophic science itself." This is an unequivocal statement of the theistic
foundation on which his thinking rested.

He then proceeds to an analysis of the theory of knowledge "which is directly implied in the theory of the Christian life, as portrayed in the Christian Scriptures," showing
his inherently rational presuppositions when he points out
that the Christian life is intimately if not indissolubly
bound up with knowledge of some sort. Quoting the say-
ings of Jesus to the effect that "I am the Way" and "I am
the Truth," he explains that the way is something for "living, intelligent men, not for unconscious automata or
machines," and that truth is nothing "out of relation to
intelligence." Indeed, "it is only through his participation

in an eternal life," such as Morris himself was now able to rationalize through the Hegelian organicism, "that man ever truly *is* himself." This is not subjectivism, hence Morris denies all validity to the "phenomenalism of Hindu religious philosophy," or the idea that "sensible knowledge and sensible existence are an unqualified illusion." Yet the notion of an individual knowledge which is purely sensible is "an absurdity and an impossibility." The individual spirit of man, "in respect of its intelligence," is a lighted "candle of the Lord." The type of knowledge "which the theory of the Christian life, as expressed in Scripture, implies and requires, is 'spiritual knowledge.' It is a knowledge which the individual possesses, not as mere individual, but only by virtue of his organic, living connection with the universal and absolute. It is a knowledge, which, in form and kind, corresponds perfectly to the definition—universally accepted, either expressly or implicitly—of scientific knowledge. It is not, as is too often supposed, something absolute *sui generis,* inexplicable, miraculous, and without scientific rhyme or reason."

This means that the "functions of the human spirit may proceed normally and accomplish their due result in the practical knowledge and possession of the truth, and of eternal life through such knowledge, even in the absence of explicit knowledge (scientific information) respecting the process of its own intelligence." However—and here Morris emphasizes the important purpose the Ely Lectures were expected to serve—this "does not prove that religious disciples, and, above all, religious teachers, can afford to slight or to undervalue the benefits of such scientific information. For although, without it the truth *may* be lived, felt, and even correctly spoken, yet, being unable to give a rational account of itself, it is, as history is ever showing, thus rendered liable to wander in all sorts of devious and unwholesome ways, and, above all, is unable to defend itself before that very forum of intelligence, before which, by virtue of its very nature, as an ostensible function of intelligence, science is with justice ever citing it to appear." It is a point which becomes especially vital in connection with revelation, and so Morris turns to this, again taking his ground in the functional psychology on which all his analyses are based. "From the point of view of the mere individual, all true knowledge, all genuine science, is of the nature of revelation," that is, it seems "purely mechanical" in the sense of "being brought or *shown* to the knowing agent. It does not appear to belong to him as his own, or as a part of himself." Here of course, in the mind of Morris, is the same old specter of sensationalistic scientism, and the shadow of the British observational theory of knowledge lying behind it.

But Morris has identified theism as the great corrective of modern philosophy. The personal experience of God, or at least of God's presence and participation in the intimate issues of life, denies all reasonableness of an "inscrutable grace" revealed "from without. . . . We now know, on the authority of philosophic science, as well as of religion, that all this is so only in appearance. . . . No knowledge whatsoever is possible on purely mechanical conditions. The Scriptures, therefore, when received in a purely mechanical way, are no revelation. They are then simply a dead letter, which kills, instead of enlivening and quickening, intelligence. The only authority which such a 'revelation' possesses is that of accidental might, but not of real and effective, because recognized or recognizable right. It may be accepted through fear, but it may also, as daily observation informs us only too well, be rejected and shaken off through arbitrary and capricious wilfulness. No, . . . all 'understanding' or knowledge proper is of the nature of revelation in another and truer sense. It is of the nature of self-revelation. And here we may lay it down as an axiomatic truth for all intelligence— whether the latter be termed 'religious' or 'philosophical' —that all genuine, or complete and effective, revelation is, *in form and kind,* self-revelation. . . . Revelation is of the same nature or genus as intelligence itself. . . . We truly are, and we truly know, only as we become 'partakers of the divine nature.' If, therefore, it is the voice of God which is heard in the word divine, it is also, and for that very reason, also the voice of man—the voice of man, namely, according to his true nature and intent."

Morris is expressing himself in a theological climate of opinion, and he uses language familiar to his listeners in instrumenting his Hegelian concept of an assimilation by human and divine personality into each other. Since the whole purpose of Christianity is to bring about man's "organic union with God, the Absolute . . . the bond of organic union for spiritual personalities is and can be nothing other than Love, the voice is the voice of love and the effective hearing of it is conditioned by love. From all this it follows that the true revelation does not fundamentally consist in the communication of dates and figures or of any other sort of purely historic information," i.e., the things appealing to the practical senses. "It may be given through these, but is in no sense merely identical with them. It is a revelation by, of, and to the spirit, and can be only spiritually discerned. Its proper content is the absolute and not the relative." Nonetheless, however much a matter of love and fullness of personality, "the content of revelation can be nothing which is essentially out of relation to intelligence. It must be of, from, and for the world of intelligence as such. In this sense it cannot be essentially 'mysterious.' To the 'natural man' it may indeed be mysterious. To the sensational agnostic it not only may be, but is confessedly, mysterious, and for that reason incredible. But so also, to him, all philosophy proper, all absolute truth, as well as all absolute religion, is a mystery and theoretically incredible. . . . For the true and proper man, for him who has reached the stature of real, and not merely nominal, spectral, manhood . . . no truth is or can be essentially mysterious, and none can be revealed as such. It may not, in all its details, be completely apprehended, but it must in its substance be comprehended. . . . Truths which are of the very essence of reason and of reality cannot be revealed, as they cannot be known, except as in harmony with both reason and reality and as throwing an illuminating light on both." [12]

The following three lectures—the fifth, sixth and seventh—are a unit in the sense that they deal with Biblical ontology in its threefold aspect of the absolute, the world and man. Morris begins by explaining that "the Absolute . . . is strictly continuous or co-extensive with all existence." How can this be, if the Absolute as such is to have any meaning and not disappear because "absorbed in na-

[12] *Ibid.*, pages 89–91, 96–8, 102–3, 106, 111, 113–4, 118–21.

ture?" The answer of Morris is unvarying. God is personal, i.e., not a mechanical or encompassing reality of some mysterious and larger sort, a space-and-time delimited superself or Stoic world soul. "For philosophy, the knowledge of the infinite or absolute, as spiritual personality, is founded in and rendered possible through the spiritual personality of man. The conscious thought and knowledge of man, as such personality" involves "the present power and light, and thought of the universal, living, and absolute Spirit. . . . Philosophic science" as "the pure and complete science of experience, finds the absolute object of knowledge to be, not dead, but living, not mechanical and sensible, but organic and spiritual," and so "perceives and demonstrates that in the spiritual realm of absolute reality limitation is not negation alone, but is also, and primarily, affirmation. Here the dictum is, 'All limitation is self-limitation, and so is self-affirmation.' The limitation proceeds from a self, which, by the very fact and act of limiting *itself*, affirms itself. It is thus that philosophy finds in the very life and thought of the finite and relative individual . . . the true infinite and absolute, not negated and obscured, simply, but affirmed. The true finite, or the finite truly *known* . . . reveals the true infinite," i.e., the knowing as completely functional is, however paradoxically, an experience of illimitability.

Morris proceeds to support his point of view by broad Scriptural reference, developing his ideas in a discussion of the Trinity, and interpreting absolute being "in the forms of absolute intelligence, absolute life, and absolute love" as a representation of the "pure, essential activity" of which the triune modes or attributes of "intelligence, life and love are three organically inseparable attributes." The niceties of theological analysis here are close to the type of verbal exposition to which Morris had particularly objected in his criticism of Shadworth Hodgson some sixteen years before, however, and he realizes that there is danger of losing the Trinity in a theological exercise of the dialectic process. "The third term, the 'synthesis,' as it is called, of the other two, were not, it is true, without the latter, but it does not result from their mechanical composition. It were not without them, but it is not abstractly identical with them. It has reality only in and through them, but its reality is not absorbed in them. On the other hand, it is just as true that the first two, taken either singly or together, in separation from the third, are dead, unreal, inexperimental abstractions. They, too, on their part, have their reality only in and through the third, while yet their reality is not absorbed in the latter." Thus the newer Hegelian orientation is proving of great value to Morris, but it may be observed that the verbal defects of a purely rational idealism have not been screened out sufficiently to give him a fully formulated system of a Hegelian order, and so to free him from his basic dependence on Trendelenburg.

When Morris comes to a consideration of the world, he finds himself in a less rarefied sort of theological atmosphere. Here is the "whole realm of the finite," the "universe as known to physical science" or the "realm of sensible phenomena," which is the first one of which man is aware through "the temporal order of our knowledge," and Morris' experiential or psychological perspective again is emphasized when he explains that his concern is not so much with the sensual aspects of this world as with its meaning or implication in human consciousness. Since the interest of the philosopher is "not the determination of nature's particular mechanical laws," which is the work of the special sciences, "nor of her universal mechanical law," which is "the task of pure physical science . . . but the ascertainment of the power, by whose presence and agency the mechanism of sensible phenomena is to be explained," and since "philosophy looks for the inner reality, the controlling reason, and looks for this, not in an inexperimental vacuum of pure abstraction, but within the present and by no means inaccessible depths of man's real, concrete experience . . . it is all-important to note that the interest of religion, in this regard, is in kind identical with that of philosophy." Here is much repetition of ideas brought out by Morris, both earlier in the Ely Lectures and in his other writings—and with ample Biblical quotation to support the points he is making—but his discussion of creation, and his objection to any assimilation of procedures characteristic of the visible world to God's act in creating the universe, are significant in revealing the slanting of his ontology away from the earlier Aristotelian use of final cause to explain the teleological character of any spiritual insights, and the substitution of the Hegelian organicism as this now is giving final form to his voluntaristic or dynamic idealism.

He explains that "there can be no doubt that the present relation of God to his work is represented as both active and incessant. It is living and, according to the conception which we have now formed for ourselves of the divine nature, godlike. It is a constant witness to the glorious activity of the divine intelligence, life and love. . . . The processes of organic nature—in other words—do not go on of themselves alone, but in dependence on the present power and activity of the Lord of all. But the processes of organic nature are built up, as we know, out of processes, or on the basis of the so-called forces, of that which we are pleased to term inorganic nature. The power that sustains the former must therefore bear a like relation to the latter. And as motion, change, process, activity, is, according to the testimony of both physical and philosophic science, an universal category—a category of all finite existence—it follows that nothing whatever in physical nature is withdrawn from that 'operation.' . . . The works of nature, no less than those of grace, are, according to the truly philosopical view of Scripture, not only 'begun,' but also 'continued, and ended,' in God. The 'heavens' are not simply the finished 'work' of his 'fingers;' they are also, and far more characteristically, the constant working of the divine hands." This is incompletion, complementing creation. Hence there is also "a side of corruptibility and change . . . the whole realm of things which are specifically characterized by their subjection to the forms and conditions of space and time. The universal and inherent destiny of such things is, not to abide forever, but to pass away."

Here comes forward what seemed so odd an achievement to John Dewey, the successful amalgamation of Aristotle and the newly formulated German idealism by Morris,[18] who goes on to say, in summary, that "in brief, then, and employing the experimentally accurate language of Aristotle, natural existence is a compound of potentiality and

---

[18] *Cf.* above, page 160.

actuality; or, more strictly, every natural existence is involved in a process, whereby a definite, typical, ideal potentiality proceeds towards its own realization." Fusing his philosophical and theological ideas into each other, Morris presents "the true process or history of the universe" as "not one of bankruptcy, but of rescue, of redemption, of realization," and ends up with the statement that "we have yet only to see how the 'reason' for this work, as a work progressing and continuing in time, is founded, according to the Christian conception, not in any casual, empirical impulse or determination on the part of Him, the essential and constitutive process of whose nature, being non-temporal, is exalted above time and is eternal, but in this very nature itself. We have to see how creation, as a temporal process, is grounded in creation as an eternal process." Hence "creation and redemption, then, in the very largest and deepest sense of these terms—creation and redemption, two names for one fact or process—express the eternal nature of God in his concrete unity, of God as Intelligence, as Life, or as Love, of God as triune—in short, of God as Absolute Spirit. They express this nature; their 'reason' is this nature." Morris' view of nature, therefore, is rational and not sensational, organic and not mechanical, and he is ready now to examine the Biblical view of man in the light of these concepts.

"Man is, on the one hand, part and parcel of the created universe," but he differs from the physical world in representing something more akin to God. "While nature bears and reveals everywhere the name of God, man is to be made in his express image. To this end man must be and is made to bear the image of the divine absoluteness and independence. Like God, he must be an independent 'worker.' Like him he must be and is a self-centered, self-conscious personality, and has within the sphere of his own being a precinct, in which his sway resembles by its absoluteness the sway of God. . . . Here he has a personal, independent work to do . . . none other than the realization, the rescue, the redemption, the salvation of the divine possibility that is lodged in him and is entrusted, as a talent, to his keeping." The evangelism of Morris is emphasized now in his discussion of the ethical consequences following on the theories he has enunciated. "The whole object of Christian morality, it seems to be thought, is to dehumanize man and to make of him, not a perfect man, but an angel—*i.e.*, something too good for this present world, and about which, for the rest, man must forever remain in substantial ignorance, so long as he continues to inhabit the earth. Christian ethics is thus viewed as a system of arbitrary 'moral injunctions,' in the form of 'divine commandments,' whose sanction and authority are derived exclusively from 'their supposed sacred origin.' " But "man is man only as he realizes in himself the image of God. He is perfect man only as his perfection resembles that of his 'Father which is in heaven' " and "God is a Spirit," so that "the perfection of man will therefore be characteristically a spiritual perfection." Here is no conformity of a fragmented creature to a pattern of necessities exterior to himself.

Does this mean then that "man . . . realizing this perfection" becomes "an independent rival of God? By no means. Not in separation from God—still less in opposition to or rivalry with God—but in living, organic, effective union with him is man made perfect." The philosophical and psychological point of importance—vital to theological understanding at this stage of the exposition—is the presupposition basic in all Morris' writing and thinking, namely, that all existence ultimately is a pragmatically conditioned self-consciousness. Man "cannot be in the image of God, he cannot be a spirit, except he really possess and exercise the power of self-determination. In order really to be man, he must be responsible. But, I repeat, the power that he uses is not self-given or self-created. It is a power of God, lent or committed to him as a sacred trust. The individual is not absolute. His highest privilege, and his highest possibility, is to be a coworker with God." This is a species of social interaction elevated into a spiritual or Biblical ontology for man, and well buttressed by Scriptural reference as are most of Morris' points in these Ely Lectures. Man is organic in far more than a merely biological sense. "The type of the purely individual is," Morris remarks, quoting his own earlier observation, "the mathematical point, which is without inward difference or complexity and equally without external relation to aught other than itself; unextended in time or space, and complete in itself—complete, the rather, in its absolute incompleteness or substancelessness," while a person, contrariwise, has volition.

In all these considerations Morris is finding the ontological bottom for his voluntarism, not in a mechanical process ending up with an infinite regression, but in an eternal and functional assimilation through the microcosmic-macrocosmic organicism developed out of Hegel. "The will, therefore, which identifies itself with the will of God

—the will which, primarily or in the first instance, wills nought but God, and then wills all else from the point of view of God or of the absolute and divine will—possesses that absolute substance of freedom, wherein consists the perfected reality of the spirit. This is freedom through knowledge, love, and practical realization of 'the truth.' It is a steadfast freedom, for it is founded on the only rock that never moves. It is unlimited, for the reason that it is the attribute of a will whose object is the Absolute—*i.e.*, that which itself conditions and so transcends all limits— and that in so doing—or in willing him in whom are the very springs of its life—it has willed itself. It is strong, for it makes God its strength. This is the freedom of those who can say, 'Of his fulness have we received'; of those, whose bodies are 'temples of the Holy Ghost'; of those who, dwelling in love, dwell in God and God in them . . . and who, increasing in love, 'increase with the increase of God.' " The pietism of Morris' boyhood, the simple devout faith which had so naïve a record left of itself when he resigned his position as headmaster of the Royalton Academy, has come back full-tide with the matured intellection of the scholar, and found itself much as it has ever been, steady and unchanged through the years.[14]

The final or eighth lecture, on the comparative philosophical content of Christianity, is concerned principally with the distinction between the type of knowledge which may be known directly or inwardly and introspectively and that which is the demonstrable type of knowing characteristic of science. Morris' effort here, and throughout his life

---

[14] *Op. cit.*, pages 122–3, 128–31, 138, 145, 158–9, 164, 172–3, 184–5, 188, 191–2, 194–5, 197, 204–6, 213, 218, 237–8, 242, 243.

work, has been to preserve the dualism without permitting it to take on any kind of an ontological character, that is, to keep it a division of labor or a purely functional distinction. "In brief, religious ideas relate, as, in the particular case of Christianity, we have already seen, both directly and indirectly to the same topics which are the characteristic and final object of philosophical inquiry. The difference is simply this: religious ideas, speaking universally, express that which has the appearance of being the instinctive judgment of mankind respecting subjects, about which philosophy seeks to reach a reasoned, demonstrative conclusion. In religion man apprehends or claims to apprehend that which philosophy aims to comprehend. And, further, religion involves the living and practicing of that which philosophy, as such, only contemplates and endeavors, with cool and unbiassed judgment, to understand," hence, in summary, his view is that "the revelation of God in Christ and in the Christian consciousness is not the contradiction, but the fulfilment, of the revelation of God in nature and in the universal or generic consciousness of man. . . . Christian knowledge is completed knowledge. The perfect differs from the imperfect, and the completed from the incomplete, rather in degree than in kind." [15]

---

[15] *Ibid.*, pages 258–9, 265–6.

MORRIS' PHILOSOPHY IN GENERAL LINEAMENTS

THE world is ideal, but its ideality is expressed by its continuous maintenance of itself, not by an intellectual derivation of its existence from an idea (or from any agent or source fundamentally or originally exterior to itself). It is at no point the end result of a process, or the product of mechanism. Rather it is organic and both (1) material, as encountered by the senses or measured by science, and (2) rational or ordered by law and principle when approached through the mind or intelligence. Man by the same token is ideal, with an ideality revealed in his moral nature or inner life, and he is no less a material and rational being through his everyday manifestation of a physiological and a social identity. The world and man are directly complementary to each other, and experience per se is the actuality of interaction involved. Experience is (1) inclusive, since it represents nothing other than itself, and (2) competent, since it is always a conjoining of cause and effect. Anything is defined by its characteristic act. The distinction between sense and reason is a functional division of labor, not the representation of a dichotomy supposed to exist in nature. Philosophy is the history of philosophy, and its ultimate corrective is through a Platonic or non-Calvinistic theism, that is, a conception of all existence as personal, or as conscious in the philosophical

315

sense of self-responsible. Here in epitome is the dynamic idealism of Morris. His point of view is an integral part of the Fichtean tradition but, as Dewey says, he was almost a common-sense realist. He was likewise almost a pragmatist and approached the sociological theory of mind and self.

The most dominant trait in Morris was his self-containment, marked in his (1) extreme personal reticence, (2) complete intellectual independence, (3) broad rational opportunism, and (4) highly evangelical single-mindedness. Only two appreciable transitions in his point of view may be traced out, in consequence. Of these, one was completed with the period of European study, while the other paralleled the transfer in university teaching from foreign languages to philosophy. The first change was his intellectual abandonment of the Scottish intuitionalism in which his early thinking had been framed. His sensitiveness to the constant interaction of an inner life and an outer materiality is found from the beginning, and hence is part and parcel of his naïve experientialism and the accompanying and unquestioned theism, but at the start he was inclined to assume a predominant reality for the intangible elements of experience. The fact that the mind is involved in any analysis of itself is ever an encouragement of the psychologist's fallacy, but yet Morris could see that this also is a great advantage in the analytical processes. He well understood that subjective and objective considerations must be given a theoretically equal rank, if one of the terms in the distinction is not to disappear in the other. His difficulty was the lack of intellectual resources for avoiding a heavier weighting of the one as a condition for a grasp of the other, however skillfully he had reasoned the matter through in his review of Hodgson's *Time and Space*. Only after his contact with Trendelenburg was he able to realize that his idealism could be epistemological, or dynamic, with all ontological elements seen to be pre-suppositionary as a convenience of mind, and thereupon —or from 1868 onwards—he took his uncompromising stand against the genetic approach per se, opposing mechanism whether this was to be presupposed in either material or rational form.

The second marked transition in the thinking of Morris was his reworking of the Aristotelian perspective developed under the influence of Trendelenburg into a version of Hegel freed from mechanism. This change, in Dewey's description, was actually an amalgamation, or perhaps more specifically was a realization that the concept of final cause, which he used at first to describe the teleological constitution of the universe, could all too easily slip off into the acceptance of motion as mechanism in another guise, whereas the highly convenient development of Neo-Hegelianism in England offered him the uncompromising organicism which his own insights required. His voluntarism transferred itself easily from the category of activity to that of self-consciousness, enabling him, however instinctively, to feel himself less the physicist and more the true philosopher. Mansel at least, if no one else as early, had suggested to him that any reference to greater and more wonderful things need not be a dismissal of relationship to nonexistence or unknowability, but rather could equally well be a means for bringing more pertinence into a given consideration. This was what Trendelenburg had emphasized in explaining that final cause was to reason what efficient cause was to fact. The Aristotelian continuity of nature reveals a compulsion on human existence which, other than merely causal in the various sequences of events, is the necessity that everything maintain its own characteristic act. Until Hegel there had been no adequate language for this latter conception, so that what really was a pure functionalism had somehow always appeared in the habiliments of mechanism. Morris emphasized the Aristotelian continuousness in his experimental papers of 1875–6, and it is probable that the ineffectiveness of this presentation was behind his recourse to the reinterpreted and essentially nongenetic Hegel in 1877. At root the new Hegelianism was the organic metaphysics of Heraclitus and Plato. As reinterpreted it gave Morris an ontology without dependence on process or ordering in either time or space, thus supporting both material or mortal and spiritual or immortal existence without logical contradictions.

When it comes to the extant writings of Morris, the matter of most consistent concern to him is obviously the rejection of mechanism in favor of organicism. Hegel was in no way the source of his own conception, but the newer Hegelianism definitely shaped his later formulation. At the beginning the influence of Henry B. Smith and Schleiermacher is to be recognized, perhaps in the spirit of the latter's famous "no God without a world, and no world without a God." Darwin unquestionably contributed to an appreciation of the necessity that nature be given a complete and over-all integrity, since this would be no less incumbent upon the theist than the secular materialist. If the real is the rational—the basic thesis of all idealism—

then the rational is immediately real, and this converse of the proposition screens out the fallacy in the original Hegelian notion that the ultimate self-conscious and spiritual intelligence of the world as a whole is exterior to the finite mind of any individual thinker. With the organic and complete assimilation of the complementary subject and object into each other, an entirely logical rationalization is given to spiritual experience. True self-consciousness transcends the individual in the phenomenon of ordinary social existence, and history in a still larger dimension is the logic of events, that is, the manifestation of the transcendent factor in all being as that universal integrity which comes to be experienced directly in thought as such. Thought and being are one, but this is not solipsism or any extreme of subjectivism such as would match the reverse intemperance of a wholly behavioristic naturalism. The striking insight of Morris—and one which might have been epochal, had he lived to give it specific formulation on its own account—was that the organic concept instruments a way of life as well as providing a corrective for the atomistic fragmentations. In everyday terms it is simple theism, or the realization that man as a person is in continual and full fellowship with the cosmic personality which constitutes the objective world in every aspect. Here is what John Dewey described in 1886 as the psychological standpoint, demanding that nothing be admitted to philosophy that does not show in experience.[1]

The rejection of mechanism by Morris, consequently, is paralleled by his acceptance of social functionalism as a self-sustaining rather than an externally-determined or

---

[1] *Mind*, London, Vol. II, page 3.

genetic process. He refuses all traffic with the popular and almost superficial tendencies in the German philosophy of his time, as represented by Herbart, who was too rationalistic, and by Lotze, who was too personalistic. While agreeing with Trendelenburg that man has to have a philosophy in the sense of building a rational house for himself in the realms of mind, Morris yet cannot accept system-building as valid if it only produces a machine, a *deus ex machina.* Nonetheless he realizes that every individual organizes himself in a pattern, and that this takes a directive role in the events of life. He expands the ideal of Kant's categorical imperative and makes it a much more organic channeling of personal talents and capacities into the racial métier. The focus in act, of course, remains entirely individual. Man is hardly a cog in a structure of meshed and articulated compulsions, but is ever a person able to take advantage of his potentials and opportunities. The individual is not conditioned genetically but rather is self-determined organically. Thus the categories, as the ultimate synthetic capacity of thought, can only describe reality on its rational side. Like the basic hyle of the physicists, they give presuppositional support to thinking, but they do not delimit the real in any actual remove from experience. While believed to impersonalize both knowledge and the world of which it is an account, they end only in making man's knowing entirely mechanical, and hence unreal. Even supposedly spiritual knowledge or revelation, if presumed to be given man by exterior agency —or independent of his own experience in and through it —loses all reality. Because human personality is marked by volition, in full organic interactivity with the world as a whole, spiritual revelation is a positive expression of universal potentials and in consequence is the ultimate promise to man in the fact of his own person.

The key to Morris, therefore, is interaction. The complementation of inner and outer, spiritual and material, thought and being, mind and matter, and so on through all manifestation of any sort, is the functional dualism or division of labor which constitutes his logic. He is not holding to distinctions which disappear in a superior synthesis, but to those which mutually and co-operatively reveal each other, and which also and thereupon make man the point of their reconciliation in the immediateness of his continuing and personal experience. In a sense —although Morris himself never so intellectualizes the proposition—he is making knowing per se the constant mean between typically Aristotelian extremes, the latter always a matter of convenience in the light of the particular frame of reference. His idealism is dynamic because the ideater (or any given reality becoming a point of attention in mind) is indomitably central in all possible ramifications of the corresponding experience or relationship. The synthesis is not progressive, tending to an infinite regression, but is a continual self-reconstruction, cr the functional immediacy identified by Morris in his concept of maintenance. Men live and work, not as they are conditioned except in passing, but rather as they are constantly reconditioning both themselves and their world. Fact and value are two sides of the same coin, and the act of personality in remaining itself is in reference to both elements. There are no ultimate dualities, only the one possible dichotomy of logical relations which despite its protean forms can always be caught and held, and found to be the continual interplay of experiment and consequences. The attempts to achieve a speculative conception of things-in-themselves, in the presumption of an ultimate and self-contradicting staticism, are fruitless. Man's efforts instead should be for gaining the knowledge by which he can manipulate or control his experience. Only experience provides a unifying potential for the fragmentations and divisions on every hand, since these latter constitute the subject and object relations in which all being inheres. There are the two kinds of knowledge, but subjective and objective knowing ultimately can but confirm each other, and man needs both in order to have this confirmation and to achieve any unification of his own personal world.

The functional dualism upon which Morris fundamentally has built his own thinking is established by his experientialism, on the one hand, and his voluntarism, on the other, and it is in this connection that his contribution may prove to be the most unique. His complete acceptance of experience at its face value is the basis of the continuity in his formulation, precisely as his unlimited and almost asocial encouragement of individuality is an articulation of the corresponding discontinuity or recognition of private identity. Thus he holds to a postulated theism, which assumes an unwavering maintenance of the whole universe through an all-encompassing intelligence of almost Vedantic scope, but he complements this with the unquenchable evangelism, not only in religious but also in philosophical and esthetic spheres, which keeps the general conception personal at all points. The experientialism is uncompromising. Thus mind has an advantage because it is in-

volved in the analysis of itself, thinking as much a matter
of participation as acting, and its reasoning powers because
wholly concerned are entirely competent in their own
special milieu. The only continuum known to reality is the
continuing act of something in being itself, and the only
possible nature of this act—as its part in the interaction
supporting its existence—is experience. Morris actually
lived his concept, clinging to the familiar with a fidelity
which might have been sheer stupidity in a less imaginative
or intelligent person. By the same token he reached out
into all possible areas of self-experimentation and made all
that happened a grist for his busy rational mill. Because
he was the rationalist by temperament, he was more interested in the history and potentialities of ideas than in
institutions and social organisms as such, and so he became an omnivorous reader, but he yet held that everything had to be verified in experience, or validated eventually by an entirely personal although perhaps vicarious ex-
perimentation. Hence he realized that there could be no
truly logical appeal except to an experiential continuum,
which means historical criteria at the end, and his emphasis upon this appeal to past experience is the mark of
Trendelenburg's most important contribution to his philosophical maturity.

The voluntarism of Morris, as an evangelistic expression
and reflection of his underlying theism, has its roots in the
necessity that for an idea there be a thinker, or that for
existence in a personal world there must be a person with
a power to act other than as a conditioned automaton.
Morris saw early that while free will could not be absolute,
it yet could be competent in the given milieu, that is, in

the interactive relationships of a man and his particular situation. The fervent evangelism characterizing the New England life known to him was a convenient instrumentation for his conception of a human individuality which was realized and fulfilled in its inner potentials, rather than merely conditioned outwardly, and also for his view of a spirituality which, instead of a progressive fragmentation down from the absolute, was the immediate realization of the absolute in the core of a self which theistically was of wholly like nature with itself. Morris reasoned through this matter initially by seeing a historical progression from disorder to order, but with the order first and inadequately imposed from without, so that the given individual had to learn self-ordering before he could achieve his spiritual self-discovery. Here is the insight for which the Aristotelian mean of Ulrici and Trendelenburg first gave a rationalization, but one which hardly had clear statement until the later Hegelian organicism provided the necessary language. Man is free as he puts the potentials of himself and his environment to use, a principle which becomes the very core of a dynamic idealism. Morris has departed from Trendelenburg in this connection, however, finding his German mentor deficient through his failure to recognize an active potency in consciousness as the complement for the physical motion described by Aristotle. Man's true nature is but half-recognized when this moral dynamic or evangelistic power is not taken into account, and the most curious phase of Morris' exposition is his turn to Shakespeare and the British poets for evidences of it in the environment where it has otherwise been inhibited by the prevailingly mechanistic philosophy.

The theism which remains the most fundamental factor
in the intellectual background of Morris is something to
which he never gives any real philosophical analysis. Despite his desire to enter the ministry, it became obvious
to him as well as to his advisers—and even to his highly devout father—that he was better fitted for a philosophical
chair than the pulpit. He grew up in his faith, and his conversion at Meriden was unquestionably a purely emotional
ripening. Before his self-conscious thinking had at all
matured he had transformed his religious orientation into
the deep and underlying continuum of his experience, so
that it never was a matter of logical or metaphysical presupposition. In his Ely Lectures, therefore, his appeal is
either directly to experience in general as warrant of the
truth he presents—on the analogy of his own orthodox
background—or else to Scripture as a rational but purely
historical verification. Wenley presents Morris as coming
close to the mystic, but Morris at no point has any revelation to give, or subjective insights to share, over and beyond
the everyday life which is commonly encountered by everyone and which is always ready for a spiritual touching to
some enrichment of itself. His concern through so many
years over the problems of Christianity was certainly a conviction that it was necessary to give the Protestant doctrines
a better intellectualization, to the end that they might have
a greater evangelistic power. Morris' trouble was not with
belief per se, but with the need to act on belief, and to get
others to do so. His theism gave him what he needed logically—that is, a postulate in the acceptance of God—and
in consequence he stood at the other pole from Descartes
who, in the complementary postulation of himself, had

given idealism a first modern impetus. Morris was aware of the difficulties stemming from Aristotle and the Cartesians—that is, the delimitation of an ego and a divine thinker by disjunction—and so he postulated instead the personal and continuous assimilation, into the image of each other, of God and man—which was the non-Calvinistic theistic position—and therefore presented the organic concept in outline even through his earliest thinking. He was able to show that Spinoza had led men astray by his impersonalization of reality. Only a living personality can express the unity of absolute spirit. Ultimate reality is personal, hence responsible in any individual aspect of itself. In the light of these factors the idealism of Morris becomes, in Dewey's phrase, an essentially ethical idealism.

The Enlightenment in its broader or humanistic terms left Morris entirely untouched, since to him the whole purpose of education and any other refinement of social and esthetic skills was ethical and religious. Thus his own understanding and appreciation of the arts, other than music, was quite devoid of critical competency. He was exceptionally sensitive, contrariwise, to the necessity for the communication of values through social and esthetic agencies, realizing that only as experience was shared would it be possible to establish a culture and refine a civilization. Mere beauty or secular norms were of no worth in this connection, however. Even his music—vital as it remained in his own personal living—never crossed the bridge between his life work in philosophy and his strictly private enjoyment of its catharsis. Hence the musical phase of the total continuum which was Morris was never of philosophical service to him, even in illustrating various or sundry points in his writing, and despite his characteristic opportunism on the rational side of things. His ethical perspective is centered entirely on the need that men be brought to realize the moral ideal developed through the whole course of history. This to Morris is a spiritual compulsion, the recognition of which constitutes the starting-point in any proper system of ethics. What is especially to be noted in his case is the pragmatic nature of his approach, ever standing in contrast with any system based on revelation as in the usual ecclesiastical or theological climate, or on rational speculation as in the positivistic systems springing into being with the advancement of physical science. Morris' ethics is neither hedonistic nor perfectionistic, but in germ at least is a highly original organicism on the ethical level. In principal part it envisions a full capture of self in a theistic fellowship with the divine reality. As against a subjective and ecclesiastical spiritualism, or a secular and entirely social-behavioristic scientism, Morris presents a cosmic potentiality of selfhood as a strictly ethical responsibility, and so here is in many respects closer to Greek and American roots than to the German system-builders.

Morris early presents his conception of philosophy in these personal and ethical lineaments when he says that the genuine philosophers always have attempted to "reduce, to logical and intelligible expression, the truth of a living, experimental and essential reality," and thus have sought to lift men up to "that plane of philosophic insight on which genius stands." This to him has best been typified by Plato, and he feels that philosophy did not have "any existence except in name" whenever it fell away from the

Athenian's vital knowledge. The empirical approach is utterly inadequate because it restricts itself to the sensual side of knowing, and sees all things in terms of mechanism. Rational positivism, by the same token, is deficient in experimental contact or validation through an actual or everyday life. Philosophy ultimately is the historical account of the rise and practical application of man's metaphysical ideas and logical concepts, so that the present builds on the past no less in intellectual realms than in biological and social domains. Unless there is an intellectual experience, or a direct reworking of the contents of thought, there is no philosophical realization of any consequence. "Philosophy may well be defined, in distinction from all other sciences, as the science of experience as such," Morris explains, summarizing his entire doctrine. "It determines . . . the absolute nature of experience, and . . . that nature of being which is given in and is organically one with experience." Hence the abstract or the general is only a rational construct after all, or is that which is fragmented or atomized by man in his personal intellectualization, whereas the concrete or the true reality is that which stands or comes whole in experience. Twice, in the history of philosophy, Morris points out, men have come to the flood tide of insight, and have seen this vital wholeness of the cosmos made manifest to the individual in his everyday potential, first in Plato and Aristotle, and then again with the Kantian succession and its climax in Hegel.

"Philosophy," Morris remarks, "as Trendelenburg loved to repeat after Plato, is the real sentinel on the boundaries of the other sciences" and "furnishes principles" for them as well as establishing "harmony among their results," and so is properly neither purely empirical nor purely *a priori*, but "ideal-realism" in any true description. Thus "true philosophy is catholic" and "welcomes science as in truth its handmaid" even as it "reveres religion, which is but the faithful love and service of the supreme object of philosophy's demonstrations," although it sees difference as real and hence "insists that things distinct shall not be identified with each other." Contrariwise, however, distinctiveness shall not be established as a metaphysical reality, which is the great sin of modern thinkers, so that when Aristotle—whom Morris identifies as the true if critical disciple of Plato—speaking through Trendelenburg, showed that Kant's "proof of the exclusive ideality of time and space" was incomplete, this rejection of absolute discreteness cut away the ground from "beneath the whole subsequent development of German idealism," and paved the way for Morris' contribution. While modern philosophy has reached its "most perfect systematic expression in Hegel" in Morris' eyes, because "the science of being has been approached by way of the science of knowledge more explicitly than in ancient philosophy," yet the real roots of Morris' thinking are in Aristotle. The unified methodology which ultimately became the whole view of organicism is actually the ideal of science as Morris first encountered scientific thinking, an Aristotelian spirit which had not been screened from him by the narrowed view of the empiricists. The indigenous American thought in which he had matured had largely obliterated the dichotomy of sense and rational criteria, thanks probably to the whole mobilization of self required by the rigors of pioneer living.

The notion that one method is necessary for physical science, and another for spiritual truth, is a fallacy against which Morris protests from the very outset of his intellectual career. Faith was commonly demonstrated by works in the New World, where there was little leisure or professional life separated in sharp social fact from the labor done by hand. Inner experience was not developed in an ivory tower, but as a concomitant of hard toil. Everyday living certainly seemed to show that these extremes did not cancel out each other, but rather contributed to a common milieu and thereupon revealed the in-betweenness of illimitable potentialities which marks man as the divine entity, and shows the extent to which he possesses a true volition. Therefore the primacy of rank and power given the idealistic element in human nature cannot be the exaltation of one as against the other factor in the cosmic dichotomy, but only the recognition of an individual's spiritual power, such as is given its broad manifestation in the physical actuality. In an Aristotelian sense the continual reference of the to-be-known to the already-known is the sole basis of scientific or demonstrated knowledge, with the result that new knowledge arises out of the old and hence remains essentially a part of it. Verification is the seating of the present in history (time) and in logical relationship (space). Morris never repudiates the desire to ascertain absolute truth, but rather the attempt to get at this by purely intellectual means, an approach which was contrary to his whole American heritage. The refinement of rational powers without a spiritual quickening of the experience in which they would be of use would again be a half-approach to man's nature, and the persisting influence of the British empirical as against the American functional tendency.

Thus George Sylvester Morris reflects his fundamental background at all points. By temperament, first of all, and to some extent by training and later self-development, he was as much the scientist and the theologian as the philosopher. His attacks on a sterile scientism and an empty rationalism (whether ecclesiastical or secular) comprise the larger part of his existing writings, and hence it is necessary to realize that he did not reject the reality but only the false shadow of these disciplines. He saw that science did not exist to challenge Scripture, or to confirm revelation, except most incidentally. Its primary work was to provide man with tools for better living, and to make man the all around citizen of a whole world in true American fashion. Morris therefore repudiated an absolute or transcendent knowledge, but was scientifically inclined by instinct to demand an unimpeachable knowing, that is, a knowledge subject to verification in all details. He understood that its boundaries need not be fixed, but that it must have a rational reliability and a practical dependableness. No less than the empiricists, whom he scorned so bitterly, he had an intense dislike for metaphysical subtleties and the hair-splitting of the Scholastics. Reality was always to be enthroned in experience, and this meant that in its turn it was to be centered in a person and not generalized in a lifeless and unintelligent objectivity. His attack upon any mere verbal rationalizing was consistent with the basic organicism, which led him to recognize the continual necessity for a restatement of truth, that is, its expression in language immediately communicable in an individual understanding. Any metaphysics which dealt with the supposed possibilities of knowledge out of all practical relation to the conditions of material existence was to him no more than a manipulation of words, and quite meaningless. To a true philosophy the fragmentation of reality was not only unnecessary, but an indication that the thinker was divided within himself, or that his approach to the world was ever the partial analysis which could end only by defeating itself.

APPENDIXES

FRIEDRICH ADOLF TRENDELENBURG

(Article by Morris in *The New Englander*, Volume 32, April, 1874, pages 287–336)

"THE kind of philosophy which one chooses," says Fichte, "depends on the kind of man one is; for a philosophical system is not a lifeless piece of household furniture; on the contrary, it is animated by the soul of the man who has it." "Philosophy is the history of philosophy." Doubtless every man, even the lowest, has his philosophy. He has a distinct set of beliefs, positive or negative, respecting the nature and origin of things, the government of the world, and his own destiny. They are his, even though derived from "the tradition of the elders," his forefathers; they are his, in a still more eminent sense, if they are the outcome of his own thinking or of his moral preferences. Philosophy, in this wider sense, is the most perfect indication of character, and the ideal of a noble man is of one whose philosophy, intelligently thought out, rounded off, and adopted, is but the conscious, theoretical accompaniment and reflex of a noble life and character. A most striking illustration of this interpenetration of life and theory is

---

1. *Logische Untersuchungen,* von A. Trendelenburg, Zweite ergänzte Auflage. Leipzig, 1862.
2. *Historische Beiträge zur Philosophie,* von A. Trendelenburg, 3 Bände. Berlin, 1846–1867.
3. *Naturrecht auf dem Grunde der Ethik,* von Adolf Trendelenburg, Zweite ausgeführte Auflage. Leipzig, 1868.
4. *Kleine Schriften,* von Adolf Trendelenburg, 2 Theile. Leipzig, 1871.
5. *Elementa Logices Aristotelicæ.* 6te Ausgabe. Berlin, 1868.
6. *Erläuterungen, etc.* 2te Ausgabe. Berlin, 1861.
7. *Zur Erinnerung* an Friedrich Adolf Trendelenburg, Vortrag gehalten am Leibniztage, 1872, in der Königlichen Akademie der Wissenschaften von H. Bonitz. Berlin, 1872.
8. *Adolf Trendelenburg,* von Dr. Ernst Bratuschek. Berlin, 1873.

furnished by the biography of Friedrich Adolf Trendelenburg, for whom also, philosophy, in a special, but not in the
narrowest sense, was identical with the history of philosophy.
It were easy, by reference to the history of philosophy and
the biographies of its representatives, to show how, universally,
the personalities of the leading philosophers have found expression in their systems. The aristocratic Plato has a more
than wholesome horror of the so-called pollutions of matter,
and identifies true reality with the ideal. And, for the rest,
modern philosophy has not found it easy, as yet, to determine
what reality, if any, belongs in fact to the material as such—
that is, what matter truly is. Aristotle, more involved in the
practical problems of life, plants his theory more cautiously on
the palpable earth. In modern times, the calm and consequent
spirit of Spinoza gives birth to the all-comprehensive system
known by his name, in which God is all, and tranquil, unfretful submission to the necessary laws of the universe (of
God) is deduced as the corollary, and is exemplified in the
philosopher's life. The pietistic training of Kant's youth leaves
its traces in the well-known, life-long conscientiousness of this
founder of modern critical philosophy, and re-appears still
more conspicuously in the notion of duty, on which his moral
philosophy is founded, and in the categorical imperative, in
which its fundamental requirement is formulated. From facts
like these, what is to be inferred? That philosophy is simply a
system of beliefs, the expression of personal traits, and that it
moves hence, eternally round in the vicious circle of the
ever-varying but substantially unchanging opinions and characters of mankind? This was not the view of Trendelenburg,
who sought in the systems of the past for the elements of
permanent value, and sought to add to these and to build upon
them, as upon a basis of historically demonstrated solidity.

Friedrich Adolf Trendelenburg was born in Eutin, in the
principality of Lübeck, Nov. 30th, 1802. His father, who had
studied law, was in the employ of the Danish government as
postal agent at Eutin. He lived in simple but comfortable
circumstances, caring intelligently for the education of his
children and being the "model of a German father and
citizen." Trendelenburg's mother, the daughter of a country
clergyman, was a woman of gentle, simple tastes, abounding in

charity, and inspiring the affection of her children. The influence of both parents in determining the loyal, genuine, earnest character of the son was great, and the latter rewarded their love and devotion fully and in kind. Of Trendelenburg's four uncles, on the father's side, one was a physician and another a lawyer in Eutin, while the other two were teachers of the classics in the gymnasia at Dantzic and Lübeck. These, and other, older family associations seconded the natural desire of the father and the inclination of the son in the matter of the acquisition of a thorough, liberal education for the latter. Happily, although Eutin was and is still but a small town, of less than 4,000 inhabitants, the school advantages there were good. Trendelenburg was early placed in the gymnasium, which was under the direction of one König, and there he remained until the completion of his studies preparatory for the University. He learned not without difficulty; but his conscientious, eager industry enabled him nevertheless to prosecute his studies in mathematics and other German branches, and in the classics with marked success, so that on leaving the school at the end of a course, the last year of which was partly spent in teaching lower classes, he received a specially commendatory, documentary statement of his character and acquirements, at the hands of his teacher. "One," Trendelenburg used subsequently to say, "can do anything which he is earnestly resolved upon," and in the spirit of this maxim he had successfully, but laboriously, gone through the first, long stage in his student life. The germs of much that was characteristic in the life, character, and teaching of Trendelenburg, were laid or partly developed in this early period of schooling. In an address delivered in 1857, on entering upon the rectorship of the University of Berlin, Trendelenburg says: "The ancient languages and the mathematics are the way to the heights of humanity and into the innermost nature of things." The foundations of this opinion were laid under König, under whose direction the reading of the classics was to him (as he himself says) "a stimulus, leading him to seek for the spirit of the ancients in their writings, to strive to learn how to think after the model of the great thinkers, and to clothe his thoughts in similar, beautiful form." Under the same teacher, also, Trendelenburg enjoyed the advantage of private instruction in logic and philosophy, Kant's works being made especially the subject of sympathetic and careful study, while the sentiment towards Fichte was cooler, and Hegel was declared by the instructor to be to him incomprehensible, and his "pure thought" the πρῶτον ψεῦδος of modern philosophy.

It is impossible to represent in too strong a light the benefit to the future philosopher of this early period of ten years of training in the gymnasium. What earnest American scholar will not look with envy upon one who had the advantage in his youth of reading through "nearly all the Greek and Latin authors that are ever read in schools," some of their works being read "several times," and all this under a teacher of broad philological and literary training and of independent philosophical intelligence? And we say nothing of the thorough course in mathematics, rhetoric, and other German branches, nor of other languages, as Hebrew, English, French, learned either in the gymnasium or under private teachers. All this careful and extensive study and training, which do not stop short with the elementary, but actually take the student into the inner sanctuary of learning, give the German student a preparation for future study and labor, at the University and in subsequent life, which we Americans must also secure for ourselves, would we ever become alike competent and independent in our philosophical and literary judgment, and respected in the world of scholars.

At the same early period in his life, also, Trendelenburg became specially penetrated with a sense of the importance and sacred character of the teacher's vocation, to which he resolved completely to devote himself.

The four years from Easter, 1822, till Easter, 1826, were spent by Trendelenburg in University studies. Until the autumn of 1823, he studied at Kiel, devoting his attention to philosophy, history, theology, and philology. His instructors in the first of these branches were Reinhold, who in Jena, thirty years previously, had with such brilliant tokens of success expounded the philosophy of Kant, and von Berger, a philosopher of Danish origin, familiar with the then current phases of German philosophy and seeking to unite the teachings of Fichte and Schelling. These men, by their moral

and scientific enthusiasm, and the latter by some of his
fundamental teachings, left a deep impression in the mind
and opinions of Trendelenburg, an impression which subsequent years did but confirm. From the fall of 1823, till
the corresponding period in the following year, Trendelenburg
studied at Leipzig, attracted thither, especially by the unusual advantages then, as now, offered by the University
in that city, for the prosecution of philological studies.
There, among others, Gottfried Hermann, "the first Greek
of his times" lectured. Here Trendelenburg devoted his
attention principally to philology, Greek, Latin, and Hebrew.
But his relations to his teachers were less genial than they had
been in Kiel, and after some hesitation between Bonn and
Berlin, Trendelenburg repaired, with his father's consent, to
Berlin, where he finished his studies and graduated, after
hearing one course of lectures by Hegel, who failed to inspire
conviction in him, and others by Schleiermacher (on Æsthet-
ics), Neander (on Church History), Ritter (on Geography),
Hagen (on German and Northern Mythology), Bopp (on
Science of Language), and Steffens (on Physical Philosophy),
and studying Gothic with Zeune, Sanscrit with Rosen, and
learning fencing and gymnastics with Eiselen. In his whole
course of University studies Trendelenburg proved himself
an earnest student and independent thinker. Conscientiously
did he devote himself to the study of the great thinkers of
ancient Greece and modern Germany, with a view to the
determination of his own philosophical beliefs. The necessity
of a definite and intelligently adopted and well grounded
system of such beliefs was ever present to his mind. "One
must have a philosophical system, just as one must have a
house," he wrote, while at Berlin, "and this house each must
build for himself; it must be almost moveable, like a tent, and
susceptible of enlargement;" accordingly he labored diligently
in his years of preparatory study to bring together the materials for the final structure of his system. His attention was
nearly equally divided between philology and philosophy, but
his interest lay chiefly in the direction of the latter, the studies
in philology being prosecuted largely with a view to their
bearing on the investigation of the doctrines of the ancient
philosophers. He took his degree after having sustained the

usual disputations on theses selected by himself and preparing and publishing a Latin dissertation on "Plato's doctrine of Ideas and Number, in the Light of Aristotle's Criticisms." The theses defended by him are characteristic of the direction of his mind and of his philosophical convictions at that time; and these convictions remained with him subsequently unaltered. The theses were the following: "The study of Etymology discloses a popular philosophy of conceptions;" "In philosophy, as elsewhere, belief precedes knowledge;" "As negation without presupposed affirmation is impossible, so also is pure skepticism;" "Kant's incognoscible 'things-in-themselves' do not follow even from his demonstrations concerning the nature of space and time;" "As space and time are pure and primitive forms of intuition, so also is motion such a form."

The first and the two last of these theses mark in particular the tone and direction of much that was of prime significance in the later philosophical investigations and doctrines of Trendelenburg. The dissertation showed how Platonism was to be corrected by Aristotelianism; the bond of connection between the immaterial ideas and the concrete things whose reality is derived from their participation in the ideas, was to be supplied by the addition of the Aristotelian principle of motion, and the (Aristotelian) principle of finality, obscured or inadequately apprehended by Plato, in his identification of the Good with Absolute Being, was also to be distinctly introduced.

For seven years after his departure from the University, Trendelenburg—in this following the example of other, more eminent German philosophers before him, Kant, Fichte, Hegel—was occupied with the duties of a private tutor. Brilliant openings had indeed not been wanting to him; the professorship of philology at Kiel and a position in the gymnasium at Lübeck were offered him. His reasons for declining these positions were characteristic of the man. The professorship at Kiel, great as were its attractions for him, would have demanded of him the preparation and giving of lectures in a wider field than that which his philological studies had fairly covered. "I have freely told you," he writes to Twesten, theological professor at Kiel, "how in the last years I have occupied myself very particularly with Plato and Aristotle and the history of ancient philosophy. I have indeed sought to keep myself in near and living relation to all the other parts of philological science. But I would now first accomplish something worth the while in the one direction mentioned. Were I now to undertake to teach in the whole field of philology, I should be unable to carry out the golden maxim: *to concentrate in the smallest point the greatest force*. I should perhaps render myself and others superficial; myself, for the whole field of philology appears to me as too extensive; and others, because in numerous branches I am too scantily prepared to teach. Were my acquisitions more solid in that department in which I desire at some time to accomplish something creditable. . . . I should perhaps ask you whether I might not be useful to the University of Kiel in a position in which philology and philosophy should be united. But I am unwilling to appear as unripe fruit, and the evidence of ripeness I can acquire only as I feel it within myself. To the eye the apple often appears red before it is ripe within." And so Trendelenburg deliberately chose the more modest position of private tutor for the son of Postmaster-General von Nagler at Berlin, having rightly apprehended the lesson of laboring and waiting. The acceptance of this place afforded him the leisure and freedom from responsibility necessary for the continuance and relative completion of the work of "gathering the materials" for his philosophical house, although the demands which it involved upon his time and energies were not slight. The position had the further advantage of bringing him into desired relation to a circle of refinement and culture, and of increasing his knowledge of the world by occasional journeys with his ward.

One principal work occupied him during his life in the family of von Nagler. This was the preparation and annotation of an edition of Aristotle's *De Anima*, the publication of which marked an epoch in the careful study and correct interpretation of the Greek author. "The study and investigation of Aristotle's doctrines," says Bratuschek, "appeared to him [in his earlier period] ever more and more as his life's work." Fittingly and brilliantly did he continue this work—begun in the study of Plato with Aristotle's eyes—in the publication just mentioned.

The remainder of Trendelenburg's biography may be briefly summarized. Thus much of it has been given relatively in detail, since it throws such instructive light on the conscientiousness and thoroughness which not only marked the scientific career of this particular philosopher, but must be illustrated in the life of every true student.

In 1833, while at Paris, Trendelenburg received from Minister von Altenstein his appointment to an "extraordinary" professorship of philosophy at Berlin. The salary was to be moderate, but was to be supplemented by work performed in the commission for the examination of candidates for positions in the public schools of Prussia. Trendelenburg accepted the position gladly, and entered upon the performance of his duties as professor with courage and hope. In 1837, on the occasion of his receiving a call to the place left vacant by H. Ritter at Kiel, his professorship was changed to a full or "ordinary" one, and in this position the remainder of his life was passed. In 1846, he was elected a regular member of the Berlin Academy, and in the following year was made secretary of the section for the history of philosophy, an office which also he continued to hold until about the time of his death.

Trendelenburg's lectures extended over psychology, logic, history of philosophy, ethics, and the philosophy of law. His lecture-room was usually crowded. His genial manners and the simple fitness and felicity of his style and delivery rendered him unusually attractive. As an examiner in the above-mentioned commission he acquired great influence among the higher class of teachers in Prussia and throughout Germany. His devotion to labor was unflagging, his health always perfectly good until very near the end of his life, his family, social, religious, and political relations agreeable, and his death (Jan. 24, 1872) widely regretted.[1] His principal works, are

---

[1] Of Trendelenburg's dogmatic views in theology, the writer of this Article has no information which descends to details. Rationalism had entered his father's family before his birth, but it evidently coexisted with warmly devout feeling. This feeling, wholly separated from fanaticism or mysticism, continued to permeate Trendelenburg's character through life. It is strikingly and most orthodoxly expressed in a poem composed by

in addition to the edition of Aristotle's *De Anima,* his *Logical Investigations* (1840, 2d ed., 1862, 3d ed., 1870), his *Natural Right* (1860, 2d ed., 1868), and his *Historical Contributions to Philosophy* (vol. i, 1846, on the History of the Doctrine of Categories; vol. ii, 1855, vol. iii, 1867, mostly critical articles on ancient and modern philosophers and philosophical systems). Numerous addresses, chiefly delivered in the Academy and relating to questions philosophical, historico-political, and æsthetic, are published in his *Minor Writings* (2 vols., 1870). He also published *Elements of the Aristotelian Logic* (a compilation of select passages from the Organon, with Latin notes), which went through four editions at least, also a volume in German of elucidations of the same, which reached the second edition, and both especially designed for use in the higher schools.

While the life and philosophical career of Trendelenburg furnish an extremely attractive object of study and attention, on account of the harmonious, happy flow of the former and the discreet method and practical fruitfulness of the latter, the special importance of the man and his doctrines are founded on their relation to the historical development of philosophical thought in Germany.

The philosophy of Germany had ever been and still is prevailingly idealistic. Its founder, Leibnitz, an Aristotle by his encyclopædic knowledge and his thoughtful union of the theoretical and the practical, had identified matter with active force and had conceived the latter after the analogy of spiritual, conscious existence. The life of the monads was ideal; it consisted in the possession of more or less distinct

---

Trendelenburg in his school-days, and given by Bratuschek in his monograph on Trendelenburg. Later it appeared in such expressions as "It is a great and glorious thing to call up the simple gospel into intimate life within one's self," in the tendency to repel all "construction" of Christianity from the stand-point of philosophical systems, in the profound belief in Divine Providence and apparently reverent and loving acceptance of the authority of Christ (cf. *Kleine Schriften,* i, p. 73). But with Trendelenburg, as with German philosophers, generally, who are not professed theologians, philosophy was an independent science, which was, if any thing, to confirm, and not to be confirmed by, religion, so that it is only virtually (but none the less truly), and not by reason of any distinct utterances or claims in his writings, that Trendelenburg could be termed (by his friend Mayer, see Bratuschek, p. 222) a "Christian philosopher."

perceptions. With Kant the cardinal point in philosophy became, under the influence of the English philosophers, Locke and Hume, anthropological and, if it may be thus termed, cognitional, rather than ontological or cosmological; the question of first importance was, what can man know? and not, as it had been before, what is the nature of things? The skeptical conclusion, by which theoretical knowledge was confined within the limits of the subjectively phenomenal and relative, and the moral conclusion, resting in the postulates of God's existence, of human freedom, and of the immortality of the soul, led, as is known, in the system of Fichte to the doctrine of complete subjective idealism: since, of the two factors, by the coöperation of which Kant accounted for the facts of human knowledge, namely, the mind with its innate forms and functions, and the unknown and unknowable "things-in-themselves," the latter had inconsequently had ascribed to them by Kant a causative agency in the production of impressions and ideas in the human mind (inconsequently, for Kant had elsewhere sought to demonstrate that the range of causality was confined absolutely to the sphere of phenomena, in distinction from "things-in-themselves"). Fichte, with characteristic logical boldness and recklessness, resolved to derive the whole universe from the subject alone, *i.e.*, from the *Me,* and hence was obliged also to identify God, the Absolute, with the absolute subject. Philosophy, thus fairly launched on the sea of pure speculation, with no acknowledged guidance but that of a purely *a priori* or dialectic method, did not delay, with the aid of Schelling and Hegel, to run to the very end of the idealistic tether, landing in the system of absolute idealism. In this system the absolute, apprehended in pure thought as identity of thought and being, figured as the source whence the dialectic method was to trace the development of the whole universe of reality. The real was to be construed—ideally constructed—*a priori.* Rich in grand conceptions and suggestive thoughts, this philosophy, nevertheless, did such insolent—had it not been ludicrous—violence to established facts of positive science and of history, that, while the crowd of men aspiring to be accounted the possessors of philosophical opinions, but too indolent or impotent to form them for themselves, were sunning themselves in the

light of the new intellectual luminary, others, more suspicious
of appearances, could not but inquire whether the original
source of all this glow were perhaps, after all, but the
phosphorescence of unsound materials, or, in other words,
whether the authority by which the new philosophy ad-
judicated *a priori* upon the facts of the universe was really well
founded or not. This philosophy wrenched by its demands
and claims too violently the fibres of average human belief, not
to be followed by reaction and resistance. Criticism would
naturally seek to detect flaws in the principle and method of
the new philosophy, and when these had been discovered
and set forth with sufficient evidence to shake the convictions
of unprejudiced believers, the query would naturally arise:
what philosophy shall we fall back upon—or, what does the
history of philosophy teach us to rest upon as solid ground of
theory? The exponent, *par éminence,* of this criticism and
this inquiry was Professor Trendelenburg, and it is because
he is thus the representative of a new tide in the historic
progress of German thought, that his life and philosophy are
specially worthy of our study.

What Trendelenburg accomplished may profitably be considered under the successive heads of,—1. Criticism of recent
methods; 2. Historical and critical investigation and rehabil-
itations of the true results of earlier, especially ancient philosophy; 3. Positive development of doctrine on the basis of
historically assured results.

I. Trendelenburg's positive aim was the establishment of a
philosophical theory which could stand the test of comparison
with the results of modern science, nay, more, which should be
confirmed by and, so far as practicable, founded on those results. Recognizing fully the necessity of experience for all concrete knowledge, respecting the various positive sciences as
sovereign within their respective spheres, he sought in philosophy the common band which should unite these sciences,
and not a speculative principle which should produce them
a priori. Philosophy was to be, in some sense, the one eye
overseeing them all, the one mind comprehending them in
their mutual relations and as parts of one ideal whole; it was to
recognize in the case of each science, whether concrete or
abstract, its place and use in the whole *organism* of knowl-

edge; it was to be consummated in an "organic conception of the universe" of thought and being.

But philosophy was not to dictate to positive science what its methods or its results should be; it should not attempt to control scientific fact. In this spirit, it differed from post-Kantian philosophy. (Hegel, for example, concluded, on speculative grounds, in favor of Gœthe's luckless theory of color, and could speak, in that connection, of the "insipidity" and "disingenuousness, even" of Newton!). On the other hand, it agreed with the spirit of Kant's and of the English philosophy, and indeed with the tendency of modern philosophy as a whole in regarding the problem of knowledge—its possibility and veracity—as the fundamental or initial one. Now, as a philosophy, fundamentally speaking, must err, if at all, either in its assumptions or in its methods, and as the current results of philosophy convicted the latter of error, Trendelenburg's first search was for the false methods or assumptions from which speculation had been proceeding. He found them, naturally, both conjoined and, as it were, intertwined, and his first work was to show their weakness or falsity.

As to method (logic), German philosophy had partly developed, partly adopted two views of logic. Kant, substantially the founder of the one view, had regarded logic as a purely formal science, having to do simply with the forms of thought, —motion, judgment, inference—without reference to its content. And in this view he had been and is still followed by numerous and influential imitators. (Sir William Hamilton's Logic is the notable embodiment of this view in English literature). The other view, founded proximately in the method of Fichte and Schelling, came to perfection in the celebrated Logic of Hegel and is known by the name of the dialectic method. Against both views Trendelenburg directs his criticism. (It will be borne in mind that the German conception and consequent treatment of logic differ measurably from the English, in uniting this science closely either with the discussion of the problem of the possibility and nature of knowledge, or with metaphysics proper. Only the adherents of the formal view of logic treat it as exclusively conversant with the laws of thought as thought, without reference to their metaphysical meaning or objective validity. Trendelenburg, true to his organic conception of the world, regards thought as, "so to speak, the highest organ of the world, so that, if understood in its forms, it points to the nature of the things which it is destined mentally to apprehend and to comprehend.")

To the formal view of logic, then, Trendelenburg objects that it regards thought without due reference to the organic end and use of thought, and that its pretended consideration of the forms of thought apart from all relation to what is thought, is impracticable (*Logische Untersuchungen,* vol. i, chap. 2). From the truth of formal logic would follow the impossibility of a philosophical development.

But it is Trendelenburg's criticism of the Hegelian, dialectic method, which did the most, not only for the celebrity of the critic, but also in the way of clearing up the speculative fog in the midst of which German speculation was floundering. Eduard Zeller, whose competency as a judge none can deny—himself originally a Hegelian—terms Trendelenburg's criticism of the dialectic method "sharp and successful" (*Geschichte der deutschen Philosophie,* München, 1873, p. 908). In fact, it was annihilating; and the breaking up of the Hegelian school simultaneously with the publication of the *"Logical Investigations"* and with the public discussion which they stimulated, was by no means accidental. The objections of Trendelenburg are directed against the primal assumption of the method, "pure thought," and against the alleged process of immanent, dialectic development. The former is shown to be impossible and the latter to be not what it claims to be, viz: a purely *a priori* process, independent of experience.

Empiricism and dogmatic idealism, in attempting to answer the fundamental questions of philosophy, become involved in contradictions or else demand of the unprejudiced inquirer the admission of what he is unwilling to admit without better reason than any alleged. Absolute idealism requires its adepts at the outset *simply to think* (*rein denken zu wollen,* Hegel, *Encyclopädie,* § 78, *Logik,* Book I, *init.*). The assurance is then held out that through an inner necessity pure thought shall move forward, developing, according to a necessary law peculiar to itself, the whole scientific system of the universe. What must otherwise appear simply as an inexplicable riddle, will be seen in its true nature; God, the universe, and humanity, with their laws, will be seen, as it were, in their growth, and the how and the why of all things shall be revealed to the satisfied gaze of men. Out of the Absolute the finite, the real, shall be construed, or, rather, developed. The beginning, then, is pure thought, without definite, concrete content, other than pure being, which, after abstracting from all concrete objects, must remain as the necessary (at least formally objective) correlative to thought. But then pure thought and pure being will be identical, and it may, therefore, also be said, and is said, that the beginning is pure being. This "pure being," the product of "pure abstraction," is, however, obviously enough "purely nothing;" or pure being and pure nothing are the same. Thus far, apparently, little has been won; how shall further progress be made from a beginning which seems so unpromising? Answer: The identity, thus established, of pure being and nothing is contradictory; thought cannot endure a contradiction; hence it determines itself, and Being along with it, to a higher notion, to which notion a corresponding higher reality corresponds, namely, to the notion of Becoming, in which, as in a higher unity, the contradictory terms are both contained and their contradiction resolved. This first stage in the dialectic process illustrates, then, the whole method. First, thesis; second antithesis; third, synthesis. The synthesis serves, however, at once as the starting-point for a new progress, the moving impulse being the new contradiction which itself is found to involve and which urges on (in the form of a new antithesis) to the determination of a new synthesis; and so on, *in indef.* In the above exposition is seen, also, in its primal manifestation in Hegel's system, the celebrated law of the identity of contradictories, as also, in its first operation, the propelling principle which lies at the basis of the speculative development. (We do not here inquire whether the antithetic terms are true contradictories, nor whether, supposing them to be such, the strange perception of their identity would not be sufficient to satisfy the curiosity and the interest of thought and so to arrest the progress of the development by taking away all motive for pursuing it further. The former point, at least, Trendelenburg, as we shall see, has considered for us.)

The first requirement of the dialectic method being that we shall simply think, the question arises as to the possibility and import of this pure thought. Admitting its possibility for the moment, we remark preliminarily that it will be of no value or concern to us, unless it shall possess some important content and advance in some definite direction. This much is by universal recognition essential to all thought worthy of the name.

The expression "pure thought" is an inconveniently indefinite one, since it may be made to stand for an important truth or to conceal an impossibility. It may denote and would perhaps most naturally suggest "the Ideal," which in the human mind depends upon a previous knowledge of the Real; or it may express the characteristic quality of rationally conscious, as distinguished from non-conscious, being; or, finally, it may be employed, as it is at the beginning of Hegel's *Logic,* as a name for thought engaged with no *definite,* concrete object and independent of sensibility. Has pure thought, in this last sense, an important content and can it move forward in a definite direction? If what Hegel claims were true, the question, in both its clauses, would have to be answered with a decided affirmative. This we have already seen. But let us look a little more closely, seeking to be guided only by the old-fashioned and scarcely yet antiquated principle of the identity of things identical and of the contradictory and hence mutually exclusive nature of things contradictory. We are required by Hegel to abstract from all that which sensation offers or imagination constructs. Complying, we find our thought occupied with nothing in particular and with everything in general, i.e., with the simple notion of being, for "everything," in its "general" aspect, is simply being. Now, could we arrive even at this indefinite result, if sensation and imagination had furnished us nothing from which to abstract? He would be rash who should assert the affirmative. Nor has this general notion of Being any significance or value for us, except in its relation to that from which it is abstracted or to those possibilities of being, unknown in reality, which we represent to ourselves only with the first or indirect aid of the imagination. If, now, this notion be viewed in the light of that from which it is abstracted, it has a certain value, but is not an independent possession of pure thought; if not thus viewed, if thought, seeking to regard it, repels all reference to the sources through which the notion was derived, it becomes nothing and the thought of it impossible. The thought of it is possible for Hegel, only because he combines in his conception of pure thought two notions, which exclude each other, and with the one of which he practically works, while the other is falsely imagined to be the true working conception. These notions have been both indicated in the above definition of the "third sense" in which pure thought may be understood. They are: absence of any definite, concrete object (but not of negative reference to sensible intuition), and independence of the forms and at least ideal activities of sensible intuition. The former is the working notion in Hegel's system; the latter is a mere figure-head, contradictory and impossible *in re,* but put forward as the all-effecting agent. In the latter sense, purely to think is purely to do nothing, and hence, evidently enough, progress is out of the question. And it is because the beginning is made by Hegel, not in the "element of pure thought" taken in this really unthinkable sense, the sense required and professed by the system, but in the former sense, i.e., it is because the beginning is made by him in a realm thickly surrounded by the shadowy forms of banished objects, which imagination is constantly ready and urgent to reintroduce upon the scene, that any kind of progress is possible for him. Without the felt presence and influence of these forms, not thought, which is life, but the absence of thought, or mental death, would ensue. For thought is suffocated and withers without the air and light of the sensible cognition of the world of real things and the creative aid of the imagination, which works with materials derived from such cognition. Pure thought, in the sense required by the Hegelian dialectic, is impossible. What is thus shown by reflection and analysis, is confirmed by Trendelenburg in the demonstration which he gives in the *"Logical Investigations"* (chap. iii, *init.*), of the fact that the first stadium, through which pure thought is alleged to pass, is not traversed without the aids now pointed out, and hence, by analogy, that the whole assumed progress of pure thought depends on the same aids. But before accompanying our author in his analysis, let us call attention to another fundamental assumption of the Hegelian system.

While the beginning, as above stated, is, in its subjective aspect, pure thought, it is, objectively speaking, pure being; and these, says Hegel, are one. Identity of thought and being, or, rather, their inseparable union as different but accordant aspects of the same thing (the Absolute), this is the assumption common to all systems of absolute idealism. The assumption in German idealism had its origin with Kant, who concluded that the whole sphere of known Being was phenomenal and hence subjective, and that true being (in "things in themselves"), though real, was unknowable. Fichte, detecting (with others) the formal inconsistency with which Kant had concluded to the existence of things in themselves, denied their existence, deriving the whole universe from the activity of the "me," the subject of thought, and so founding the system of subjective idealism. In this system obviously enough, being could not but be identical with thought. But the basis of the system was untenable, the fancied demonstration of it (through Kant) having (now, at least) been shown, on the one hand, to be unsound, and, on the other, not to warrant, in so far as it may be sound, any such conclusion as that drawn by Kant and his successors. The theorem of the identity of thought and being became therefore, instead of a demonstrated principle, really a postulate of the whole school of absolute idealists from Fichte onwards.

What it means with Hegel is, doubtless, in the main (as with Spinoza), that the content and connection of necessary thought corresponds with the content and connection of being, and further (in advance upon Spinoza) that thought is the "truth of being," as its genius and its end. In the Absolute, according to Hegel, thought and being are one, and since, according to the same authority, the Absolute can be comprehended in pure thought—can be seen in dialectical development—it follows that the dialectic development of thought is at once an expression of the necessary development or being of things. If, in what follows, the demonstration shall be completed that pure thought is impossible for man (or, at least, that Hegel's attempt at it was unsuccessful,) the above

conclusion will also fall, with the assumption on which it
rests. (For the rest, Hegel himself found insuperable obstacles
in nature to the realization of all which he had proudly
claimed for pure thought. "The development of the particular," he admits, in his *Philosophy of Nature,* "is exposed to
external and foreign influences; in this is seen an impotence
(?) of nature, which sets limits to philosophy; that which is
most particular in nature cannot be ideally exhausted [ex-
pressed in adequate conceptions]." See Ueberweg's *History of
Philosophy,* New York, 1874, vol. i, p. 531.) We call attention
here simply to the circumstance that Hegel seems to envisage
the postulate of thought and being as identical, in different
manners, in different parts of the *Logic.* At the beginning we
are told that the commencement is made with "pure being,
which is also pure thought." Here the identity is evidently
purely psychological; pure being is a "pure abstraction," and
an abstraction has no being except in thought. It is evident
that from this identity there does not follow the real identity
of definite physical being with the thought which apprehends
it or even with the thought which (in man) is assumed "dialectically" to develop it. Nor is either of these forms of
identity synonymous with that other, which Hegel affirms in
his *Philosophy of Law,* when he says that "whatever is real
is rational, and whatever is rational is real." It is this latter
conception of identity which determines Hegel's practical
developments, and in the affirmation of its truth, but not in
its application, few metaphysicians, we fancy, will disagree
with him.

That, now, the progress from thesis, through antithesis, to
synthesis, in the successive stadia of the dialectical development, is not a progress of pure thought, is shown by Trendelenburg in an examination of the first stadium. "The beginning," says Hegel, "is pure being, which is, at the same time,
pure thought." "This pure being," he continues, "is pure
abstraction, hence the absolutely negative, which is nothing."
"Nothing" (in this view) "is the same as being. The truth of
being, as also of nothing [*das Nichts,* taken, it should be observed, with the article, hence substantively, hence treated as
though it were after all something more than bare, absolute
negation] is therefore the unity [identity] of the two; this unity

is [ideally, and hence also really] Becoming." Pure Being, the
beginning, is Nothing, and Nothing is pure Being; both are
identical, and yet they are contradictory; the contradiction is
resolved, for thought, in the notion of Becoming, and for the
corresponding world of reality, in the corresponding real
process. That becoming contains a positive and a negative
element—being and non-being—is obvious enough, as Trendelenburg now says, when we consider the notion in the light
of sensible intuition or observation. "While, for example, it
is becoming light [while day is dawning], it is both light and
also not yet light." But pure being, says Trendelenburg, is
repose: and pure nothing is repose. Becoming (development)
is motion; where, in the elements which Becoming involves
and whence it issues, is found the element of motion which
appears in the resulting higher idea? It is not contained in
them: and pure thought being unable to draw from them
what they cannot yield, nor to add this to them from its own
resources, is really compelled, tacitly, but surreptitiously, to
call in the required idea of motion from the sphere of sensible
intuition.[2] "Thus Motion, without a word of explanation, is
assumed by the dialectic method which pretends to assume
nothing." "The beginning of the dialectic is subsequently
represented as being like the beginning of the geometry of
Euclid. The postulate of logic, it is said, is Think, just as
the postulate of geometry is 'Draw a straight line.' In and
through these actions both of these sciences then proceed
systematically and naturally forwards. That which is involved
in the requirement to 'think' is presupposed, and nothing
else. But the difference between the two cases is easy to be
perceived. Geometry requires something simple: something
equally simple was to be required by the dialectic method;
hence its requirement was termed *pure* thought. But, behold
what happens: this pure thought, presupposing only itself,
can, notwithstanding its simplicity, not advance without aid,
and it shows itself in its very first step indissolubly joined to
[making use of] an idea, in which space and time are perceived
to be involved; it is therefore not pure thought, completely

---

[2] We use the expression "sensible intuition," in this Article, as the
equivalent of the German term *Anschauung*.

unfettered from external or concrete being." Trendelenburg points out, with less of detail, how motion, with space and time, is in like manner tacitly assumed in subsequent stadia of the alleged progress of pure thought, and in particular, in the section relating to Quantity, where such notions as continuous and discrete magnitude, the "Extensive," the "Intensive," and Number are considered. He calls attention to the fact that the terms of language confirm the assertion of the natural and necessary involution of motion, time, and space in the notions in question. (The reader will recall the "Thesis" above cited, in which Trendelenburg asserts the philosophical significance of etymology. Trendelenburg constantly looked to the forms of language for the confirmation or correction of his views.) "External motion is thus, in the first place, the postulate of this non-postulating logic. It is impossible to tell how much is thus secretly introduced—the whole wealth of constructive mathematical intuition, the clearness of an accompanying sensuous image. This postulate is immeasurable in its consequences. For motion, when present in the slightest measure, gives an image and so conducts directly into the realm of sensible intuition. Thus thought has at its disposal an image, which it uses whenever it needs it, but which, agreeably to its principle, it repels from itself, whenever it withdraws into the realm of proud abstraction." So, then, the "pure thought" with which the dialectic method claims to begin, is impossible, for it cannot exist without content, nor, if it could thus exist, can it live without progressing, and both content and progress depend on the presence and aid of elements derived from or indirectly related to the sphere of the sensuous imagination.

The dialectic method proposes to construct the universe of thought and being by speculative development from the datum of pure thought. Its procedure is professedly a priori. It would show the genesis and necessary connection of things, as they might lie in the consciousness of a divine mind. A posteriori, i.e., empirical, aid, the aid of sensation and imagination, is to be excluded. By what means, then, is the construction to be effected? It has been above indicated that the notions of contradiction (negation) and identity are the prominent means used for the end proposed. Trendelenburg proceeds to show the defects and the inefficacy of these means. Negation, he points out, may be either logical or real; the one is formal, contradictory opposition (A and non-A); the other is real (material) opposition—the opposition of contraries (white, black). The former is purely mental, the work of reflection, and requires no positive image of the second term; the latter alone exists in nature, whence both its terms are derived through sensuous intuition. By an examination of various stadia at which the principle of negation is seen at work in Hegel's system, Trendelenburg shows that it is not logical, but real opposition which is in play, and that consequently its employment requires and has led to the constant use of sensible intuition and its products, which are foreign to pure thought, and concludes his consideration of the first one of these "means" as follows: "There results from all this, for the dialectic of pure thought, an inevitable dilemma. Either the negation, by the aid of which it leads to antithesis and synthesis, is pure, logical negation (A, non-A)—in which case it can bring forth no *definite* product in the antithesis and can not combine thesis and antithesis in the synthesis; or it is real (contrary) opposition—which, however, can not be arrived at by the way of logic alone, so that the dialectic is not a dialectic of pure thought. . . ." The other means employed, identity, establishes the reconciliation of what was before opposed, as, above, Becoming was termed the identity or unity of Being and Nothing, and "their truth." But this identity, as Trendelenburg shows, is an identity of reflection or comparison—an identity, that is to say, at the perception of which the dialectic philosopher arrives only by the way of comparison with what, *ex hypothesi*, his pure thought does not contain, namely, with the world of real, sensuously apprehended forms; hence the employment of this means involves again the abandonment of the ground of pure thought. While it is claimed to have concrete significance, it is purely abstract, and is ludicrously inadequate to the accomplishment of the results claimed for it. This is shown by Trendelenburg in numerous examples taken from Hegel's *Logic*, among others, in the development of the notion of Freedom. Here the thesis is causal substance, causality; the antithesis is the effect; the synthesis is reciprocity of action (action and reaction). The effect reacts, is itself therefore causal. Cause becomes effect, and effect, cause. In this identity of cause and effect, the underlying substance remains "at home" ("with itself," *"bei sich,"* a phrase denoting a moment subsequent to that expressed by "in itself" and "for itself;" the indefiniteness of the expression, as applied by Hegel, is fitly pointed out by Trendelenburg.) This being "at home" (having come home) on the part of substance is, therefore [!], the truth of necessity, or freedom! Trendelenburg very justly and mildly remarks, that the dialectician thinks he has more in this train of development than he really has.

The remainder of Trendelenburg's criticism—which we cannot be expected further to reproduce here—is directed to showing that the argument from a *regressus in infinitum* is frequently and incorrectly employed by Hegel as positive proof of a contrary; that the terms "immediate and immediacy," present in every page of the Hegelian *Logic,* conduct unseen from the assumed realm of pure thought into the realm of sensuous representation; that in place of the asserted immanent connection of the Hegelian system, there is, rather, a constant solution of continuity; that the dialectic process, contrary to its claims, is the reverse of the genetic. Particularly entertaining is the manner in which Trendelenburg convicts of logical error those steps in the dialectic process in which, by virtue of the ostensible Principle of Identity, thesis and antithesis are united in synthesis. In these steps we discover "the second syllogistic figure of Aristotle, but—what logic interdicts —with an affirmative conclusion. E.g., Pure being is 'immediate;' Nothing is 'immediate': hence nothing is pure being; or, the premises being interchanged, pure being is nothing. Logic warns us against such syllogisms. . . . From the nature of the case, syllogisms of the second figure with affirmative conclusions are fallacies or sophisms. Since Aristotle's time it has remained a demonstrated law that in the second figure none but negative conclusions are possible. Hegel counts the second figure as the third—which does not alter the case; but he treats with contempt the rules to which it is subject; since he adds in a note *(Encyclopädie,* § 187): 'The inquiry, for the rest, as to the conditions necessary to correct conclusions in the various figures—whether these may be universal, etc., or

negative—is a *mechanical* one, which, on account of its senseless mechanism and essential insignificance, has justly fallen
into oblivion.' That which is termed mechanical in this passage, is really, the rather, an instance of mathematical exactness and necessity, which no one has ever yet disregarded with
impunity. He who considers the observance of an elementary
principle to be beneath his dignity, will surely be tripped up
by it." In like manner, errors in conversion and instances of
a fallacious *quaternio terminorum* are pointed out.

Such, then, are the principal points in the criticism by
Trendelenburg of Hegel's dialectic method—and he who will
may read the whole expressed in the author's meaty German,
Logische Untersuchungen, 2d ed., ch. iii.[3] In this examination
of the dialectic method and in this exposure of its defects,
Trendelenburg claimed that he had placed the life of the
system of absolute idealism at stake, since the latter lived only
through the former. He recognized, with all others competent
to express a judgment in the matter, the grandeur of Hegel's
aim. But this aim of Hegel's was and is substantially identical
with that of all philosophy, to comprehend, namely, all things
in their necessity, to make it evident to thought how and why
things are and must be as they are, and to discover the principle of life on which the procession of events in the universe
depends. But were the means chosen by Hegel sufficient for
the end proposed, "was the earth, on which he stood, firm
enough to support such a heaven-storming construction?"
This is what was to be decided, and Trendelenburg's dissec-
tions and demonstrations were "epoch-making" in leading to
that negative answer, which has already become so nearly the
judgment of history. If we have dwelt so long upon it, this
has been because of the importance of the achievement in it-

---

[3] In the *Journal of Speculative Philosophy*, ed. by W. T. Harris, St.
Louis, No. 20, 1871, Nos. 21, 22, 24, 1872, may be read a translation of
articles written by Trendelenburg in defence of his criticism, after the
publication of various attacks upon it. While these articles, well translated,
furnish an admirable specimen of the reposeful, pregnant, almost antique
style of the author, it is surprising that the translator did not instead give
the readers of the journal the original criticism as published in the
Logical Investigations; for the "articles" deal only by way of brief re-
capitulation with the criticism itself, and are largely taken up with
personal or local discussion of relatively transient interest.

self, and also because the interest among American students of philosophy in Hegel, and the disposition among many of our best philosophical minds to study the scientific merits of his method, are so marked, as to make the exposition given both welcome and, possibly, useful.

But not only did our philosopher thus seek negatively to determine his own ground by showing the untrustworthiness of others among his immediate contemporaries; in the further development of his own doctrines he has constant reference to the theories of others, seeking to prove all things, to hold fast that which is good. Thus, to take one example and that a most important one, in connection with his own derivation of the notions of time and space, Trendelenburg seeks to justify his disagreement with various philosophers, whose theories on the subject were most worthy of attention. It is in this connection that he first developed, in a manner to attract attention, his criticism—now become notorious, if not also famous—of the Kantian doctrine of time and space; the doctrine on which the whole *Kritik of Pure Reason* essentially rests, and which affirms the exclusively subjective and *a priori* character of these intuitions, as forms of perception and imagination, valid *for us,* but unrelated to things-in-themselves—necessarily applied by man, but only within the sphere of experience, which sphere covers only phenomena and does not extend to the true things as they are or may be in themselves. Trendelenburg maintained that Kant's arguments for the subjective and *a priori* nature of the intuitions ("forms of intuition") in question did not exclude the hypothesis that space and time have also objective reality; Kant, according to Trendelenburg, seemed to have fancied that space and time must be either exclusively subjective or exclusively objective, and not to have considered the third alternative, viz: that of their being at once both subjective and objective. It is pretty nearly literally true to say that the *cudgel* was taken up by Kuno Fischer, the historian of Modern Philosophy, in Kant's defense, in the second edition of his *History.* The dispute became in the end extended over a wider ground than that of the doctrine in question, in consequence of the intimation made and supported by proofs, on the part of Trendelenburg, that Kuno Fischer's exposition of Kant was not authentic;

and it must be admitted that it also became personal and criminatory to a degree not creditable to the influence of divine philosophy on the passions of its votaries. Numerous parties have expressed their views on the main subject of the dispute, in pamphlets and review-articles, and the matter will still be held by many to be *in judice.* The present writer, after a tolerably careful review of the arguments and proofs on both sides, can not but express his agreement with many whom he believes to be among the most impartial of philosophical judges in Germany, that Trendelenburg was triumphantly in the right, as he was far superior to his opponent in point of temper. We should be glad, did the limits and proportions of this Article permit it, to develop the grounds for agreement with Trendelenburg in this matter. It will be evident, at all events, to all familiar with the philosophy of Kant and of his successors, how this demonstration of the incompleteness of Kant's proof of the exclusive ideality of time and space, cuts away the ground from beneath the feet of the whole subsequent development of German idealism.

II. The degree to which, during the past three or four decades, historical studies in philosophy have taken the place, among the Germans, of original system-making, has been often enough remarked. The causes of this lie near at hand. Modern philosophy had grown up without due reference to the investigations of earlier thinkers. Bacon, Descartes, Kant, had treated ancient philosophy with neglect, when not with contempt. The same inattention to ancient thinking had prevailed, relatively, with the immediate successors of Kant. Hegel with his comprehensive, all-embracing desire for knowledge, had indeed studied the history of past philosophical systems and lectured on the same. But his study and his exposition had been prejudiced by the desire to find exemplified, in the succession of philosophical stand-points, the all-compelling sway of the dialectic process of development. It was not history as such, but history as testifying to the truth of the Hegelian system, that was sought. The tension of the general philosophical mind after the publication and wide-spread adoption of the Hegelian philosophy was extreme, and could not but generate in the end a reaction of fatigue. When finally, after the death of Hegel, history began to make up a verdict unfavorable to the truth of the Hegelian method and teaching, it is not strange that a general distrust of system-makers followed, and that those who did not abandon philosophy entirely, sought rest for their minds and a sure footing for their remaining philosophical convictions in the calm study of the past. And especially was it the grand, reposeful forms of the Greek masters towards which many eyes turned. It was as if the resolve had been made to institute a new investigation, which, covering the whole ground of the past, should determine what results, valid by the fiat of history, and consistent with the results of modern science, had been arrived at by all preceding philosophers. And this impulse towards historical investigation was and is but a part of the wider movement in the direction of historical study in general. "Seldom is sufficient emphasis laid upon the fact, that our century, by the historical direction given to its investigations, has brought about a second Renaissance—a Renaissance extending to all that is great in the past, but yet restricted to that alone which is ascertained to be truly great—a Renaissance on the basis of an all-inclusive criticism, and not, like that of the 16th century, borne on the inspiration of an one-sided, naive enthusiasm." (Alfred Dove, in *In neuen Reich*, 1872, No. 7, p. 242.) In this study and restoration of the past Trendelenburg took a conspicuous and earnest part. His philological studies had specially prepared him for the critical study of Greek texts. (The union in him of philological and philosophical attainments led to his being termed, revilingly, "the philologist among the philosophers, and the philosopher among the philologists.") The fruits of such study appeared in the historical works above named. The first part of the *History of the Doctrine of Categories* is especially devoted to Aristotle's doctrine. The result of the investigation is that Aristotle arrived at the statement and definition of the categories in his table, through the study of the logical elements of grammatical discourse. While this result was not received, in the case of weighty contemporary authorities, without protest, it could not but be especially interesting to Trendelenburg, as furnishing a new exemplification of his favorite thesis of the intimate connection between philology and philosophy. The other volumes of the *Historical Contributions* contain articles and addresses relating especially to the history of modern philosophy, Spinoza, Leibnitz, Kant, and Herbart receiving most attention. The numerous addresses reprinted in the *Minor Writings*, relate in large proportion to Prussian history, and are to a considerable extent an historical commentary to Trendelenburg's work on Natural Law.

The characteristic of all of Trendelenburg's historical investigations is the scientific objectiveness with which he apprehends and sets forth the historic facts and their substantial import. Not that he regards the various philosophical systems and doctrines of the past with the dry light of the understanding alone, as a botanist dissects a plant or an anatomist a corpse. From the time of his graduating from the gymnasium, he sought to combine with intellectual light the warmth of feeling; indeed, according to him, feeling and not thought, was the fundamental and characteristic mark of humanity. So, then, the artistic in form and the ideal in inspiration and content, in Plato's works, excited his special and enthusiastic approbation, as did also the sober exactitude and much in the method and specific teachings of Aristotle; while doctrines, such as some of Spinoza's, Kant's, Hegel's, and Herbart's being, in his opinion, demonstrably false and in some cases pernicious, he treats them with all the severity of logical rigor and, sometimes, of a just moral indignation. Never, however, does he confound an intellectual opinion with the personality of its defender, when measuring out his blame; his decided reprobation, on scientific and logical grounds, of the pantheism of Spinoza and Hegel, for example, never blinds him to their personal, moral worth nor to the magnitude of their substantial contributions to the development of philosophic thought and knowledge.

But while Trendelenburg's historical investigations were thus carried on in a truly scientific spirit, they all had, as above mentioned, a direct and intended bearing on the construction of his own philosophical system and the discussion of living questions. "We desire," he says, in his *History of the Doctrine of Categories*, p. 197, "to contribute to the result, that historic investigations, from their broad basis in the past, shall raise their summits into the present. It is where history ceases to be simply past, that it furnishes the most active impulses for the present." While philosophy must ever seek expression in a system, it could not disconnect itself from its past. The past contained for it results and warnings, from which the philosophy of the present could and must derive profit. "Philosophy will not recover its former power, until it acquires permanence, and it will not become permanent until it shall grow in the same way in which the other sciences grow—until it presents a continuous development, not taking a new start, and then abruptly breaking off with every successive thinker, but taking up the problems of thought as given in history and carrying their development further on."

"The Germans must give up their erroneous idea, that a new principle must be found for the philosophy of the future. The principle *has been* found; it is found in the organic conception of the world, founded in Plato and Aristotle, continued by subsequent philosophers who followed in their steps, and which must be developed and gradually perfected in a profounder investigation of the fundamental conceptions, as also of the special minor sides of the problem, and in mutual *rapport* with the concrete sciences.

"Had a powerful mind, like Schelling, begun with Plato and Aristotle the philosophical studies which, in the succession of his works, he went through with 'before the public,' instead of proceeding in inverted order backwards from Fichte and Kant to Herder's analogies, then to Spinoza, then to Plato and Giordano Bruno, then to Jacob Böhme, and only taking up Aristotle at the last and at a time when, in spite of his most earnest attempts to penetrate Aristotle, he could only use him —as he does in his rational philosophy—as a kind of elastic springboard, whence and by the aid of which to hasten himself and the reader into the monstrous 'Potenz'-doctrine, which is wholly unrelated to Aristotle's principles—had, I say, Schelling not pursued this, but followed the contrary, course, one portion of German philosophy would have turned out otherwise than it did—greater, more enduring, more fruitful. So important is it to keep company with history and to follow the historical development of great thoughts in humanity."

It was, above all, Aristotle without the knowledge of whom "the true source of modern philosophy would remain unknown." During every semester, accordingly, it was Trendelenburg's custom to spend two hours in each week in the public explanation of some portion of Aristotle's writings to a voluntary class of students. His method in these lessons was not doctrinal or magisterial; on the contrary, he sought to make his pupils investigate for themselves, and his method was adapted to draw them out and assist and stimulate them. The result of the impulses thus communicated became subsequently apparent in the lives and works of more than one of his pupils, who have made substantial contributions to the study and interpretation of ancient—especially the Aristotelian—philosophy.

As to the sources, in ancient philosophy, of Trendelenburg's own system, they are to be sought in Plato's and Aristotle's doctrines. The spirit of Plato's dialogues, in which thought—the "Ideas"—are made so decidedly, not simply the *prius,* but the only and true reality of things, elicited from Trendelenburg a hearty and sympatheic response. But he was not blind to the indefinite and the fantastic in Plato's philosophy, in whose theory of ideas and of the cognition of ideas he discerned the ancient prototype or beginning of the modern notion of pure, unimaged thought. The Platonic Idea was true and real, but not such, nor cognizable, apart from "things"—the reality and scientific cognoscibility of which latter were, according to Trendelenburg, not to be contested. In Aristotle he found a more discreet, because more realistic theory of cognition, a conception of nature and spirit which so commended itself to Trendelenburg that he made it the ground-work of his own theory, and, what was of no less consequence, an organon of method—the Aristotelian logic—confirmed in the experience of centuries, and not superseded by the dialectic method of the new philosophy. In Aristotle, too, he found the idea by which the formal ethics of a Kant was to be corrected and supplemented, and on which Trendelenburg's own ethical theory was founded.

On the basis of his careful study of the past, and with constant reference to the results of modern positive science—which he studied with unwearied application in the midst of most engrossing labors—Trendelenburg founded his own system of philosophy.

III. Trendelenburg was, evidently, not one of those who,

disheartened by the disastrous end of the labors of the Titans in speculative philosophy, passed to the conclusion that no philosophy was possible. We have already seen that his own experience taught him, what it requires of course but little reflection to perceive, that a system is as necessary for a thinker as a house. Plato, or Aristotle, or Kant, or Hegel, as a system-maker, may fail, but every one will still require that the connection of his own thought shall correspond in some manner or other with the connection of things.

Trendelenburg not only perceived the folly of shutting one's eyes to the verifiable results of earlier thought; he also recognized the inseparable connection of philosophy with the other more concrete or specialized sciences. "Properly speaking, there is as yet no philosophy there, where as yet there exist no special sciences; for it is only in relation with these that philosophy receives its problems and its significance." The special sciences are restricted to limited portions of the realm of reality; their results are but fragments of the whole sum of real or conceivable knowledge; all that we learn is fragmentary, and every philosophical theory is an attempt to reconstruct from the torso the image of the god, or with artistic divination to reunite the scattered limbs in one beautiful body." Philosophy, as Trendelenburg loves to repeat after Plato, is the sentinel on the boundaries of the other sciences, fixing and preserving limits, uniting, demonstrating, and in all this morally purifying. "Philosophy is the religion of science." The special sciences point to the universal; philosophy seeks to realize this universal. She "furnishes principles for the beginnings of the special sciences, establishes harmony among their results, and maintains a living *rapport* among them; she is thus at once *a priori* and *a posteriori;* the latter, because it is in the other sciences that she finds her material, and the former, since she must go beyond and above the material thus furnished in order to seize and exhibit the living band that unites the whole." Philosophy must then bear a due relation to the real and to the ideal; she can be neither purely empirical nor purely *a priori.* Ideal-realism will be her proper name.

The universe exists for thought; the one thing desirable and essential is, that our thought about it shall be true.

Knowledge is something we all imagine ourselves in greater or less measure to possess. The sciences claim to arrive not merely at knowledge, but at necessary knowledge—knowledge of necessity. They prove, in a manner, the legitimacy of this claim by their verification in the application. So, in particular, pure and applied mathematics. The former proceeds by axioms, principles, and constructions, resting on a basis of *a priori* intuition; these axioms, etc., furnish points of view—categories, in a secondary sense—which are verified or concretely illustrated in applied mathematics. The fact of the existence of the sciences is the starting-point for the first philosophical problem, for in this fact is involved the conception of scientific knowledge.

It will be objected (and has been, for example, by Dr. Ulrici, of Halle), that the acceptance of scientific knowledge as a fact, implies what the sceptic may deny, the existence of an objective realm present directly or representatively to the mind. But the question of the reality of an objective world of external things is one upon which practically there is no disagreement among men. The discussion of the grounds of our belief in this reality is essentially one belonging to physics and psychology, and to logic. The explanation of the necessity of this belief is, however, "tacitly contained in logic, which seeks to open the way for an insight into the nature of necessity and into the process by which our knowledge of it arises."

The theory of vision assumes provisionally the reality of the thing to be explained, viz: sight. The nature and significance of the phenomena of sight are to result from the ascertainment and scientific elaboration of the facts. So, in the case of the theory of cognition, the difficulties of the subject can not be expected to disappear before the correct doctrine—statement and comprehension of facts—shall have been developed.

The axioms, principles, and constructions of pure mathematics are not forms or notions found unaccountably in the mind *a priori*, but are seen and known in their mental genesis; our trust in them reposes on our genetic comprehension of them. In so far as our knowledge—thought—in general contains necessary or universal elements, it can be comprehended only when we comprehend, in like manner, its derivation.

.At the outset, therefore, nothing is to be declared inexplicable or unknowable. Any limitation of the field of knowledge, which may eventually be shown necessary, will result from our genetic insight into the nature and possibilities of thought.

Other ways of beginning a system of philosophy, which will occur to the reader of some English systems, are, to write first, for example, a section labelled "The Unknowable," wherein, on the basis of concurrent testimony and alleged "inconceivabilities," the most difficult problems are from the first brushed aside, the subsequent development, running through volumes, being devoted to questions in physics, empirical psychology, or social science (worthy and extremely important subjects, but not questions relating to the essential problems of thought and being); or, on a similar basis, to prove to a probability that certain notions can not but be held, without showing the source of this necessity. If thought and its objects were petrified, and not living, there can be no doubt that the English method of reflective analysis, carried out with sufficient patience, would suffice. But since the contrary supposition is the true one, nothing remains but to find a primal germ and follow it in its development. Philosophy is explanation; but explanation gives the how and the why, and the former can be stated only in terms of motion—terms which describe a genesis.

All the sciences—such is Trendelenburg's development—have to do with somewhat that *is,* and they treat of this "somewhat" through the organ of thought; or, each science has its special subject, a portion of the realm of being, and makes use of thought in the treatment of it in a definite way, or, in other words, has its peculiar method. As, then, the part points always to the whole, so each science points to the science which treats of the whole of being, or of being as such (Metaphysics), and to the science of thought as thought (Logic). "If the sciences will become completed, they need precisely that to which—though it lies beyond their separate, special spheres —they point. Logic and metaphysics are in so far the proper implication, the consequence, of the essential life of the sciences."

The theory of science will hence include a reference both

to metaphysics and to logic, and it is this theory which the *"Logical Investigations"* would establish.

In every act of knowing is involved the antithesis of being and thought. The former is taken up into the latter; the latter penetrates the former. How is this possible?

It was a saying of the ancients that like is known by like. Knowledge, as the union of thought and being, can be possible only in virtue of something which belongs equally to these two factors, something in which each resembles the other. And since thought is essentially active, this element common to thought and being must be some form of activity. The first mark, then, of that active principle which shall mediate between thought and being, must be that it shall be common to both. It must, secondly, be primitive and therefore need and admit no explanation, and hence, thirdly, simple, for the complex is not, logically, primitive.

For the discovery of the principle in question, says Trendelenburg, two ways may be pursued. Either the activities manifested in thought and in being may be analyzed, with a view to ascertaining that ultimate one in which both agree, or, some activity known to sensible intuition may be assumed hypothetically, with a view to seeing whether it meets the required conditions. The latter course is adopted.

The activity thus hypothetically selected is motion. Aristotle declared that "he who knows not motion, knows not nature." Modern science is demonstrating with ever increasing completeness the universality of motion in nature. Our perceptions of nature, sight, sound, etc., are found to depend on external motion. Even for the explanation of matter, the image of motion is found necessary: matter is comprehensible for us only in terms of balanced or specific positive forces, and the conception of force, if realizable at all, is not so without the aid of the conception of motion.

On the other side, thought depends in all its phases on the ideal counterpart of motion. In vision we describe the outline of the object in thought, though with lightning-like rapidity—a form of ideal motion; in sound we "follow" the succession or prolongation of sounds—again a form of ideal motion. The terms and processes of the abstract or logical understanding, such as distinguishing, combining, classifying, inferring, its ideas, such as causality, finality, all imply ideal or *constructive* motion, the counterpart of external motion.

Motion, then, would seem to satisfy the first of the requirements for the desired principle mediating in knowledge between thought and being, the requirement, namely, that it be common to both thought and being.

Motion is, further, both in the sphere of being and in the sphere of thought, primitive, as being underivable, indecomposable, indefinable. No definition of motion can be given which does not presuppose the thing defined.

Thirdly, motion must, in order to meet all the requirements of the principle sought, be simple. It is claimed by some that motion is the product of space and time as its factors. But the ideas, factor, space, time, all involve, in order to their realization in thought, the idea of motion. Or is it claimed that activity is more universal than motion? But no specific difference, by which motion may be distinguished from activity, can be stated, which does not itself imply the conception of motion. Nor is the idea of change more general, though more abstract. Motion is simple, and not compounded. (Since activity and change are more abstract than motion, they cannot serve as principles in a theory of cognition. For a principle is needed which shall conduct thought into the realm of the concretely real.)

Motion is a fact of nature, and "the fundamental phenomenon of all nature." It is claimed and shown to be, in its ideal form, also a fact of mind, and that, not as a mere representative image derived from without, but as original, spontaneous, the counterpart of motion in space, and taking place in the ideal space of thought. Since motion is thus common and fundamental to thought and being, it is possible to conceive how that which is necessarily involved in external motion may be comprehended—may find its necessary counterpart—in thought, which is ideal motion. And *per contra*, that which follows from motion as an ideal possession, those ideas which are seen in thought to result from motion as implied in it, we may expect to find realized in the world of outward, real things. How much, then, and what, is involved ideally in the fact of motion?

First, Trendelenburg examines Kant's arguments for the exclusively subjective nature and validity of the notions of space and time, and finds, as above stated, that they are not conclusive; that, while they prove that space and time are subjective intuitions, they do not exclude the possibility that space and time may have also objective validity. As directly following from the idea of motion, these ideas are observed by Trendelenburg to be at once subjectively and objectively necessary and valid. They are hence not empirical, their number (which, on the Kantian theory that they are *a priori,* purely subjective forms, remained unaccounted for) is explained by the fact that no other similar ideas actually flow from the idea of motion, and their peculiarity as belonging to the sphere of sensible intuition, in distinction from the sphere of abstract conception, is comprehended (for motion, from which they result by implication, is an idea of sensible intuition), as is also, for an analogous reason, their infinitude. The harmony of the subjective and the objective, the union of thought and being in knowledge, is, in so far, made intelligible. Space may then be termed "the external product of motion, and time the idea of the inward measure of motion." Trendelenburg examines various other theories of space and time, arriving at results which confirm indirectly his own conclusion.[4]

From what has now been set forth, it will be evident how, in the view of Trendelenburg, motion, as a physical and ideal (theoretical) activity, is to be regarded as the *prius* of experience, "the *a priori* before experience," and how it is the medium of experience. In an examination of the fundamental notions of mathematics and physics (point, line, figure, number, matter), he shows how, with the aid of space and time, products of motion, through the constructive (intuitive, not abstract) motion of the mind, these notions (intuitions of the sensibility) are, with the exception of matter, evolved *a priori* by generic necessity and are necessarily outwardly manifested and confirmed in the physical world, the radicle of which is also motion. Not as though these notions were developed *a priori,* in such sense as to be anterior to experience and an

---

[4] On the objections to this theory of space and time as related to motion, see Dr. Porter's *The Human Intellect,* New York, 1867, pp. 560, 561.

independent possession of pure mind; (pure mind, mind unrelated to empirical objects, we do not know;) on the contrary, "the *a priori* is only what it is, in so far as it confirms and reveals itself externally." As to matter, although all our attempts to analyse or comprehend it result and end in the apprehension or idea of some form of motion, yet it is admitted that there remains in it something as yet inexplicable.

From Aristotle's time until now, philosophers have been more or less accustomed to distinguish a certain number of fundamental notions, of more general application than others, which have been termed categories. These notions represent mental points of view, from which we apprehend and judge of objects or relations; or, they are fundamental notions, on which all our thinking rests. The ten categories of Aristotle are well known in the history of philosophy, and the twelve categories, in three classes, of Kant, will be familiar to every student of modern philosophy. With Hegel, every new stage in the dialectic development of thought furnishes new categories. In Trendelenburg's *History of the Doctrine of Categories,* he had examined the various forms which this doctrine had assumed in the history of philosophic thought, and had pointed out that, wherein each successive form seemed to be defective. In the last chapter of vol. i. of the *"Logical Investigations"* he names and explains the derivation of eight categories or ideas which follow from the idea of motion and are therefore valid wherever motion is found. These, in distinction from the subsequently investigated "modal" categories, are termed "real categories, following from motion." Thought, since it is self-consciousness, can regard itself in its motion; it knows what it does and sees what it has done. As, now, it observes motion, and its products and relations and distinguishes the latter, there arise for it the categories.

Of these the first and most important is causality. Motion, it has been shown, produces. The apprehension of the product takes place in forms of motion; the product is comprehended only in terms of motion. When, now, we follow backwards the motion of production, we see whence the product came. This derivation of the product is termed causality, which accordingly denotes simply the "direction whence." "The law of causality expresses nothing but this continuity of development." Since motion is in all thought and in all things; the notion of causality is universal and necessary in thought and things.

Motion and counter-motion limit and determine each other and the result is a product relatively at rest. This is termed thing or Substance—the second category. Quantity, the third category, needs little explanation. The fourth, Quality, is causality in substances. A substance, product of motion, is not absolutely at rest. From it motions go forth, producing specific effects. Thus a substance is "through its surface" the occasion of ethereal vibrations, which are perceived by us as color. The other "real" categories (termed also "mathematical") are Measure, Unity in plurality, Inherence, and Reciprocity of action (including force). The significance of all these categories, when the principle of the system is admitted, is absolute, and not merely relative. If motion is the "first energy" of thought and of being, the categories which follow from it express relations at once ideal and real, subjective and objective. "In this view the chasm does not exist, which in other theories separates the categories of thought and the principles of things, as though they belonged to two worlds, which it is impossible to bring into relation; for in their origin all are one." The reader will easily see the coherence between the general theory here propounded and the further view of Trendelenburg, that in cognition, judgment (which corresponds to activity, motion) precedes conception (whose products represent the products of motion).

Thus far we have remained in the physical realm, the realm of the working cause, the sphere of mathematics. Is this the only realm?

The organic world stands before us apparently an imposing monument of the power of thought over the elements of things. In it the part has significance only in relation to the whole—the root only in relation to the tree it nourishes, the human hand only in relation to the person whom it serves. So intricate are the combinations by which the ends of the organism are reached, so inexplicable, at the first glance, except upon the theory that the end has determined the means, that a modern "Positive" philosopher, while refusing to affirm the reality of final causes, has somewhere said that in the investigation of nature we must often proceed as if such causes really existed and acted. In the organic realm, what before was effect (in the sphere of efficient causation) seems now to become the cause, or, in other words, the preconceived idea of the end appears to have determined and directed the means. The phenomenon is at least extremely striking, and the idealistic theory by which it is accounted for is so plausible and so superior in point of evidentness and facility to any other, that it should certainly not be set aside without sufficient reason. The ancients, Plato, Aristotle, accepted the fact and the explanation, the one seeing in the fact the imperfectly realized power of the Idea, and the other not only following out the notion of purpose, end, in the whole sphere of physically organized existence, but also founding on it his conception of the ethical life of man as organically developing itself in the individual, the family, and the state. The notion of purpose, inherent end, as manifested in organic existence, is for Trendelenburg the second fundamental notion in philosophy. Motion—the efficient cause—forms the basis and becomes in the organic sphere the material of purpose—the final cause —and thus philosophy and nature are carried up above the purely mathematical and physical realm into the organic and ethical. There is differentiation, but not opposition. The real categories receive a new and profounder significance, but do not disappear, when permeated by and in the realm of the organic.

The adoption of this second principle required a more explicit and detailed justification than that of motion. The latter was furnished to hand, so to speak, by the sciences, which are but constantly completing the demonstration of its universal presence in nature. The former is very widely ignored or denied by the representatives of the positive sciences. Trendelenburg seeks to show that finality is a natural conception, one furnished by the facts of natural science. For this purpose he examines the structure of various organs and the adaptations of organs to the circumstances in which they are to be used and for the specific uses to which they are put. In these examples the philosopher finds it impossible to exhaust the whole truth of the case with the application of the physical or mathematical categories, and is hence obliged to recognize a new principle, that of intelligence or finality. The difficulties of the case are not ignored. In the organism the efficient cause produces the whole from the parts, while the final cause determines the parts from the whole. "The circle is distinctly revealed. The organ in its activity falls under the sphere of the efficient [physical] cause; but by its structure, which reveals design, it falls under the law of its own effect. The eye sees, but it is sight itself which constructed the eye. . . . The organs of the mouth speak, but it is speech itself, the necessity of expressing thought, which beforehand framed them pliant to their designed use. This circle is the magic circle of the simple fact; and the pre-established harmony seems to point to a power superior to and including both efficient and final cause, and in which thought is the Alpha and the Omega."

The final cause, controlling the efficient cause, the force, identifies itself with the same. Its results are always a form of activity, not of rest; and thus motion which was at the beginning, reappears in the later and higher results to which thought contributes. Thought, finality, takes motion up into its service; "the idea persuades necessity," as Plato says, to become its servant. The efficient cause becomes a means.

Trendelenburg examines the theories of Bacon and Spinoza, who denied or limited the employment of the principle of finality, as also Kant's and Hegel's derivations of the notion, and finds in all no valid objection to the reception of the principle. The principle is assumed, because physical, mechanical causation is as yet insufficient for the facts. "True," says Trendelenburg, "the possibility still remains that a more complete knowledge of the efficient cause would dissolve the theory of finality into mere show. Such an attempt must be expected. But until the attempt shall succeed, the impotence of the efficient cause is the indirect proof of the necessity of design. Light cannot be comprehended as the product of darkness and consequently we assume it to be a distinct form of activity. But light is self-revealing, and this is its proper evidence. So also is it with finality."

The possibility of finality, as an objective form of cognition, is grounded, for Trendelenburg, in the fundamental theory of motion as common to thought and being, and as being hence the agent or *tertium quid* through which thought and being can come together. Being acts upon thought and becomes thus the *ratio cognoscendi* through the medium of motion.[5] In like manner is given the possibility that thought shall act upon being, controlling its motion—its efficient causes—for ends conceived by thought. "As we know external motion only through the mind's own motion, so we perceive the external ends, which nature has realized, only because the mind itself proposes ends and can therefore reproduce in thought the processes of finality in nature." It is true that design—thought —cannot be observed like an outward phenomenon. But no more can physical cause,—for example, the cause of the phenomena of color. One thing only remains indemonstrable. "We observe nowhere in nature the point at which thought seizes hold of force and directs it to ideal ends, and speculation is unable to indicate the point. The philosophy which seeks the inner ends or purpose, founds the ideal in the real; but it as yet knows not how the ideal comes, enters, into the real. Just as the ancients represented the sun-god standing boldly erect in his chariot, and guiding his steeds with his hand, but placed in his hands no reins, instruments of human driving: so thought, as finality, rules the efficient mechanical forces of nature with invisible reins. Human intelligence has under its control an executant hand which provides for the bringing into realization of the means required by intelligence for its ends. But in nature the equivalent for the hand fails in our knowledge, and it is especially through this gap that the doubt enters in which regards finality with incredulity. It is not impossible that one day this defect of knowledge may be made good. For the present, let it suffice to be aware what we do and what we do not know." It remains true, however, that "finality is a fact in the world, and the question is simply, whether it is a universal one or not. If not, then its existence in the world is an inconsequence."

As the physical realm is broader and higher than the mathematical, which latter it takes up into its service, and as the organic, in which the new principle of finality plainly appears,

---

[5] The reader may recall here Spinoza's definition, in his *Ethics*, of the condition of causality: "If two things have nothing in common, one of them cannot be the cause of the other."

stands in a similar relation of superiority to the two preceding, so finally the ethical sphere rises out of and above the organic. In the ethical realm the end is an idea, the idea of the perfection of human nature—an idea given, it is true, in man's existence, but freely accepted and realized by him. The intellectual recognition of this ideal end of existence, and the free consecration of one's powers to its realization, are the characteristic conditions of the ethical. "The will is desire, permeated by thought." "The will is then first will in the full sense of the term, when it is able to act in response to the motion of thought [more especially, in response to the conscious idea of the end to be realized in human existence]. When it thus acts, when therefore it is moved by the idea of the nature of man, it is the good will." "This ability, in opposition to the desires and independently of sensuous motives, to have for one's motive only the Good as conceived in thought, we term Freedom of the Will." Truly free acts are necessary acts, because determined by the immutable idea of the nature and design of man, and by what necessarily flows therefrom.

The "real categories" are raised to a higher and most significant form in the light of the principle of finality. Efficient Causality becomes Means, Substance becomes Organism, Inherence—the relation of parts to a whole—becomes the relation of members to the organism, Quality becomes Organic Activity, and so on.

Of the modal categories, which are peculiarly categories of logic or of thought, Necessity, the most important, rests on the mutual permeation of thought and being. The impossibility of the contrary, by which phrase it is often defined, is measured only by comparison with fixed points in knowledge, which are won only by the mutual interpenetration of thought and being, or by the comprehension of being in thought, on the ultimate basis of the element—motion—common to both.

The method of philosophy is at once analytic and synthetic. A model of all such cognition may be seen in the process by which an obscure passage in the writings of any author is studied and interpreted. The words are analyzed in their etymological forms and syntactical relations, and the sense thereby obtained is confirmed or corrected by comparison with the whole thought, of which the passage is but a partial expression.

"Only in the idea of the whole does the restless movement of the mind find repose." The part points to the whole, the relation to the unconditioned, the finite to the infinite and absolute. In the infinite as its end and cause rests the thought of the finite. But unmistakably as finite science points to the infinite, yet the endeavor to apprehend the infinite must necessarily fail, and the proof of its reality must be indirect; for all direct proof is genetic; but of the infinite there is no genesis. Yet the indirect proof becomes more and more convincing, in proportion as the points of view, the necessities of thought and fact, on which it rests, are made in the progress of science more evident. "God alone can comprehend God." No one is angry with the eye, when it acts with the unexpressed consciousness that the realm of its activity is not that of unchanging, pure light, but of light that is modified, reflected or refracted in the various play of color, that it lives not in the brightness of the sun in the heavens, but in the sphere of terrestrial light. But human thought is reproached with incredulity or indolence, when, like the eye, it knows that the circle of the finite and conditioned, which is surely broad enough, is the limit of its free and joyous activity. When the eye is ravished by the harmony of colors, it does not deny the sun; on the contrary, it knows, so to speak, that the colors are born from the light. When thought exercises itself successfully in finite things, it does not deny God, but sees Him in the reason that is in the world and knows that this reason comes from Him. But by the sight of the sun the eye is dazzled, and it sees then only phantasms of its own production; and so by the intuition of God finite thought is swallowed up and in this fancied intuition it produces only a reflection of the finite. "All proofs of God's existence resemble the attempt to find out the pure light by reasoning from color, in which light is as it were clouded—as though man could remove the cloud." "Or, the world may be compared to one among the poems of a master mind, a partial expression of his thought. We read the poem and infer what must have been the whole, the general thought of the poet."

"The knowledge which the finite spirit has, however, extended is yet, for each individual, bare patch-work, fragmentary; and whether one's knowledge extend only to a particle or to a part of the world, yet the thought of God is ever the completion of this patch-work." "Science completes itself only in the hypothesis that there exists a spirit, whose thought is the origin of all being. The principle of cognition and the principle of being are one. And because this idea of God underlies the world, the same unity is sought in things and, as in an image, found again. 'The act of the divine knowledge is the substance of being for all things.'"

If in this last division of our Article we have presented so extended an abstract of the contents of the *"Logical Investigations,"* an excuse may be found in the importance of the subject-matter, both in itself and as something which might well be incorporated into the current of English and American philosophic thought. The public mind in England and America is or is not now particularly adverse to philosophic exposition and inquiry, according as the latter is conceived as purely *a priori* speculation or as dealing with palpable questions of fact. In this the public mind is partly right; for, if anything has been demonstrated by the history of philosophy, it is the utter sterility of purely speculative inquiries, unrelated to demonstrated fact. But concrete questions in philosophy, no matter how specialized and empirical, cannot be successfully treated when isolated from a more general metaphysical theory. Philosophy is an organism, because all truth is organic. Each special truth is related organically to the whole sum of truth. Truth is one, and a partial truth is never rightly and fully understood except as related to the one whole of which it is a part. A metaphysical theory is therefore necessary, but not one manufactured at pleasure out of the philosopher's *a priori* consciousness. On the contrary, it must be born of the widest knowledge of the actual methods of the sciences and of the facts of existence as scientifically established. And it is because English and American philosophy has been so often fragmentary and superficial (has the influence of the so-called eclectic school in France, together, alas! with the tradition of English philosophy, had nothing to do with this?) that, though writing, fundamentally speaking, rather in the spirit of an historian than of a propagandist, and acknowledging the influence in the right direction which is exerted by illustrious exceptions among our philosophical writers, we have been influenced by the thought that the further infusion, into our current thought, of something like the grave, comprehensive, universal doctrine of Trendelenburg would, if it could be accomplished, be in the least degree beneficial.

English philosophy is now separated into two camps, in the one of which the fundamental assertion is a negation—the denial of necessity in knowledge or thought—while in the other the opposite is affirmed. And how do the followers in the opposed camps go about to convict each other of error? By firmly based and comprehensive inquiries, resting on a correct appreciation of the whole breadth and depth of the problem? Not, certainly, in all cases. In the first place, the necessity in question is quite commonly conceived as psychological compulsion and philosophers have gone bravely to work to disprove the necessity (for example) that a child of two years should assume a cause for every effect or insist on the identity of A and A! As though any amount of anthropological knowledge or psychological history or analysis were going to show how and why we know (in so far as our *scientific* knowledge extends) that any things are necessarily as they are! For the necessity in question is not the necessity of psychological experience, alone or in any eminent degree, but the scientific necessity of things, and the determination of the basis and rationale of *this* necessity depends on a broad theory of the conditions and foundations of thought and existence, or of scientific knowledge. And if then certain ideas—so-called "forms of intuition," or categories of the understanding— reveal themselves alike to the unsophisticated and to the philosophically educated as necessary to thought, their necessity will neither be demonstrated as the result of any number of ages of habitual experience, nor will the temper of the times nor the true spirit of philosophy admit of their being explained (?) as existing in the mind by a divine creative fiat, but they will have to be comprehended as involved in the simple basis of all thought and of all our conceptions of existence. It should be borne in mind that thought, ideas, are nothing except as belonging to an organism of knowledge. Ideas are not necessary in themselves, but only as elements in knowledge. "The *a priori* is what it is, only as it reveals and confirms itself in the knowledge of reality." The question of the origin and nature of necessary ideas is not, therefore, one of empirical psychology. It *can* be treated only in a separate science, the Science of Cognition, or the Theory of Science, which must rest at once on a physical and metaphysico-logical basis—the latter in so far as it relates to the fundamental quality and implication of thought, and the former inasmuch as it requires the widest knowledge which the physical sciences, and they alone, can furnish of the nature of being.

A philosophy like Trendelenburg's claims no greater completeness than that which the positive sciences have themselves attained, for it depends on those sciences for its data and its confirmation. It is frankly avowed to be an hypothesis which must be tested by the results of its application. The requirement that a philosophy should be stated as absolute truth is absurd, when we reflect that the philosopher is mortal and fallible, and that what is to be explained is much more difficult to seize than are, for example, in physics the causes of light, heat, and the like, of whose nature, however, our knowledge, though hypothetical, is none the less for that reason respected.

It is not our business nor our purpose to undertake here an absolute defence or criticism of the philosophy of Trendelenburg, yet a few words of cautionary explanation may be allowed.

First, then, let the error be guarded against, of decrying the theory of Trendelenburg as materialistic or in the bad sense empirical, because it rests on the hypothetical identity in nature of the basis of thought and of physical existence. Once for all—and this is a late day at which to be repeating the statement of a thing so obvious—man is not a pure spirit, and as conscious existence in general depends, at least in this our earthly condition, on physical organization, so thought itself, even in its freest activities, depends on the presence of an image, which image may be received from without or construed from within. Even the most immaterial conceptions, as God, truth, are realized, if at all, only in direct (positive or negative) relation to sensible intuition and imagination and their products. The rule of the physical universe is the rule of the human mind. In each there is gradation, and in each higher grade the preceding is involved as a means. The artist's thought is revealed in a physical material chosen for the purpose; thought, finality, in nature finds no expression except in and on the basis of physical or efficient causation. And so the higher operations of human thought rest upon and involve the lower; conception implies previous perception and imagination and, as an instrument, the ideal, constructive motion which runs through both. The theory, then, instead of being monistic and materialistic at its commencement, is the rather dualistic, since it postulates, starting from the realm of first appearance and from a positive fact implied in all the sciences, the distinction of thought and being. It is not stated, be it observed, that motion exhausts the conception of thought and being, but the hypothesis—in developing which the tendency is to proceed from the known to the unknown—is simply propounded, that motion is universally common to both. What each may have or be in addition to motion is, for the time, set aside. If the analysis of thought and the results of the scientific investigation of nature go to confirm the hypothesis, this is enough to suggest the further supposition that it is through this common element that thought and being can come together in the act of knowledge. However immaterial thought and its substrate may be, neither can come into relation to material, physical existence without some middle term of relation; thus, at least, judged so great a philosopher as Descartes, who accordingly, since he recognized the existence of no such middle or common term, accounted for the interaction of soul and body (which is but a specification of the problem of the interrelation of thought and being) by the assumed and essentially miraculous concourse of God. If the beginning, then, though in the better sense empirical (as starting from a given fact to be accounted for), is yet dualistic and hence not materialistic, much more, as has been seen, is the end adverse to materialism, since it recognizes the presence and power of thought in nature, ascribing to the former the supremacy and to both a dependence on the Unconditioned.

But, again, it may be said that motion presupposes something that is moved and a moving force, and that the former is in the theory not specified. This may be true; but the theory is not *ab initio* a metaphysics; it is a theory of cognition. It seeks primarily not the essence of existence, but the conditions and implication of thought. It runs incidentally—or, if one will, necessarily—upon the irrational conception of matter, which it frankly confesses its inability wholly to unriddle, although showing that all we can say about it must be said in terms of motion.

The fundamental emphasis which is laid upon finality in nature, is calculated to shock the prejudices of positive philosophers and of some scientists. But the legitimacy of their seeking only for the efficient cause or the mechanics of the phenomena which they investigate, is fully admitted. Since intelligence, if it rule at all in nature, can rule only through the agency of physical causes and on the basis of physical laws, every organism presents a problem in mechanics, which science has to solve. If by usage or courtesy the realm of efficient causation, and that alone, is set apart for science, yet philosophy, whose glance is more comprehensive, must regard phenomena in all their aspects, and if an aspect of them is found which, though not contradictory to the scientific aspect, is yet decidedly different and seemingly higher, the truly scientific spirit will be the last to object to anything being inferred from that aspect, which the facts may warrant or the analogies of thought may necessitate. In the face of opposition, however, philosophy must here stand upon her right and deny the right of the part to dictate to the whole, or of the basis (science, efficient causation) to dictate what superstructure (not in contradiction therewith) shall be raised upon it.

Trendelenburg's *Philosophy of Natural Law (Naturrecht)* is founded on ethics, and the ethical, as has been above intimated, is with him but a higher stage or potency of the organic—it is "the organic become free." Space does not remain for an examination of his doctrine of natural law, agreeable and full of instruction as the examination might prove itself. Yet the founding of the ethical in the organic may strike some strict constructionists among our intuitional moralists as bringing the theory of morals too near to the realm of empirical philosophy, and theologians may reproach it with naturalism. The former objection will tend to disappear when it is recalled that for Trendelenburg the organic is the expression of thought, the illustration of an Idea; not, however, of an idea known apart from experience, but of an *a priori* revealed and confirmed in experience. Nor is the theologian's objection more substantial, for the theory expressly admits and claims that the Idea and its requirements (e.g., the idea, end, of man, and the duties following from it) are the revelation in human nature of the will of the infinite, unconditioned God.

It is a peculiarity of truth, resulting from its organic nature, that, just as, for example, in the human organism, no member can be understood out of relation to the whole organism, and the complete comprehension of any member involves a general comprehension of the whole, so the complete consideration of any part of truth leads, when correctly carried out, to the consideration and knowledge of the whole. And since truth is multifarious and many-sided, the approaches to it are correspondingly numerous. The philosophy of Trendelenburg is an approach to truth and an attempt to comprehend it, from one direction. Equally possible were it, however, conceivably to make the approach, as others have done, from other directions and to arrive at substantially the same results. A philosophical system conceived in this way does not admit of partisans, since a system thus conceived does not and can not claim to be the only true avenue to truth. Only a system, which pretends to take its stand *a priori* at the centre of absolute knowledge and thence to derive by necessary deduction all truth of fact, must have one-sided partisans for its disciples. But it is hoped that all who shall read the first division of this Article, will be disposed to allow that such a system is impossible for man. Nothing hinders, then, our conceding the general truth of Trendelenburg's doctrine, without, however, granting that his theory is the only one which a true philosophy may adopt. Nor in accepting conditionally his doctrine is it necessary to accept all the minor statements, although we believe that remarkably few just grounds of criticism will be found in them, when all are considered with reference to the whole doctrine of which each statement is a part. Thus what is said (and above expounded) in regard to causality may well strike one as furnishing a strikingly inadequate account of the motion, unless it be borne in mind that it is only causality in the mechanical realm which is being considered. In the higher, organic sphere, the idea becomes deepened and spiritualized. This only must we say by way of criticism, namely, that the reduction of force, as a physical category, to motion, does not seem to us to have been properly supplemented by Trendelenburg in the part devoted to the treatment of the organic sphere. Here force appears as that which we know it in consciousness—not separate from motion, it is true, but with a significance which includes much more than motion. To find this pointed out we have sought in vain in Trendelenburg's works.

We may add, supplementarily, that Karl Rosenkranz, the gifted veteran in the ranks of the Hegelians, who has lectured and voluminously written to the delight of so many thousands —thanks to the charm of his style and the wealth of his erudition and intelligence—in an Article on Trendelenburg and Hegel, in *Die Gegenwart*, August 3, 1872, repeats, against the fundamentally important principle that thought without image (*Anschauen*) is impossible, the charge that such logical conceptions as "causality, necessity, universality, identity, difference, and the like," can absolutely not be imaged. In reply: it is not claimed that motion, and sensation, as dependent in cognition on ideal motion, exhaust the nature of thought. But it is claimed and shown that the universal and abstract conceptions above named come to consciousness and are realized only through the aid of constructive motion. This has been pointed out in particular, as regards the first named of them, in the third division of our Article. As to necessity, the most familiar manner in which we clothe the conception to our thought is by regarding it as identical with a repellent force which forbids—wards off—the contrary. In like manner, universality, identity, difference, while, like necessity, they are conceptions peculiar to thought in distinction from being (they are not "given" in sensuous intuition, in the same sense in which, for example, color or sound is), have yet no sense and no application, and hence no existence in consciousness except as they reveal themselves and are confirmed in motion (real or ideal) and its products. Rozenkranz's comparison of

Trendelenburg to Cousin is infinitely more complimentary to the latter than to the former. There can be only a superficial resemblance between the German philosopher, who from youth to old age was self-consistent in his thought and ever self-possessed and indefatigable in his judgment of the results of the philosophic thought of the past and in his endeavor to confirm his theory by comparison with the scientific results of the present and by testing it in the application, and the French "orateur-philosophe," a philosopher, in some sense, by commission, changeable in his fundamental views, and deterred by no philosophic bent from turning his attention, when his philosophic "business" was accomplished, to the study of female characters of the reign of Louis XIV.

Appendix B

REVISED DRAFT OF UNUSED
INTRODUCTION

(For Morris' translation of Hegel's *Philosophy of the State and of History*, Published by S. C. Griggs & Company, Chicago, 1887, including the footnotes in Morris' manuscript and occasional notations attached to the pages by Morris and here added to footnotes.)

I suppose that the two greatest masterpieces of political philosophy, belonging to the history of European thought, are the Politics of Aristotle and Hegel's Philosophy of the State (*Philosophie des Rechts*). Appreciation of the former, on the part of thoughtful students of politics, grows rather than diminishes with time; so that at this day a writer, after reviewing the history of the "Science of Politics" in ancient and modern times, declares that, for the answer to so simple, fundamental, and practical a question as, "What does the State exist for?" the best thing we can now do is to raise and follow the cry, "Back to Aristotle." [1] And of Hegel's work, notwithstanding the sharp criticisms that have been passed upon it, I think that the final estimate is likely to be similar to that expressed, in a recent work, by one of its author's countrymen, who places it in "the foremost rank of the classical productions of the science of all times." [2] Both of these authors stand at the culmination of classical epochs in the history of philosophic thought. Both lived at critical periods of political evolution; and both at once gathered in and went beyond, or beneath, the results of brilliant predecessors in political inquiry.

Hegel's Philosophy of History [3] may be termed a continua-

[1] Frederick Pollock, "History of the Science of Politics," *Fortnightly Review*, Jan., 1883, p. 99.
[2] Adolf Lusson, *System der Rechtsphilosophie*, Berlin, 1882, p. 104.
[3] *Vorlesungen über die Philosophie der Geschichte*, Hegel's *Werke*, Vol. IX, English translation by Sibree; *Hegel's Philosophy of History*, in Bohn's Philosophical Library, London, 1861.

tion of his Philosophy of the State. For the proximate factors
of Universal History are States. It is in the movement of universal history that the larger and essential nature of the state
is exhibited. If the state is man "writ large," history may be
termed the state "writ large." So, at least, the matter is viewed
by Hegel. Accordingly, the political student of Hegel, who
should confine himself to the *Philosophie des Rechts,* and neglect the *Philosophie der Geschichte,* would miss our author's
most luminous generalities respecting the universal nature of
the state; while, on the other hand, the historical student, who
should confine himself to the latter of the two works named
and neglect the former, would lose the substantial benefit and
assistance to be derived from a knowledge of our author's
views concerning the elementary composition and specific
character of the very elements of history themselves. (The foregoing sufficiently explains the reason for the union of the
two works in this exposition.) I may add that, in my judgment,
Hegel's Philosophy of History must share in whatever praise
is justly bestowed on his Philosophy of the State.

The State is indeed, as above intimated, man "writ large."
It has, by a recent writer, been aptly described as "simply the
res interne of human nature changed to a *res publica* or *ex-
terna";* and what is thus said of the state may, in a still more
comprehensive sense, be said of history. In other words,
history and the state are the objective manifestation of Man.
The state is a human organization. History is the course of
human events. It is man who is the immediate soul of the
state. It is the life of humanity which is the immediate woven
into the fabric of history. In studying the state and history,
man is engaged in studying himself. In comprehending them,
he is comprehending, *pro tanto,* himself. The philosophy of
the state and of history is an essential part of the philosophy
of man. In the picture drawn by the former, man is the central
figure.

The foregoing statements being accepted, it is obvious that,
while, in prosecuting the scientific investigation of the state
and of history, as in all other scientific inquiry, what is known
as the "personal equation" must be carefully eliminated, the
human equation, as I may term it, is here the all-important
and essential thing to be retained and considered. The elim-

ination of the former must not be carried out with such vengeance as to involve the suppression of the latter. This would be done, if, for example, one were to look upon the state and history as wholly comparable, say, to a geological formation or a biological process—phenomena existing for man, but not through man, objects offered and presented to human intelligence, but in no sense dependent for their existence upon the intelligence, the conscious activity, the will of man.

On the other hand, the attempt to regard and solve the "human equation" purely by itself, or to comprehend the state and history as the work of man standing quite alone, independent of factors external to himself, and operating, as it were, *in vacuo,* must end, not less surely, in disaster. In the picture drawn by the science we are about to expound, man, as above intimated, is only the "central figure." He is not the only figure. The representation of him alone does not constitute the whole picture. One of the elements of a good picture, as an artist would say, is its composition. It is made up of several parts, yet standing to each other in such unity of relation as to form a natural whole. The part that is of special and commanding interest is, indeed, the central figure; but the intelligibility, as well as the beauty, of this part depends essentially on the relations by which it is joined to the others. So man, in history and in politics, while unique in character and occupying a central position, does not stand alone. He has an environment. With this environment he is connected by vital and hence essential relations. Separated from this environment he is little more than an abstraction. To attempt to comprehend him in such separation is to follow a chimera.

The human equation, *plus* its external or extra-human factors, and not one of them to the exclusion of the other (or others), must be considered in any complete science of man or of any of man's political or historic works and ways. The fulfilment of this condition is the fulfilment of the first condition essential to a philosophy of man, or, in particular, (to keep to the special subject before us,) of a philosophy of the state and of human history. For, subject to conditions whose nature is obvious, "philosophy" and "complete science" are equivalent expressions. Philosophy resembles art in at least one particular: it has to do with wholes. The artist sees and seeks to represent things as wholes. The philosopher aims to see and to comprehend them in like manner.

The human mind is so constituted that it can never long rest in any set of views which has not the form or pretension of absolute totality. It is on account of this innate tendency—a tendency flowing from the very nature of intelligence—that all men are truthfully said to be implicitly philosophers. It is on the same account that they are with equal truthfulness said to be by nature religious; for all religion involves the application to conduct, and the development in the sphere of feeling, of notions that claim to be universal and ultimate in their authority and significance, i.e., that claim to be notions of the whole. Now, it is the peculiarity of nearly all special investigation, that it methodically and for a particular purpose sets a limit to this philosophical tendency. It marks off for itself a limited portion of a larger territory, a single aspect of a complex whole, a single factor or set of factors entering into a complex product; in other words, it methodically limits its range of vision by what is essentially a process of abstraction, by abstraction, namely, from all but the special "portion," "aspect," or "factor" chosen for investigation; and it then proceeds, by a process of analytical examination, to take, as it were, the inventory of what is left. The mathematical sciences thus abstract from all but the pure relations of space and time, or of quantity. The "pure physical science" of modern times abstracts from all but "phenomena" consisting in "changes of configuration and motion." The lawfulness, the practical necessity and utility, of this method are, of course, beyond question. It is by it that the sciences mentioned become what is termed "positive," and "exact," and are so rendered definitely capable of subserving the uses and enhancing the power of man. So conspicuously true is this, and so deeply rooted has the predilection for this method of abstraction and specialization become in the modern mind, that the term "science," with its cognates, has come in our day to be technically restricted, in the common language of discussion, to denote only inquiries, and the results of inquiries, conducted by the method in question. The express or implied model and ideal of all "science" is mathematics, and of all method, the "physical" (strictly, the *mathematico-physical*) method.

The dangers that attend the cultivation of the "scientific" habit of mind (as we may now term it) are such as have often been remarked upon. They may be summed up in the two words, narrowness and dogmatism. First, narrowness. For, the natural bent of all intelligence being toward totality of view, the "scientific" man is secretly thrust on to forget the limitations which, by abstraction and specialization, he has methodically placed upon the special activity of his own intelligence, and thus to treat, so to speak, his own ordinary scientific horizon as though it were the outermost boundary of the intellectual universe. And, secondly, dogmatism. For, under the same condition, our man of "science," if he does not deny the existence of a region beyond his special view, is fain to form and express judgments about it after the restricted analogies, and according to the restricted method, of the particular science, or order of sciences, in which he is adept; or else, while admitting the "beyond," to declare it "unknowable"; and to pursue either of these courses is essential dogmatism. In this case, "science" definitely undertakes to fill the *rôle* of philosophy, or to be the science of the absolute whole, the science of first and universal principles, the science of being as such, the science of universal truth.

It is scarcely too much to say that the origin of all the narrownesses and dogmatisms of modern "philosophies" is of the nature now described. And political philosophy has not been the last and least to suffer in consequence. Thomas Hobbes, sharing with the other most influential thinkers of the seventeenth century in a regard for the method of mathematics, which became extravagant only by being exclusive, and instinctively perceiving that the only definite existence capable of mathematical treatment is moving bodies, led the way, among English writers, in treating society, or the state, as a "civil body," whose constituent and, in the "state of nature," mutually-repellent, elements (individual human beings) became united in society, or in one "body," not spontaneously, not in the free fulfilment of a common, substantial, and good will, and still less in the realization of the essential potentialities of an ethical substance termed human nature, but by a mechanical necessity. The problem of political philosophy was practically a problem in social mechanics. The like tendency has continued in the main dominant among the most conspicuous leaders of English discussion to the present day. It is illustrated, in the present century, with differing degrees of completeness or exclusiveness, in the works of the Benthams, and Buckles, and Spencers, and others devoted to the elucidation of the "physics of politics." The final scientific ideal is the reduction of society and history to the mere quality of a complex mode of motion. Freedom is resolutely denied—is fairly argued,[4] out of existence. Thought, "looking before and after," is viewed exclusively as the dependent function and instrument of physical processes. "Ideas and justice" are held to be determined by the physical evolution of society; they are not comprehended as at once the final and efficient causes of social development. In brief, the independent influence of anything, which is usually termed "subjective," as a factor in the public and historic life of man, is not admitted.

That such "philosophy of the state and of history" has much that is abstract and arbitrary about it, that it does not correspond to the concrete fulness and reality of the facts of man's social and historical experience, and that it thus fails sensibly to establish the needed equation between fact and theory, is probably obvious enough. So far as it is still occupying the field or is still a claimant for the suffrages of the thoughtful, the philosophy of Aristotle and Hegel is its rival. So the whole is ever the rival—and the rival predestined to victory—of the part, the concrete of the abstract, the positive of the negative, and the complete *truth* of the one-sided "fact." For, indeed, the mechanistic theory of society and history is founded on facts, but only on a part of the facts, relevant to the subjects in hand. It is no news that man is, among other things, a physical being; that the physical enters, as a factor, into the composition of his nature; that it constitutes an essential part of his environment; and that it furnishes a visible scene and an organic instrument for the social and historic activity of man. These truisms have escaped the notice of none of the great philosophers, whether in ancient or in

---

[4] It is well known that by "argument" any thing can be "proved."

modern times. And it is superfluous to say to any one who is
a successful student of *philosophy*, as well as of "science," that
a far deeper and truer comprehension of the essential nature of
the physical, and of what may even be termed its organic unity
(not its abstract identity) with the nature and life of man, is
to be found in the works of Aristotle and Hegel, than is revealed in the speculations of our modern mechanistic philosophers. The true problem of the comprehension of physical
nature is more than a mathematical or mechanical one. Nature
is more than modes of motion. It is more than a blind and
automatic composition of forces. It is substantial, as well as
phenomenal. And if the phenomenal side of nature is a complex of modes of motion, capable of perfect scientific expression in nothing but mathematical formulae, the substantial side, which alone (as was well shown by Leibnitz) contains the "sufficient reason" of the phenomenal, consists of
living forces, spontaneous, bathed in ideality, and connatural,
in their inferior degree, with that force of practical intelligence
in man, by which he is constituted a thinking, willing spirit.
Nature, in short, in her interior substance, is concretely logical.
She is, in her degree, incarnate *logos*. Of nature, thus conceived and comprehended, man is the crown. In her he finds
a friend and ally, and not merely a resistant enemy or an inflexible tyrant. Man and nature are of the same spiritual household. The dependence of the former on the latter (usually
spoken of as the "subjection of man to physical law") is not
abject and dead, but free and living. It is like the "dependence" of an organism on one of its own members. Instead of
prejudicing the freedom of man, it is one of the conditions of
the latter. The freedom of man fulfils, rather than contradicts,
the prophecies of nature.[5]

Such are, in kind, the notions of Aristotle and Hegel regarding the essential nature of the "physical factor" in human
existence and human activity. The physical, as is seen, is, for
these philosophers, not in abstract identity with that which is
most characteristically human, namely, the living, thinking,
willing spirit of man; nor are these two merely in abstract op-

[5] The true idea of nature cannot be attained except when it is viewed
in its relation to that being who is at once its culmination and its explanation." Caird. *Comte* 135–6. *Cf. ib.* 133–6.

position to each other; the rather, they are in concrete unity with one another. Nature prefigures man, and man is the fulfilment of nature; while both nature and man are full of ideal "riches," which bear witness to their divine origin and end. Accordingly, both of our philosophers are so far from forgetting, in their treatment of man and of his works and ways, in state and history, duly to appreciate the "physical side," that, the rather, it may truly be said that no others have come so near to a full appreciation to be impossible rightly to comprehend their philosophy of the former, without understanding their notions about the latter. And the account which, in dealing with the products of human activity, they take of the physical, is not restricted to a few universal notions, but extends also to more definite particulars. "The political constitution of a people," says Hegel, "constitutes one substance, one spirit, with its religion, with its art and philosophy, or at least with its ideas and thoughts in general culture—not to mention also the other, external factors, such as · climate, neighbors, geographical boundaries, and place in the temporal order of universal history." To the consideration of these "external factors" Hegel, in his Philosophy of History, gives distinct and conspicuous attention. But he does not treat them as first and final in the order of rank and influence. For man, according to his concrete and broadly experimental view, is not a mere appendix or accident of nature. He is not simply the mechanical product of "external factors." The rather, man is man, and he accomplishes a constructive work in society and history, only by making nature and the external an appendix to himself, the organ of his own thinking will. One may say that the aim of our author is, not to put asunder things which in the order of concrete reality are joined together, and, also, not, in that theoretic transcript of reality which all science seeks to create, to invert the true order of reality by putting what is secondary in the place of what is primary; and still less, again, substantially to efface or abolish one of the terms of the union by completely merging it in the other (as when man is treated as only a physical being, and the process of history as wholly identical with a physicomechanical process).

The procedure mentioned in the preceding parenthesis is

the one that is peculiar to the mechanical theory of the state and of history. It consists, negatively, in eliminating, from the problem in hand, what was above termed the "human equation." And this elimination may be said to be the necessary logical result, not only of an initial act of abstraction, by which attention is withdrawn from that which really constitutes the human equation, in distinction from the physical, but also of a further act, by which, in contemplating the physical itself, abstraction is made from all that is interior and essential, and fixed exclusively on the external and phenomenal.[6] Thus viewed, the physical is nothing but a moving system of mathematical relations, among which a constant equation is maintained. The formal logic of this abstract system is then treated as the real logic of all concrete reality. Life, spontaneity, freedom, having been banished from the premiss, disappear from the conclusion. Individual human beings, who constitute the visible elements in the composition of society, are treated like the hypothetical atoms of speculative physics. Each individual represents a definite atom of brute force, and social and historical activities are the result of the mathematical composition of these forces, following mechanically the lines of greatest traction and least resistance.

In this theory, which has been called that of the "atomy of the state," is grounded the excessive individualism of our times, with its morally and socially destructive consequences. The ideal of this individualism is the liberty of each one to "do as he likes," the "unchartered freedom" of mere license.

But the theory also contains another side and another ideal, contradictory to those just mentioned and more logically involved in it. It is what may be termed the side, and the ideal, of mechanical solidarity, or of the determination of all the actions of each individual by an all-absorbing social mechanism. This indeed, and not individualism, is alone according to the essential logic of the mechanical theory. In the strict sense, as we have seen, all free individual initiative is ex-

[6] The view of men, who
  "judge all nature by her feet of clay,
  without the will to lift their eyes, and see
  Her godlike head crowned with spiritual fire,
  And touching other worlds."
      cited by Funan, S. after God, 294.

cluded. Whatever takes place, occurs on account of what had taken place before, by a law of iron necessity; and the future will be the similarly necessitated child of the present. So the "socialists" of our day, in predicting and inviting the social revolution, that is to usher in the day of the accomplishment of their plans, announce themselves as simply prophets of that which any scientifically instructed intelligence must perceive to be inevitable: they are the irresponsible prophets, as they will also be the irresponsible leaders, of a revolution, which will be nothing more than a necessary, and necessitated, evolution.

Is it not plain that the time has come for a revival of political knowledge, for the renewed and most thorough cultivation of political and social philosophy, for the establishment, on the broadest possible basis, and in the completest manner possible, of the whole and full science, the philosophy, of Man, and of his social and historical relations; a science, or philosophy, which, by taking account of the whole man, the man whose life is in the spirit, no less than the man whose life is in sense and physical nature, the spiritual and "ideal," no less than the mechanical and sensibly "real" side of man and of his relations, shall be able at once to recognize and be just to whatever of positive truth may underlie the mechanical conceptions and to deprive them of their power for evil, by demonstrating and enforcing their limitations? Or, has not the time come, when, from our theorizings about human relations, and, consequently, from the determining bases of our practical action in regard to the latter, the "human equation" can no longer be eliminated, without the gravest and most immediate peril to all essentially humane interests? Is not the frequent and despairing repetition, in our days, of the question whether life is "worth living," the result of the fact that man, in his theories, and in the modern progress of his science, has lost the sight of himself, has ceased truly to know himself, and has come to think of or treat himself as if he were nothing but a helpless and irresponsible physical value?

There can be, I fancy, no reasonable dispute as to the answer to any of the foregoing questions. Certain it is, at all events, that the prevailing and, within its peculiar sphere—the sphere

of man's command over nature—triumphantly fruitful pre-
occupation of the modern mind with the mathematical and
physical sciences has led, not only to the construction of abstract, mechanical "philosophies," like that above criticized,
but also, in increasing measure, and where all pretense of
ultimate philosophical generalization is expressly disavowed,
to the exclusive application of this method in the cultivation
of sciences, which, by their titles suggest matter closely related
to, if not essentially identical with, the characteristic spiritual
nature of man; the result being, again, naturally and necessarily, the elimination from these sciences of the essential and
characteristic "human equation." So it is that, in these days,
we have a "new psychology," which, says M. Ribot,[7] "differs
from the old in its spirit: it is not metaphysical; in its aim: it
studies only phenomena; and in its methods, which it borrows,
as far as possible, from the biological sciences." It is, in brief,
a *"psychologie sans âme,"* or a "science of the soul, minus the
soul." It is the analytic science of a class of "phenomena,"
which for convenience are termed "psychical," considered with
reference to their duration, to the space they occupy in the
area of consciousness, to their associates within this area, and,
above all, to the physical phenomena of the nervous system,
with which they "coexist" and of which they are often said to
be the simple "obverse." Any offensive "metaphysical" assumption, such as that man has indeed a soul, as well as a body,
and that "psychical phenomena" are to be considered as
evidencing both reality and positive nature of the former, is
carefully avoided. In like manner, the name, "Science of Man,"
or "Anthropology," is now given to a body of doctrine or of
still progressing investigations, concerned, not with the essential nature of man, but (in the language of one of our
leading anthropologists, Mr. E. B. Tylor,) with the "natural
history of mankind"; which latter involves such questions as
those relating to "man's place in nature," the temporal "origin
of man," the "races of mankind," and the "antiquity of mankind." And so, again, and lastly, "sociology," which, by etymology should be the "science of the social nature of man," is
cultivated, in like professed abstraction with the foregoing

---

[7] Th. Ribot, *La Psychologie allemande contemporaire.* (*École Expéri-
mentale.*) Paris, 1879, p. viii.

from all "metaphysical" assumptions and pretensions, as an analytic investigation of the natural history of society.

In these sciences the "physical method" is employed, or imitated. The use of the physical method implies abstraction from everything but the physical aspect of phenomena. The object of the cultivation of psychology, anthropology, and sociology, by the physical method, is, accordingly, the determination of the laws or empirical rules of psychological, anthropological, and sociological phenomena in respect of space and time, or the laws of their coexistence and sequence. From all else abstraction is, by a strict construction of the method, made.

Now, that such a procedure is completely scientific and legitimate, is plain enough. But it is such, only within the strictly defined limits involved by the physical method. I only wish the reader to be reminded that the predominant engrossment of the modern mind in the analytic investigation of physical phenomena has led to a like engrossment, on the part of a very large and influential number of those who are engaged in the prosecution of sciences ostensibly related to the mental and moral nature of man, in the study of mental and moral phenomena under their unquestioned physical relations, to the exclusion of their more essential and important spiritual side; that the resulting, abstractly correct and commendable, science of the part, or of the single aspect, has too often been put in the place of the true science, or philosophy, of the whole; and that thus sciences, cultivated professedly in independence of any and all metaphysical suppositions, are made to support the impression that, as regards the spiritual and free nature of man, agnosticism is the last word of philosophy, or else that the mechanical philosophy is to be out and out adopted. And so the modern man loses sight of himself. The command of the Delphic oracle, "Man, know thyself," on complete obedience to which the self-mastering freedom of man and the accomplishment of his true destiny in history depend, is left unfulfilled. And the result is individual recklessness and despair, and, *pro tanto,* the development of the germs of social disintegration.

Hegel, notoriously, was one who possessed not only the "courage of truth," but the patience and endurance requisite for the prosecution of the "acrid labor of thought" to any degree that seemed to him necessary for the attainment of a view of the truth in its totality. If his works on the State and History have any value, this is due to the fact that he would not consciously allow any side of the truth to remain foreign to him.

Man, viewed in the totality of his nature, is for Hegel a spirit. The state and history, as the corporate expression of the nature of man, are spiritual values.

It is man, I say, in the totality of his nature, who is, in Hegel's view, a spirit. This totality has its different sides, aspects, parts, or factors, as one might be variously tempted to term them. Man, in popular conception and phraseology, is perhaps most frequently bisected into the two parts termed body and soul, viewed as wholly and essentially distinct from and opposed to each other. The unity of his nature is then only superficial, and consists merely in the chains which, for the present at least, are supposed to hold the soul attached to the body.

For Hegel man is indeed a body, and he is a soul. But man, as a totality, is more than the mere arithmetical sum or mechanical aggregate of the two. He is both in the organic unity of a spiritual nature, which at once transcends both body and soul and also historically realizes itself in and through them as its organic members and instruments.

To study and comprehend man as a spiritual being is therefore to study him in the wholeness of his nature. It is to take a view of him, "standing complete and wanting nothing." It is to take an artistic view of him. It is to take that view which was above characterized as alone in truth philosophical.

The view of Hegel is, further, that not only the body and soul of man are spiritually conditioned, but that universally, or throughout the whole cosmos, the material and the psychical are similarly conditioned. If man, taken absolutely or in the totality of his being, is to be termed a spirit, so, with his attention fixed upon the totality of existence, or on being "taken absolutely," Hegel says, "The Absolute is Spirit." In like manner, and with the like sense, the apostle of the absolute religion declares, "The Spirit is the truth." "Matter and mind," the "physical" and the "psychical," viewed apart from their spiritual condition, are indeed disparate, incommensurable. Neither appears to have any thing essentially in common with the other. Neither can find in the other its own explanation. And of neither of them can the explanation, or "sufficient reason," be found in itself. Thus regarded, they can be recognized (distinguished), but not cognized. They are at bottom "unknowable." They become intelligible only when they are seen in the light of their spiritual condition, in the light of the totality in and through which alone they dependently subsist, or in the light of that Spirit, "in whom they live, and move, and have their being." Then they are seen to be full of divine, i.e., spiritual "riches." Nay, these "riches," of divine power and purpose, or of "force" and "law," are seen to constitute their very essence. (The mechanical conception, whether of the world of matter or of the world of mind, results from the attempt to comprehend both "in themselves," and apart from the totality in and through which alone they subsist and are essentially intelligible.[8]) Thus to *comprehend* all existence whatsoever as a spiritual value, and not to mistake for such comprehension the ready response of human *instincts* or *intuitions* to declarations (inspired, or otherwise) to the effect that it is such a value, is no light matter. No labors of science are more arduous than those which this problem must demand; and from such labors the great philosophers have not shrunk. The largeness and essential truth of their aim may and should be recognized, even by those who do not make it their special task to take up and carry on their work. For, indeed, their work is to be taken up and carried on. It is not ended. The specific task of philosophically comprehending the whole of existence or of any natural portion thereof, the task of viewing either and taking its whole measure as a spiritual totality, is, like every other broad scientific undertaking, an ideal destined to occupy the intellect of man to the end of time. But here a distinction is to be made. The end in view, in all philosophic investigation, is, as Hegel rightly terms it, "absolute knowledge." But this expression is ambiguous. Absolute knowledge may mean knowledge of totality, of the

---

[8] The Divine Spirit, acc. to the biblical expression breathed into man a living soul—thaumaturgically or magically not miraculously *created* one *for* him.

whole, as such, and of its essential nature as a whole; it is in this sense that philosophy may and does claim to possess and demonstrate an absolute knowledge. Or the expression may mean a knowledge, every detail of which has been filled, and in which every subordinate question has been answered; this is the ideal of all science, of every kind; it is not peculiar to philosophy; and in no science is there any prospect of its premature fulfilment.

It will now perhaps be evident in what sense Hegel can say that the "absolute object of knowledge is spirit." Absolutely, or in the full sense of the word knowledge, like can only know its like. The human spirit can truly and fully know only that which is spiritual. Indirect evidence of this is furnished in the circumstance above mentioned, that matter and "mind," the physical and the psychical, or objective motion and subjective feeling, can, by notorious admission of all who have made the attempt, not be comprehended when taken in abstraction, or "by themselves." We may know something *about* them, we may even have "clear and distinct ideas" of them as, respectively, a space-occupying substance and a sensitive state of consciousness; but we do not and can not *know them;* they remain for us, so long as we continue to look at them in this way, "final inexplicabilities." *A fortiori,* man, viewed only on his material or physical side, as a mere natural object, is strictly uncomprehended and incomprehensible. Something is indeed known about him, but he himself, in his essence and in the fulness of his nature, is unknown and "unknowable." The like is true if the attempt is made to comprehend man, by taking account only of the exclusively subjective side of his nature—of his life in feeling, passion, and emotions. The "physiology of society" and the "psychology of society," for example, do not establish a philosophical comprehension of man, in the totality of his nature as a social being. Taken by themselves, they leave this nature uncomprehended. They end at most only in a "faith," which it is the work of philosophy to turn into "knowledge." But they are, or represent, the ideal preconditions of philosophical comprehension, just as the body and soul of man are the actual preconditions of the historic existence and activity of man as a spiritual being. Philosophy is not their enemy, nor their rival, nor their pre-

tended substitute, but their complement. In the realm of real
knowledge there are no rivalries; there is simply organic unity.
Man, in the totality of his nature, as a spirit, is a thinking
and willing being. Confronted with nature, he treats her varied
kingdoms, aspects, forms, as so many pages or characters of a
printed language. His acquisition of knowledge of nature takes
place through his learning to read this language; and the result is, that he rethinks the thought expressed therein, or,
better, the thought of which nature is the express substantia-
tion. But, in his thinking, man goes beyond the mere passive
reception of lessons dictated by objective nature. He actively
grasps thoughts that nature only suggests or prefigures. He
sees new possibilities, which are open to him through the
cunning combination and application of nature's laws; and, in
the exercise of an intelligence, now no longer merely theoretical, but also practical, he proceeds to the active realization
of these possibilities, and thus to the immense extension of his
command over nature. First, his thought was determined by
objects. Now it is objects that are determined by and in accordance with his thought. But nature does not only suggest
new applications of her own laws. She prefigures a thought,
which man conceives—the thought, or ideal, of a self-conscious,
practical intelligence, determining itself spontaneously, yet,
with an invariability like that of nature, in accordance with
a law or laws determined by its own being. It is the thought,
ideal, or "conscience," of the ideal man, of the "best self," of a
spiritually perfected humanity. Supremely, it is the thought of
God. The struggle to realize this ideal is a moral struggle. Its
aim is the establishment of a reign of ideas and justice, of the
true, the beautiful, and the good. The results of this struggle
are organized in institutions and constitute the true substance
of history. But, once more, the thought of man finds its own
substance, content, or material, not only in the thought substantiated and presented to him in nature and in the thoughts
that nature practically suggests or ideally prefigures, but also
in an infinite and absolute thought, which the thought in
nature evidences as its own eternal pre-condition, and to
which the thought of man also points, as not only its pre-
condition, but also its goal. For it is of the nature of pure,
absolute, or perfect thought, that it thinks itself. It knows

itself. It is self-conscious. In it subject and object of thought are inseparably joined—existing in concrete unity, the one with the other. So inseparable and vital is this unity, that it cannot be absolutely—but only relatively, or apparently— rent in twain. The *appearance* of a thought purely subjective is the evidence of thought correlatively objective (a correlative "object of thought," as is usually said); and the *appearance* of thought purely objective (as in nature) is the evidence of thought correlatively subjective (or of a "subject of thought," a "thinker"). The objective thought in nature is the evidence of an absolute thought, in which the former is enclosed, or in which it "lives, and moves, and has its being." And the like is true concerning the thought which nature, not objectifies, but only partially prefigures, and which man more or less clearly conceives as the thought or ideal of the perfect man, or of a perfected humanity. For this thought is, alas! largely, not to say mainly, "subjective," and, according to the first appearance, only subjective. The ideal man has, with one exception, never existed, and "perfected humanity" is a dream of the future. Yet this subjective thought, which slowly but surely, with the progress of the ages, assumes greater clearness in the minds of men and is growingly realized in the objective realm of history, demonstrates, by its own existence, the existence of its objective correlate, not in the realm of history, but in a realm, or centre, of absolute thought, which is the eternal precondition of all history, as it also is of all the processes of nature. This absolute and eternal thought is the function of an absolute and eternal Spirit; for thought, universally, was defined as a spiritual function.

In thinking, then, the thought of nature, man rethinks, as Kepler said, the thoughts of God. And in striving, by every form of moral endeavor, whether individual, social, or "world-historical," to give present, earthly reality to the ideal of a perfected humanity, he is really laboring to realize the thought of God. His mission is thus to accomplish the divine will (which is one with the divine thought). To do this will he is come upon the earth. And the end, so far as it is achieved in the setting up on earth of a true kingdom of man, is in like measure the establishment of a true kingdom of heaven, or of God.

Recapitulating, and partly expanding the foregoing, we may say that, according to the thought of Hegel, man is characteristically and totally man, only as he is a spirit. As such, he is not preternatural. Allied, through his body and soul, with the realms of "matter" and "feeling," he transcends both, but contradicts neither. The characteristic function of his spiritual being is thought, under its two forms of theoretic knowledge and practical willing. In all of his spiritual, i.e., thinking functions, man may be called essentially a social being. His thought requires an object, and in the relation of his thought to its object he enters into a most intimate and, as it were, organic companionship with the latter. He, as a thinking being, and the object of his thought become or prove themselves, in a deep sense, "members one of another." Thus, he successfully makes nature the object of his thought, only because there is thought already in nature, so that nature is not wholly foreign to him, but in an essential measure, spiritually bone of his bone and flesh of his flesh. So, in thinking the thought of nature, in knowing or acquiring knowledge of nature, man can and must assume toward her the attitude of the little child, allowing, or, by experiment, forcing, her to speak for herself, unquestioningly receiving as a lesson the tale that she tells, permitting the blanks in his own thought to be filled up with the material which she supplies, and so, *pro tanto*, acquiring spiritual substance, nay, paradoxical as this may seem, developing his own spiritual substance, by inviting and compelling nature to share her own with him. In the strictest sense of the term, man's knowledge of nature is a communion with her, the thought of nature becoming the thought of man; or, man is potentially the thought in nature. This relation between man and nature is essentially a relation of society, though on terms that are unequal for the two parties involved.

The great theoretical problem for man is self-knowledge; and the great practical problem for him is self-realization. (I speak now not merely of man, as an individual, but of mankind or humanity as a whole.) An essential part of both these problems is, and can only be, solved through knowledge of nature and the consequent development of human power over nature. Man is thus first taught the lesson that his own spiritual substance, his thought and will, or, more technically expressed, the true self-consciousness in which is to stand his spiritual completeness, is not something that belongs to him in individual isolation and abstraction from all relations to nature, to God, and to his fellow-men, but is essentially dependent on them and only in them can become actual. Man, as a spiritual being, was "not made to be alone" and in the strictest truth can not be alone.

But the more immediate and essential sphere for the solution of the problems of human self-knowledge and self-realization is found in the realms of human society and history. Man first begins to know himself as a specifically human, and not merely natural, being, when he sees himself in the faithful mirror of others of his kind, and enters into active relations with them. In his communion with nature, as previously contemplated, man addressed himself to an existence that was dumb. The language of nature was written, not spoken. It was written in rock and stream and sea, in tree and flower, in bird and beast and fish, but was accompanied by no voice. It was like a dead language, to which man was obliged, by laborious searching, to find the key. But his fellow-men, like himself, exercise the divine gift of significant speech. Thoughts are easily interchanged. The development of thought, and its application as a guide of practice easily and necessarily becomes a common labor. Men find themselves animated by a common consciousness. And this consciousness is a strictly human one. Its subject-matter is man and human relations; and it becomes clear and definite only as it is practically exemplified and objectified in institutions having the character of natural moral organisms—family, tribe, community, city, state, and finally universal history. Human self-knowledge or self-consciousness is found to be attainable only in the way, in which it actually is attained, namely, in and through the organization of social relations in which that consciousness is expressed; so that if, to be truly and specifically a man, one must have in some sense obeyed the Delphic command, above cited, it may be truly said that to obey the command one must have lived in social relations with one's fellows.[9] In other words, man, by his

---

[9] "In order thoroughly to realize ourselves, we must be conscious of our absorption, or at least of our inclusion, in a greater and grander system

spiritual nature, as realized, necessarily, through thought and self-knowledge, is a social being.

The communion and society of man with his fellow-man, while specifically different from his relation to nature, remains yet in organic continuity or unity with the latter. The former rises up on the basis of the latter, is vitally connected with it, and can never be separated from it. In nature man finds law— types, uses, beauties—established: nature *is* established, real- ized law. In society and history man creates the realm of a higher nature, through the active establishment of laws and the realization of typical aims, and of specific uses and beauties, which are organically continuous with the laws and prophecies of nature, but are specifically differentiated by the circum- stance that they express the thought and will of man, or the spiritual substance of human nature. The reign of human law, says Aristotle, is the reign of "intelligence without passion"; and the end of its establishment is the attainment by man of human perfection. "The universal sphere of human responsi- bility," says another, "is the State." It is the "laboratory of moral experiment." In it—i.e., in all his social institutions, and finally in history, the world-parliament of men organized in states [10]—the will of man seeks to be true to itself, to re- spond to its true and essential motives, to realize the spiritual substance of humanity. And it does this, I say once more, not in blank opposition to and forgetfulness of the spiritual and intrinsically social connection of man with nature, but in harmony and organic unity therewith. The circle of man's social relations with his fellow-man includes, not excludes, the circle of his relations with nature.

But the circle of man's relations with his fellows is not only one that is larger and higher than the circle of his re- lations with nature, and one that is ever growing in extent and —what is of still greater consequence—in fulness and richness

---

than that of our individual surroundings; in order to find our lives, we must first discover the art of losing them." Professor Fowler, *Progressive Morality*, p. 144, London, 1884.

[10] "The whole of universal history is a labor on man's part to give reason an organized existence in the sphere of reality, and it is through this labor that cultural humanity has won the reality and the consciousness of a rational existence." Hegel, *Philosophie des Rechts, Werke*, Bd. VIII, p. 336.

of content; it is itself a circle within a still larger one, in which are included man's conscious relations with the Absolute Being. This is the sphere of religion. "In religion a people defines for itself what it regards as the essential and ultimate truth." [11] What it thus defines, it seeks in its philosophy to comprehend and demonstrate. And what it thus defines it also seeks to realize in its social and historical relations.[12] "Hence it is, that the state reposes on religion." "Like religion, like state and political constitution." [13] Absolute religion and absolute philosophy respectively recognize and comprehend the Absolute as Absolute *Spirit*, and as God. The state is a *spiritual* construction, "standing in the world." [14] It is an imperfect and a growing one. The true guiding-star and the true norm of the activity of its members are found in the thought of the divine Spirit, who is the perfect truth and the perfect life, or, in the will of God. Lower motives—passions, selfish interests, rivalries—indeed exist, and have influence. But these are not the motives of the true citizen, who is the member of a social organism, where all are members one of another, animated by a common consciousness, the consciousness of a common and ideal good, to the realization of which the supreme energy of the whole organism is directed. On the contrary, where these false motives rule unchecked, the state, not subsists, but perishes. The true statesman, as a true citizen, makes the motives in question, ineradicably implanted as they are in human nature, the instruments and levers for the accomplishment of the higher end of the state. And above all, the divine Spirit, whose thought constitutes the explicit or implicit substance of the true statesman's motive, cooperates with the latter. God, according to Hegel, as also according to the conception of the Christian scriptures, is not idle. He is the eternal and omnipresent worker. The universe is not merely

[11] Hegel, *Philosophie der Geschichte; Werke,* Bd. IX; p. 62.
[12] Even those who make of irreligion a religion, see in the realization of an irreligious ideal the highest end of the state. To the French socialist, as above noted, the brute mechanical conception of the universe is supreme, and it is such a conception, accordingly, which he aims and expects to have carried out in the perfect state.
[13] *Ib.* pp. 63-4.
[14] " . . . der staat aber der Geist ist, *der in der Welt steht.*" Hegel, *Werke,* VIII, 333.

the finished product, but the scene of the constant operation of his hands. This operation, considered especially in its relation to the affairs of men, is popularly termed Providence. It is particularly thought of as "special" and relating peculiarly to the fortunes of individual human beings. "But in universal history we have to do with individuals, that are peoples, and with wholes, that are states: here, therefore, we can not stop short with this small-trade faith in providence (so to express it), and just as little can we rest in the merely abstract, indefinite faith, which only goes so far as to admit the general proposition, that there is a providence, without recognizing its presence in definite acts. We must, the rather, in all seriousness, seek to recognize the ways of providence, the means it employs and the manifestations it makes of itself in history, and to connect these with the divine Spirit as their universal principle." [15]

We have, then, once more, man recognized as a spiritual being; constituted a spirit by his thought; his thought, theoretical and practical, or manifested in knowing and willing; this thought, again, first kindled and nourished by the thought in nature; then rising out of and above nature to find its object proximately in the ideal man, perfected in truth and goodness and slowly organizing itself in universal history, and finally and absolutely in the absolute and living Spirit, who is the intrinsically necessary correlative and absolute object of man's thought, and who is not simply an ideal, but the reality, of perfect truth and perfect being. We have man in an organic-social relation with nature, with his fellows, and with God; the three relations vitally connected in a concrete unity that can not be ruptured without fatal consequences; and the whole course of history illustrating the growth and gradual perfection of this unity, in a process, in which nature, man, and God work together to make manifest the power and sovereignty of spirit.

The foregoing may have something of the appearance of the description of an ideal. It is indeed one of the necessary singularities—let us say, rather, distinctions—of all truthful descriptions of man and of human relations, that the consideration of

[15] *Werke*, IX, 18.

an ideal enters into them. But it must not and, I presume, can not be supposed that Hegel, in building on such foundations as I have been trying, partly to describe and partly to illustrate, is simply constructing, or aiming to construct, what is vulgarly termed the "ideal" of a state of things that might be, that he would personally think it desirable to have brought about, but which could not be realized without laying violent hands on the natural constitution and tendency of things. If he seems to foresee a condition of perfection, to which man, in state and history, has not yet attained, he does not do so by virtue of any professed prophetic foresight of a future break in the continuity of the present order of things, but simply because of his faith in the impossibility of such a break. The present is itself big with a better future. Really, however, Hegel wastes no words over pictures of a possible, or even probable, future. His concern is with the actual, whether in the present or in that past which is continued, in its results, into the present; and this, in accordance with his well-known and oft-repeated dictum, that philosophy can never be in advance of the time in which it is cultivated. "This treatise," says Hegel, in the preface to his *Philosophie des Rechts,* "must, as a philosophical work, be farthest of all removed from an attempt to construct an ideal state; as a work of possible instruction, its end can not be to instruct the state how it must be [or, be constituted], but rather how it, the ethical universe, is to be comprehended." And our author immediately adds, "The task of philosophy is to comprehend that which is; for that which is, is Reason. The individual man is always a son of his times; so, too, philosophy is the time, in which it exists, apprehended in thought. It is just as foolish to fancy that any philosophy is in advance of its present world, as to suppose the like in regard to any individual. If the theory of an individual does in fact transcend [and so exist out of direct relation to] the actual world of which he is a member, if in his theory he constructs himself a world, 'as it must be,' then we may say of his theory that it exists indeed, but only in the wax of his fancy—a pliant material, in which all things indifferently may be represented." [16] To the eye of an unfriendly criticism Hegel has

---

[16] *Werke,* VIII, 18.

seemed, in his *Philosophie des Rechts*, to carry out these views so rigorously, as to warrant the charge, that this work was occupied only with the attempt to comprehend, as the perfect work of civic reason, "the practical and political conditions existing in Prussia in 1821" (the year of the original publication of the work).[17] Whatever of justice, real or apparent, there may be in the charge, there is not enough to deprive Hegel's work, in any sense, of its conspicuous worth and character as a contribution to the "philosophy"—i.e., the science of the essential and total nature—of the state and of social relations, taken universally.

Before closing this introduction, it is necessary to say a few words with reference to Hegel's method. A great deal of nonsense, in the judgment of the writer, is contained in the speeches and written arguments of many respecting the subject of scientific or philosophic method. From much that is said, one would infer that the question of method, in any science or order of sciences, is one to be arbitrarily and abstractly determined, independently of any consideration of the nature of the subject-matter which is to be methodically treated. This state of things has doubtless arisen from the circumstance that the science of method, commonly termed "logic," has come to be treated so generally as a purely formal science—a science concerned solely with certain forms of thought, irrespective of their possible "content," or, of the subject-matter to which these forms may be "applied." (Or should we rather say, that the mentioned treatment of logic is simply the most pronounced symptom of the diseased "state of things" alleged?) But forms of thought, taken in abstraction from any particular subject-matter, are empty. These forms, in current logic, are the so-called "principles" of abstract identity and contradiction: A is A, and A is not B. These can scarcely be called "principles," otherwise than by courtesy. Being abstract and empty, they are not principles of movement, of development, of self-development. They end where they begin; and the actual worker in any science, who should resolve to be guided exclusively by them, would never take the first step forward. Sciences are actually built up, not indeed by ignoring or

---

[17] See Haym, *Hegel und seine Zeit*, p. 366; Berlin, 1857.

violating the principles of abstract identity and contradiction, and still less by merely following them alone—how can that be "followed" which leads nowhere?—but by following the method or order which the material to be scientifically treated has itself objectively and really taken and is ever taking. In other words, the specific method of a science can not be determined antecedently to all knowledge of the special nature of the concrete content of the science. Most especially is this true with reference to the whole order of sciences, which are strictly to be termed philosophical. For these sciences, having to do in each case with a concrete totality, are least able to make any advance while employing a formal and one-sided method of abstractions. Their end, I say, is in each case, the knowledge of the subject-matter chosen for treatment, in its totality—the inside (if one will so express it), as well as the outside, the essential and noumenal, as well as the superficial and phenomenal, and the specific, as well as the general. Here, therefore, less than any where can progress be made in specific knowledge by simple fidelity to the principles of abstract identity and contradiction. The state is the state; it is not a mineral kingdom. A state is made up of many individuals; and the latter, considered as many, are not one. The state subsists through living, dynamic processes; it is not unchangeably petrified or embalmed. All of these statements may be and, let us hope, are true. They illustrate the application of the principles of abstract identity and contradiction; but their conformity to these principles does not stamp them with the quality of scientific truth. So far as it appears, they are at best only unreasoned statements of immediate, empirical fact, or allegations founded on current, but not scientifically tested, belief. In order that they may be changed (for us) from the quality of "right opinion," or mere matter-of-fact truth, to that of truth which is comprehensible and is comprehended, these, and as many other similar "statements" as are relevant to the subject in hand (the nature of the state), must be seen and exhibited in their necessary connection and in their common relation to the one comprehensive and substantial reality, of which the historic state is the manifestation. The state, in other words, must be comprehended, not merely as an abstract and general unity, but as a concrete and specific one, having a complex ideal content of its own, and following a law that in some strict sense is its own and not another's.

Now the substantial reality of the state, in which is founded its concrete unity and individuality, is, according to Hegel, Man. It is Man, viewed in the totality of his nature, as a spiritual being. The state is the sphere of human personality. Still more exactly and technically, the substance of the state is the human Will.

The unity of the state is therefore the unity of man, of human personality, of human will. The various specific truths about the state are truths concerning man and that practical intelligence, in which the developed will of man consists. And the one all-comprehensive law of the state's existence must be the law of man's self-developing and self-realizing substantial will.

But the true will of man is "practical reason." It is intelligence in action. The law of the will must therefore be, if not in specific, yet at least in generic, identity with the law of all, and especially of theoretic, intelligence, or reason. The specific difference of practical from theoretical intelligence consists in the circumstance that the latter is a process in which "external reality" is transmuted into the quality of "inward thought," while in the former the transmutation takes place in the reverse direction. But this difference is, as one may say, a difference lying on the surface. It does not touch the essential nature of intelligence, which remains the same, whether its function be theoretical or practical. I may add that these two functions themselves are never completely separated.

Now it is the peculiarity of all intelligence, or reason, that it is self-conscious—not in the morbid, psychological sense of this expression, but in the philosophical sense. It involves a double aspect, an objective and a subjective one, or, as is more commonly said, two factors, termed subject and object. The universal and essential law of intelligence is the law of the equipoise of these abstractly different aspects or factors; or, it is the law of their concrete unity. In all intelligence, whether theoretical or practical, subject and object, or inward thought and external reality, become in some very intimate and vital sense one, without losing their abstract difference. The history of philosophy may be said to be a progressing demonstration of this truth and of all that it contains, in the realm of theoretic intelligence, while the social, political, and historic relations of men with each other are a growing demonstration and illustration of the like thesis in the realm of practical intelligence.

Now it follows from the foregoing that a purely objective intelligence, whether theoretical or practical, without any admixture of a subjective element, is strictly impossible. It is in contradiction with the essential nature of intelligence, just as the equality of all the angles of a plane triangle to three right angles would be in contradiction with the nature of such a triangle. The same is to be said respecting the idea of a purely subjective intelligence, separated from every thing that is objective. But it may be said with truth that in the natural history of intelligence, the involuntary tendency of the latter is to seek to manifest or realize itself, first, in purely objective fashion, abstraction being unconsciously made from all subjective conditions; and, secondly, in purely subjective fashion, abstraction being consciously made from all that is objective. The result is, necessarily, relative contradiction and failure, or the perception of the fact that to the manifestation of the full nature of intelligence there is needed a third step, leading to the harmonious synthesis of the subjective and objective in an organic unity. These steps are severally illustrated (to mention but one historic example) in the early natural philosophy of the ancient Greeks, which began with a purely objective direction of intelligence to the search after the unity of the natural universe; in the later abstract idealism of the Eleatics, which would turn all that is concretely objective into illusion, and the subjective phenomenalism of the Sophists, which denied the attainability of an objective standard of truth; and, finally, in the culmination and perfection of Greek philosophy (Socrates, Plato, Aristotle), which rested in the completed conception of the organic interpenetration and unity of the subjective and objective, or of the ideality of the real and the reality of the ideal.

The social and historical relations of mankind, the soul of which is practical intelligence, or Will, illustrate, in a sphere and in specific forms peculiar to themselves, the same law, rhythm, or succession, as that just described. The philosophy, or essential science, of these relations consists in the detailed demonstration that this is so. The articulation, the subdivisions, great and small, of Hegel's works respecting these relations, are founded on or correspond to the law now stated. In particular, the Philosophy of the State (literally, the "Philosophy of Right"; the title might also well be translated as the "Philosophy of Social Relations"), with which our exposition is to be first concerned, after a brief "Introduction" containing mainly abstract definitions relating to Will, is subdivided into three main parts. The first relates to Will, or the social-practical intelligence of man, in its abstractly objective aspect, and is entitled "Abstract Right." The second considers the same subject in its abstractly subjective form, and is termed "Morality." The third considers it in its natural, concrete fulness, the equipoise in concrete unity of objective and subjective as exemplified and realized in Family, Civil Society, and State, and is termed "The Ethical World" (Die Sittlichkeit).

BIBLIOGRAPHY

The Published Writings of George Sylvester Morris

(Note: A few items by Morris which involved no expression of his own ideas, several others concerned solely with the teaching of modern languages, and several abstracts or announcements of no reference value are omitted.)

1867, "Hodgson on Time and Space" (*The American Presbyterian and Theological Review*, New Series, Volume V, pages 217–38)

1871–3, Translation of Friedrich Ueberweg's *History of Philosophy from Thales to the Present Time*, including footnotes and addenda by Morris (2 Volumes, New York, Scribner, Armstrong and Company)

1874, "Vera on Trendelenburg" (*The Journal of Speculative Philosophy*, Volume VIII, pages 92–4)
"Friedrich Adolf Trendelenburg" (*The New Englander*, Volume XXXIII, pages 287–336)
"The Final Cause as Principle of Cognition and Principle in Nature" (*Journal of the Transactions of the Victoria Institute, or Philosophical Society of Great Britain*, Volume IX, pages 176–204; reprinted as a pamphlet, London, Robert Hardwicke)

1876, "The Theory of Unconscious Intelligence, as Opposed to Theism" (*Journal of the Transactions of the Victoria Institute, or Philosophical Society of Great Britain*, Volume XI, pages 247–91; reprinted as a pamphlet, London, Hardwicke and Bogue)
"The Philosophy of Art" (*The Journal of Speculative Philosophy*, Volume X, pages 1–16)
Review of "Philosophy of Trinitarian Doctrine: a Contribution to Theological Progress and Reform," by Rev. A. G. Pease (*The Journal of Speculative Philosophy*, Volume X, pages 111–2)

"The Immortality of the Human Soul," A University Address. (*The Bibliotheca Sacra*, Andover, Volume XXXIII, pages 695–715)

1877, "Spinoza—a Summary Account of His Life and Teaching" (*The Journal of Speculative Philosophy*, Volume XI, pages 278–99)

1878, "The Johns Hopkins University" (*The Michigan Chronicle*, Volume IX, page 180)

1880, *British Thought and Thinkers: Introductory Studies, Critical, Biographical and Philosophical* (Chicago, S. C. Griggs and Company)

1881, "Kant's Transcendental Deduction of the Categories" (*The Journal of Speculative Philosophy*, Volume XV, pages 253–74)

1882, *Kant's Critique of Pure Reason. A Critical Exposition* (Chicago, S. C. Griggs and Company)
"English Deism and the Philosophy of Religion" [Abstract]. (*Johns Hopkins University Circular*, Number 13, pages 177–8)
"Philosophy and its Specific Problems" (*The Princeton Review*, Volume IX, pages 208–32)

1883, "Dr. Cocker's Philosophical Attitude" (*The Michigan Argonaut*, Volume I, pages 245–7)
Philosophy and Christianity: a Series of Lectures Delivered in New York, in 1883, on the Ely Foundation of the Union Theological Seminary (New York, Robert Carter and Brothers)

1883–4, Articles on "Agnosticism," "Causation," "Conception" and "Consciousness" in *The Encyclopædia Americana*, A supplementary Dictionary of Arts, Sciences and General Literature, Illustrated; in Volume II for which the title has been changed to *American Supplement to the Encyclopædia Britannica*, Ninth Edition, with the same subtitle (Philadelphia, Hubbard Brothers)

1886, "The Philosophy of the State and of History" (*Pedagogical Library*, edited by G. Stanley Hall, Boston, D. C. Heath and Company, Volume I, Second Edition, pages 149–66) "University Education" (*University of Michigan Philosophical Papers*, Ann Arbor, Andrews and Witherby, First Series, Number 1)

1887, *Hegel's Philosophy of the State and of History. An Exposition* (Chicago, S. C. Griggs and Company)

1888, Review of *A Brief History of Greek Philosophy* by B. C. Burt (*Michigan Argonaut*, Volume VII, pages 67–8)

The Morris Collection at the University of Michigan

This comprises the extant unpublished materials, and there are two sections, both uncatalogued. The *George S. Morris Papers, 1857–1935* have been arranged chronologically by type, and consist of one volume and fifty-seven pieces. The *George Sylvester Morris Papers, 1852–89, 1909–15*, are unarranged and include seven volumes, approximately four hundred pieces and one bundle. Aside from the correspondence (which includes letters written to Robert Mark Wenley in response to his inquiries concerning Morris) the items of principal interest are (1) Morris' private journal covering the years 1856–61, the journal of his first European trip in 1866–7 and the diary of the second and shorter visit abroad in 1885, (2) the preparatory school material consisting of nine compositions, various school notes and his commencement oration, (3) the college and allied materials comprising forty-three compositions, together with miscellaneous papers mostly concerned with contemporary problems from the period of his senior year as an undergraduate through his first semester at Union Theological Seminary, six addresses to a group of his former students of Royalton Academy who were with him in Virginia, serving in the Sixteenth Vermont Regiment of the Union armies, and his master thesis presented at Dartmouth after his discharge from military service, (4) his summary of Friedrich Trendelenburg's lectures on psychology during the winter semester of 1867–8 in Berlin, thirty-three pages of divers notes on philosophy, a bibliography of books on philosophy, two drafts of an unused introduction to his volume of Hegel, an undated lecture on philosophy, and university class lectures on political philosophy, esthetics, ethics and logic.

Principal Secondary Sources

1893, *Henry Boynton Smith* by Lewis F. Stearns (Boston, Houghton, Mifflin)

1917, *The Life and Work of George Sylvester Morris* by R. M. Wenley (New York, Macmillan)

1926, *Philosophy of the Recent Past, An Outline of European and American Philosophy Since 1860* by Ralph Barton Perry (New York, Scribner's)

1930, *Contemporary American Philosophy* edited by George Plimpton Adams and William Pepperell Montague (New York, Macmillan)

1939, *Philosophy of John Dewey* edited by Paul Arthur Schilpp (Chicago, Northwestern University)

1943, *The Growth of American Thought* by Merle Curti (New York, Harper)

1943, *The Origin of Dewey's Instrumentalism* by Morton G. White (New York, Columbia University)

1946, *A History of American Philosophy* by Herbert W. Schneider (New York, Columbia University)

INDEX

Adams, G. P., 158n.
Adamson, R., 209
American Presbyterian and Theological Review, American Presbyterian Review, 115f.
Amherst College, 34n., 42n., 89, 244
Analogy, 36
Andover theological seminary, 89
Angell, J. B., 183
Ann Arbor, *cf.* Michigan, University of
Aristotle and Aristotelianism, 5ff., 40, 44f., 59, 62, 73f., 117, 122, 153, 160, 163f., 169ff., 174ff., 194, 202f., 244, 247f., 251, 260f., 263, 288f., 292, 297, 308f., 317f., 324, 326, 328ff., 336, 340f., 356, 360ff., 367, 370, 372, 385, 390f., 404, 411
Arnold, T., 96
Astié, J. F., 148ff.
Auburn Seminary, 30

Bacon, Francis, 58ff., 123, 158, 211, 224, 229f., 359, 373
Bacon, Roger, 228

Baltimore, *cf.*, Johns Hopkins University
Bampton Lectures by Mansel, 44ff.
Bangor Theological Seminary, 239
Bentham, 390
Berger, von, 338
Berkeley, 42n., 232f., 251
Berlin, University of, 167, 337
Bethel, Vt., 18, 64
Bible and its inspiration, 50, 57, 67, 298ff., 325, 331
Biographical History of Philosophy, 61
Böhme, 362
Bowdoin College, 183
Bradley, 209f., 214, 244f.
Brattleboro, Vt., 29
Bremen, 135, 200
Brewster, W., 26n.
Bridgman, Laura, 41
British empiricism, 108, 115, 122ff., 162, 192, 219ff., 243, 257, 303, 331
British idealism or British Hegelianism, 6f., 13, 104, 208, 216, 237, 242, 317
British Thought and Thinkers, 73ff., 111, 209ff.
Bruno, 362